WITCHES, WIFE BEATERS,
AND WHORES

The science of law should, in some measure, and in some degree, be the study of every free citizen, and of every free man. . . . Happily, the general and most important principles of law are not removed to a very great distance from common apprehension. It has been said of religion, that though the elephant may swim, yet the lamb may wade in it. Concerning law, the same observation may be made.

—James Wilson, *The Study of Law in the United States* (1790–92)

WITCHES, WIFE BEATERS, AND WHORES

COMMON LAW AND COMMON FOLK IN EARLY AMERICA

ELAINE FORMAN CRANE

CORNELL UNIVERSITY PRESS
Ithaca and London

First published 2011 by Cornell University Press

Printed in the United States of America

Library of Congress Cataloging-in-Publication Data

Crane, Elaine Forman.
    Witches, wife beaters, and whores : common law and common folk in early America / Elaine Forman Crane.
        p. cm.
    Includes bibliographical references and index.
    ISBN 978-0-8014-5027-3 (cloth : alk. paper)
    1. Common law—United States—History—
17th century.   2. Sociological jurisprudence—
United States—History—17th century.   3. Women—
Legal status, laws, etc.—United States—History—
17th century.   4. Domestic relations—United States—
History—17th century.   I. Title.
    KF394.C736 2011
    340.5'7097309032—dc22   2011011617

Cornell University Press strives to use environmentally responsible suppliers and materials to the fullest extent possible in the publishing of its books. Such materials include vegetable-based, low-VOC inks and acid-free papers that are recycled, totally chlorine-free, or partly composed of nonwood fibers. For further information, visit our website at www.cornellpress.cornell.edu.

Cloth printing   10 9 8 7 6 5 4 3 2 1

Contents

For the Men in My Life
Steve, Monroe, Milton, CR, Jimmy, Sam, Jack, Wil
And for the women of the twenty-first century
Liliana, Juliet, Sage, Madeline

Acknowledgments

Steve, of course, comes first. It has been extremely handy to have a lawyer on hand for a book like this, not to mention an enthusiastic supporter and gentle critic who is as familiar with archives in New England, Bermuda, and Maryland as I am. It was probably above and beyond the call of duty to drive with me in a heavy snowstorm to Rhode Island in late December 2008 to confirm that Comfort Taylor's screams could be heard across Narragansett Bay, but he did that too. I am greatly obligated to him for all his efforts, although I paid some of it off with rum swizzles in Bermuda, lobsters in Rhode Island, and crab cakes in Maryland.

Fordham University has been a longtime supporter of my efforts to research and write. Grant money, course reductions, and leaves of absence all furthered the project. The Walsh Library Interlibrary Loan Office was as helpful as it has been in the past. No sooner did I put in a request than I received word the obscure book or article had arrived. Individual colleagues rendered assistance each time I badgered someone with a question: my thanks to Maryanne Kowaleski, Richard Gyug, and Susan Wabuda. Susan Ray's assistance with translations from German to English meant that I could use important foreign language books. My graduate students, Samanta Brihaspat, Efrat Nimrod, Elizabeth Stack, Melissa Arredia, and Noël Wolfe read and criticized the introduction without worrying they would fail my course for doing so. Jenna Silvers assisted me by finding illustrations. Ken Kurihara and Mariah Adin, former graduate students, were no less helpful.

Colleagues around the country read various chapters, answered questions, and made helpful suggestions. They include Nina Dayton, Edith Gelles, Joyce Goodfriend, James Green, Jack Greene, David Hall, Bruce Mann, John Murrin, Mary Beth Norton, Elizabeth Reis, Susannah Romney, Sheila Skemp, Terri Snyder, and Mike Zuckerman.

Since several of the chapters deal with incidents that took place in Rhode Island, I spent considerable time in the archives there, and my gratitude is extended to those who assisted me in various repositories. At the Rhode Island Judicial Archives Steve Grimes and Andy Smith went out of their way to

provide me with needed material, as did Bert Lippincott at the Newport Historical Society and Gwen Stearn and Ken Carlson at the Rhode Island State
Archives. This is the third book of mine these professionals have nurtured.
My thanks also to John Torgan, baykeeper of Narragansett Bay, who discussed arcane issues of sight and sound with me. Richard and Joan Youngken
tolerated the questions asked by a researcher who writes about New England
but who knows less about boats and sailing than most landlubbers.

Participants at the Boston Area Early American Seminar, sponsored by the
Massachusetts Historical Society, offered constructive ideas for the chapter
on Comfort Taylor and Cuff. I thank Conrad Wright for inviting me to
participate in the seminar series and Gerald Leonard for his perceptive comments on my paper. Similarly, I am grateful to Dan Richter for inviting me
to present "A Ghost Story" at the Friday McNeil Center seminar series, and
to the seminar participants for their welcome suggestions.

The chapter on witchcraft in Bermuda is indebted to Karla Hayward,
Richard Lowery, and Joanne Brangman at the Bermuda Archives; Ann Upton,
special collections librarian at Haverford College; as well as to Clarence
Maxwell, Michael Jarvis, Virginia and Jim Bernhard, and Jennifer Hind.

Ghosts can be very elusive, and I am grateful to the many Maryland-
ers who helped rouse Thomas Harris from the dead: State Archivist Ed
Papenfuse, and Owen Lourie, Joyce Phelps, and Jean Russo at the Mary-
land State Archives. Scott MacGlashan, clerk of the Queen Anne's County
Courthouse, provided invaluable assistance. Rob Rogers and the staff at the
Maryland Historical Society were extremely helpful as well. My old friend
Janet Johnson provided good company during the off hours when we could
just talk about the day's finds.

Jaap Jacobs, Joyce Goodfriend, and Karen Kupperman were instrumental
in refining the chapter on slander in New Amsterdam. That chapter could
not have been written without the assistance of Virginie Adane, a graduate
student fluent in Dutch, who checked the English translation of the Dutch
court records against the original seventeenth-century manuscripts.

Samuel Banister's story was reconstructed with help from Elizabeth Bou-
vier at the Massachusetts Archives in Boston and Ann Tate and Scotty Breed
at the Stonington (Conn.) Historical Society.

There are people whose efforts significantly affected this book in different
ways. Wilton Tejada, my physical trainer, spent countless hours listening to
and commenting on the chapter about Comfort and Cuff. His insightful
comments made me rethink several points, and I will not forget the moments,
gasping for breath as he forced me to do five more reps, that I asked him
to e-mail me the thought he had just conveyed. Sheri Englund, my former

editor at Cornell University Press, is now a literary consultant. She read, commented on the entire manuscript, and offered thoughts about organizing the material that I implemented before daring to submit the book for publication. Rosemarie Zagarri, an exceptional early American historian and good friend, took time out to read and comment on the manuscript once it was submitted, and her creative suggestions about framing the introduction made a difficult task considerably easier.

It has been a privilege to have Michael McGandy as my editor at Cornell University Press. His thorough reading and thoughtful proposals have made considerable difference in the clarity of presentation and cohesiveness of the manuscript. It was also a pleasure to work with Sarah Grossman, who was very patient with me as I tried to navigate the world of electronic images. Thanks also to Ange Romeo-Hall and Susan Barnett for their effective and competent assistance and to Glenn Novak, whose copyediting skills smoothed the final manuscript. Finally, none of my books would be complete without an index compiled or supervised by John Kaminski. This time kudos to Jonathan Reid for assembling a cohesive index from six diverse chapters.

ELAINE FORMAN CRANE

Introduction

Jacob Vis had run up quite a tab at Geertje Teunis's New Amsterdam house where Teunis tapped beer for her thirsty neighbors. Shocked at the amount of his bill, an incredulous Vis questioned the accuracy of the account: "How can it be, that I am so much in debt here?" Teunis and Vis quarreled, and according to Salomon La Chair, who witnessed the shouting match, Teunis called Vis a drunken rogue—a nod, perhaps, to both his excessive consumption and unwillingness to ante up. Perceiving her verbal slap as an attack on his reputation, Vis demanded reparation of his honor (a legal formality that included an apology and cash).[1] Defending herself in front of the authorities, Teunis acknowledged the insult but insisted she hurled it only after Vis called her a whore and a beast. Thus, she reacted to his vocal assault with equally stinging words: "I hold you for a rogue and knave, until you have proved, that I am a whore," and, she declared, "I am from no beasts stock." Because the offensive accusations constituted slander, the court insisted that both Vis and Teunis provide proof of their cross-charges. Unfortunately for the warring litigants, Vis could not prove Teunis was a whore any more than Teunis could offer evidence that Vis was a drunken rogue. And since two other witnesses to the altercation claimed temporary deafness, the matter was dropped.

This historical shard is very telling, even if it only pinpoints a few isolated moments in one small community. The Vis/Teunis story is important because it reflects the texture of early American life through the intimate experience of ordinary people. The episode involving these few people shows, on a very personal level, how matters with legal implications saturated everyday activities and how often people's lives were woven together through them. A tapster, a customer, a contested bill, witnesses, a social moment that turned into a slander case. This is only one example of how, on any given day, the law affected early Americans in various ways, whether they were at work or at leisure. Ordinances regulated the hours and days during which Geertje Teunis could sell beer. Ethical standards required Jacob Vis to pay his bill. Statutes prohibited slanderous language that impugned reputation. Judges demanded proof of the provocation. From an interpretive standpoint, the incident raises questions about the meaning of the word "whore."

All this is to say that Americans were keenly interested in and influenced by legalities, which on a quotidian basis included an assortment of dos and don'ts that separated right from wrong. Yet, if most people tried to balance life on a foundation of codified moral and ethical rules, it is equally true that the daily treadmill offered endless opportunities to stray from communal values. Occasionally men and women found themselves frustrated by situations with no easy resolution, which meant that they sometimes bent the law or defied it altogether.

The vignette about Geertje Teunis and Jacob Vis is what historians have dubbed microhistory. Although microhistory comes in many shapes and sizes, its value, as Richard D. Brown explains, "lies in its power to recover and reconstruct past events by exploring and connecting a wide range of data sources so as to produce a contextual, three-dimensional, analytic narrative in which actual people as well as abstract forces shape events." Directing attention to "the multiple contexts in which people made their decisions and acted out their lives," Brown makes a strong case for the importance of microhistory as a tool for unearthing the past.[2] In some ways it does so with greater effect than other strategies, since microhistory's narrow focus enables researchers to ferret out historical nuggets that wider studies overlook or ignore.[3] A deeper, more focused probe also reveals ambiguities and complexities that resist definitive historical answers. Such cases encourage as well as legitimize an informed speculation that offers tentative or alternative interpretations. Truth, after all, is elusive and, arguably, a matter of competing perspectives.

If small stories contain a potential to reveal aspects of the larger culture, devotees of microhistory are somewhat divided over any approach that assumes conclusions from one time and place can be extended to others. Allowing for wider implications if corroborating evidence permits a broader brush, I would argue that such a debate deflects attention from the importance of microhistory as a historical tool. Microhistory has another, equally important role: it reinforces and humanizes traditional studies written on a grander scale. Since microhistory is so very personal, it draws the reader into a relationship with the protagonists who move the narratives. History in microcosm uncovers emotion in ways that more impersonal studies rarely do. Fear, frustration, and anger undulate through the pages as microhistory inverts the social order by exposing assertive females and passive males. It defies stereotypes by showing women mauling each other and men gossiping while shopping for dinner. Furthermore, by describing behavior that the community rejects, microhistory reveals the perimeters of permissible conduct. If historians are still ambivalent about microhistory's role in the development of a sweeping national thesis, it still contains the potential to change the way we think about the ongoing flow of history. Even more important, microhistory introduces the reader to the unexceptional people who make history happen.

As for the records from which microhistories are created, legal documents play a unique role. If the early American past is hard to pin down in the best of circumstances, the use of sworn statements—as opposed to other documents—has the capacity to close in on incidents deliberately or innocently shielded from view. Diary entries are composed by people who construct the self they want others to see. Letters contain just as much information as the writers want to share with the recipients. Newspapers sensationalize. But testimony, although based on personal perception, is taken under oath and therefore may represent (or even force) a less distorted version of an event. Did witnesses lie under oath? Sometimes they did, but perjury was a criminal offense. Besides, there is little doubt that many, if not most, early Americans took oaths seriously and that their statements were accurate reflections of memory. Not exactly "truth," perhaps, but the next best thing.

In this book I have used microhistory as the lens through which aspects of early American legal culture will be explored.[4] Unlike the vignette that opened this introduction, however, the following narratives are drawn from extensive bodies of evidence. I have written each chapter as a self-contained account, an independent story that provides an engaging way of reimagining the meaning of law as experienced by common folk. Jointly, the six chapters might also be thought of as the nonfiction equivalent of a fictionalized short story collection. Put another way, to the extent that they appeal to the reader by concentrating on individual lives captured at a dramatic moment, they have something in common with their fictional counterparts. Indeed, with murder, illicit sex, shifty deals, ghosts, and witches rife throughout the pages, how could they not?

Despite these similarities, however, the following pages never blur the line between fact and fiction. If novelists and short story writers invent imaginary speech and incidents, I have drawn on trial transcripts and other relevant documents to "hear" what people actually said and "see" what they saw. No need for docudrama here: depositions and examinations make it easy to eavesdrop on the colorful statements of ordinary people. The book may read like fiction in places, but these are all factual accounts.

All this is another way of confirming the Bard: life was indeed a stage where everyday tensions and conflicts were played out as legal dramas. Values—carried across the Atlantic or born in North America—took effort to uphold, but were worth the struggle because they represented ideals that stood the test of time and place. That such contests were staged under cover of law suggests a trust in the power of formal legal proceedings as well as in improvised folk law. Moreover, I have deliberately chosen topics that span centuries and cross borders because the issues themselves are not bound by either chronology or geography. People assaulted and maligned each other in Virginia as well as New Amsterdam; witches (under other names) threatened Americans in the seventeenth century—and thereafter. Domestic abuse pervaded the colonies and then the states. Sexual assault and its collision with race and gender were never limited to Rhode Island, while debt and inheritance controversies plagued Americans wherever and whenever they lived (and died). Law mattered—and matters—because reputation, negotiated limits of violence, sexuality, race, economic standing, familial and communal relationships were and are issues of deep concern.

The topics of these microhistorical narratives may range widely, but their focus is nonetheless narrow. My intention is to illustrate a common theme: the ways in which legal culture and the routine of daily life were knotted together in early America. Collectively, they not only reveal the values that bound Euro-Americans despite their differences, but they also raise salient questions about the consequences of decisions based on those values.[5] Can a convicted wife beater be a patriarch? Should witches have the same civil rights as other offenders? How does a society protect speech and reputation at the same time? In what way do race and gender influence legal decisions? Should debtors be sent to prison? If some of these questions are closely linked to early America, others resonate in our own time.

All of the events in this book relate to some aspect of early American legal culture prior to 1800. The six case studies are representative, but hardly exhaustive of possible examples. All of them call attention to ordinary people, which is key to understanding the complexities and ambiguities of seventeenth- and eighteenth-century society. Women as well as men amble, stumble, or collide throughout the pages, while black and white, rich and poor, mingle and confront each other. Different settlers, in various ways, turned to law not only to protect themselves but to stabilize their lives and reinforce their belief system. Drawing on actual incidents, each case illustrates the ways in which Euro-American law shaped life as it related to commerce, property, family, race, and gender—not to mention the supernatural. The array of cases, with their startling panoply of legal maneuvers, confirms the proposition that law was a matter of deep concern to the original settlers and that their knowledge of the legal process was surprisingly ingrained and extensive. It was also innovative.

Anglo-Americans did not import English precedent wholesale. They introduced and relied upon what they knew best and what had worked in the past, but questions regarding the untested conditions of North America occasionally required novel answers. Witches could not get a free ride in New England any more than they could in old England, but a vast continent seemed to offer free land for the taking, and colonists applied home-grown rules to the distribution of property. White males continued to reap benefits established by the patriarchal society across the Atlantic, but Native men on this side of the ocean became increasingly destabilized by laws that intruded on their way of life. If most English tolerated religious diversity and lawyers, Massachusetts Puritans did not. In the Chesapeake, a hoped-for cache of precious metals never materialized, forcing settlers to design and regulate an economy based on the next best thing: tobacco. All this required legal maneuvering.

★ ★ ★

To explore the intersection of people and law, a microhistorian slogs through legal documents. Starting from a simple case report, the historian tries to create a background by assembling supporting evidence from a variety of sources. Some of it will be found in published volumes. The more interesting material, however, is usually buried among the obscure handwritten documents secreted away in local archives. If the case is a criminal matter, the indictment can be quite revealing. Lists of jurors and the names of judges become as important as the identity of the defendant or litigants. Statements from witnesses help define the issues and provide details that will invariably prove ambiguous and vexing. Once the parameters of the case are established, other sources set the controversy or incident in context. Locally, census and tax data refine the identities of the participants. Collections of statutes (frequently online) establish what laws were in place at the time. Occasionally a diary or letter written by someone close to the case will contain a pertinent reference. In the eighteenth century, newspapers reported sensational cases, and these accounts frequently offer tidbits of information unavailable elsewhere. Colonywide and even international events often affected local incidents and set them in context. Luck and persistence have much to do with a successful hunt, although there are limits to what will be found even after the most vigilant search. The survival of documents is never a sure thing, and in the end, the history detective is at the mercy of a collection, a friendly archivist, and a scribe with a sharp quill. The particular subjects on which I have concentrated raise multiple issues and reveal so much about the social values that mattered because they are based on material from evidentiary treasure troves that provide entrées into the past.

As historians develop microhistories, they often rely, as I have, on legal archives and case reports. Since my research included documents from both English and Dutch America, an understanding of both common and civil law was essential to the task. As a result of colonial membership in the British Empire, English common law—custom and court decisions, but eventually statutes as well—prevailed in the English colonies of Rhode Island, Maryland, and Bermuda. The Puritan bastion of Massachusetts turned to biblical strictures for legal guidance, although colony leaders never completely eschewed common law. New Amsterdam clung to civil or Roman law, which affected the structure of the court, although the content of the cases closely resembled those of the English colonies. And even New Netherland came under the sway of English law before the last third of the seventeenth century. Maryland's laws evolved after independence, but no one called for a complete overthrow of the legal system that existed before statehood. The New England courts were layered according to the severity of the crime, with the right to a jury trial established early on. Bermuda, too small for a diverse court system, also provided for trial by jury. Until New Amsterdam became New York, its court was headed by a *schout,* who wore the hats of both sheriff and prosecutor. He, along with a bench composed of two burgomasters and five *schepens* (aldermen), heard and decided cases without juries.

Microhistorians relish unexpected details, especially ones that were broadly experienced. Thus, it was of some interest to find a kaleidoscope of civil rights enjoyed by early Americans as early as the seventeenth century. Indeed, I found it nothing less than astonishing to see the safeguards that existed—and frequently employed—throughout both English and Dutch America. In the English colonies, a criminal charge was accompanied by a grand jury indictment, bail for most crimes, the ability to challenge jurors peremptorily or for cause, and a trial by jury. Defendants were presumed innocent, and in some venues they had the right to an attorney—whether they could afford one or not. The accused were safe from self-incrimination and were entitled to face their accuser (admittedly problematical when a ghost played that role). Defendants charged with a crime could demand the papers involved in the proceedings. If convicted, they had the right to appeal the decision. White males fared best under these rules, but even if discrimination against women and people of color is readily apparent, they too were entitled to take advantage of legal protections.[6] Dutch America had slightly different rules, but there is no doubt about its commitment to proving the truth of an accusation through the judicial process.

Nevertheless, early American legal procedure was still embryonic. No police force patrolled a community. The most sought after seventeenth-century juror already knew the facts of the case and was familiar with the defendant and the incident. Was the defendant capable of the crime? His or her past history signaled yes or no. Did the body of a homicide victim bleed after the fact? If so, the person in contact with the corpse was clearly guilty of murder. Ghosts (through a human vehicle) could testify in front of a jury throughout the eighteenth century. And although the jury was the final determiner of guilt or innocence, if the judge was dissatisfied with an acquittal, he could send the jurors back without food or rest to rethink their decision. Punishments for legal infractions ordinarily included whippings and fines—but not incarceration. Warnings-out and banishment rid communities of undesirable inhabitants, as did an occasional hanging. Executions were public events and often combined with the festivities of market day. Justice was swift: most trials took no more than a few hours from beginning to end.

Folk law and custom existed outside the courtroom, which is only to say that in life "law" was an ongoing contest between formal authority and informal consensus, or a joust between those who declared themselves arbiters of right and wrong. Sometimes warring litigants in slander cases reached agreement and shook hands after a mere apology that restored honor to the aggrieved party. On other occasions a complainant, such as an alleged victim of attempted rape, might consider her best interest served by a creative accord not sanctioned by statute. The law concerning spousal abuse may have been on the books, but evidence suggests that many men circumvented it without fear of consequences, since custom recognized certain male prerogatives. Yet, as we will see in the chapter on domestic violence, sometimes groups of people intervened to ensure "justice." Not everyone was willing to participate in what might be called "community policing," but it was an integral part of neighborhood dynamics, nonetheless. Formal and informal law worked in tandem in early America, an approach to conflict resolution that gave a vast number of unknown actors a role to play in the making and shaping of history.

Indeed, among the most striking features of the stories recounted below are the different ways that law was implemented from the bottom up. Ordinary people "made" law by establishing and enforcing informal rules of conduct. Codified by a handshake or over a mug of ale, confirmed by a skimmington (public ridicule of an offender), such agreements became custom, and custom became "law." Furthermore, by submitting to formal laws initiated from above, common folk legitimized a government that depended on popular consent to rule with authority. Some white males either wrote statutes or elected the legislators who passed them. But for those outside the electoral process—ineligible white males or white women—compliance implicitly sanctioned law. Still others, such as enslaved men and women, involuntarily abided by legislation that demeaned them, because they had little choice. Compliance hardly indicated consent, but awareness of what the law required and adapting to rules in the interest of self-preservation made the enslaved an integral part of a collective legal culture that owed as much to the bottom of the social order as it did to the top.

It is difficult to overemphasize the importance of those people clinging to the middle or bottom rungs of the social ladder. Their influence as lawmakers gave them a stake in society as it simultaneously democratized one community after another. The life, liberty, and property that men and women went to law to protect were best safeguarded in a public courtroom where hot tempers were cooled in a peaceful atmosphere. Private negotiations were not always successful, and riots, protests, and beatings were hardly unknown. Yet the fact that the majority of people were willing to live by the formal and informal rules they devised and valued reinforced a respect for law that did not go unnoticed.

★ ★ ★

In each chapter I have emphasized the fresh insights that microhistory offers. The evidence I analyze in "In Dutch with the Neighbors" provides a new perspective on slander by suggesting that it was a novel response to underlying social grievances. In this context, the use of the word "whore" was less a sexual sting than a weapon of commercial rivalry, and Marretie Jorisen could not let it pass when Andries de Haas "scolded her as a whore." In court, she demanded proof of the slur, as did other women and men similarly maligned.

In the same way, when colonists in Bermuda spoke through legal documents, they confirmed that long-standing resentments could turn into metaphorical accusations of witchcraft, just as "whore" stood in for economic dislocation. "There is a witch amongst us," announced Elizabeth Middleton, and Bermudians, like colonists elsewhere, relied on law to rid the community of such a threat. More important, however, I would argue that by assuring witches of their day in court, the law humanized the spiritual world and invested man-made law with a power that trumped witchcraft.

Dysfunctional families who were troubled by domestic violence offer a rare opportunity to observe folk law in action—that is, the extralegal means by which networks of women encircled and protected neighbors who were victims of abusive husbands. Such a candidate was Sarah Rouse, who was "afraid her . . . Husband would Take away her Life." Alternatively, John Hammett's friends call attention to male bonding when they tried to shield him from the law after he pummeled his wife. The various assaults over time also raise what might be termed a revisionist question: if *prosecutions* for domestic violence declined without a commensurate decline in spousal abuse, does this imbalance call into question the rise of companionate marriage—a compatible union where a heavy-handed patriarchy allegedly fell from favor?

As Comfort Taylor and Cuff wend their way through the Rhode Island courts, the unusual imbroglio offers a rare view of the complex relationship between slavery and freedom by showing how the law mediated a system where a man was both person and property. Before the judges confronted this ambiguity, however, the protagonists demonstrated the importance of informal legal machinations as Thomas Borden considered Comfort Taylor's claim that "the Negro cuff had tried to kiss her and had bruised her very much" during an attempted rape.

By focusing on an individual, Samuel Banister's chapter captures the human side of debt and debt litigation. Much of his woeful tale takes place in a public courtroom—where the proceedings humiliated him and jeopardized his masculine role as family provider. Evicted for nonpayment of rent, Banister threatened "he would kill or Shoot the first man that should attempt . . . to take possession of his house." Set in the context of new commercial realities that stimulated both upward and downward mobility, Banister is a symbol of a man suffering from the anxieties and frustrations that are said to appear only later in the century as the American economy evolved. Legal history, in microhistorical form, pushes the clock back here, just as it does in the chapters about New Amsterdam and Bermuda.

A ghost and a disputed will are central to the last chapter. Apparitions had eagerly participated in criminal matters for hundreds of years, but the way in which the ghost in this chapter operated reveals a spirit created to meet the needs of the new nation. In short, late eighteenth-century spirits were transformed by the economy, just as the economy altered business practices. Thomas Harris's ghost still came to avenge a wrong, but money, not murder persuaded him to intervene. There was no doubt of the ghost's identity: even his former horse "knew Thomas Harris."

Notwithstanding my efforts to expose the past in a very personal way, I have been unable to induce the subjects of the narratives to yield definitive answers to some of the more provocative questions they raise. Despite the most intensive probing, we will never really know what Andries de Haas meant when he allegedly "scolded" Marretie Jorisen as a "whore," or whether John Middleton actually thought Christian Stevenson was a witch. No matter how thorough the research, even the most garrulous early Americans deny access to their inner thoughts or motives. Thus, with nothing more than circumstantial evidence proving his guilt, only Comfort Taylor and Cuff knew if he really attempted to rape her. Similarly, every effort fails to verify William Briggs's confrontation with Thomas Harris's ghost. And with Samuel Banister's jurors unwilling to share their deliberations, it is impossible to know why the jury acquitted him of murder.

★ ★ ★

Beyond consideration of fresh insights and unanswerable questions, an alternative reading reveals the common features that splice the individual chapters together. Such an analysis uncovers parallels that readily turn diverse stories into a sort of *e pluribus unum* of case studies. As complementary themes crisscross chapters, they reveal analogies that are sometimes obvious, sometimes unforeseen. All, however, confirm a connection between law and intrinsic American values.

If, for example, the various chapters appear to be based on unrelated legal issues, a closer reading suggests that in each case commerce and property were fundamental factors. While such a connection may be yesterday's news, it is still revealing to read beyond the headline into the small print. On the surface, slander hurt reputations in general, but it was reputation in the marketplace (more so than the marriage market) that counted. Neither men nor women could prosper if they were not trustworthy businesspeople. Witchcraft, too, may have been prosecuted under criminal law, but the underlying grievances revolved around marketable property: theft of hog feed, pigs that died, butter that wouldn't churn, and petty trade goods. Quakers preached egalitarian land redistribution, a terrifying prospect that threatened the economic status quo on Bermuda.

One could argue that given their rights under the law, patriarchal men considered their wives as property to be vigorously controlled. Yet if such an interpretation remains below the surface in the chapter on domestic violence, the chapter on Comfort and Cuff is overtly about property, once the criminal action is concluded. Cuff himself was property, and Comfort sought compensation in the form of property for the attempted rape. And even if Samuel Banister was ultimately charged with murder, his crime was stimulated by financial distress and activated in defense of property he believed to be rightfully his. Finally, a dispute over Thomas Harris's estate precipitated the appearance of his ghost. If Americans were fixated on the law, they were no less infatuated with the possession of property. In each of the chapters, law became the means by which individuals sought redress for actual or potential hurt to their possessions. Similarly, they attempted to resolve disputes through the acquisition of property.

Looked at from still another perspective, it is clear to me that early Americans—even those with little money and less education—had considerable knowledge about laws that mattered. Whether that information was culled from scaffold confessions, execution sermons, books, an oral tradition, or experience is of less consequence than the accumulation of legal know-how and the surprising frequency with which that general knowledge was put to use. Of even greater moment are the arcane points of law that lay dormant in the popular mind, ready to be roused as occasion demanded. In *Witches, Wife Beaters, and Whores* I illustrate both the extensive knowledge and consistent use of law by an astonishing number of people.

Take, for example, Samuel Banister. Banister's acquaintance with the legal process began long before he was tried for murder. As a bookkeeper and merchant he was a familiar courtroom figure. For a while he seems to have prospered, but eventually fortune abandoned him and debt pursued him. Defiant in the face of eviction from his home, Banister claimed "he knew something of the Law." No doubt he did.

Battered women in New England were aware that the law protected them—at least in theory—from abusive husbands. But they were reluctant to bring charges, knowing that the response of the authorities would be lukewarm at best, and that they might face reprisals from husbands angered by their defection. In such circumstances, knowledge of formal law did little to protect those for whom it was designed. Instead, folk law—popular action based on a desire to thwart a "wrong"—rescued women when statutory law deserted them.

Comfort Taylor's screams, immediate revelations, and exhibition of bruises indicate her understanding of what the law required from a woman who was pressing charges of attempted rape. She also tailored her multiple appeals to the fine print in Rhode Island's statute books, which allowed her to hold her assailant as both person and property.

Ordinary Bermudians, despite their isolation, had mastered a surprising amount of legal minutiae, the sum of which competed with whatever their brethren on the mainland had absorbed. Routine civil matters clogged the calendar, but by the time Satan settled on the remote island, the English colonists there were well prepared for a legal battle with him. Indeed, John Middleton, an accused witch, became a leading authority on the physical manifestations of witchcraft and gave detailed advice on how to "discover" a witch. John Makaraton, Middleton's accuser, was also keenly aware of the fine points of witchcraft, information he used to craft charges against Middleton.

One hundred and fifty years later in Maryland, Thomas Harris's ghost (through his interlocutor, William Briggs) employed arcane legal strategies to make sure his illegitimate children would be the beneficiaries of his small estate. Harris, however, did not have to rely on legal training that was handed down by word of mouth. As literacy expanded in early America it enhanced the ability of people to read written laws. That same extension of literacy also drew more people into the legal lives of others. A proliferation of newspapers, wide readership, and sustained interest in criminal behavior created a broadly dispersed reading public with intimate knowledge about people they would only know vicariously. Most early Americans, like Samuel Banister, "knew something of the Law."

Early Americans put that knowledge to use in defense of values that mattered. Not surprisingly, deeply held beliefs about rights to real and personal property precipitated the bulk of courtroom controversies. But people also went to law to safeguard intangible property such as honor, an amorphous attribute that was tangled up with reputation. Honor and reputation shadow the chapters because good names were valued enough to be protected through the legal process. Moreover, honor and dishonor were perpetuated by gossip, whispers that provided a window into the intimate lives of others—and eventually affected legal outcomes.

The New Amsterdam court records reveal that despite language differences in this tower of babble, gossip frequently degenerated into slander, and just as often provoked retaliation. Thus, New Amsterdam's slander suits illustrate the intersection of reputation and gossip most vividly, with insults satisfied in each case only by "reparation of honor." When Lysbet Ackermans allegedly accused Grietje Pieters of New Amsterdam of stealing a beaver pelt, Pieters worked feverishly to refute the accusation while the gossip network operated overtime to sort out what had happened. Mary Pia "heard it from others" that Pieters had pilfered the pelt. If Pieters could not prove her innocence, who would do business with her? And when Geurt Co-erten and his wife slandered Madame Beeckman, they excused themselves by "saying they heard it from the mouth of Aert Willemsen." Although the couple was at fault for "propagating the report," the law's deepest frown was reserved for "the first promulgators and calumniators" who ignited the verbal firestorm.[7]

Witchcraft thrived on gossip. Bermudians knew who was suspect and why. If butter did not congeal, if children sickened unexpectedly, if items disappeared without cause, suspicion fell on people known through hearsay to have Satan's ear. Christian Stevenson's neighbors were long aware of her ability to do the devil's work, and tried to avoid dealing with her—which only infuriated Stevenson. Alice Moore's barefoot treks and predictions about the death of barnyard animals stirred up gossip, as did the accusation that Jane Hopkins had threatened the welfare of an entire ship because of her trickery. In Bermuda, as elsewhere, charges of witchcraft always threatened reputations; but if other slanderous allegations could be forgiven and forgotten courtesy of an apology or cash, witchcraft accusations were not easily shaken off, and honor was never effectively restored.[8]

The concept of a patriarchal society rested on the premise that a male household head had the right to control his wife. For the men analyzed in the chapter on domestic violence, that control degenerated into physical violence. But small communities reveled in gossip and allowed rumors to travel quickly, which meant that domestic violence and the men who perpetrated it did not go unnoticed. Battered wives confided in friends, and neighbors interceded with abusive husbands as a result of such confessions. Furthermore, such gossip raised a perplexing question: Since justice was often blind to spousal abuse, did a wife beater retain his honor in spite of his malevolent behavior?

Comfort Taylor's reputation and her credibility were at stake when she turned down Thomas Borden's offer of a private settlement in favor of a public trial in order to shame both Cuff and his owner. Truth and falsehood were at the core of Comfort's accusations against Cuff, and the rumor mill (which must have included the entire town of Newport) churned out chatter as townspeople debated the merits of her thousand-pound claim against an enslaved ferry operator whose reputation, not to mention life, were also threatened by her charge.

The lawsuits against Samuel Banister proclaimed to one and all Banister's failure as a businessman, and as small talk traveled, the people with whom he dealt became aware of his predicament. Banister surely knew that people were speaking unfavorably about him behind his back as rumors of his insolvency motivated business associates to institute suits for debt. The public nature of the cases humiliated him and, by extension, his family. In an effort to protect the family honor—as well as his brother's reputation—John Banister paid his brother's legal fees. Samuel's damaged reputation cost him dearly as creditors lined up to sue him, and the court put him behind bars until he made good on the claims. Restitution, not punishment, was the point of his incarceration, although everyone realized Banister's ability to pay up was hampered by his confinement.

Bastardy was common enough in early America, yet bearing children out of wedlock was still a matter of some concern in a culture that strongly discouraged illegitimacy. This proscription did not prevent Thomas Harris and Ann Goldsborough from producing four illegitimate children (a feat even in fecund early America), but the affluent and respectable Goldsborough family appears to have been concerned enough about honor and reputation to keep the young couple out of court and away from public scrutiny. Nevertheless, gossip followed them years after their liaison ended. News that Thomas Harris's ghost would testify through his friend, William Briggs, was common knowledge for at least a year before the actual event. When the case finally reached court, gossip included tales about the unmarried couple, an uncle who siphoned off the inheritance of his nephews and niece, and speculation, one might suppose, about whether a ghost could be counted on to tell the truth. Honor was an integral component of legal culture in this world and the next.

★ ★ ★

An American legal culture, based on shared values, took root through a common language that sped from person to person and from place to place, confirming established principles en route. As words traveled, they created a ripple effect by expanding the circle of people drawn into an action that began with only two litigants (or a prosecutor and defendant). When New Amsterdammers debated the merits of a slanderous accusation, when travelers from Newport discussed Comfort Taylor in Boston, and when news of witchcraft executions on Bermuda reached ears and eyes on the mainland, early Americans were being immersed in a legal culture without realizing the extent of their benign indoctrination. As time went on, assorted "facts" about such incidents were spread via print media as well as through personal contact, and by the mid-eighteenth century backdoor newsmakers competed with front-stoop newspapers. With no pretense of neutrality, tabloid items about

Samuel Banister's murder of James Osborne and Cuff's attempted rape of Comfort Taylor helped sensationalize the legal process. How far words traveled, how deeply they became embedded, is best illustrated by the Harris ghost case, a controversy that crossed an ocean and survived a century of print.

Notwithstanding the ways common social values operated under a legal umbrella in early America, they may also be read from a competing perspective. By resisting the established order, people offered counternarratives as well as mainstream ones. Parsing even further, I would argue that most men and women flouted the established value system by deviant behavior; fewer rejected that value system altogether. Slanderers did not advocate a competing social order; none of the word-slingers objected to laws controlling speech. Samuel Banister did not campaign for a retraction of statutes governing debt. Thomas Harris's ghost argued for the implementation of well-settled inheritance laws, not the repeal of those laws. Accused witches took no stand against witchcraft itself, nor did they protest punishment for convicted perpetrators. Conversely, Cuff's values—his sense of right and wrong—were at odds with early American society. By stealing himself, Cuff spurned the consensual view that it was lawful for one person to own another. His escape was a personal challenge to laws favoring slavery. Abused women took a position somewhere in between: they surely favored laws that condemned spousal assault, but they just as surely rejected the social climate that exonerated men who battered their wives.

Since Nathaniel Alcock, Samuel Banister, and Comfort Taylor were all mid-eighteenth-century Rhode Islanders, they may have known each other—even though they appear in different chapters and for different reasons. Yet even if none of the other characters I have written about ever crossed paths, they all illustrate the ways in which law permeated daily life and created a legal culture. I agree with David Hall that "religion was embedded in the fabric of everyday life" in early America, but I would emphatically add that law was woven into that fabric as well.[9] Notwithstanding the complementary (if sometimes fractious) relationship between religion and law, there are major differences in the way the two influenced belief and behavior. Religion abetted privacy in a way that law did not. Belief itself remained fixed in the recesses of the heart and mind, and although church membership was encouraged, no colony or state demanded it. But if law required group affiliation (that is, universal adherence to it tenets), as well as faith in the judicial process, then there was no escape from its oversight. Legal culture was inherently inclusive and public. Law—that is, its basic principles—also unified early Americans, whereas competing religious doctrines were divisive factors that left bitter conflict unresolved.

More often than not, disputes parried in a formal legal setting avoided street fights and battlefields. That being so, going to law frequently resulted in peaceful settlements and a harmony that might otherwise have eluded the litigants. Yet positive results came at a cost: law imposed itself into the most personal human relationships: sex and marriage. Not satisfied with regulating the lives of one generation, law determined inheritance rights and divided property. It defined the boundaries of speech by deciding what one person could say to another. It eased access to commercial markets for some, and built roadblocks for others. The law advanced upward mobility and severely punished debt with a bias that enhanced or destroyed reputations. Law irreparably damaged race relations by establishing rules making some people freer than others and creating societies where skin color offered privileges—or not—and where there was little refuge from discrimination.

Collectively, the individuals portrayed in these chapters illustrate these issues as well as others, and as they do, they confirm the omnipotence and omnipresence of value systems that transcended geographical boundaries. The glut of "matters" in early America (that is to say incidents, cases, negotiations, folk law remedies) reflected an unwavering confidence in and reliance on legal devices to uphold values and to solve problems. So widespread was law's influence, so inextricably intertwined with everyday experience, legal culture ultimately became fused with other enduring American traditions. This synergism not only cemented American society, but also perpetuated social stability by transmitting cultural messages over invisible wires to future generations. The people introduced in the following chapters were probably unaware that they would leave such a legacy, but there can be little doubt that early American common folk and common law shaped what would become a uniquely American national identity.

CHAPTER 1

In Dutch with the Neighbors

Slander "in a well regulated Burghery"

It is difficult to imagine the Manhattan of soaring skyscrapers as New Amsterdam. In the early seventeenth century, trees blanketed the greater part of the island, while hogs and dogs ran wild in the small town clinging to its southern tip. Occasionally, an agile canine would catch a slow-moving hog and chomp on a porcine ear. Less often, a scrawny mutt would bite an even mangier goat to death. Indians, English, and Swedes threatened from all sides, while the well-being of the Dutch colony rested on soldiers who spent as much time drawing knives on each other as on their enemies. Rich and poor alike scandalously and shamefully engaged in "unseasonable drinking," so that by 1648 "nearly the just fourth of the city of New Amsterdam consist[ed] of brandy shops, tobacco or beer houses." Complaints of drunken Indians, cheating, fraud, and smuggling followed the excessive consumption of alcoholic beverages. Tavern fights erupted with alarming frequency, and some unlucky patron—like that unfortunate pig—could lose his ear, albeit to a cutlass rather than to a cur.[1]

If, as estimated, some five hundred men lived in New Amsterdam prior to the devastating Indian wars of the early 1640s, and if those wars considerably reduced that number to one hundred males in 1648, then it is possible the town may have contained no more than a thousand people and 120 houses in 1656. On the other hand, only a building frenzy would account for the 350 houses said to exist by 1660, although the number of dwellings may have been enhanced by the theft of timber, an ongoing problem.[2] For reasons of their own, builders also constructed chimneys of wood and roofs of reeds, a combustible combination not outlawed until 1648. Owners and renters chose to preserve the cleanliness of their interiors by disposing of "rubbish, filth, ashes, and dead animals" in the streets.[3]

Despite their difficulties, however, the inhabitants of New Amsterdam did not seem starved of either food or material goods. Bakers provided bread, butchers prepared meats, fishermen hooked and netted fish, farmers grew vegetables, and traders/spinners/weavers/tailors sold sheets, pillowcases, garments, and stockings to the local populace. A few women wore pearls, but whether the jewelry arrived by ship from Holland, Brazil, Guinea, the West Indies, or courtesy of the indigenous oyster population is unknown. Beaver skins found their way into the local economy as a trading commodity, a component of the local currency, and as wearing apparel. Sewant (or wampum) and tobacco were mediums of exchange as well.

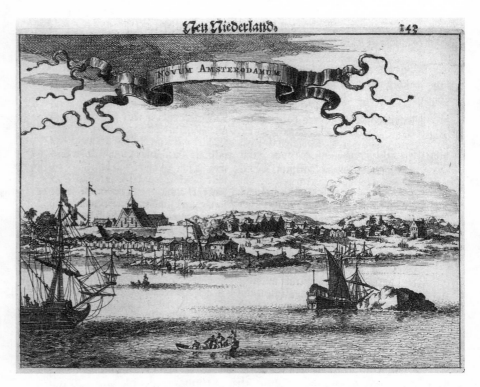

FIGURE 1.   New Amsterdam by Arnoldus Montanus (c. 1625–83). First published in 1671, this view shows New Amsterdam in 1651. Bert Twaalfhoven Collection, Fordham University Library, Bronx, New York.

New Amsterdam was ethnically and religiously diverse. Unlike their New England neighbors, who were far more homogeneous, the Dutch in Manhattan rubbed elbows with French, Spanish, Portuguese, Swedish, and English inhabitants on a daily basis. Jews, Catholics, and Baptists established homes there as well. Enslaved Africans contributed to the labor force, and the Dutch maintained an uneasy relationship with the Indians who surrounded—and outnumbered—them. Given this assortment, it is easy to conjure up a baffling babble of languages as people went about their business or paused for a short conversation. It would be too much to say that the Dutch welcomed this diversity, but the inhabitants did coexist surprisingly well, given time and place. Local ordinances played no role in promoting such coexistence; the Dutch West India Company demanded it in the interests of a flourishing trade. If, thousands of miles from Amsterdam, the colonists could claim a small degree of local power, the Dutch West India Company trumped that power with long-distance authority. In turn, the colonists were resigned to using ethnic and religious slurs in an occasional display of one-upsmanship.

The elite governing body of New Amsterdam understood all too well the volatility of the small community and was committed to taming it in the interest of good government. In its early years, theft, violence, and a general immorality among soldiers were "matters of serious consequence," which could not "be tolerated." Indeed, "leading a scandalous life" was "highly dangerous" in an "infant Republic." That they thought of themselves as a republic suggests a desire to emulate the world they left behind; but whether infant republic or trading outpost, no matter—for the next several decades the authorities drove home the same point: physical violence and unbecoming behavior were offenses "not to be tolerated in a well ordered province." To the end of their half-century rule, burgomasters and schepens (aldermen) attempted to confine the community to people worthy of living "in a well regulated Burghery."[4]

Slander was among the many wrongs that needed to be addressed. Thus, the small coterie of settlers was put on notice that "speaking ill of someone" or using "bad and unbecoming language" would not be tolerated "in a well ordered place," a utopian vision that remained an aspiration rather than a reflection of the current state of affairs. Nevertheless, it was commonly held that "injurious and foul words" undermined authority, ruined reputations, and destroyed honor. Furthermore, as the unruly inhabitants were reminded, such language was "directly contrary to the customs and provisions of the laws."[5]

The laws that governed New Amsterdam were the same laws that governed the colony of New Netherland as well as the provinces in the Netherlands. These laws rested on the writings of Hugo Grotius, a legal scholar who, in the course of a much-quoted treatise, defined defamation as "wrongs against honour," or "the good esteem in which others hold us."

> All persons are liable for defamation who by word of mouth or in writ-
> ing, in a person's presence or absence, secretly or openly, make known
> anything which impairs another's honour, though what he says be true,
> except when information is given to the authorities with a view to the
> punishment of a crime.[6]

According to Grotius, in order to compensate someone who had been defamed, the person liable for the injury was ordered to admit guilt, pray for forgiveness, declare that the statement was untrue, and confirm that he or she "knows nothing of the person defamed but what is upright and honourable." If the statement was true but "improperly brought forward," the defamer was required to declare that he or she acted inappropriately. In addition, character repair demanded compensation, which consisted of "honorable and profitable reparation for the insult—honorable, by acknowledging that he is sorry for having insulted the plaintiff, begging forgiveness of God, Justice and the plaintiff; and profitable by paying a fine," the amount of which would be determined by the court.[7] Reputation and remuneration were inseparable, although awards usually went to the poor or the church rather than to the victim.

The court in New Amsterdam adhered strictly to these guidelines. It did so because disorder was disruptive of good government, and good government required justice. To the Dutch, and to the inhabitants of New Amsterdam who abided by Dutch law, justice was "the foundation of the Republic." The court consistently equated "a well regulated place" with one "where justice is administered."[8] And the delicate balance between justice and order could only be maintained by emphasizing the community over the individual. In short, it was better that an "evildoer be punished than that a whole country and community suffer through him." Punishment was a deterrent— "an example to other violent and disorderly persons." If fines, house arrest, or corporal punishment proved unconvincing, banishment awaited unrepentant transgressors "in order that the few people here in New Netherland may live together in peace."[9]

Justice was a priority in the English colonies as well, and they similarly meted out punishment as a deterrent. In both Dutch and English colonies, however, the concept of "justice" was still in a rudimentary stage. Seventeenth-century religious scholars were surely aware of the biblical axiom (embedded in later Anglo-American jurisprudence) that favored the innocent over the guilty. This tenet originated in the book of Genesis and a conversation between Abraham and God in which God, in a surprising twist, deferred to Abraham's reasoning on the subject. But seventeenth-century magistrates were more concerned about the corruption of a community by an individual, and more fearful of God's wrath if an evildoer went unpunished. As a result, both Dutch and English authorities in the 1600s ignored the biblical injunction and privileged the group over the individual as they dispensed "justice." It was left to Enlightenment thinkers to revert to scripture. As William Blackstone concluded in his magnum opus: "the law holds that it is better that ten guilty persons escape, than that one innocent suffer." Voltaire subscribed to the same principle.[10] Thus, eighteenth-century commentators appear to imply that it was better to jeopardize society by freeing a potential recidivist than to punish an individual innocent of wrongdoing.

Before 1647, the director-general of New Netherland and his council oversaw legal disputes and criminal proceedings; between 1647 and 1653 arbitrators assisted them. When municipal government was established in 1653, New Amsterdam instituted a more formal court system as well. The schout (who wore two hats as sheriff and prosecutor), two burgomasters (who acted as co-mayors), and five schepens (the equivalent of aldermen) heard cases on what was roughly a weekly basis.[11]

Slander prosecutions dotted the calendar from the beginning. Between 1638 and 1649, the court heard approximately 82 cases; settlers brought roughly 129 defamation actions before the authorities between 1653 and 1674.[12] In her pathbreaking article on slander in seventeenth-century Maryland, Mary Beth Norton unearthed and analyzed 145 defamation cases during the seventeenth century in a colonywide population that was far larger than the town of New Amsterdam.[13] One hundred six of those cases took place between 1654 and 1671, when Maryland law applied fewer restrictions on slander suits than it had in the past—or would in the future. In other words, this study and Norton's closely parallel each other chronologically, albeit not numerically: 129 cases in New Amsterdam versus 106 in Maryland during the same two decades.[14] Marylanders may have been more respectful to each other than New Amsterdammers, or more likely to shrug away speech that impaired their honor. On the other hand, the rural nature of Maryland may have scaled back the contact between people that gave rise to abrasive language.[15] Whatever the reasons, residents of New Amsterdam were considerably more thin-skinned when it came to accusations that undermined their reputations.

But the quantity of cases is not the only difference between New Amsterdam and Maryland. Cross-sex slandering was more evident in New Amsterdam than it was in the upper South. The words "rogue" and "knave," for instance, used interchangeably to mean someone corrupt or underhanded, were hurled at men only by other men in Maryland, but the records reveal nine women verbally accosting men with the same words in New Amsterdam. Adding rascal, cheat, thief, or a general accusation of dishonesty to the list increases that number by five.[16] A "despoiler" (who was also a "bloodsucker") ups the count by one more, making fifteen verbal assaults by women against men out of a total of thirty-nine nonsexual slanders. Clearly, women in New Amsterdam were not as reticent about slandering men as were their southern sisters. Nine men took enough offense at the accusations to respond with defamation suits.[17]

During the same period (1653–74) in New Amsterdam, twenty-one men accused other men of being rogues, knaves, thieves, and/or scoundrels and villains. Moreover, both men and women employed colorful language to exaggerate their accusations. A man was not only a rogue, but "a rogue of rogues" or a "consummate rogue," a clear escalation of the charge. He was not just a villain, but a "squint-eyed villain." Non-sexual slanders by men against men also included such creative expressions as Indian dog, *spitterbaard,* black pudding, "Dutch pock face," and devilish Jew, a medley that hints at ethnic and racial equality when it came to meting out slander.[18]

Unlike in Maryland, no women were defamed as witches in New Amsterdam. This is unsurprising, since persecution of alleged witches in Holland ended at the beginning of the seventeenth century, even as the rest of continental Europe continued to hunt them down.[19] At the same time, accusations of theft parallel Norton's findings: in the eight cases where women were defamed by accusations of theft, six of the defamers were female. Nevertheless, Dutch women were accused of stealing a more diverse assortment of articles than the plain vanilla textiles purloined elsewhere. Pork sausages, livestock, beaver skins, decedents' estates, gold rings, and tinware were among the items that unaccountably disappeared along with the usual linens.

Sexual slanders also chart differently in New Amsterdam. According to Norton's table, eleven Maryland women were called whores, with accusers divided among seven men and four women.[20] In New Amsterdam, at least twenty-seven women suffered that insult (or words to that effect) between 1653 and 1674, with the slur (or some combination containing the word) being uttered by sixteen men and eleven women.[21] Thus, although the male/female ratio of accusers is roughly equivalent in both places, the total number of slander accusations involving the word "whore" was considerably higher in New Amsterdam—and relatively more so considering its smaller population. Ten women in New Amsterdam sued their defamers directly, and of those particular defamers only two were men. Thus, women were more likely to sue other women for sexual insults, which speaks either to the relative importance of female accusations or a hesitation about taking on male defamers.

In New Amsterdam, men were often the objects of sexual slanders as well, the insults mouthed by men in all but two of twelve cases between 1653 and 1674.[22] Men were charged with being a cuckold (or a cuckold by implication), a bastard, a bigamist, an adulterer, a whore's son, or even a "hoore and Burthen's whore" (a possible reference to a beast of burden).[23] In the ten cases where one male defamed another, both plaintiff and defendant were male. In the two remaining cases, a man sued a woman who had accused him of displaying "carnal lusts," and in the last dispute, two women fought it out over a torn cap, "a slap or two," and a sexual slight against the plaintiff's husband. In the latter case, however, the insult seems to have been less important than the assault in which the defendant (Anneke Kocks) kicked the plaintiff (Geertruyd de Witt) "in the side and bit her in the ear."[24] Indeed, de Witt may have been less concerned about her husband's reputation as a cuckold than her own character as the wife of one—by definition an adulteress.

Adultery was another category of sexual insults, which theoretically, at least, is hard to separate from other sexual charges. Most of the women who were insulted as whores were married and thus technically being accused of committing adultery. Yet a man who accused a widow of being a whore and then added "your late husband did not make your children" was actually separating the two offending remarks.[25] Besides, if a married woman was accused of being a whore, the allegation implicitly made her husband a cuckold. Between 1638 and 1649, three women, one man, and one couple were accused of adultery—each time by a man. One of these women (a widow) sued her defamer directly, and two were represented by their husbands. One implied accusation of cuckoldry resulted in a defamation suit. In the period between 1653 and 1674, only four slander suits involving adultery made their way to court, although in two of them the charge was implicit rather than explicit.

The small number of adultery suits compared to other sexual slander actions may be explained by the way in which the law was enforced (or not enforced, as the case may be). Fornication did not top the list of criminal activities, as it did in New England. No ordinance specifically prohibited it, no punishment awaited it, except for the one or two instances of consistently debauched behavior. Adultery, however, was subject to prosecution. A local ordinance, passed in 1638, insisted that "every one must refrain from Fighting, Adulterous intercourse with Heathens, Blacks, or other persons . . . and other Immoralities."[26] Perhaps married couples remained faithful to each other for the most part. Otherwise, people were careful not to get caught, or their neighbors looked the other way. As a result of this indifference, even if a law prohibiting adultery was on the books, transgressors had little to fear from enforcement. The definition of "other immoralities" remains a mystery, although fornication could have fallen into this catchall category.

There can be little doubt that not all instances of defamation in New Amsterdam made their way to the courtroom. Yet what is striking about the ones that did is how often they provoked violence. Indeed, it is the assault component that becomes the focus of a slander case nearly 20 percent of the time.[27] In every instance where the sequence of events is clear, pushing, shoving, stabbing, and blows followed (rather than preceded) slanderous remarks. And honor notwithstanding, the court frowned more severely on the assaults than on the defamatory exclamations.

Not surprisingly, violence, slander, and alcohol often formed a triangle. In 1659 Reinier Gaukes was charged with "great violence at the house of Clery Aart." He "abused the widow as a bawd and the daughter as a whore and struck Hendrick Pietersen, who strove with gentleness to get him out the house; also Jan Gillesen Koeck, wherefore Mr. Paulus Leendertsen van der Grift . . . had him removed." Asked if he was guilty of the charges, Gaukes responded that "he knows nothing about it, as he was drunk." Questioned about a subsequent assault shortly thereafter, Gaukes waffled: although "he knows nothing of it" (presumably because he was smashed), he "does *not* deny, that he has *not* struck" two other people.[28]

If New Amsterdam was a sexually permissive society—or at least more permissive than New England—it seems paradoxical that the word "whore" aroused such ire and provoked such a backlash. Yet it is a paradox only if the word is narrowly applied in its sexual context. In a broader sense, however, a whore represents instability. Married or unmarried, she cannot be trusted. She has no loyalty to her husband, and as a mother she brings forth children whose paternity is uncertain. On one level, then, a whore destabilizes the institution of marriage and the descent of property. Were her children the legitimate heirs of her husband, or weren't they? As a result of her indiscretions, a married whore emasculates her husband and opens him to the accusation that he is unable to control his household. Married or single, a whore upsets the social order by questioning its legitimacy.[29]

As it happened, nearly all of the women slandered as whores in seventeenth-century New Amsterdam were married. But it is unlikely that many were involved in extramarital affairs. Nor is it likely that more than a few widows and single women passed their time bedding down other New Amsterdammers. Furthermore, gossip being what it was in that time and place, family and neighbors surely knew as much. So if a woman's sexual probity was not at issue, why lash out at her as a whore?

Only if the word is understood to be ambiguous and, consequently, interpreted in a wider social context do the accusations make sense. New Amsterdammers came from an Old World culture where Dutch women were excluded from formal politics yet maintained important economic and social roles. They were traders and shopkeepers and took a keen interest in the business affairs of their families. In the seventeenth century they also took part in riots and disturbances in Dutch towns, which gave them a say in the informal politics of the republic.[30] Under Roman-Dutch law, wives and husbands owned property jointly, and she was equally liable for their debts. Unlike her married common-law sisters, a wife could own property herself. Furthermore, a married woman could make contracts and sue to implement them.[31]

In response to these conditions, Firth Haring Fabend raises a question that complicates slander suits and the use of the word "whore." She asks whether the prevalence of women in the marketplace, and the "economic leverage" that Roman-Dutch law encouraged, exacerbated tensions between men and women. It is likely that female mobility did make economic competition more stressful, and that if a "whore" is more broadly defined as someone who traffics in goods instead of bodies, the content of whore-related slander cases in New Amsterdam becomes saturated with subtleties. Put another way, if the word "whore" was actually a metaphor rather than an explicit accusation, it suggests that New Amsterdammers were using the legal system for subliminal ends. In short, they were motivated by underlying rather than obvious issues: commercial rather than sexual intercourse was the core of these disputes.[32] Calling a woman a whore was tantamount to saying she was an untrustworthy businessperson whose transactions were duplicitous.

As it happens, the culture of Amsterdam in the mid-seventeenth century lends credibility to this interpretation. According to Lotte van de Pol, who has studied prostitution in the early modern Netherlands, Amsterdam was Europe's seventeenth-century "city of whores." Distinguishing between whores and prostitutes, van de Pol points out that even if a whore did not support herself with proceeds earned from illicit sex, she was indecent nonetheless. A whore was a woman who engaged in scandalous behavior, and she lacked morals. She was godless, bawdy, and lewd even if she did not make a living by prostituting her body for money.[33]

Honor was an important concept in seventeenth-century Amsterdam (as it was in the rest of Europe), and whores were, by definition, dishonorable.

Calling a woman a whore in public disgraced, shamed, and humiliated her. It questioned her honor. As van de Pol explains, in the popular literature a whore was equivalent to a bankrupt man. Not only that, but whores were actually thieves who lured men with the promise of sexual favors only to rob them.[34] And that is precisely what unscrupulous businesswomen were accused of: they promised a fair transaction, but in fact robbed their clients.

If rethinking the word "whore" reveals less-obvious meanings, so do two other slanders cast at women: "swine" and "baggage." A second look at these words also suggests that control of the marketplace was in question— and the courtroom was the forum where this contest was played out. In the seventeenth century, "baggage" was equated with rubbish or corrupt matter—a trashy article. More to the point, it meant a worthless, good-for-nothing woman who led a disreputable or immoral life: a strumpet. Given the obsessiveness with which Dutch women were said to clean their houses, "swine"—a word associated with squalor—was a particularly inappropriate charge. Yet swine was also equated with greediness, and might be applied to a sensual, degraded, or coarse person. In the New Amsterdam court records, the word was often coupled with whore, as in "whore and swine." In fact, swine was used indiscriminately with trollop, jade, slut, and bawd, combinations that speak not only to the linguistic creativity of Dutch slanderers, but to the word's use as a synonym for whore.[35]

Lewd women were compared to unclean animals not only in New Amsterdam but in Amsterdam as well, where the word *dreckig,* literally translated as "dirty" or "filthy," may also be interpreted as a dishonest or sexually perverse person. Van de Pol notes that Dutch insults often contained animal analogies such as cow, "street swine," pig (a dirty animal), or dog—the last "an animal that makes a point of displaying its sexual organs and copulating in public."[36]

A further reason for believing that overtly sexual words masked covert meanings involves high culture in Amsterdam in the mid-seventeenth century. The golden age of Dutch painting was also the era of Jan Vermeer, whose sensual yet seemingly innocuous canvases of maids, mistresses, courtship, and farm scenes contain sexual allusions to male and female body parts (i.e., eggs = testicles, and pitchers = voluptuous women). Such images would have been appreciated by Dutch art lovers in this sophisticated city of one hundred and seventy thousand. Pictures and words might appear to mean one thing, yet could simultaneously deliver a sly yet sub rosa message to an observant viewer or listener.[37]

All this is to say that slander, in both Amsterdam and New Amsterdam, was a power play. As psychologists well know, people engage in slander to elevate themselves above others. In such a way slander becomes a strategy by which people demean or denigrate those who compete with them or threaten their status. Moreover, slander is often a response to anxieties and insecurities.[38] Set in the context of the Netherlands and its North American colony in the mid-seventeenth century, words mattered because the economy mattered.

If the Dutch West India Company took little interest in New Netherland to begin with (other than a halfhearted attempt at a trade monopoly), it removed itself from serious competition altogether when it finally opened trade between the colony and mother country to all citizens after 1638.[39] In this ripe economic climate, New Amsterdammers scrambled for gain in the race for economic advantage. Given the strong patriarchal nature of the society, coupled with the economic rights accorded by law to both unmarried and married women, it is hardly surprising that commercial clashes took on gendered overtones.

The timeline corroborates this interpretation. According to Dennis Maika, sojourners, or outside traders, had threatened New Amsterdam's commerce by circumventing the town en route to upriver markets. The upshot of a 1657 complaint to the director-general and council about this trade resulted in the establishment of great and small burgher rights. Outsiders would be permitted to trade only if they opened a shop in New Amsterdam, a requirement that included the purchase of a burgher right. New Amsterdam's residents secured their citizenship and burgher rights free of charge, but a burgher's oath was a prerequisite to this elite status, just as it was for outsiders. The rights, which could be inherited and conferred by marriage, conveyed advantages that were shared by women as well as men, and wives as well as husbands.[40] Between 1657 and 1661, 210 tradesmen paid twenty guilders for small burgher rights.[41] That number is deceiving, however, since men and women qualified for burgher rights either through inheritance or marriage. Thus, the number of small burghers was considerably higher than the list implies. Whether it was as high as Russell Shorto claims is questionable, but regardless of the actual number, the economy was moving in the right direction. As Peter Stuyvesant noted in 1658, God had showered the province with "prosperity, abundance, [and a] remarkable increase of population and trade."[42]

There can be little doubt that competition for customers and goods was keen, especially with the price of essential goods skyrocketing in 1659. Taken together, these local conditions may very well have precipitated the rise in slander cases between 1658 and 1663. Sixteen of the twenty-seven instances where a woman was defamed as a whore occurred during those years. The preponderance of assault cases associated with slanders was clustered during that period as well (thirteen out of twenty-four). Equally important, nearly all of the women who were either plaintiffs or defendants in cases involving the word "whore" (and who can be traced) appear to have been engaged in some sort of business activity. Marretie Joris trafficked in oysters and brandy, among other items. Madaleen Vincent and Geertje Teunis were tapsters, Metje Greveraat took the burgher oath and traded business tools, Geertje Hendricks had commercial dealings, Abigail ver Planck was a fur trader, and Elsie Gerrits surely carried beaver pelts with her on her trip to Fort Orange.[43] Twenty-three husbands associated with either defamers or objects of defamation were among the small burghers. What all these fragments of information seem to suggest is that the competitive atmosphere in New Amsterdam may have created underlying economic tensions that were overtly expressed through allegations of sexual misconduct. They may also be read as an attempt to create a distrust of women in the marketplace. At another time and place these same women might have been accused of witchcraft.[44]

Sexual slanders against men are more difficult to assess, yet it is hardly a reach to suggest they may contain subliminal attacks on commercial (as opposed to bodily) trafficking. Since studies show that slanders against married women are often concealed attacks against their husbands, the reverse is potentially true as well. The wife of a cuckold was, by definition, a whore or adulteress. Thus the wives of the three men who were defamed as such either explicitly or implicitly may have been the actual targets of the slander. A man addressed as a *"hoore"* was the direct butt of a linguistic lob—or he may have been defamed in his wife's stead. To call a man a "whore's son" or a bastard implied a mother's whoredom. Even an accusation of bigamy conveyed the notion of whoring, since it involved illicit sexual activity on the part of the male. Were these sexual assaults on the character of men (or the covert attacks on the women with whom they associated) a way of reducing competition in a hotly contested commercial market? Maybe so.

To be defamed as the "son of a dog" implies sexual promiscuity as well. And being slandered as a "pokie rogue" or a "pocked rogue" not only linked an unsightly appearance to a scarred character, but was tantamount to calling the male target a whore, since *pokken* may be translated as syphilis, a disease transmitted through indiscriminate sexual liaisons. In her book, Lotte van de Pol explains that in Amsterdam a man could be insulted as a rogue, rake, or knave, all of which contained sexual connotations. He might even be cast as a male whore. If pokken was a reference to syphilis, whoever engaged in any sort of traffic—sexual or economic—with pokie-ridden men or women risked contagion, literally by contracting the disease, and figuratively by being tainted with dishonor.[45] Jacob Teunissen, an alleged pokie rogue, was a small burgher, and his accuser, Elsie Gerrits, a trader. This was not the first time Elsie had insulted a man; she had already defamed the very affluent lawyer, estate manager, surgeon, and merchant Jacob Hendricx Varrevanger in language that emphasized her point. He was, she said, "a rogue of rogues."[46] Varrevanger sued Gerrits and won.

If name calling was motivated by a desire to cast doubt on the reputation and integrity of the competition, it was a clever ploy. Many defamers were probably never hauled into court, and those that were, walked away after a request for forgiveness and/or a small fine. Meanwhile, their targets were subjected to negative advertising, while the legal system aided and abetted the pursuit of profit in an unintended way. Apologies notwithstanding, words once said can never be unsaid.

New Amsterdam was not Boston. The Puritans were probably not as prim as Hawthorne portrayed them, and the Dutch not quite as brash as Diedrich Knickerbocker parodied them. Yet truths are occasionally embedded in stereotypes; both Boston and New Amsterdam contained people with hollow legs. At the same time, New England miscreants did not flout either the law or communal sensibilities quite as flagrantly as the inhabitants of New Amsterdam. It would be difficult, in other words, to picture a visible saint requesting permission from a neighbor to sleep with his wife, and even more problematical to envision a Boston matron drawing a knife from her boot to threaten a rival. Personal confrontations took place in both venues, yet religious oversight and prescriptive literature seem to have modified behavior in Massachusetts. A rebellious Anne Hutchinson took on the clerical establishment, but she did so as a matter of conscience. She did not, like Grietje Renier in New Amsterdam, accuse a minister of swearing falsely, nor did Hutchinson raise her petticoat and moon an amused crowd. Surely, a few Bostonians frolicked "in the bush," but unless historians have misread them, they did not engage in the same raucous speech and coarse conduct that perturbed the Dutch authorities. If the documents are at all reflective of the people whose words and actions brought them before the court, New Amsterdammers were far more often in Dutch with their neighbors than were the English colonists to the north. The following cases in which males sue males, males sue females, females sue males, and females sue each other allow the antagonists to speak for themselves.

The seventeenth century was the golden age of Dutch painting. Willem Claesz Heda may not be as well known as his contemporaries Rembrandt and Vermeer, but his work has made its way to the Metropolitan Museum of Art, where his 1635 painting *Still Life with Oysters* graces a wall. Some years after Heda completed the painting, a New Amsterdam burgher—who may or may not have known of the artist—contemplated a lawsuit against a few loudmouthed men who challenged his manhood. The case began with oysters.

According to Joost Goderis's complaint, he was returning from Oyster (now Ellis) Island, where he and a boy had been gathering the shellfish. On his arrival, he ran into a group of acquaintances, among whom were Gulyam d'Wys, Isaack Bedloo, and Jacob Buys. They "called out loud . . . you cuckold . . . Joost Goderis ought to wear horns."[47] The men continued to taunt Goderis, saying "Allard Antony" [a public official] had Goderis's wife "down on her back."[48] That being alleged, Buys asked Goderis for a "*lettre repressaille*"—a letter of reprisal granting Buys permission to sleep with Goderis's wife. Subsequent testimony indicated that Goderis responded genially, "If you can induce my wife to do it, I am satisfied." Although some of this must have been banter, Goderis took it badly. Confronting Bedloo on the Strand, Goderis inquired "why he had so insulted him," to which Bedloo replied, "you fool, I have said nothing, you said it yourself."[49] Goderis then slapped Bedloo, who immediately drew a knife and slashed Goderis's neck.

On Monday, February 10, 1653, an irate Joost Goderis demanded "law and justice" for the insults. He made no mention in the complaint of the knife assault. The defendants denied the charges and began haggling over details. The Magna Carta may have established important legal principles in the English world, but Roman-Dutch law as applied in New Netherland took no backseat to the procedural rights enjoyed by English colonists. The defendants demanded, and received, copies of Goderis's complaint. The court ordered Goderis "to prove his accusation," an inviolate legal requirement at that time and place. To do so, Goderis summoned (or, more precisely, sued) four witnesses: Gysbert Verdonck, Jan Vinje, Harmanus Hartough, and Anthony van Hardenbeger. Each of these "defendants" received an interrogatory—a list of questions—from Goderis, which required answers. "Their Worships, the Burgomasters and Schepens," appointed a committee to hear the witnesses and "report to the full Board."

Guliam d'Wys, one of the original defendants, decided that a good offense made the best defense. Thus, on March 3, 1653, he countersued and declared himself "insulted" by Goderis's complaint against him. D'Wys then insisted that Goderis "give security for the expenses and damages" should he fail "to prove his allegations." In a fit of pique, d'Wys demanded reparation of *his* honor. Goderis reacted to this move with a procedural claim: since his own witnesses had "not yet handed in their testimony," he argued, "d'Wys's complaint cannot be received." Goderis then demanded that his witnesses swear to his "declaration," an order that prompted an instant refusal from each one. They would be willing to testify to the sequence of events, but to do it under oath was another matter altogether. Indeed, as Harmanus Hartough heatedly insisted, he was "not bound to swear to such trifles." The court thought otherwise, and since they were obliged "to uphold the respectability of Goderis and his wife as far as law and justice demand," on March 4 they put Van der Donck, Vinje, Hartough, and van Hardenbergh under house arrest until they declared "under oath" what they had seen and heard.

Whether or not Hartough actually believed that Goderis's claims were "trifles," his opinion is less important than the fact that oaths were not to be taken lightly in New Amsterdam. On another occasion, when the court ordered a plaintiff to confirm a debt by oath, the judges reminded him to "think well of what an oath is; and should he take a false oath his soul will be damn'd."[50] In that case, the court gave the plaintiff eight days to think about the consequences.

It only took the defendants in the Goderis case four days to reconsider. They confirmed Goderis's claims in vague language, remembering some things, conveniently forgetting others. Twenty-four-year-old Hartough swore he heard Bedloo shout "cuckold, horned beast," but said he did not know to whom Bedloo referred. Van Hardenbergh took a "solemn oath" that Buys asked for a letter of reprisal from Goderis and that Goderis said he would leave the decision up to his wife. At the same time, Van Hardenbergh tried to minimize Allard Anthony's role in the sequence of events. He may have been intimidated by Anthony's presence in his official capacity, or he may have been trying to protect a fellow member of New Amsterdam's elite leadership. Another witness, Van der Donck, argued that since he was only nineteen years old he would prove "by several authors and men learned in the law, that he is not obliged to take an oath." He was right; Roman law rejected witnesses under the age of twenty in criminal cases.[51] Nevertheless, in spite of precedent and Van der Donck's protests, the court remained adamant and resolved to keep him in detention until he "voluntarily" swore to his statement. Van der Donck caved on March 24, and although he surely took the oath involuntarily, his "so help me God Almighty" released him from confinement and enabled him to "attend to his business." Jan Vinje, the fourth witness, disappeared to think matters over but returned on March 17 to swear to his answer in front of the court.

The surviving records of the Goderis case do not reveal its final disposition. His case proven, his honor restored, perhaps Goderis did not press for monetary damages. Nevertheless, the case suggests that humor eluded men who found themselves the butt of jokes concerning their wives' fidelity—

assuming, of course, that it was in fact a joke. Goderis must have known that the law of slander was on his side and that the court would not tolerate, as a matter of masculine (or even cultural) consciousness, slurs that challenged sexual standards. Yet Goderis put his witnesses in a difficult position when he required them to swear to the events of which he complained. In so doing, he raised the bar, so to speak, and made the content of the defamation all the more important. Goderis took advantage of the legal remedies to which he was entitled, but by forcing his witnesses to testify against affluent men such as d'Wys and Vinje, he opened the possibility of repercussions somewhere down the line.[52]

The case also hints that both plaintiffs and defendants knew something of the law and how the legal system operated. And in a bind, they were aware that they could call on precedent and legal scholars to bolster their arguments. Given widespread community consensus involving matters of right and wrong, and an understanding that wrongs must be redressed, the legal culture of New Amsterdam functioned (house arrest notwithstanding) much as it did in the English colonies.

Marretie Joris was involved in two slander cases: the first in 1655, the second in 1660. So, too, were Maria Joris, Maretie Jorisen, Merritje Boot, Maria Boot (or Boodt), Mary Jores, and Mary Boot. This is not surprising, since only one woman answered to each of the various names.[53] To be fair, she was the wife of Nicholas Boot, which accounts for several of the surnames, but what was apparently common knowledge about her identity among her contemporaries is a nightmare to historians whose comfort zone is limited to English naming practices. Her name aside, we know something more about Marretie because of the volatile relationship between her and her husband, Nicholas (a.k.a. Claas) Boot, which came to a head in 1663.

The initial slander case was much like the others that wend their way through the court records, even if there is some confusion over the name of the defendant (as well as the plaintiff). In May 1655 Marretie Joris instituted a suit against *Gabriel* de Haes. After a series of defaults by one or both parties, on June 14 Marretie Jorisen told the court that two weeks previously, *Andries* de Haas "scolded her as a whore, and her husband as a rogue . . . in their own house." She named two witnesses: Claes Michelsen and Claes de Sweet. As usual in such cases, Marretie demanded that Andries prove that she was a whore or else satisfy her with "reparation of honor." De Haes denied the charge and, in a formulaic response, insisted that Jorisen prove he uttered the defamatory words.[54] Three weeks passed before the parties returned to court on July 5, but this time the docket once again referred to the defendant as Gabriel de Haes. It is verifiably the same case, even if the identity of the defendant is ambiguous.

Joris presented witnesses who confirmed her account, after which de Haes (Haas) entered an objection. "They are the pltfs' [plaintiff's] servants," he observed, suggesting that they had perjured themselves in support of their mistress. The witnesses, properly insulted, denied they were Joris's servants, and their testimony stood. With no other defense to fall back on, de Haes explained what had precipitated his slander. It involved a business transaction: "she said she was not indebted to him,—he replied whores and knaves act so," a reference to both Marretie and her husband, Nicholas Boot. Apparently Nicholas was not as concerned about being labeled a knave as his wife was about being called a whore, because it was Marretie alone who charged Gabriel (or Andries) with slander.[55]

Exactly what their business transaction involved is not disclosed in the records. Marretie appears to trade, but other than a shipment of 443 florins' worth of beer charged to her account and a transaction involving "freight for 5,000 oysters," there are no other specifics. Joris traded with both men and women, sometimes engaging in litigation when friendly transactions turned bitter. That some men, at least, were uncomfortable dealing with her in her role as a businesswoman is clear from the record. When Marretie sued Jacob van Couwenhoven for 234 florins "according to a/c," Couwenhoven requested "that pltf's husband come to a settlement with him." As to the case at hand, Andries de Haas was a baker—and a successful one at that—if his "voluntary contribution and taxation" of twenty florins in October 1655 is evidence of his economic standing. Gabriel, the more likely of the two possible defamers, was a tobacco farmer who was in and out of court on a variety of counts, but more to the point, he had a subsequent dispute with Nicholas Boot over the payment of eight beavers.[56]

With no defense, Gabriel De Haas could only apologize in prefabricated terms: he knew "pltf. and her husband only as honest and decent man and wife, and that the words were expressed in haste." De Haas's uncontrolled tongue cost him "six guilders for the behalf of the deaconry," and so ended a classic slander case that conforms to Mary Beth Norton's analysis: women were defamed as whores, men insulted as knaves.[57]

Five years later in 1660, Maria Boot was involved in another defamation case, this time as a defendant. In the new proceedings, Pieter Jansen, a mason, appears to have taken offense when Maria defamed him as a thief and a rogue. Maria admitted the slander but defended herself by explaining that "he first scolded her and . . . he ought to quarrel with men and not with women," a curious comment that may speak to gender role expectations.

Huybert deBruyn and Jacob van der Bos allegedly witnessed the altercation and supported Jansen's version of events. But as Boot maintained, "had she brandy to spend," she, too, could have purchased testimony, a comment that showed she could play impugn-the-witness as well as anyone. Jansen, as was his right, demanded that she prove her accusation, and the court "postponed the matter" in order to give Boot time to do so.[58]

On May 4, 1660, the parties were back in court, where Jansen demanded reparation of character from Boot for the slander. Boot reiterated her defense, pleading that if Jansen "had not troubled her, she should not have scolded him."[59] When asked if she could prove that Jansen was a rogue and a thief, she admitted she lacked evidence. "No . . . I know not what he is." Further pressed to prove that "he troubled her" and questioned as to whether "there were anyone present," she acknowledged Bruyn the Mason, but then added once again, "the witnesses have testified for a pint of brandy."

Since Maria admitted the slander but could not prove the truth of it, the court ordered her to apologize to the authorities, to Jansen, and to pay a fine of twenty-five guilders plus the cost of suit. She asked to postpone the sentence until her husband's return, a request that the court considered frivolous. The magistrates condemned her "for her bad and unbecoming language," adding the usual formulaic admonition that such behavior "ought not be tolerated in a well ordered place, where justice is maintained."[60] The schout (prosecutor) asked the court to confine Boot to her "chamber" until she fulfilled the sentence, but there is no indication they complied with his request. Had they done so, Maria Boot would have been under house arrest for a considerable amount of time. According to Schout de Sille, Mary Boot refused to pay the judgment. Whether that meant the entire fine or just the costs of suit is unclear, but in September 1660, after several unsuccessful attempts to collect from Boot, Pieter Janzen threw in the towel.[61] He "should take no more trouble about it," he said—which was surely what Maria Boot (or whatever name she went under) had counted on.

But there is a subplot to this slander story. In the intervening years between 1655 and 1660, Maria's husband, Nicholas, had obtained burgher rights, which meant that his wife could claim them as well.[62] Yet all was not peaceful in the Joris/Boot household. Thus, when the court indicated that Maria Boot had "frivolously" objected to her sentence by requesting a postponement until "her husband's return," they were probably reacting to rumors they had heard about the couple's deteriorating relationship. There was little chance that Nicolas Boot would be sympathetic to his wife's predicament, much less pay her fine. Two years earlier, in February 1658, Boot "complained of his wife" before the court. If she did not repair her "irregular life," he wished to "separate" from her. The court immediately summoned Merritje Joris and questioned her about her allegedly unquenchable thirst. Why does she go "drinking in all the groggeries and holes," they queried? Consumption aside, she responded that she paid for her habit out of her own purse and that Nicholas also went drinking, "rollicking and full," a common enough activity in New Amsterdam.[63]

But then, in a surprising revelation, she told the court something more than they expected to hear. "She has not slept with him for a long time," she explained. Yet "were she a young woman he would have more affection for her." The bench ignored these humiliating disclosures and in a remarkable display of male bonding told Maria to live in peace with her husband so that he would have no reason to complain about her. Seeing that her attempt to gain their sympathy had failed, Maria offered another scenario to capture the court's attention. Her husband "frequently beat her," she testified, "and he divers times shut her out." Worse, "he had not put either wine or beer in the house for her," which was why she went "now and again for half a *Mutjie* and a couple of puts of beer and he does not pay the cost."[64]

These allegations had their desired effect. The tables now having turned, the schout accused Nicholas Boot of abusing his wife, "shutting her up in her house . . . nailing to the windows and doors, and also beating her, as she declared." Following standard procedure, the court ordered proof of the charges, all of which Nicholas denied. As the prosecutor, Schout de Sille summoned "Boodts wife, daughter and servant" in order to interrogate them. Unfortunately, Merritje changed her story between February and April 1658, denying what she had previously admitted. Moreover, the court concluded that her testimony lacked respect for the men who judged her, tending to "vilipend or scoff at the Court," which, of course, could not be tolerated, etc. etc. They fined Merritje twelve guilders and once again sent her back to Nicholas, telling the couple to "remain at peace."[65]

Although the court records do not disclose any marital disputes between 1658 and 1663, the peace must have been fragile at best. In September of the latter year, the schout accused Merritje of creating "a noise both in the street and in the house," breaking windows and making "a riot." She admitted all, "saying that her husband shoved her out of doors, at which she was so vexed, that she acted so." Nicholas once again asked for a separation; once again the court ordered them "to live together in peace." This was not to be. By summer or early fall, arbitrators were called in to decide what to do with Marritje Joris and Nicholas Boot. They had the good sense to urge separation of the warring couple, advice the court finally followed. The settlement required Nicholas to give his wife a yearly maintenance of twelve hundred pounds of good Virginia tobacco. In return, Merritje was to "place in his hands under inventory what silver ware she has."[66]

Merritje's shouting matches with her husband are intimately connected with her involvement in the slander cases. While she may have been slightly more vociferous than her female acquaintances, her volatility, her visibility in the marketplace, and her economic standing as a burgher made her a target for the men with whom she did business and a court that was well positioned and culturally ingrained to keep women in their place. In one court appearance she accused her husband of being an inadequate provider. Not only did she lack wine and beer in a society that considered such potions as necessities, but "he has not a stiver."[67] Such indictments were tantamount to slander as well, since a wide circle of people would have been aware of Nicolas's failures. His reputation as a husband and a businessman were at stake, just as Merritje's character—expressed in sexual terms—affected her business dealings.

Merritje Joris was among the very few women who were involved in two slander cases in which integrity, not to mention chastity, were questioned. In the de Haas case, the slander erupted over a business transaction, which suggests once again that the word "whore" had a subliminal meaning. At the same time, calling Merritje a whore implied that she was an adulteress and Nicholas a cuckold. Nicholas could not have been happy to hear that or to have been called a rogue and a knave, but for reasons of his own he decided not to extend his wife's suit to include his own grievance. Perhaps he knew that whore was less a sexual slur than an economic one. Moreover, if his unwillingness to support his wife's claim was testimony to their unhappy marriage, the reverse may be true as well: her harangue against Pieter Jansen may have been the result of displaced anger toward her husband.

Jacques Cousseau may have been a formidable member of the New Amsterdam community, but he was not immune to a verbal assault that maligned his reputation and ethnicity. A large-scale wine importer, a mediator of business disputes, a three-time schepen nominee (who was finally confirmed in 1663), Cousseau was clearly respected by his fellow New Amsterdammers. Yet they never forgot he was French.[68]

Cousseau first brought Jemima Moreau to court in May 1661. She injured him without cause, he charged, and he demanded an apology. Cousseau and Moreau exchanged papers throughout the rest of the year, and it was not until January 1662 that the court finally heard the case.[69] Nothing beyond the case is known of Moreau, although her name and marital status indicate that she was either born or married into the French community of

New Amsterdam. If the former is true, her willingness to malign a French-man comes as a surprise—or, on second thought, perhaps not.

According to Cosseau, Jemima Moreau insulted him by calling him "a cheat," which was nothing less than a stab at his business reputation. She did not utter these words to his face—and Cousseau admitted "he had no witnesses"—but rather to two other men, Jacques Fletchart and Francois Gee, whose gossip eventually reached Cousseau's ears. Under what circum-stances Moreau complained to Fletchart and Gee is unknown, but her griev-ance was laid out in simple terms. Speaking of her husband and herself, Moreau said that Cosseau had "sold their grain without their knowledge, and had delivered them summer, in place of winter grain." Worse, according to Moreau, Cosseau had supplied "leveled measure, whilst they gave him heaped-up measure." In short, their transaction was not measure for measure, which gave Moreau reason to label Cosseau as a cheat. All this was related to the court before Cosseau entered the courtroom, a sequence common to legal proceedings in New Amsterdam, where the bench heard testimony sequentially and defendants did not initially face their accusers.

When Cosseau finally made his appearance, he produced declarations that "some Frenchmen had sent him without having asked it," and which, presumably, proved his case against Moreau. Then, in another ritual com-mon to defamation cases, Moreau was asked "what she had to say against Jacques Coesseau." More specifically, the court inquired what she meant by her ambiguous comment that "people know well, what Jacques Cosseau is." In response, "she answers, that he is a Frenchman and that he presumes too much." Presumes too much about what? This was an odd comment, par-ticularly if she herself was of French extraction. Has she really "anything to say against him," the court persisted. "No," admitted Moreau, "she railed so strongly against him" because she "was angry" at the way he treated her and her husband. Why then, the court continued, did she collect "a mob about his door?" Her surprising answer reveals something about ethnic relations in New Amsterdam. She did not collect a mob, she responded. "They spoke French to one another," and "everybody stopped."

Even more revealing are the business dealings between the Moreaus and Cosseau, matters that show a contentious relationship long before Cosseau's slander suit. According to Cosseau's statement, he had shown favor to the Moreaus during the previous two years and had "advanced" Jemima "over a thousand guilders." And just as Jacob van Couwenhoven preferred to settle with Marretie Joris's husband rather than Marretie herself, Cousseau looked to Jemima's husband "for payment" of the loan. This may have been a mis-take, since Jemima's husband paid the debt in tobacco at a much-inflated price—over Cosseau's objection. In this instance, Cosseau was the injured party, but even though "he suffered considerable loss" from the transaction, he did not make a claim against the Moreaus at the time. Perhaps Cosseau bided his time and waited for a more propitious opportunity to vent his resentment against the Moreaus.

In the end, the court demanded that Jemima Moreau declare that she had "nothing to say against the person of Jacques Cosseau except what is honorable and honest." For calling him "a cheat" the court fined Jemima twenty-five guilders and the cost of the suit. In a gesture worthy of courtroom theatrics, Cosseau responded that he did not "require from her the costs he incurred, but [would give] them to the poor." The court gave Jemima eight days to pay the rest of the judgment, a sum Cosseau did not decline.

This defamation case is classic to the extent that a man had been slandered in terms that offended his business reputation. What is less typical is that the slander emanated from a woman, although she did not accuse him of dishonesty in a heated moment during a face-to-face quarrel. More striking is that Cosseau responded with a lawsuit, despite the fact that Jemima and her husband did not seem to have much influence in the community—at least as measured by their lack of visibility in the records. The number of people involved in this case also confirms that words, especially slanderous words, mattered. And if it is true that "a mob" collected at the scene of the incident, the scenario raises even more questions about language, ethnic compatibility, and the absorption of the "other" into the dominant society—even one as heterogeneous as New Amsterdam.

Grietje Pieters was a businesswoman. She was, to be sure, a married businesswoman, which meant that her carpenter husband, Frederick (or Frerick) Aarson, occasionally stood in as her courtroom alter ego.[70] Nevertheless, even if Frederick and Grietje were interchangeable in a legal context, he was not her business partner. Frederick was, however, a burgher, which automatically conferred burgher rights on Grietje, as well as rank and privilege in New Amsterdam's commercial community. Grietje was a small entrepreneur who traded in linen. She bought the fabric in various quantities and then farmed it out to workers who made shirts and caps. If this agreement between owner of material and hired labor was equivalent to the putting-out system, the arrangement appears to have been an early foray into proto-industrialism.

Grietje's success in the business world depended on her reputation—just as it did for a man in the same circumstances. Good business followed a good name; any hint of dishonesty compromised Grietje's honor and thus her livelihood. As a result, her presence in the courtroom as either plaintiff or defendant suggests that women in New Amsterdam took very seriously comments that questioned their integrity. Moreover, the cases in which she was involved confirm that if women cooperated and assisted each other on a regular basis, they were not above using vicious slander and rumors as competitive strategies. And if women, as well as men, publicly defended their probity against accusations of malfeasance, such slurs become less useful as a tool with which to distinguish gender roles. Both men and women were expected to act honorably in matters of commerce. The cases in which Grietje Pieters was involved also suggest that even nondefamatory accusations that hint at improprieties jeopardized her reputation and that New Amsterdammers walked a thin—and sometimes humorous—line between permissible speech and slander.

Grietje Pieters first appears in the court records as a plaintiff in a 1659 case involving ells of linen. Speaking on her behalf, Frerick Aarzen, Grietje's husband, demanded that Jan Eraat "repair honorably and profitably the injuries done to his wife," in language resonant of slander litigation. Eraat had apparently accused Pieters of short-changing him by reducing the amount of linen he, Eraat, received. Aarzen admitted that his wife possessed ten and three-quarters ells of linen but he "knows nothing of it."[71] The court demanded Grietje's appearance "on the next court day," to fill in the missing pieces of the story.

When Grietje faced the court over a month later, in mid-January, she persisted in her demand for repair of injuries. Eraat, in turn, produced declarations from witnesses who maintained that Pieters had "received a piece of linen for six shirts from Mighiel, a sailor," which Pieters was "to hand to Jan Eraat." As a result of their inquiry, the court ordered Pieters to deliver fabric equivalent to six shirts. Pieters complied by sending ten and one-quarter ells of linen to Eraat, hoping, no doubt, that this would satisfy him.[72] Since her husband had already admitted to possession of ten and three-quarters ells, the discrepancy did not sit well with Eraat. By October 1660 the two faced each other in court once again. "There is not sufficient linen for him to get six shirts," claimed Eraat. Pieters insisted "she had no more linen," whereupon Eraat produced a witness who asserted that Pieters admitted to having "enough of linen . . . for six shirts." Hearing that the witness swore to this statement under oath, Pieters retreated. "I will pay it," she agreed, a concession that suggests not only the seriousness of sworn testimony, but that her best interests lay with a quick settlement.[73]

To add to Grietje's legal troubles, in September 1660, a month before the conclusion of her case with Eraat, she was involved in yet another proceeding, this one brought by the schout on Grietje's behalf. According to the pleading, one Jan Rutgerzen struck "the wife of Frerick Aarsen." In response, Rutgerzen denied that he had assaulted her, "saying, that Frerick Aarsen's wife berated him for a *rich beggar* and rascal and he pushed her from him." According to Rutgerzen, the shoving match followed slanderous remarks about his character.[74] Grietje was involved simultaneously in two defamation cases.

A week later, Rutgerzen reappeared in court armed with a witness, Merritje Pieters. Merritje stated that "she did not see him strike Frerick Aarsen's wife," equivocal testimony that stopped short of exculpating Rutgerzen. Merritje's testimony was less than Rutgerzen hoped for, and was rendered moot when Grietje herself described the encounter in dramatic terms. She declared "that Jan Rutgersen struck her, and if she had not prevented it, he should have beaten in her brains; relating the causes which gave rise to it." Reading between the lines, it seems as though Rutgerzen objected to being called a *"rich beggar* and rascal," although he was not wounded enough by her barbs to bring suit against Grietje for her outburst. His lack of response supports Mary Beth Norton's conclusion that women's taunts about men were not usually damaging enough to inspire legal retaliation. Nevertheless, the court did not let Grietje off the hook. In the end, they fined Rutgersen six guilders for striking Pieters, and Grietje three guilders "for her evil speaking."[75]

Grietje Pieters and Lysbet Ackermans were both burghers. What's more, they were neighbors in a patch of New Amsterdam called the Marketfield. Ackermans, among her other commercial ventures, was a tapster. On a thirsty Thursday in March 1665, Grietje paused for a pint of beer at Lysbet Ackermans's house. Shortly thereafter, Lysbet, according to Grietje, "accused her with having stolen a beaver from her house." When sued by Grietje for slander, Lysbet denied the charge.[76] Carefully choosing her words to prevent them from being construed as defamatory, Lysbet told the court that she had said to Grietje, "I have lost a beaver, have you got it?"—a seemingly innocent question that circumvented a direct accusation of theft. Grietje remembered otherwise. Lysbet, she recalled, had "stated to her, there was no one else in the house but you"—an implication of theft that closed the gap between an innocuous question and slander. This was an important distinction, because truth was no defense to slander. Even if the accusation of theft was true, it would still be considered defamatory unless the accuser intended to bring a crime to the attention of the authorities. If Ackermans could not prove Grietje was a thief, Ackermans was in trouble. She stood a better chance of making the slander case go away if she denied she had accused Grietje of stealing the beaver.

In the end, it mattered little what Lysbet actually said, because gossip took over where the incident left off, and Grietje's reputation stood on the brink of collapse if she could not quash the rumor quickly. Matters worsened when Mary Pia assumed the worst and confronted Grietje about the incident in an accusatory tone. She "had heard it from others" that Pieters "had stolen a beaver from Lysbet Ackermans."[77] A week later, on March 7, 1665, Grietje sued Marya (Mary) Pia, demanding that Pia prove "that she had stolen a beaver from Lysbet Ackermans," a charge that redirected attention from the theft to the source of the gossip about the theft. Pia explained that she had heard the rumor from Sara Teunis. Called as a witness, Teunis testified that "she being at Tomas the baker's house," she learned from Jesayntje Verhage "that the pltf stole the beaver from Lysbet Ackermans." The court ordered Sara Teunis to submit proof of her testimony. In June, Grietje Pieters sued Sara Teunis.[78]

In court once again, Teunis repeated her earlier account and pointed a finger at the other rumormonger, Jesyntje Verhagen. Summoned for her version of the incident, Verhagen stated that "Lysbet Ackermans told her, she missed a beaver, but did not know who had it and that Grietje Pieters had brought a pint of beer from her house and left the door open and that an Englishman and an Indian were in her house, but she did not know, who took it." As the cast of characters increased and the plot thickened, each woman twisted the event to avoid a defamation charge. Teunis, however, rejected Verhagen's innovative retelling and insisted that Verhagen specifically said "that Grietje had taken the beaver." Since other witnesses were present at Thomas Laurensen's house where this scenario—in whatever form—took place, the perplexed court decided to "inquire further into the case." Grietje continued to demand "reparation of character, inasmuch as she is accused of having stolen beavers."[79]

Having gotten nowhere up to this point except to call attention to the charge against her, Grietje added to the list of defendants by suing Josyn Verhagen (who is "Jesayntje," despite the name difference). The new charge claimed that Josyn "told Saertie Teunis in presence of Marretie Cornelis and the wife of Tomas Lourens, that Grietie Pieters had stolen a beaver from Lysbet Ackermans." Not so, declared Josyn, who denied accusing Pieters of theft. Speaking with measured words, Josyn recalled that "[she] stated, that a beaver was stolen from . . . Ackermans and that [she] heard, there was no one in the house but . . . Grietie Pieterson." This was sophistry at its best. The other potential witnesses refused to get involved. Marretie Cornelis and Tomas Lourens' wife had no idea what Josyn Verhagen had said "as they were occupied about their own business."[80]

By this time, the mayor and aldermen decided they had let this morality tale play out long enough.[81] Concluding, with good reason, that they would never sort out who said what, the court required Grietie to pay the costs incurred in the various actions and further ordered "that it be not hencefor-ward troubled with such unfounded doings."[82]

If this series of cases involving Grietie Pieters contains elements of humor today, it is unlikely that anyone involved thought so at the time. Given that Grietie pursued the last action from February to July 1665, she must have assumed that the accusation of theft was, in fact, damaging to her reputation and worth her time to rebut it. With this in mind, she made every effort to clear her name. As it turned out, none of the defendants, male or female, was willing to admit accusing Grietie of theft. Language mattered, unproven accusations could be costly, and the court was hard put to distinguish be-tween slanderous and not-quite-so-slanderous words. Either way, until their patience ended, the authorities considered the case very seriously. The tes-timony emphasizes the prevalence and importance of gossip as a means of establishing or undermining reputations, as well as the value women placed on their nonsexual honor and integrity—the sum of which translated into their ability to conduct business.[83]

Indeed, there was a thin line between nondefamatory words and slander-ous accusations, as the following scenario described by an outmaneuvered male trader illustrates: "the wife of Wolfert Gerritsz came to me with two otters, for which I offered her three guilders, ten stuivers.[84] She refused this and asked for five guilders, whereupon I let her go, this being too much. The wife of Jacob Laurissz, the smith, knowing this, went to her and offered her five guilders . . . Thereupon to prevent the otters from being purloined, I was obliged to give her five guilders."[85] Since the narrator, Isaak de Rasiers, refers to both women by their husbands' names, he appears to see them as adjuncts to a male figure rather than as individual female merchants in their own right. Wolfert Gerritsz was a small burgher, which gave his wife burgher rights as well. De Rasiers's use of the word "purloined" is suspicious and hints at a potential theft, but by and from whom is unclear. Was the high asking price a theft, or did "purloined" refer to the attempt by Laurissz's wife to buy the pelts from under de Rasiers's nose? Either way, his use of the word bordered on the slanderous.

What is striking about slander cases is the way each incident circulated, drawing more and more people into a web where gossip and rumor spun out stories that affected reputations. The law banned defamatory speech, yet even though townspeople knew better, they consistently flouted the prohibition. Such unrestrained speech was not premeditated; it usually arose from anguish, anger, or alcohol. But it was not just the ubiquitous confrontation between two people that made slander part of New Amsterdam's legal culture. Shouting matches drew a crowd, especially when one of the participants was an officer of the law. It is, perhaps, a paradox that the law initiated and sanctioned the economic competition that triggered so much of the slander.

Schout Pieter Tonneman was "insulted, affronted and illtreated" by Joannes Withart, an attorney and large-scale merchant. The two men had been involved in litigation, and Withart apparently could not contain himself in the aftermath of the court's decision in Tonneman's favor two weeks earlier. "In the presence of more than twenty persons" Withart slandered Tonneman "as a rogue, villain, cheat, swindler," and, to make certain no one missed his point, "a dishonest person." In response, Tonneman demanded honorable and profitable reparation, adding a formulaic (albeit stage-worthy) phrase that was ordinarily omitted in like circumstances: "he is willing to declare on oath that he would not suffer such insults for such a sum,"—in this case twenty-five beaver pelts—"nay for any worldly wealth." Despite the public nature of the slander, Withart denied "having said such injurious words," leaving the court no choice but to demand proof. Unfortunately, the document trail ends at this point, and the records do not disclose whether the court resolved the spat or, conversely, the litigants reached a private settlement.[86]

Another incident illustrates how one slander could embrace an entire community. In order to catch the thief who had stolen a quilt from the house of "Jan the soldier," the constable of North Haarlem, Resolveert Waldron, "searched all the houses" but "could not find it." Determined to oust the culprit, "he assembled all the townsfolk together in the square and told them that a quilt was stolen, and as no stranger had been in the village, some of the inhabitants must be guilty." On hearing this, Pierre Croyson came forward and said that one day before the quilt disappeared, Jan Teunissen had told him that the victim "had only an empty chest in the house." Suspicious because of a previous allegation against Teunissen, and reasoning that Teunissen would have knowledge of the empty chest only if he had seen it, Constable Waldron accused him of stealing the quilt. Teunissen sued Waldron for slander. That case went nowhere, and although Teunissen was not convicted of theft, the court reprimanded him for vaguely defined "improper behavior" and required him to compensate Waldron for his "lost time" and court costs.[87] Meanwhile, everyone in North Haarlem knew that Jan Teunissen had been accused of stealing a quilt. Whether this was Jan Teunissen the miller or Jan Teunissen the carpenter or Jan Teunissen the tapster, such a reputation was not good for business.

Words matter. Their power is such that societies have defined the permissible boundaries of speech for centuries. They mattered because according to the worldview shared by New Amsterdammers, a "well regulated burghery" functioned best when the law controlled speech, and discourse was limited to words that did not wound. To the extent that words were weapons, they had to be restricted, and although the authorities in New Amsterdam never specified by placard (a statute or ordinance) precisely which words were to be condemned, townspeople were generally aware of linguistic land mines and what could or would be challenged in a court of law. By common consent—and this is what is meant by "legal culture"—words that demeaned female chastity or marital fidelity, speech that impugned the honesty of either sex, and language that ridiculed authority were banned from ordinary, heated, or drunken dialogue. Words mattered because they had consequences. When emotion overcame respect, and caution gave way to intemperate speech, the citizenry allowed the governing authorities to impose sanctions on those who maimed others with verbal slings and arrows.

Although unsupported accusations that undermine female chastity or threaten economic viability may still be tested in a court of law, the modern world has added new categories, such as "hate speech," to the litany of unprotected words.[88] It is unclear, however, how New Amsterdammers reacted to religious or ethnic slurs. References to Turks (Muslims) or Jews in the court records were frequently cutting, although there is sparse evidence that the targets of such insults were willing to confront those who taunted them. More to the point, however, the voices of New Amsterdam as recorded in legal documents indicate that even though heterogeneity trumped homogeneity, people of different ethnicities and religions were in agreement about what they should and should not say. It was common knowledge that civil authorities were quick to take offense and even quicker to punish insults that mocked their status. It was understood as well that blasphemy rarely produced more than a legal yawn, a moral dereliction that sets New Amsterdam in stark contrast to New England.

Finally, although slanders were a rebuke to the laws that prohibited them, New Amsterdammers showed their commitment to a "well regulated burghery" by prosecuting offenders. And even if the insults appear to have been spontaneous outbursts uttered in haste or by tongues loosened with drink, they more likely reflected long-standing resentments that were set off by a sudden spark. Since the litigants in defamation cases were usually well acquainted, callous words and the assaults that frequently followed may have masked underlying grievances or larger struggles, particularly in a preliterate society dependent on the spoken word to communicate its values.

The Dutch surrendered to a fairly lenient English government in 1664. Apart from replacing a few key political figures, English authorities allowed the legal system to function as it had in the past. Nevertheless, common law eventually usurped civil law, New Amsterdam slowly shed its Dutch identity, and New York emerged as a bona fide member of England's colonial empire. This could not have been an easy transition, since different attitudes toward crime, punishment, and perpetrators must have challenged the judicial system. Witches, for example, did not present a legal problem in a Dutch venue, but their unwelcome presence in an English colony demanded legal remedies to rid the community of such disruptive and malevolent forces.

CHAPTER 2

Bermuda Triangle

Witchcraft, Quakers, and Sexual Eclecticism

Three thousand people, twelve accusations, five executions. Proportionately, Bermuda's witchcraft outbreak between 1651 and 1655 rivals the worst of the seventeenth-century episodes.[1] Chronologically, the epidemic triangulates with other midcentury witchcraft frenzies in both old and New England, as religious factionalism erupts and then disrupts the 1640s and 1650s. Similarities with English and mainland incidents abound: suspected witches curse neighbors, kill turkeys, and bestow evil gifts. Victims fall sick, lose property, see specters. Accusers turn to the law for redress, and witnesses quickly confirm dark deeds. Familiars scamper about. Some of the witchcraft flare-ups in Bermuda, England, and New England begin with petty quarrels among neighbors; others with an ominous gift or the death of a child. Yet there are differences in this world gone awry. On Bermuda, the absence rather than the presence of ministers dominates the story. Equally important, the roles of accused and accuser are inverted, with the most marginal members of the community becoming finger-pointers. In this topsy-turvy legal world, slaves, servants, and prisoners of war bring charges against owners and masters. And as they do so, the law temporarily empowers those on the fringe of society by giving equal weight to the testimony of rich and poor alike. Moreover, if the standard profile of an English witch consigns her to the ranks of the unmarried, most of the accused witches on Bermuda have living spouses.[2]

Some of them deny their involvement with Satan. Others confess their allegiance to the devil.

The most complete trial records involve those unfortunates destined for execution. Depositions, heavily weighted toward the prosecution, hint at the inner workings of seventeenth-century Bermudian society as well as the mental anguish of the accusers. Testimony from the accused reveals hesitation, uncertainties, and only ambiguous denials of guilt. Taken together, the documents confirm a widespread and deeply held belief in witchcraft; and even if charges of *maleficium* are metaphors for personal and social grievances, it is significant that those resentments are played out within the context of Bermuda's legal framework.

★ ★ ★

By the time his two-day trial began in May 1653, John Middleton was convinced he was a witch. He came to this conclusion slowly, alternating between confessions, uncertainty, and denial. As early as August 1652, Margery Tucker had heard Middleton say several times "that he was a witch," and such dangerous admissions—uttered for whatever reasons—were not without consequence. Once rumors began to circulate that "Leiftenant White entended to question him for a witch," Middleton backtracked. "If I be a witch, it is more than I know." Yet if John was ambivalent, his wife—accused of witchcraft herself toward the end of 1652—was not. Her testimony must have resonated powerfully. "There is a witch amongst us," Elizabeth Middleton assured the grand jury in December—but "it was her husbande and not herself." Elizabeth eventually recanted during John's trial five months later, insisting then that "they have taken a wrong hogg by the eare" and that she had "no ground to accuse her husband to be a witch." Since the grand jury had not returned an indictment against her the previous winter, she could safely admit now that she had spoken "in the tyme of her distemper"— presumably to save herself at her husband's expense.[3]

If Elizabeth Middleton's accusation and retraction reveal something about the state of the Middletons' marriage, her conflicting testimony must have puzzled the grand jury convened for her husband's trial on May 3 and 4, 1653. Many of the grand jurors who had previously refused to indict Elizabeth had been recalled to hear testimony against her husband.[4] Yet it was surely John's admission after failing the ducking test that sealed his fate. Two observers, Thomas Hess and Michael Burrowes, accompanied a very wet Middleton back to prison and asked him what he had to say for himself. "Confess the truth," they demanded en route, to which Middleton responded that "he was a witch and that he knew that not before."[5] And Middleton

confirmed this damaging admission during his trial. Hoping, perhaps, that a
confession might save his life, Middleton tried to redeem himself: "I thought
that a man could not do the thinges I was accused for and prayed that god
would show his judgment upon me as you do. But since I came to prison I
prayed to the Lord to discover that to me, and now he hath found me out and
made me know that I was a witch, which I knew not before." Swift trial, swift
punishment: John Middleton swung from the gallows on May 9, 1653.[6]

Middleton's self-knowledge aside, of what did his witchcraft consist, and
why was he convicted? For the record, at least, the jury agreed that the
"severall signes and markes upon his Body" were conclusive evidence of
witchcraft, as well as the way he "vexed tormented and disquieted" one
John Makaraton, "a skotsman of about the age of 50 years."[7] The additional
wrongdoings that Middleton confessed to at the "place of execution" only
reinforced the judgment of the court. Among his transgressions were several
that were common to condemned criminals throughout the seventeenth-
century Anglo-American world: disobedience to parents, theft, drunkenness,
swearing, cursing, lying, and lack of godliness. Besides these formulaic talk-

FIGURE 2.   Witch dipping. English woodcut, seventeenth century. The Granger Collection, New York.

ing points, however, Middleton admitted to adultery with both "English and Negroes" and to running away from school (a fact confirmed by the presence of a mark rather than his signature).[8]

But there were other deeds, particular to John Middleton, for which apologies seemed in order at this precarious moment. He had consented "to the stealing of turkeys," and he "did curse John the scot for cutting his pastuer [pasture]." The latter admission is all the more striking since Makaraton had denied that Middleton cursed him—and it was the closest Middleton came to an admission of witchcraft that day.[9] In these last minutes of life, Middleton also attempted to make amends with his wife. Whether their marriage had fallen apart before or after his adulterous liaisons is uncertain, but he was remorseful, or so he implied, "for making awaie my wives estate. And making her case worse than it was when she was in trouble for witchcraft and for her goods I put awaye and denyed them until she found them with other folks." Under these circumstances, Elizabeth's original testimony against her husband is anything but surprising.

A further revelation from Middleton suggests he stirred up controversy by "making debate between neighbours," a reference, perhaps, to the religious disputes that had rocked the island colony for a decade and more. Yet only one disclosure would have sent Middleton to the gallows if he had been caught in the act: bestiality. Middleton confessed that when he was sixteen he "Buggered a heifer."[10] Buggery was no small offense in Bermuda; in Middleton's lifetime four men had been tried for the crime, two of whom were hanged. Indeed, less than a year before Middleton's trial, William Morth was convicted of buggery "upon the body of a young heifer" and was executed for this "abominable and wicked crime."[11]

Taken at his word, John Middleton was not a pillar of the community. Yet the first evidence of his presence on the island in 1624 hints at a young man with an ethical streak. Ordered to build a tobacco vault in which his master, William Peele, could conceal tobacco to sell privately in England, Middleton hesitated. Since tobacco was Bermuda's cash crop, and its sale strictly regulated, Peele was demanding that his servant break the law. As Peele's servant, Middleton would have been required to keep his master's secrets, but Peele's dishonesty put Middleton in a delicate situation. Worried that the authorities might get wind of Peele's scheme, Middleton told Peele "that hee heard the servants should bee put to their Oath what Tobaco was made as well as their masters." Peele warned Middleton not to betray him: "I tell thee Middleton, if thou doest reveale it I will make thee an example to all the men in the land, for I am a Jury man and so am like to bee and my word will be taken before thine." Apparently undaunted by this threat (much less by any deference owed to his "master"), Middleton refused to lie for Peele, and testified against him in front of the governor in February 1625/26.[12] No records attest to Middleton's age, but it is likely he was either in his late teens or early twenties, working off an indenture or term of servitude.

Given Middleton's age and station, this show of bravado is surprising. At the same time, it might be explainable if John counted on other Middletons of higher standing to back him up. Richard Middleton, who was a Somerset burgess in 1623, a grand juror in 1625/26, a man involved in business of the colony's governing council the same year, and a judge the following year, was undoubtedly related to the younger Middleton.[13]

Family connections notwithstanding, the next time John Middleton appears in the records, he is on the wrong side of the law. Ordered to deliver a bing (heap) of something to Henry Whethersbie in the spring of 1626 shortly after the above incident, Middleton refused. Charged with contempt against the governor, Middleton paid for his stubbornness with fourteen days' work at the King's Castle "at the Governor's pleasure." A little less than two years later, Middleton was fined and admonished for being drunk. But these were minor infractions, creating no impediment to his advancement in the community. By the end of March 1629/30, Middleton could be found on the "Jury for Life and Death," which despite its ominous sound was the petit jury for criminal cases.[14] And in 1636, Middleton leased twenty-five acres of land for seven years from John Ball, presumably to grow tobacco. The lease was short-lived, however. Scarcely two years later, for unrecorded reasons, he transferred the lease to Thomas Walker. It is unknown whether Middleton ever owned real property on Bermuda, but he appears to have made his living off the land. Documents recorded during his trial in 1653 refer to him as "a planter."[15]

The date of Middleton's marriage and whether he and his wife had children are beyond the reach of surviving records. That the Middletons had some personal property is evident from Alice How's attempt to steal it aboard the *King of Poland* as the ship crossed the Atlantic during the summer of 1652. Whether one or both of the Middletons were actually aboard the vessel, or whether they had ordered the goods from England, can only be conjectured, but the accessories themselves—cuffs, aprons, waistcoat, handkerchiefs (and handkerchief buttons), strips, and bandstrings—suggest the couple's genteel aspirations. Conversely, the items are consistent with a shopkeeper's inventory and might suggest that the Middletons were involved in petty trading as a sideline.[16] Aspirations aside, before the year was out Elizabeth Middleton had been brought up on witchcraft charges, and within ten months' time

John Middleton had been executed for doing the devil's work. Why? Why Middleton?

The formulaic nature of Middleton's indictment—that he had partnered with the devil—is less than helpful in understanding the accusations against him. The signs and marks on Middleton's body are part of a larger story, however, as is the alleged harm he perpetrated on the body of his accuser, John Makaraton. Bodies are central to the tale, and Makaraton—a Scotsman of no account—is readily believed because Middleton, probably in his early fifties by this time, may have already acted in ways that made him anathema to people who did count in this island community. In short, Bermuda was better off without him. They were also better off without three other witches: Christian Stevenson and Alice Moore, who were executed two weeks later, and Jane Hopkins, who followed them to the gallows in January 1654/55. Unlike Macbeth, this Scotsman got the better of the witches.

John Middleton was taken up "for bewitching . . . a skotsman called John Makaraton." Middleton initially denied the charge, maintaining that he had done "good" rather than "harm" to Makaraton when he "healed his legg which was hurt at the catching up of calves that were lose." Subsequently, however, the two men had a falling out over Makaraton's attempt to gather "hogsmeat" (food for hogs) from Middleton's property. Governor Josias Forster had issued a proclamation less than a year earlier that prohibited any person from trespassing on another's property "to digge Crabbe" or "to gather hogsmeat" without "licence from the owners." The penalty for ignoring the law was ten pounds of tobacco, unless the culprit was a servant, in which case he or she would be "emediately carried to the Justice or constable from whom they shall receive correction by whipping without remission." Unfortunately, Makaraton had been caught flagrante delicto, and he was a servant—to the same governor who had issued the proclamation. Middleton's initial reaction when he discovered Makaraton was "to strike him," but "he turned to him agayne so they parted that tyme."[17] In short, for whatever reasons, Middleton decided against a violent altercation on the spot, and subsequent testimony from both Middleton and Makaraton suggests that at the time Middleton neither struck nor cursed the intruder. So far, Middleton appears to have been the aggrieved party.

It is unclear whether Middleton and Makaraton parted in anger or friendship, but either way Makaraton may have been worried that Middleton would turn him in. If this fear preyed on Makaraton's mind, he may have conducted a preemptive strike against Middleton designed to divert attention from himself. But on what grounds could he incriminate Middleton? Since Middleton's wife had been accused of witchcraft the previous year, it was not unreasonable to think that her husband might be tainted as well. The sequence of events suggests that Makaraton accused Middleton of bewitching him, and it was only after Middleton's arrest and examination on Wednesday, April 13, 1653, that he revealed Makaraton's theft. Makaraton was "brought to prison" on April 15 and eventually tried for an unspecified crime—probably for trespassing and gathering hogsmeat.[18]

Shortly after his arrest, Makaraton was sitting just outside the prison door. Suddenly, he fell into one of the "strange fitts" that had recently plagued him and that were, presumably, the result of Middleton's power over him. He "grew so stiffe that they could not bend him in body legg or arme." After being carried into the prison, Makaraton "came agayne to his senses and talked very Discreetly," ate, and prayed. He included in his account "how he came hurt on his legg," a wound that he seems to have attributed to Middleton's malevolence as well. In short, Middleton had lamed Makaraton. Makaraton added that his fits rendered him incapable of "perfect understanding" and therefore he could not be "examined at all tymes." Thinking that a language barrier made interrogation even more difficult, Governor Foster sent for two of Makaraton's "countrymen that best could understand him" to inquire about Makaraton's relationship to Middleton. Makaraton related his story to James Blake, whose sworn testimony was later presented at trial.

According to Blake, Makaraton claimed that his "griefe and distraction" came upon him "by degrees," a development that took place over a two-week period. "At first he grew solentary," and it was during his "solentary fitts," while he was in bed, that he twice perceived "a thing in the shape of a man, black in culler . . . who sate upon him very heveyley and asked him if he would love hym and he answered noe. I will love God." Although spectral evidence was common enough in the seventeenth century during witchcraft trials, this particular scenario is unusual with its ambiguous hints of a homosexual and/or interracial encounter. Makaraton's rejection of the overture was formulaic: "I will love God"—yet Makaraton was, quite literally, in no position to reject what might have been a carefully crafted allusion to Middleton. If the subliminal reference is indeed to Middleton, the "man, black in culler" could have been Middleton as devil. If not an allusion to Middleton, Makaraton's fantasy involved an interracial liaison.[19] Either way, the apparition incapacitated the prone Makaraton by straddling him and rendering him unable to overcome his alleged tormentor. Makaraton also related that he roared and cried out to God. Blake was apparently ordered to keep close watch on Makaraton, who in one of his nightly fits exclaimed that he was "terrified enough for Midleton's hogsmeat"—an indication that the potential repercussions of the incident still tortured him. Blake testified that Makaraton frequently repeated Middleton's name and, in the midst of yet another fit, insisted that Middleton "came to strike him."[20]

Although Makaraton alternately confessed and denied his desire to even the score, he consistently maintained that Middleton was to blame for his misfortune. Indeed, Makaraton was certain "that he should never be well until he saw Midleton hanged upon the Gallowes." And in a scene rife with drama, Makaraton described Middleton's attempt to silence him: "Ah ah Middleton art thou come to choake me," he cried out.[21] Yet Makaraton claimed in one of his more lucid moments that he was imprisoned not "as a thefe or a rogue but because the Lord's hand was upon him." Presumably, he was taking no chances. Jurors rejecting claims about Middleton's involvement in Makaraton's mysterious ailment might be less reluctant to hold God responsible for Makaraton's fits. Either way, Makaraton must have hoped that the hogsmeat charges would disappear in the hands of a sympathetic jury.

If Makaraton's conscious or subconscious visions led him to describe an illicit sexual encounter with Middleton, Makaraton had once again trespassed dangerously. Prosecutions for sodomy were as rare on Bermuda as they were in the mainland colonies, but a consensual relationship between two men would have been frowned upon, to say the least. In March 1653, six New Haven youths who had engaged in such nefarious activity were publicly whipped. Given the trade between New England and Bermuda, such sensational news might have reached Bermuda close to the time of the Middleton/Makaraton altercation.[22] From Makaraton's perspective, whipping was better than hanging, but if the specter Makaraton described had incapacitated him, Makaraton could be seen as the victim of a forced assault, rather than a willing partner in what was ordinarily described as an unnatural act. And if Makaraton could convince a jury that Middleton not only attempted to victimize him sexually but caused his fits, they might waive the penalty for stealing hogsmeat from Middleton's grounds. Moreover, if rumors about Middleton's sexual eclecticism were already circulating, such common knowledge would also explain why the jury was so ready to believe Makaraton's accusations.

The striking feature of Makaraton's testimony is his familiarity with the fine points of witchcraft prosecution. That witchcraft reposed safely on every list of capital crimes was surely a matter of common knowledge. Yet how did Makaraton know that laming someone through witchcraft would send the perpetrator to the gallows? Where did he learn that "the intent to provoke any person to unlawfulle love" was part of the revised witchcraft statute of James I in 1604? The latter offense was a capital crime only if committed twice, which suggests that Makaraton—or whoever was priming him—was wily enough to emphasize that the black man accosted him "two severall nights." Who told Makaraton that the best time to name Middleton was while he was "in his fits"—just as Michael Dalton, the seventeenth-century jurist, proposed?[23]

Elizabeth Middleton had reason enough to be angry with her husband after he alienated her property without her knowledge or consent—an exercise of his rights under common law, but infuriating nonetheless. Yet to accuse him of witchcraft—as she did during her own presentment—was a heavy-handed and disproportionate response to his rights under common law.[24] But if he had given her reason to suspect infidelity with a man, woman, or beast (he admitted adultery and buggery in his confession), she may have felt that an accusation of witchcraft was commensurate with the injuries he inflicted on her. When she recanted at his trial, it may have been because she realized that if her husband was convicted and executed, the state might replace her as the beneficiary of his property.[25] Notwithstanding such speculation, the record emphasizes the sexual component of the evidence against Middleton. John Middleton, like his contemporaries, associated witchcraft with specific marks, and the committee whose diligent physical search substantiated his guilt took their assignment to extreme and peculiar lengths.

Following Middleton's arrest on April 13, 1653, John Burch testified that he had been present at the house of Captain Robert Pulford, where he witnessed Middleton making over his estate by a deed of gift—an irrevocable transfer of property. Subsequently—and inexplicably—the question of witchcraft arose in conversation, at which time Middleton denied any involvement with the devil. To reinforce his disclaimer, "he put downe his Breeches and showed a marke," adding that "he had showed that marke to the Guvnor and to Mr. Paynter and that it was all the marke they could find about him."[26] The previous August, however, Margery Tucker heard Middleton admit that he was a witch and that, as confirmation of the fact, he had "two private markes about him," "the one between his fundament [anus] and his Codd [scrotum] the other on the inside of his thigh."[27] Not only did Middleton drop his breeches at the slightest excuse, but he was quite willing to disclose intimate details about bodily abnormalities to anyone who would listen. Whatever happened to modesty?

Because seventeenth-century rules of evidence demanded corroboration, the governor appointed six men to search Middleton's body for signs of witchcraft. Their thoroughness is reflected in their testimony. After stretching out Middleton's body on a chest, they found "one teate or dugge" and then another. The first was moist, the second dry. The committee further affirmed "that they found on his body divers suspitious markes and spots Blew in culler." Although it was common practice to conduct an invasive body search for signs of witchcraft, it was the committee's response to its discoveries that draws attention. "Because they desired to be better satisfied amongst themselves they concluded to search each other, to see whether there might appear any such marks upon any of themselves which they did accordingly, but they affirm that they found not any, nor the likelihood of any."[28] With the location of Middleton's self-disclosed abnormalities in mind, the vision of these six men groping each other leads to serious speculation about their motives. At the same time, the circumstances shed light on the way in which the law legitimized such examinations and legalized what at another time and place might be highly suspicious and bizarre behavior.

Although Elizabeth Middleton would have been privy to marks on her husband's body when she accused him of witchcraft in 1652, she never mentioned any deformities—at least none that made their way to the record. Her major complaint seemed to have been that "she suffered for his cause." Yet even when Elizabeth Middleton retreated from the accusation after her husband was charged the following spring, her testimony did not exonerate him completely, and her innuendos connected their intimate relationship to the possibility of witchcraft.[29] Elizabeth Middleton stated that "when her husband had been lying with her she hath felt some thing in the night lying [in] her stomach and much tormenting her in her body—she conceives that might prove from natural causes for that she hath been so troubled before she knew her husband." Whether she meant "knew" in the biblical or social sense is uncertain. But even if "she had no ground" to accuse John of witchcraft, the torment during intercourse with her husband only "might" prove to have been from natural causes. Left for consideration was whether Elizabeth Middleton "might" have had intercourse with the devil. Once again the legal context provided justification for these pronouncements. Although none of these revelations would have surprised the neighbors with whom Elizabeth Middleton gossiped, under cover of law the bedroom activities engaged in by John and Elizabeth became a matter of public discussion, jurisdiction, and intervention.

Although John Makaraton was the chief witness against John Middleton, and it was Makaraton's accusation that was Middleton's undoing, other witnesses added weight to Makaraton's account with suggestive embellishments. "A negro Boy called Symon being in prison, in another roome where this Makeraton was prisoner, he saw through a great hole in the wall a thing of a blacke culler come from towards the place where he laye and ran so swiftly that he could not well tell the shape of it, which thing went out of the privy hole. Att that instant he heard the man give a thump and make a noyse which before he thinks was fast asleep."[30] Under ordinary circumstances, a "thinge of a blacke culler" scurrying through a cell would have been a rat, yet Symon was clearly implying that Middleton's familiar disturbed Makaraton's rest.

Similarly, when Robert Priestley was at work near Middleton's house on April 15, he saw a "Black Creatuer . . . in the shape of a catt but farre Bigger, with eyes like fier, and a tayle near as long as a man's arme." "Daunted" at first, Priestley "tooke courage" and investigated the creature. Bravely, he drew his knife "to strike at it." Yet even though he was "a strong man, he found he had no power to strike it." Priestley became so "amazed and affrighted that his hayre stood up right on his head," at which point he took flight, notwithstanding how "wishfully" the beast looked after him.[31] Which barnyard animal—if any—turned menacing on the evening of Friday, April 15, matters little, but Priestley's testimony taken the following Sabbath was undoubtedly stimulated by Middleton's arrest earlier in the week. Sometimes a knife is just a knife, but in describing a tail "as long as a man's arm," Priestley may have been "wishfully" engaged as well. It would be interesting to know what other fantasies were running amok to make Priestley's hair stand on end.

If John Middleton's neighbors were provoked by his sexual escapades, they may have been equally disenchanted by his religious persuasion. John had allied himself with the radical Puritan faction on Bermuda in the midst of a civil war that battered not only England but also its colonies across the Atlantic. In 1644, three of Bermuda's ministers, Nathaniel White, Patrick Copeland, and William Golding, renounced their membership in the Church of England and declared their intention of establishing an Independent church on Bermuda along the lines of those in Massachusetts Bay. To the dismay of the authorities and the larger Presbyterian population, a small but vigorous group supported them. A 1645 petition lists the followers of this radical faction, and among the ninety-one names are John and Jonah Middleton—the latter one of the many other Middletons who dotted Bermuda by this time.[32] Banished to Eleuthera in 1648/9 to thwart an uprising against Church of England supporters, the Independent exiles were not invited home until the Protectorate was firmly established in England. Not everyone returned at once, and it took years before time soothed the religious passions of the most ardent believers. Jonas Middleton was likely to have been one of the exiled Independents; records show him arriving from Eleuthera on the ship *John* in March 1656/57.[33]

Whether the authorities attended John Middleton's execution on May 9, 1653, is unclear, but their examination of a woman, Christian Stevenson, on the same day suggests the haste with which they sought to rid Bermuda of witches. Middleton was responsible for her arrest since he had been all too ready to implicate other witches when prodded to do so a few weeks earlier. After the chilly April water in which he had been ducked cleared his head, he revealed that Christian Stevenson was a witch—indeed "as badd a one as any in the world." Upon further reflection, he named Goody North, but hesitated to "positively accuse her."[34] Questioned also about Goody Moore on April 17, Middleton replied that "he feared that she was a naughty woman . . . because he saw her in her window in a witches hatt." Clearly warming up to his task and obviously delighted to be the center of attention, he elaborated on Goody Stevenson's nefarious activities with imaginative detail. Immediately summoned to court to respond to Middleton's allegations, Stevenson denied the charges but quickly became the focus of an investigation despite her protests.[35]

If, on some level, the charges against John Middleton appear to be grounded in a local squabble between two men, the accusations against Christian Stevenson indicate that she was the very model of an English-style witch (her marital status notwithstanding). After the examination of the evidence against her, there can be little doubt that the long tentacles of English legal culture (as well as commonly held ideas about witchcraft) extended to this remote Atlantic island, some six hundred miles off the coast of North Carolina. Forced by law to accuse Stevenson face to face, Middleton responded to her denials by insisting that she was a witch, and as such, he said, "I would have thee judged." This dramatic confrontation (which was, one imagines, accompanied by a finger thrust toward her face) must have been followed by some tumult, forcing the officials to clear the courtroom of spectators. "None remayneing in the sessions house"—except presumably the court, John Middleton, and Christian Stevenson—a women's committee "were appoynted to search Goody Stevenson."

As the only confessed witch in the immediate neighborhood, Middleton suddenly became the leading authority on this subject, and the person to whom the women's committee turned for advice. It is somewhat puzzling that the newly formed committee did not seek guidance from Elizabeth Stowe, the one committee member with practical knowledge. Two years earlier, Stowe had been one of the jurors who found evidence of witchcraft in the form of a "blewe spott" in the mouth of Jeane Gardiner, a mark that cost Gardiner her life.[36] Lack of experience notwithstanding, Middleton now commanded the spotlight, and before the day was out the group had "some conference" with him. Middleton urged haste: "if at any tyme, they intended to discover witches by signes and markes they must not delay it but goe about it suddenly." As for their task, Middleton drew on a century of English lore:

> And as for their Teates or markes wch the ympes do suck; after their sucking these Teates wilbe pale & hard soe that if you offer to enter them wth an Instrument you shall hardly enter them, but if you do try them with yr Instrument Crie Twang: and as for those that do not suck after their desire, that those teates or Mkes will be redd because of moystuer in them, and they being prickt they will seem to bleed but it is not blood, but redd waterish blood & not blood although it may appear so to you.[37]

That Middleton was au courant is beyond refute. That he savored the physical details of this intimate examination is evident as well. Compared with the detached description of the marks in Jeane Gardiner's mouth, Middleton's instructions were overtly sexual in nature and consistent with the assertions he made about his own body.[38]

It is not surprising, however, that Middleton was so knowledgeable. Seventeenth-century English literature was rife with descriptions of witches' marks and advice as to their location, although the English pamphlets were rarely as precise as Middleton's prurient account. Whether Middleton could read is debatable, but even if he was illiterate, information about witches was surely transmitted orally. Testimony in a later witchcraft case indicates that word "about some Lancaster witches" had made its way across the Atlantic to Bermuda.[39] Moreover, the practice of pricking suspicious marks to see whether they bled or caused pain was widespread in England, and by the seventeenth century, witchcraft detection had become something of a trade. In 1649 a Scotsman who had acquired an expertise and reputation as a "pricker" was invited to Berwick and Newcastle to ferret out witches there.[40]

The women who were impaneled to search Christian Stevenson took their charge seriously, and what they lacked in expertise they made up in diligence. When they pricked "two small Teates or Duggs" in Goody Stevenson's mouth with a needle, no blood "came forth," and Stevenson "confest" that she felt no pain. Such a disclosure was tantamount to an admission of guilt, since the absence of pain and blood was the hallmark of a witch.[41] Stevenson must have been well acquainted with this aspect of witchcraft lore, making her confession a startling departure from the expected. Either she was so committed to the "truth" that she was willing to risk her life, or on some level she believed in the "proof" that the test revealed. This is to say that folklore became authoritative once it was transmuted into folk law.

Long-standing and widely held beliefs commanded greater respect with the force of law.

Because of the serious implications of the initial results, the entire committee—seven members—"did all severally search her mouth and prickt these Teates." Their painstaking efforts paid off with the discovery of "a blew spott or like wart . . . very suspitious & against nature out of which came waterish blood when they prikt it." These discoveries confirmed John Middleton's detection skills and were inspired, no doubt, by the power of suggestion: the committee members saw what they expected to see. It was common knowledge that Jeane Gardiner had had an abnormal blue spot in her mouth and John Middleton's body contained "suspitious markes & spots Blew in culler." A conspicuously blue mark attracted immediate attention, since it was one of several signs indicative of a witch's presence. According to Michael Dalton's widely consulted *Countrey Justice,* "the Devil leaveth other marks upon their body, sometimes like a blew spot."[42] Thus, the alleged anomalies in Christian Stevenson's mouth reinforced what her neighbors had long suspected. Goody Stevenson was a witch.[43]

For at least eight years Christian Stevenson had done all the things that witches usually did in seventeenth-century England. After having "consented to and with the Devil to become a witch," she killed children and farm animals, tormented adults, and interfered with the productivity of neighbors. None of this was news to Stevenson's neighbor-victims in 1653; according to testimony, they suspected Goody Stevenson of witchcraft all along, despite her persistent denials. Moreover, her profile boded ill: an older woman of little means.[44]

Thomas Seeward remembered that his healthy one-year-old daughter suddenly went into "strang fitts" eight years prior to Stevenson's arrest. He was advised by "Mrs. Seymer" that the child might be "bewitched"; Seymer then related a story about her own grandchild who also fell into "strang fitts" after an encounter with Stevenson. Seeward admitted to Seymer that Goody Stevenson "was very busy with his child and would ever and anon be giving it green plantains & such things." He subsequently forbade Stevenson to offer the child anything, to which Stevenson responded "do you thinke I am a witch?" Seeward's edict and Stevenson's reply confirm that both were acting out their prescribed roles according to their understanding of witchcraft lore. Seeward tried to prevent Stevenson from having any contact with his daughter, but despite his best efforts Stevenson would suddenly appear "with the child," exactly as witchcraft treatises described. As further proof of Stevenson's malevolence, one of Seeward's shoats (young pigs) died after Seeward refused to sell Stevenson a comb and "she went away mumbling."[45]

Played out in these vignettes were traditional witchcraft themes that were familiar to English audiences on both sides of the Atlantic. Witches gave gifts, they appeared out of nowhere, they harmed children and animals, they mumbled, and they avenged insults.

The most unintentional rudeness could provoke a witch's wrath. Mary Hopkins, a young servant, recalled an incident "4 or 5 yeares since" when en route home she "overtook Goody Stevenson." Stevenson indicated that she would follow Mary, which "Mary refused to doe because she [Stevenson] was her elder & told her it was not meet for her to goe before her." Presumably Mary was acknowledging local custom, but Stevenson rebuffed this common courtesy. "Wth that she [Stevenson] came to her & pusht her forwards." Later that evening, Hopkins "felt herself bitten on the arm."[46] Sarah Denicombe (Dunscombe) confirmed and embellished Hopkins's story. Denicombe "herd her cry out & say oh lord oh lord goody Stevenson was pinching her or biteing her." Mary's arm looked "as though she had bin Bitten."[47]

Mary Hopkins's mother also had a run-in with Stevenson. She was a recent widow at the time of her testimony, and the confrontation between Hopkins senior and Christian Stevenson involved a butter-churning incident. Stevenson had lent Hopkins some butter, but when Stevenson approached Hopkins for its return, Hopkins was unable to churn enough butter to repay her neighbor in kind. Despite Hopkins's best efforts, "her butter would not come," and a disgruntled Stevenson departed. Hopkins's husband finally threw the mess "into the Piggs," with the ominous comment, "pray god that this woman be not a witch." Henry Hopkins should have considered this possibility sooner. Guidelines for trafficking with witches specifically warned against trading butter with a suspected witch. To make matters worse, Stevenson returned to the Hopkins house later that day and insisted "that neither she [Stevenson] nor her husband had bewitched her butter," a remark that could only have stoked the other couple's discomfort. Whether or not the obstinate butter was Stevenson's fault, the widow Hopkins subsequently suffered at Stevenson's hands. As a witness to the committee search of Stevenson's body after her arrest, Hopkins testified that "she was taken with divers paynes & tortuers in her body so that she lost her child that she carried in a strang & unnaturall manner."[48]

Witches in English tradition not only produced miscarriages but were likely to harm children as well. And on Bermuda, as in England, youthful victims traditionally suffered lingering rather than sudden deaths. Thomas Seeward's daughter "pyned away" after experiencing considerable distress. So too did Thomas Murrill's infant daughter, Sarah, who "felt extreamly

sick & it continued with sore & unnaturall paynes until it died."[49] Both children were described as having grotesque physical symptoms of witchcraft on
their bodies. Seeward's daughter died after "her side hunched up & her eyes
grew out of her head & a great bunch grew upon her head." Murrill's child
had "boils upon the breast, wch had a black speck or spott on the head."
Subsequently the child's "flesh grew away from the bones so that they might
see the ribs very greavous to behold."[50]

In both cases, Christian Stevenson had suffered rejection from the parents
of the child, a classic precursor to a tragic event. Seeward resisted Stevenson's
attention to his daughter; Murrill refused to trade with Stevenson. Murrill's
wife also turned Stevenson away, after Stevenson offered a remedy to relieve
sore breasts. "Goody Stevenson bid her lay a ragg dipt in rayne water to her
breast. But she [Murrill] told her that she would have none of her medicines," which was a proper response given Murrill's suspicions. Nevertheless,
such a rebuff was fraught with risk. "After this her child was taken with a
greavous groaning & paynes until it died." If Thomas Seeward was consumed
with guilt over the role he alone played in his daughter's death, both Thomas
Murrill and his wife could share the blame. The records do not disclose
whether they berated or consoled each other, but surely they were haunted
by the belief that Stevenson's response to their rude and unneighborly behavior was somehow warranted.[51] The "charity refused" model in English
tradition was usually interpreted as a refusal to give rather than to receive
from the poor, but regardless of the precise circumstances, the two families
had acted in a disrespectful manner toward Stevenson.[52] Whether Stevenson
believed she played a role in the death of these children is unknown.

Petty economic disputes also incited revenge. Thomas Murrill explained
that when Stevenson came to his house to sell "a croseleth wrought with
gould . . . he refused it & would not meddle with her tone." She then offered to "buy some paper for a dollar," but "he refused that alsoe at wh. she
went awaye very much discontented," a portent of things to come. That day
"his child fell extreamly sicke."[53] Again, when Thomas Seeward refused to
trade with Stevenson, she took this snub badly: a shoat pined away and "af-
terward died." Seeward's reaction to the death of the piglet might also have
been expected, given his understanding of witchcraft: "He cut the tayle &
left eare & threw them in the fier saying it may be Goody Stevenson will
come by and soe she did." Seeward knew exactly what to do, since burning
a bewitched animal was usually meant to bring a witch back to the scene
of the crime. In some cases the witch would be beaten for the misdeed, in
others she or he would be prosecuted. It is not clear how this would have
helped the dead pig, but in cases where an assault fell short of causing a

victim's death, the subsequent execution of a witch was said to provide relief and even a cure.[54]

Henry Bishop also attracted Stevenson's ire when he only reluctantly agreed to trade with her. At first Bishop denied that he had some "hookes and lynes" to sell, to which Stevenson replied that even "old lynes would doe her turne for her, some to catch her some small fish." Bishop subsequently "picked some . . . & sold them to her." But his fear of reprisal for the unfriendly way in which he transacted business manifested itself in a dream that night. In his nightmare, Bishop fled from a spirit and fell into a cave, where he told a friend that "Stephen Stevenson had bewitched him." Matters only worsened upon awakening, when "going to turn himselfe in his bedd was not able to stirre & so continued for the space of a month not able to turn himselfe without great paynes, wch griefe caused him to cry out grievously."[55] Although one of the Stevensons may have been responsible for Bishop's distress, stress—caused by Bishop's fear—was the more likely culprit.

The torment that Prudence Seares underwent after an altercation with Stevenson was far more intense than Bishop's, even though Seares was merely acting as a mediator rather than on her own behalf. Seares "was entreated by Mrs. Burrowes to demand 12d of Goody Stevenson due for a payer of Spectacles," or "2 fowles if she had not money." Seares and Stevenson argued; Stevenson "called her plunder mouth & said that she coulde teare her flesh from her bones . . . & that very night . . . her tongue was puld out of her head and hanged out like a beastes tongue . . . so that she could not eat nor goe to church by the space of many days." Furthermore, "it was 3 tymes that she had differences with Goody Stevenson & all these tymes her tongue was drawn out & rufe [rough] like a beastes tongue."[56] How Burrowes persuaded Prudence Seares to represent her is unknown; why she sent a delegate to negotiate on her behalf is obvious.

Despite the gothic nature of the account, however, the connection between witchcraft and the female tongue was anything but coincidental. The tongue was not only associated with female sexuality, but with evil as well. Female tongues and malevolent speech were inseparably intertwined in the form of curses, as when Stevenson referred to Seares as "plunder mouth." The word "plunder" was very new to the English language in the 1650s, and on whose tongue it arrived in Bermuda is a question that involves the spread of language from the metropole to the periphery of empire. Linguistics aside, plunderers robbed people; presumably a "plunder mouth" would steal by the tongue—in this case by demanding repayment. Thus, Stevenson, who saw this claim as unjust, retaliated by punishing the tongue. Alternatively, Seares might have felt guilty about exacting the outstanding debt, which would explain the nature of the symptoms she described.[57] Later, when the search committee examined Stevenson's mouth, they were "examining" speech as well. It is hardly surprising that the devil's marks in the form of teats or dugs were found in the mouth of alleged witches.

Accepting any gift from a witch was dangerous business. Even a rose, a flower esteemed by lovers, artists, and poets, could wreak havoc in the hands of a witch.[58] When Stevenson offered a rose to Thomas Wiverley two years prior to her arrest, "wh he refused to take at her hand," she responded by claiming "I am no witch." Wiverley must have thought otherwise, for from that moment on, he was haunted and "fully persuaded that he saw Goody Stevenson" in her spectral shape. Stevenson tortured Wiverley in bed, turning him with violence. Wiverley was convinced that "being haunted in this manner" explained "his great weakness." His wife did not escape Stevenson's maleficium either. The side of her "that lyeth next to him in the night" was "very black," although it was not discolored "when they lye downe together."[59] Here, too, guilt over his lack of politeness may have predisposed Wiverley to fear and to expect reprisal.

The strangest story about Stevenson and a rose was related by Anne Buller, who quarreled with Stevenson over twopence. After they "grew friends again . . . Goody Stevenson came to her & gave her a Rose." For whatever reasons, Buller, a married woman, "kept the rose in her bosom all the night following." During the night, she felt a hand "in her bosom," and in the morning "herselfe & children sought for the rose . . . but could not see nor fynd so much as one leafe of it." When questioned, Stevenson denied retrieving the rose, but apparently the question exasperated her, and she took her annoyance out on Buller. Buller "was haunted every night for the space of a yeare & half." Matters worsened when "a thing having the shape of a woman came in the night" and grabbed Buller "by the throat." Buller managed to bite the apparition's thumb so hard "that her mouth was all clammy with blood." Predictably, Goody Stevenson appeared the next morning with "a clout bound about her thumbe," and subsequently Buller "was never after haunted any more," presumably because she had drawn blood of the witch.[60] Buller made the mistake of telling people about the thumb incident, however, which resulted in a search of Christian Stevenson, who reacted by effecting the death of cattle, hogs, and young pigs. Worse, Buller's infant "pyned away by the space of 3 quarters of a yeare & then died."[61]

Whether John Middleton was one of the "divers people" in whom Buller confided, or whether Middleton was repeating gossip he heard thirdhand is unclear, but when pressed to explain the accusation of Stevenson that led to her arrest, he said "he had herd that she had given Goody Butler a Rose & after she had smelt on it the woman was very much troubled and ill or sicke." Faced with Middleton's allegations, Stevenson "answered him that it was true that such a Report there was about giving her a Rose, but she gave it to her for noe hurt to her."[62] A rose is a rose is a rose. Or is it?

The records tell us nothing about past differences between Christian Stevenson and John Middleton. Nevertheless, when "earnestly" pressed "to discover other witches," he immediately accused Stevenson. Her name must have resonated among his listeners, since Stevenson had been suspected of witchcraft for many years prior to 1653. In such circumstances, she was a reasonable choice. And once Middleton uttered her name in public, other tongues were loosened. Almost all of Stevenson's accusers were neighbors from Pembroke Tribe (tribes were the equivalent of parishes) and appear to have lived within shouting distance of each other near Crow Lane, an arm of the sea now known as Hamilton Harbor.[63] Apart from their proximity, however, the records reveal little about the people surrounding Stevenson. Only the Fords and Wiverleys (Weaverlys) owned property; the rest leased or rented. Wiverley appears in the records only as a juror; his wife, Ann, as a midwife.[64] No one in the group could sign his or her name; even the men signed with a mark. Henry Bishop, a sometime vestryman and inquest juror from Hamilton Tribe, added his signature to his account; Thomas Murrill, the merchant/planter from Southampton Tribe, did not. The Dunscombes of Pembroke inscribed neither name nor mark, but the prominence of this extended family and the number of Dunscombe wills that survive for that period and beyond suggest that they were at least middling folk.

Thomas Dunscombe was a blacksmith who occasionally served as civil and grand juror when not involved with his own litigation. We are privy to his occupation because he was called upon to use one of his instruments to file "a ragged tooth" of Goody Stevenson's, which, she insisted, was responsible for one of the marks on the inside of her "cheeke." The other suspicious deformity had been caused by an "impostume"—or so she said.[65] Daniell Buller, a now-and-then juror, went head to head with the law himself when he refused to account for goods recovered from a wreck. Henry Ford both initiated and defended lawsuits. Such confrontations with the legal system seem to confirm the notion that judging others and being judged were no more at odds in this island colony than anywhere else in England's Atlantic empire.[66]

Of the Stevensons themselves there is little mention in the surviving documents. It is unlikely they were property owners. Christian appears only in the context of her trial, as does Thomas, mentioned once as her husband.

Her physical appearance is left to the imagination, other than the fact that she wore glasses, if indeed she bought them for herself. She earned her living by spinning. For Stephen Stevenson, the record is more complete. Blind and disabled as he aged, Stephen was "past labour" by 1657 and "old" in 1659. A "humble" petition in 1655 secured him maintenance for a decade, notwithstanding the accusation that he had bewitched Henry Bishop. "Old Stephenson" disappears from the records after 1666. What his relationship was to Christian is unrecorded.[67] Perhaps she bought the spectacles for him.

The timing of Christian Stevenson's witchcraft prosecution on Bermuda correlates nicely with developments in legal culture on the home island three thousand miles away. Historians of English law generally agree that middling and poor folk were more likely to seek legal remedies for their problems in the early modern era than they had been in the past. Moreover, the Reformation eschewed the use of counter-magic to thwart witchcraft, a prohibition that some historians argue advanced the use of law courts to prosecute suspected witches.[68] Yet there appears to have been little enthusiasm for bringing a witch to trial, probably because such proceedings could end badly for the accuser. True, arrest derailed a witch's capacity to injure, but an acquittal could easily spell ruthless retaliation. If there is substance to the accusations, Christian Stevenson had threatened and assaulted people for a long time. She was suspected of witchcraft for more than seven years. Given this foot dragging, it is obvious that her neighbors saw legal prosecution as a last resort rather than a line of first defense.[69] In Stevenson's case, and perhaps in others, victims resorted first to counter-magic and turned to law courts only when such tried-and-true methods failed to stymie a suspected evildoer. Thomas Seeward committed his piglet's tail and ear to the fire despite the fact that counter-magic had fallen out of favor. The Reformation may have frowned on this sort of retaliation, but it would take more than a fiat to eliminate it altogether.

Accusations against Christian Stevenson may have been rooted in local disputes rather than an abstract fear of bewitchment, but the neighbors who feared her were in no hurry to drag her to court. When she was finally brought to justice in 1653, the timing may have had as much to do with a confluence of events on the Atlantic periphery as with incidents internal to Bermuda. Yet once Middleton accused Stevenson, the legal machinery began to whirr, and Stevenson was afforded the rights that applied to any other defendant. The law required her accuser to face her in court. The grand jury handed down an indictment; twelve jurors decided her fate. The record noted whether the marks in her mouth bled and whether she felt pain when they were pierced, precisely because the law demanded proof and a record.

Did Bermudians believe in witchcraft? Yes. Were there underlying grudges that might have led to false accusations and manipulation of evidence? Yes again.

Alice Moore swung alongside Christian Stevenson on that spring day in May 1653, their gray shadows and dark deeds contrasting sharply with the shimmering turquoise water a short distance from the gallows. Yet, if strong evidence insured Stevenson's execution, the case against Moore had been weak. True, her body exhibited the usual signs and marks that her examiners had come to expect of witches, but the dramatic accusation that her "diabolicall practice" of witchcraft had "destroyed" her neighbors' "cattell and hogges" was based on little more than suspicion and guesswork—Moore's profile notwithstanding.[70] No one had actually seen Alice Moore injure any farm animals; it was her inexplicable ability to forecast the death of animals that troubled her neighbors. Unlike Stevenson, Moore never walked away mumbling who knows what.

Alice and Thomas Moore lived in Warwick Tribe, as did her accusers. The Moores do not appear to have been landholders; indeed, a dispute between Thomas Moore and John Wainwright over Moore's refusal to allow Wainwright to cross the property he rented ended badly for Moore. Wainwright, who threatened to "displace" Moore if he ever "obteyned . . . that share wch Moore lived upon," ultimately made good on his promise to evict Moore, thanks to "friends."[71] Alternately referred to as "godmother" or "mother Moore," Alice was probably somewhat advanced in age, even if her husband, "old Thomas," had some years on her. The couple had at least one son, also named Thomas.

It apparently raised eyebrows when Alice Moore ambled through the neighborhood "barefooted & barelegged." She and her husband were not only propertyless; they were probably poor, earning a little now and then from whatever work Alice could get as a spinster. According to testimony, she went to the Wainwrights' house "to buy or begg some fine thread" from Wainwright's wife.[72] The records do not disclose whether Moore obtained the thread, but in the course of conversation with Wainwright's wife, Moore inquired about her livestock. "Wee have had such ill successe with them," Wainwright responded. The hogs they bred always died. There is no indication that Wainwright's wife held Moore responsible for her bad luck, but others, suffering the same misfortune, connected Moore to their losses.

Truth be told, pigs appear to have been Moore's specialty, and their demise her expertise. Thomas Gaplin refused to sell pigs to Alice Moore, saying "they were all gone he had sould them all but two." Moore countered that it was "no matter for they will all dye"—and as it turned out, "soe they did."

In another stalled negotiation, "Goodman Moore or his wife . . . would not consent" to the price John Burt set on his sow and went away without buying the animal. Within weeks "after the sowe pigged . . . the sowe & all her pigs died." His wife's nonaccusatory attitude aside, John Wainwright testified that not long after Alice Moore "praysed" Wainwright's sow, the sow "pigged & all her pigs died as soon as they were pigged." Yet it was not that Alice Moore was held responsible for the death of these farm animals, but rather that she had foreknowledge of the event. When Dorothy Gaplin heard that Alice Moore had referred to her dead shoat before the young pig actually died, Gaplin declared "truly I think then that she is a witch."[73]

But it was John Wainwright, involved as both inquisitor and witness, who probably carried the most weight. As a Councellor, he had taken damaging testimony about Moore from Ann Holmes, Dorothy Gaplin, and Nathaniel Conyers before unburdening himself in front of the grand jury. Only Wainwright directly accused Moore of murdering his pigs. "Att the time of Captain Turners entrance into his Govment or a little after I did charg Goody Moore with these & many things else."[74] Just as Christian Stevenson had a long history of suspected witchcraft, so, too, did Alice Moore. It is unclear when doubts were first raised about Moore, but if she had been accused as early as 1646 or 1647, gossip surely predated that year. And suspicions obviously lingered, even if no further charges materialized until 1653. Wainwright had also brought to public attention Moore's uncanny ability to predict future adversity and her possession of knowledge about events beyond sight and sound. How could she know, demanded Wainwright, "that myselfe with the rest of the company who were in the ship wth me were taken by the Turkes or chased by them?"

It is the sexual component of this case, however, that is among its most intriguing aspects. As Edward Holmes and his brother William passed by the Moores' house in December 1652, they heard a voice cry "wilt thou never have done sucking. I think you will bring me off my leggs, for I must go worke now." Close to the source, William Holmes judged that "it was Goodwife Moore's voice." At first the men "thought Goodman Moore had bin in the house talking with his wife," but subsequently "they saw him on the top of the hill." The implication of this testimony would have been clear to Holmes's audience: if Alice and Thomas were not having a go at it before their morning chores, then Alice must have been consorting with the devil. The women who searched Alice's body had, after all, found the teats and dugs upon which the devil ordinarily sucked. Some were on "the right side of her body," another "in her mouth towards the almonds of her eares & another between her tooes upon her left foote."[75] Evidently, sex between Alice and Thomas—even at their advanced ages—was not a topic for wagging tongues; sex between Alice and the devil, on the other hand, was a matter of public concern.

In the end, Alice Moore, like Christian Stevenson, incriminated herself. Moore declared she felt no pain when the women who searched her body pricked the suspicious marks. She had no explanation for the "blew spots" they found. The "teates and duggs" exuded the waterish blood John Middleton had told them to expect. The searchers were preconditioned to see what their legal culture translated into evidence of witchcraft.[76]

Alice Moore's execution was not the end of the troubles for the Moore family. It is difficult to tell whether the subsequent controversies involved Thomas Moore senior (who could have remarried) or Thomas Moore junior and his wife. In any case, one couple or the other was charged with beating a female servant to death in 1656. The details of the incident suggest that the younger Moores were involved, since it is unlikely that the older Moores had servants, much less the agility to beat one with such force. William Holmes once again spoke against them. This time Dorothy Gaplin and Ann Holmes defended Moore and his wife, and the story ended with William Holmes being convicted of slander even in the face of corroborating evidence.[77]

Accusations connecting the Moores to witchcraft arose again in July 1658. This time the victim-accuser was a servant who testified that "being in bedd in his masters house . . . he was awakened by some noyse . . . and that he there saw the wife of Thomas Moore . . . or the divell in her likeness." The servant, John Richards, told the apparition "that she was a witch & he would have her hanged." After recovering from the shock of this unexpected visitation, Richards met Moore and his wife "as they were going along the Path." Moore asked if Richards had been "sicke" and "scared." Richards answered "yes." Thomas Moore then inquired whether Richards had accused his wife, whereupon Richards replied "it was eyther your wife or some in her likeness." According to Richards's master, Nathaniell Astwood, after meeting the Moores on the path, Richards "had bin very ill and . . . much impared in his body And that upon that very night he was taken very ill That he did meete the above sd parties." Fortunately for this Goody Moore, the women's inquest found no suspicious marks on her body, and she escaped the hangman's noose.[78]

The genesis of the accusation against this Goodwife Moore cannot be gleaned from the records: Richards may have had a legitimate grievance of his own against the Moores, or perhaps he sought revenge for the death of the Moores' maidservant. If so, it is curious that charges were brought against Thomas's wife rather than Thomas, since both were accused of beating their servant. She may have been an easy mark, since another female Moore had been convicted of witchcraft, and everyone knew that witchcraft ran in families. Or the charge may say something about the intersection of witchcraft and gender. However all this played out, the sequence of events suggests that Richards, a servant, knew that he had access to the legal system and that his accusations would be taken seriously enough to produce a formal inquiry. For Richards, this short time in the legal limelight was an egalitarian moment that empowered him—albeit temporarily.

Jane Hopkins was the last witch to be executed on Bermuda. But the circumstances of her case, and that of Elizabeth Page, who was acquitted at the same session, were conspicuously different from the others. The two women caused no harm to anyone, killed no animals, ruined no crops. Neither woman had quarreled with a neighbor. Neither Jane Hopkins nor Elizabeth Page appears in the records before 1654, and Page vanishes after her trial. Nevertheless, Bermudians with the names Hopkins and Page surface from time to time, making it impossible to gauge whether these particular women were newcomers to the island colony or were returning to family after an English sojourn. Their troubles began when William White, master of the ship on which they crossed the Atlantic, sought the governor's ear shortly after reaching Bermuda toward the end of 1654. The captain complained "that there were two women on his . . . ship who hee did vehemently suspect to be witches, and desiered Justice agt them." The governor "yielded," and the suspected witches "were brought to their triall" on January 1, 1654/5.[79]

All the witnesses against Hopkins and Page were passengers aboard the ship, the *Mayflower*. At least one woman, Elizabeth Cobson, had known Elizabeth Page in England, and she described an incident there three or four years earlier when she and Page were "bedlaying at the 3 tuns." According to Cobson, Page confided in her bedfellow that "she had raised the devil and whipt him with briars . . . and she had made Maidstone Jaile doores stand open, so that others might or did goe forth, but she had no power to goe forth herselfe."[80]

By the end of 1654, a reference to the infamous Maidstone jail would have resonated powerfully among Cobson's listeners. Six women had been hanged as witches at Maidstone in Kent County, England, during the summer of 1652. A number of others—men and women—had been arraigned; some received light sentences, and some were reprieved. The heinous crimes of those executed allegedly included the murders of children and adults, the destruction of cattle, and the loss of a large quantity of corn during a shipwreck.[81] If Page's account (according to Cobson) was based on anything more than fantasy, she might have been among the Maidstone prisoners. If not, the tales might have become so embedded in her mind that she imagined her presence at the jail. Page also whiled away the long days and nights during the Atlantic voyage by telling "several passages about some Lancaster witches," although a fellow traveler, Mrs. Rathorme, never heard Page admit "anything of herselfe being a witch." Her reticence notwithstanding, Captain White had good reason to fear Elizabeth Page's presence aboard his ship, particularly because she went out of her way to arouse suspicion.[82]

Thomas Crofts and Charles Hancock testified that Page had strangely manipulated the ship's compass, making it spin back and forth "from North to South." Crofts seemed amazed when she made it turn "Round, Round," particularly because Page "never touched it." Hancock, presumably one of the ship's officers, was "at the helme" when Page "had her finger over the compas," and he, too, must have been uneasy as he watched Page usurp control of the ship's navigational device. To make matters worse, Page told her spellbound audience that "any woman that was wth child may make it do soe," dramatically confirming a sexual power inherent to pregnancy, and reaffirming a commonly held masculine fear about women's bodies.

As events unfolded, however, it became clear that Elizabeth Page had been playing with her audience all along and amusing herself at their expense. Three days after this incident, Page admitted to Hancock "that she had a steele needle about her that caused it," and she once again demonstrated her ability to make the compass gyrate. What was an innocent prank to Page, however, was anything but that to her observers. Shakespeare's *Macbeth* was half a century old by the time of the *Mayflower* voyage, and although there is no way of knowing whether Captain White or his helmsman was familiar with Hecate and her sisters, it was common knowledge among seafarers that witches could stir malevolent winds and manipulate the "shipman's card" (compass dial).[83] Furthermore, William White may have had an unusually high financial stake in this particular voyage. On August 2, 1654, he had contracted with Thomas Browning, a merchant, to carry a group of servants to Virginia, for which White would be handsomely compensated. The timing is such that Page and Hopkins were likely to have been aboard this ship, although it is doubtful that they were among the servant transports, since Page was accompanied by her maid. Moreover, both women were referred to as "mistress," a title denoting high status.[84] In any case, the ship also carried a large cargo of merchantable goods, the loss of which would have been a disaster.[85] Once they were safely ashore, Captain White's vehement accusation might have been his response to a perceived threat to his vessel, or it might have been his way of retaliating against a not-so-funny caper.

If Elizabeth Page got off with a scare after the female jury did not find "any marke or spotts or signes" of witchcraft, "only something more than ordinary in her secret parts," Jane Hopkins was not as lucky.[86] For reasons that are buried in time and place, Hopkins's shipmates conjured reasons to accuse her of having "consulted and covenanted with the Devil."[87] Her association took the form of the usual physical marks, as well as the dramatic appearance of an alleged familiar whose timing suggests either coaching or rehearsal. It is unclear, however, whether any of Hopkins's shipmates knew her before they assembled on the *Mayflower.* One witness asserted that "being one daye at his Lodging And speaking of Mrs. Hopkins Mr Baker tould him that he herd a boye say that he seeing her dresse herself he saw a strange thing upon her shoulder."[88]

This last bit of testimony raises several issues. If "Lodging" meant a residence of sorts on English soil (rather than a cabin on a ship), the incident occurred prior to the sea voyage. If so, Baker and the unidentified witness had heard chatter about Hopkins before passengers boarded the ship. But no matter when the alleged conversation took place, it was still hearsay, a legal point of no concern at the time, but one that confirms the importance of rumor and gossip in the chain of events. More puzzling is why "a boye" would be present while Hopkins was dressing, and why she would confide in him in a subsequent conversation. According to this thirdhand report, Hopkins declared to the boy that "she had one marke came lately upon her which she never had before." And immediately on the heels of this damaging admission came a non sequitur: Hopkins blurted out "that she had had her desire upon her enemyes & she hoped that she should have her desiers still of them."[89] Based on this testimony, incriminating evidence of witchcraft issued from the mouth of Jane Hopkins herself. She did not disclose the identity of her enemies.

Two other male witnesses sealed Hopkins's fate. Jeames Man and Thomas Cobson were "in the caben with Jane Hopkins she . . . wished that god might showe some signe whether she was a witch or not, and emediately there was a thing in the likenes of a ratt appeared unto them."[90] The exquisite timing of the rodent's performance all but condemned Hopkins, even though an occasional rat should not have attracted attention aboard a ship. For reasons that are obscure, however, this one was identified as her familiar, and the possession of a familiar, and having physical marks, were, according to Michael Dalton, "the main points to discover and convict" a person of witchcraft.[91]

A final incident added to Hopkins's dossier confirmed her occult powers. Elizabeth Page's maid spoke of losing a bottle somewhere on the ship and complained of her loss to Jane Hopkins.[92] Under ordinary circumstances a bottle is just a bottle, but in this case the missing object was likely to have been a "witch bottle," a container filled with urine, hair, pins, and other items designed to thwart bewitchment.[93] Needless to say, the disappearance of such a protective device would have been a matter of great concern to Page. Anthony Love, another passenger, overheard the scuttlebutt about a bottle gone astray and reported efforts to locate it: "Mrs. Hopkins said that if she would crosse her hand with a peece of silver of something that she would conjure for her bottell, and that she shold have it that night or next morning. And that night she had the bottell." If this conversation actually took place, it is unclear why Hopkins would advertise her skills, knowing, as she must have, that they would be associated with witchcraft.

In any case, all this was revealed once the governor "yielded" to Captain White's demand for "justice." Whether the use of the word "yielded" suggests some hesitation on the governor's part is unknown, but clearly the evidence upon which the jury convicted Hopkins was somewhat thin—even by seventeenth-century standards. The indictment referred only to the marks and signs that the female search committee had discovered: "Jane Hopkins hath in her mouth a suspitious mke and under her arme she hath a dugge or Teat And upon her shoulder a wart and upon her necke another wart And her privy partes she hath a teat or dugg" from which "issued a kind of thicke filthy matter . . . all these were insensible when they wre prickt and tried."[94] Convinced that Hopkins had "suckled and fedd" the Devil because of the "markes & signes upon her body," the jury found her guilty of witchcraft on January 3, 1654/5. The hangman dispatched her two days later.

If witchcraft accusations against John Middleton, Christian Stevenson, and Alice Moore were based on long-standing quarrels between and among neighbors, Page and Hopkins had no history on Bermuda to explain the allegations against them. Even the accusations that derived from the long weeks at sea were weak: no persons or livestock suffered injury, and no specters appeared. It is possible, therefore, that Hopkins and Page evoked other, subliminal fears, and that the two women, traveling without male escort, were associated with an upheaval that was rocking England in the mid-1650s: the Quaker movement.

By 1652 or 1653, the Quaker invasion was well under way in northern England, and as early as 1654 Quaker communities had sprung up in all of England's northern counties, with large meetings also established in urban centers such as Bristol. From its inception, the movement attracted a disproportionate number of women. Within a decade of the sect's founding in the early 1640s, accounts suggest that there were somewhere between

FIGURE 3. Witch bottle. Ceramic Bellarmine jar of the type used in the seventeenth century as counter-magic to reverse or protect against a curse; such jars were usually filled with nails, hair, and urine. This one, found in Plymouth, England, contained pins, hair, nail clippings, and bird bones. Courtesy of the Museum of Witchcraft, Boscastle, Cornwall, England.

thirty-five thousand and forty thousand Quakers in England. The early converts rejected orthodox Puritanism; in turn, Presbyterians were particularly hostile to the new sect, even if some Quakers originally came from Presbyterian stock. From the sect's base in northern England, Quakers slowly moved southward, holding street-corner meetings, disturbing congregations, disputing with ordained ministers, and proselytizing whenever and wherever they could. Bristol and London saw considerable Quaker agitation in 1654 and 1655. Between 1653 and 1657, over five hundred Quaker pamphlets rolled off the presses.[95] Popular reaction against English Quakers was immediate and violent. They were subject to brutal beatings, painful examinations, and harsh confinement. Riots followed their appearance, and, not surprisingly, a symbiotic relationship developed between Quakerism and witchcraft, the result of the Quakers' inexplicable success in attracting converts.[96]

Exactly when the movement turned its attention toward North America has not been confirmed. References to a traveling ministry appear in English sources in 1654, but the first recorded Quakers did not arrive in New England until 1656. Mary Fisher and Ann Austin led that offensive after their ship docked in Boston harbor in July of that year. They were jailed, examined for signs of witchcraft, and banished from Massachusetts a month later. So fearful were the authorities that the two women would attract followers that their cell windows were boarded up and a fine imposed on anyone attempting to talk to them.[97] What is not generally recognized is that Fisher and Austin began their sojourn in 1655 with a trip to Barbados, the same Caribbean island to which they would be banished after their imprisonment in Boston. Barbados was already home to a smattering of Quakers, a state of affairs that would not have gone unnoticed by Bermudians who traded widely with that island.[98]

As to the *Mayflower,* the ship on which Page and Hopkins traveled, there is reason to believe it had some association with the Quaker movement. An obscure reference indicates that about the middle of June 1657 "the little 'Quaker *Mayflower* . . .' started on her perilous voyage for New England with 11 Friends on board." No further evidence indicates whether the name is a coincidence or whether the ship was known to transport Quakers across the Atlantic.[99]

Nevertheless, given the treatment of Page and Hopkins following their arrival in Bermuda in 1654, it is possible that the two women were perceived to be Quakers, whether or not they were actually in the vanguard of the movement as it progressed from east to west. But why would the Quaker message arouse such hostility on Bermuda, especially since Barbadians appear to have adopted a live-and-let-live attitude toward the sect? Coming on the heels of the religious factionalism that had roiled the island several years earlier, the strident Quaker message would have created yet more havoc. Among other startling proposals, Quakers sought to rid Christianity of an established ministry and to abolish the tithes that supported the clerical army. As it happened, Bermuda was bereft of ministers between 1651 and 1655, a situation that many found disturbing. Thus any call to perpetuate a clergyless society would have been seen as a freefall into instability. Since Quakers were already directing their attention to what one historian calls the "pastorless" English settlements on Long Island, Barbados, and Maryland, it would not be surprising if Bermuda was one of their intended targets.[100]

The Somers Island Company had been unsuccessfully trolling for ministers to send to Bermuda as early as 1649/50. As a temporary measure, the company proposed that Bermuda's governor and council install "holy and unblameable men" as "Readers" in each of the eight tribes. It took several years before enough men with those qualities could be found, but by the spring of 1655 the company had confirmed seven "Readers" for the various parishes. One of the men, Francis Eastlake, turned Quaker by 1660, and the son of another, William Righton, did the same. William Righton senior (the "Reader") ran into trouble preaching in 1656 and was relieved of his duties a year later—possibly for Quaker tendencies.[101] Other Bermudians, either early immigrants (such as the Tatums) or born on the island (such as the Wilkinsons), also became Friends, although it is unclear how early they were attracted to the ideas of the Society. Robert Ridlie, who appears to have been left in charge of the Independents in 1648, was censured rather quickly for drawing people from the established church. A rabid Puritan at the time, he, too, eventually joined the Quaker contingent.[102] The most interesting convert, however, was William White, the ship captain who escorted Jane Hopkins and Elizabeth Page to Bermuda and then ratted on them. Whether his friendship with the Wilkinsons, Eastlakes, and Rightons cemented his religious convictions is unknown, but there is a certain irony to his later change of heart, nonetheless.[103]

Bermudians had good reason to be leery of Quakers. In addition to their other failings, they opposed predestination, the nobility and gentry, and preached egalitarian ideals. Worse, as far as Bermuda was concerned, it appeared that they espoused land redistribution.[104] With the island's system of tribes and concentration of land among relatively few wealthy Bermudians, such a message would have sent shock waves throughout the island. The less-fortunate found it hard to eke out a living because they were unable to compete with those who grasped "as much land as they can." Each settler who amassed a large farm added to the number of poor who had no place to go.[105] Propertyless Bermudians would have found Quaker ideas appealing, while powerful landholders would have been threatened by the Society's radical notions.

There are other reasons to think that in this time of religious turmoil aspects of Quakerism—if not Quakers themselves—had permeated the island. One clue is the use of the words "thee" and "thou." Quaker language reflected the group's insistence on social equality; by the mid 1650s, thee and thou were clearly associated with Quaker speech patterns. Although these words had been eliminated from ordinary speech by Shakespeare's time, thee and thou could still be heard in northern England where Quakerism arose. Dismissive of the word "you" because of its elitist connotation, Quakers retained the egalitarianism inherent in the older form and applied it to everyone.[106] Yet some people clung to thee and thou even without religious conversion; farmers continued to use the words despite the controversy over them. With all this in mind, one can only guess why John Middleton responded to Goody Stevenson's denial of wrongdoing with the words "perceiving that you are a witch I would have thee judged."[107] He may have reverted to the older use of the word to address a woman he perceived to be his inferior, or he may have deliberately taken up Quaker usage. Middleton was, after all, a radical Puritan, a disciple of the group from which Quaker converts were frequently plucked.

During Christian Stevenson's trial, Anne Buller deposed that Goody Stevenson came to her in the night and said "I'le do thee no harm," but the context, as above, is ambiguous. Buller may have been hinting that Stevenson was a Quaker, which by the 1650s was perilously close to an accusation of witchcraft. Or she, too, may have been employing the archaic form. And when Edward Holmes testified against Alice Moore, he deposed that he had heard Moore say "Wilt thou never have done sucking."[108] Ambiguous again, but the lists of Quaker sufferers include many Middletons, Stevensons, and Moores, the most famous of whom was Marmaduke Stevenson, well known in England prior to his execution in Massachusetts in 1659. Closer to home, a Bermudian, George Stevenson, was committed to prison in 1676 after acting on his Quaker beliefs.[109] It is probable he was related to Christian. Finally, when the deputy governor of Massachusetts committed Ann Austin and Mary Fisher to prison as Quakers, "all the Proof he had was that one of them said *Thee* to him, whereupon he said *NOW he knew they were Quakers.*" The English Quaker Francis Howgill had already confirmed the point in 1654: "They say none speak like us."[110]

If Quakers were conflated with witches, and if Peter Elmer is correct that Quakers were beginning to replace witches in English culture in the 1650s (particularly among the elite), Bermuda's witchcraft trials hint that the mental merger may have been under way there at the same time.[111] Moreover, Quakers were opposed to the singing of psalms because more often than not, they insisted, the words were unintelligible to churchgoers. Thus, when Goody Brangman was accused of witchcraft in Bermuda at the same time that Stevenson and Moore were being tried in May 1653, Jone Bell's declaration that "Goody Stow told her that she had observed Brangman did not use to sing in the church, and that made her thinke she was a witch," makes perfect sense if it is interpreted in the context of the Quaker peril.[112]

All this brings us back to Page and Hopkins, who were traveling without male escort, and who were subsequently accused of being the devil's apprentices. The two women did not conform to the usual profile of Bermuda's indigenous witches: no disagreement over a purchase, no sick chickens, no nightmares, no physical maleficium. They weren't even typical of English witches, since 94 percent of all witchcraft indictments in the home circuit included the same sort of accusations.[113] An errant compass, warts and blue spots, a rat, and the reappearance of a lost bottle are all that tie these women to the devil's work. Still, Quakers were known to possess such enchanted bottles, from which their influence was said to emanate. By 1655 Bermudians might have even heard rumors of the notorious Quaker Jane Holmes, whose victim drank from Holmes's bottle and who immediately fell into a trance.[114]

Yet the tenuous chain of evidence linking Hopkins and Page to the Quaker movement makes their involvement more suggestive than conclusive. Bermudians with the names Hopkins and Page appear in church and court records, but whether they were related to the suspected witches or whether they were Quaker sympathizers is left to conjecture. Related or not, both family names are prominent in Joseph Besse's *Collection of Quaker Sufferings,* where three Page martyrs (William, Richard, and Mary) are memorialized after dying for the cause.[115] Were Jane Hopkins and Elizabeth Page Quaker missionaries? Perhaps. Perhaps not. But if they were persecuted for that reason, it means that "Public Friends" may have sought converts on this side of the Atlantic earlier and in greater numbers than we originally thought. And if Hopkins and Page had kin on Bermuda, it might be time to explore the earliest Quaker movement in the context of transatlantic family networks.

Whether or not Page and Hopkins traveled as Quaker emissaries, Bermuda's bout with witchcraft makes best sense in its Atlantic context. A glance at the numbers tells all: the rise and decline of witchcraft indictments on Bermuda closely parallel those of England and New England. While English witches (and the authorities who prosecuted them) were most active in the last decades of the sixteenth century, the 1640s and 1650s saw a renewed interest in the eradication of witchcraft after several quiet decades. Prosecutions in Essex County, England, peaked in 1645 with the conviction of twenty-eight witches, nearly all of whom were hanged thanks to the efforts of Matthew Hopkins, the foremost English witch hunter. Bermudians would certainly have heard of this madness, which was followed in the next decade by a craze that centered in Kent County between 1652 and 1657. There and then convictions were meted out to seventeen witches, of whom only four (including three men) escaped the death penalty. Ten of the trials took place in 1652. News of these shocking events would have reached Bermuda in time to stimulate fears about homegrown witches.[116] Indeed, John Makaraton, who was almost certainly among the Scottish prisoners banished in 1651, could have been an eyewitness to the excesses in Scotland prior to his exile.

New Englanders reacted to word of the 1645 Essex County prosecutions in England by demonstrating their own eagerness to rid the mainland Puritan colonies of suspected witches. Of the nine to eleven cases that date to the 1640s, nearly all were subsequent to the English outbreak. Yet most of the midcentury New England witchcraft cases were prosecuted in the next decade, between 1651 and 1656, with anywhere from twenty-six to twenty-nine alleged witches brought up on charges in Massachusetts, Connecticut, New Haven, and New Hampshire during these years. At the same time, the execution rate was comparatively low: no more than seven of those prosecuted met a date with the hangman.[117]

Bermuda's witchcraft episode deviates from similar events in New England in terms of its scale—that is, the high number of accusations relative to its small population. And on Bermuda, conviction was tantamount to a sentence of death. It is religion that dominates the Atlantic setting, however. All three points of this geographic triangle were conspicuously Puritan, which seems to confirm that Puritans were highly motivated to eradicate whatever it was that witchcraft represented, and that religious battles, in which Puritans were major combatants, set the scene for these particular prosecutions.

If Bermuda was a "moderate" Puritan colony in its youth, by the 1640s the island was racked by sectarian controversy as Independents and Presbyterians engaged in a bitter war for control of the island. Their quarrel paralleled that of England itself, except that die-hard royalists played little role in the ongoing battle for supremacy. Furthermore, if the usual clerical suspects were unwavering in their dedication to Puritan ideals, they were, at the same time, small in number. The secular colony leaders, however, bent in the wind, alternately showing favoritism to (and ambivalence for) Presbyterianism, the Crown, or radical Independents. In 1643, three of Bermuda's Puritan zealots, the Reverends Nathaniel White, William Golding, and Patrick Copeland, broke with the Church of England and established an Independent church in the New England way. By the middle of the decade, rumor had it that the Independent faction reigned supreme and had established a theocracy on Bermuda. This did not sit well with either Parliament or the Somers Island Company, and a new Presbyterian governor, Thomas Turner, was dispatched

FIGURE 4. Matthew Hopkins, English witch finder. This line engraving of 1792 reproduces an engraving of 1647, the year Hopkins died. The illustration shows Hopkins with two witches. The witch on the right says "My Imps names are" and lists them below, while the witch on the left points to one familiar, Holt. Other familiars are named as well, suggesting a personal relationship between a witch and her pet. The Granger Collection, New York.

to rid the island of its Independent troublemakers. Governor Turner's heavy-handed tactics following the execution of Charles I in 1649 only made matters worse. An uprising, followed by a popular election, deposed Turner and installed John Trimingham at the helm of government.

The new governor banished the Independents to Eleuthera. With the far left and almost far right out of business, moderation prevailed, although in 1650 the company—in an effort to ingratiate itself with England's new government—replaced Trimingham with a new governor, Josiah Forster, a moderate with Puritan (perhaps even Independent) leanings. The exiled Independents were invited back to Bermuda, and a tedious, long-term, and occasionally contentious discussion about reparations ensued. Nevertheless, the lingering controversy never reached the heights of acrimony that marked the preceding decade. Indeed, Forster's appointment and compromises earned him a politically peaceful eight-year term as governor (1650–58), the witchcraft trials under his watch notwithstanding.[118] Yet, if Michael Jarvis is correct about Forster's religious politics, it is not likely that the governor instigated the witchcraft proceedings against John Middleton as part of a general Puritan morality sweep, since evidence aligns Middleton with the Puritan faction.[119]

If, as in England and New England, Bermuda's witchcraft trials were precipitated by long-standing squabbles among neighbors, wide-ranging social conditions on Bermuda also contributed to the Pandora's box of suppressed grievances that exploded into witchcraft accusations during the Interregnum. Moreover, the departure of the Independent clergy left only two ministers, the Presbyterians William Viner and Thomas Hooper, to pacify a population resentful of the bleak economic conditions that prevailed.[120] Whatever restraint they might have imposed evaporated with their deaths, however, and by 1651 no clergy remained on the island. Without them, people acted "profanely." They drank, swore, and stole.[121]

Local hardship coincided with imperial chaos. Because some foolhardy settlers vigorously opposed the beheading of King Charles and vociferously supported the Crown, Parliament declared Bermuda in rebellion in 1651. Furious at being labeled "rebels and traitors," the Bermudian government sent an indignant letter to the company in London on January 1, 1651/2, complaining about the act that prohibited trade with Barbados, Virginia, and Antigua, and equally blaming the government and the forces of nature for what followed. "Because of a Great wind" in August 1651 that "blew away most of their summer tobacco," Bermudians were forced to trade with the Dutch to relieve "the great distress of the colony for want of supplies.[122] The Somers Island Company saw the situation from a different perspective. The company had no sympathy for Bermudians who collaborated with the Dutch to undermine English monopolization of the tobacco trade, and fleetingly threatened to wash their hands of the trying colony by selling it to the Dutch. Moreover, drought decimated the corn crop, creating food shortages.

By December 1653, the scarcity of corn evoked charges that some planters were engrossing and setting high prices on the staple.[123]

Two other interrelated social conditions might have compounded the general malaise, which in turn exacerbated a need to hold someone or something responsible for Bermuda's inexplicable adversities. First, Bermuda had suffered out-migration in the decades between the 1630s and 1650s as colonists sought a better life on other English islands or on the mainland. Second, it is possible that the most significant feature of Bermuda's eighteenth-century demography—its striking female majority—already existed by the mid-seventeenth century.[124] A distorted sex ratio stunted population growth, and although it is probably a stretch to say that accusations of maleficium (especially when directed toward children) were a metaphor for the way an overabundance of unmarried and childless women harmed the future viability of the island, it is still true that most female witches were past the age of childbearing and therefore could not rectify the unbalanced sex ratio or compensate for out-migration. Is it merely coincidental that women outnumbered men in Salem in 1692 as well?

If all this wasn't enough to distress the most optimistic Bermudian, in 1653 Barbados threatened to become a free state at the same time that the Council of State in London was creating more turmoil by totally reorganizing the Somers Island Company.[125] Since Bermuda had remained uninhabited until the last ghost had been routed from the island in the seventeenth century, colonists who had overcome their initial doubts about settling there in the first place might have been more than ready to believe that witchcraft was the source of their misfortunes.

As the gossip network widened and charges of witchcraft escalated, accused as well as accusers resorted to the law.[126] In the midst of the special assizes called to try Christian Stevenson and Alice Moore, Edward Brangman complained that Mary Stow had used "some slanderous speeches . . . agst his wife." Apparently Stow had spread rumors that after an aborted transaction involving Goody Brangman and a pig, "the pigg ran madd." Stow held Goody Brangman accountable, and her husband, Edward, took offense. After being summoned to court, widow Stow backed off. Admitting that she had accused Elizabeth Brangman of witchcraft, Stow begged forgiveness for the slander, saying "she had done her wrong in using such suspitious speeches agt her." The Brangmans accepted Stow's apology, and all ended well, with both sides tacitly recognizing the court's legitimate role in mediating this dispute. Two years later, William Haynes appeared in court to answer for his "uncivil behaviour." He acknowledged "in open court" that he had done Mistress Miller "& her posterity living great wrong in reporting & saying Mrs Miller was a witch." Again, apologies resolved the matter, and both parties went about their business, conscious of how central the law had become not only to their lives, but to "posterity."[127]

Counterintuitive though it may be, the law validated witchcraft by legislating against it. Legal penalties created a pseudoreality by defining and identifying witches through specific acts. And as repudiation authenticated the existence of sorcery, belief in the authority of law simultaneously instilled fear of and respect for witches themselves. At the same time, the use of law as a weapon against witchcraft was an early modern substitute for the ancient counter-magic that had thwarted the devil's accomplices from time immemorial. The Reformation and centralization of the criminal justice system drew the middling and lower sorts to the courtroom to process their claims against suspected witches, a change in venue that imbued the complainants with newly acquired public authority. If, in some way, this suspension of hierarchy was a small (albeit unintended) step toward democratization, it was, more importantly, a clear acknowledgment of the power of the law. Arrest and imprisonment stripped a witch of his or her influence, a humiliation that attested to the supremacy of man-made laws over supernatural forces. Given their obsessive belief in the potency of the invisible world, it is surprising to see the assurance with which the seventeenth-century English used a humanly devised legal system to combat the spiritual world. Having contracted with the devil, witches were part of that other world and, presumably, possessed powers that ordinary women and men lacked. To vitiate these powers with ink and quill is to have faith in the magic of the written word.[128]

Gossip may have been a prelude to indictments, but formal legal procedures institutionalized the prosecution of witches. As each stage of the action unfolded, the process validated and reinforced the ritual known as common law. At a time when rules of evidence were hotly debated, lawyers could consult Richard Bernard's *Grand Jury Men* or Michael Dalton's *Countrey Justice* in order to arm themselves with evidence that would stand up in court and ensure conviction of an alleged witch. Thus, the physical signs of witchcraft became critical corroborating evidence. It was not only what a witch had done, but that she or he possessed marks that attested to a pact with the devil and could be presented as visible evidence in a court of law. In a similar way, common gossip became transformed into legal evidence once sworn testimony about specters, familiars, and inexplicable events made its way into the record.[129]

After legal theorists such as Dalton codified rules of evidence pertaining to witchcraft, lawyers and judges confirmed them by complying with their provisions. In practice, the law corroborated the existence of witchcraft by prohibiting its practice and by establishing mechanisms for discovering a witch. At the same time, it comforted people by assuring them that witches would be punished. In this way, laws relating to supernatural crimes were incorporated into routine practice, and by giving substance to illusion, legal sorcery regulated the dark forces that threatened early America. If witches weren't exactly like other people, the rules governing their trials were still the same as those that applied to other forms of criminal behavior. Thus, suspected witches were entitled to the fundamental safeguards that other malefactors enjoyed. In such a setting, witches themselves might have been seen as a little less mysterious and threatening. Indeed, it is not impossible that by giving witches their day in court, the legal system contributed to the decline of witchcraft itself.

Accusations of witchcraft were a form of abuse. Ordinarily hurled against neighbors, business associates, competitors—indeed, against anyone who might be quarrelsome or provocative—such accusations could result in a preemptive slander charge or in an indictment, trial, and hanging. Angered by Edith Craford, Anthony Ashby of Salem, Massachusetts, announced "that hee would have Her Hanged . . . for shee was A witch & If Shee were nott A witch allreddy shee would bee won & therefore It was as good to Hang her att first as Last." Craford was exonerated, but only after spending time in prison.[130]

Family members were not exempt from witchcraft accusations. A husband might control his wife by threatening to spread rumors about her. Or he might challenge a divorce, as Ralph Ellenwood did in 1682, by hinting to a neighbor that "he thought there were witches not far off," a clear reference to his wife, Katharin.[131] *In a more chilling scenario, a son might remind his mother that "her name did stinke about the Island, or Country," an allusion to witchcraft uttered by Thomas Cornell of Portsmouth, Rhode Island, in 1673. Cornell was subsequently hanged for matricide.*[132] *Violent words about women could end in violent assaults against women.*

Chapter 3

"Leave of[f] or Else I Would Cry Out Murder"

The Community Response to Family Violence in Early New England

No records reveal whether Merritje Joris Boodt's New Amsterdam neighbors came to her aid when her husband Nicholas "beat her." No documents testify that they took her in when he "shut her out."[1] In New England, however, there is considerable evidence that community response to such public and private brutality was both anticipated and immediate. In these circumstances, popular participation was part of a culture that incorporated informal as well as formal legal remedies.

Nowhere is this phenomenon more evident than in the reaction to spousal violence in eighteenth-century Rhode Island before the establishment of local police forces. It suggests that the eyes and ears of family, friends, neighbors, and servants were not only attuned to the desperate affairs of those in their midst, but that people acted on such information—often without hesitation and at great personal risk. This is not to say that peacekeepers always prevailed, but it is likely that they were at least semi-successful at maintaining a controlled level of intrafamily violence. Children as well as adults were touched by the bitterness of angry households, as were the physicians who treated abuse victims. In homicide cases, doctors testified before judges and jurors, drawing still other members of the community into the sordid affairs of one family. Gossip extended the circle of interested parties. Unlike today, domestic violence was a public rather than a private concern, one that embraced concentric circles of townspeople, and one where community members not only took an interest in the case but might even pressure a jury to reach a particular outcome. Yet these same people knew more than they were willing to share with the future, since the pervasiveness of domestic violence cannot be determined from the relatively few cases that dot the court files.

Mary Beth Norton argues that domestic violence was underreported and infrequently prosecuted in seventeenth-century New England and the Chesapeake, although she points out that Massachusetts took wife beating more seriously than other colonies as a result of proscriptions embedded in the 1641 Body of Liberties and subsequent legislation.[2] Randolph Roth's examination of domestic violence in northern New England indicates that such abuse was related to geographical, cultural, and chronological factors, and his work is a focused starting point for further study. Pennsylvania appears to have had its share of domestic spats that turned ugly, but even among Quakers spousal attacks were undercounted.[3]

Scholars of early modern England maintain that intrafamily assaults were frequent enough there, although such commonplace battering seldom resulted in death. As far as other transatlantic comparisons are concerned, it is still an open question whether the little commonwealths in New England were any more peaceful than their English counterparts, although the abundance of food and dearth of laborers kept the child murder rate at lower levels than in old England.[4] Evidence from American colonial records raises questions about other differences as well. If, as Susan Amussen maintains, neither random violence nor wife beating that led to serious injury was acceptable in early modern England, the same cannot be said for eighteenth-century Rhode Island. If, in England, there were culturally established limits to patriarchal correction in response to a fault, it appears from colonial New England cases that uncontrolled tempers, rather than established rules, governed these episodes.[5] And even if a woman in distress could expect assistance from those around her, such aid must be evaluated by the standards of a society with a high, albeit unfixed, threshold for aggressive behavior. Long-standing and deeply entrenched patriarchal attitudes slowed the demand for intervention by authorities, who rarely intruded in spousal warfare until summoned, even though they were frequently aware of bellicose households.[6] Existing depositions demonstrate that instead of sending for a constable, battered wives called on family, neighbors, and friends as their first line of defense. And neighbors (sometimes promptly but ofttimes tardily) tried to prevent further abuse without summoning local authorities. Their roles were, as Margaret Hunt describes them, "ritualized activities."[7]

Yet certain questions stubbornly resist answers. What were townspeople willing to tolerate, and how much latitude did they grant heads of households to rule their families without interference? At what point did neighbors, friends, and authorities intervene to rein in an abusive husband? What exactly was domestic abuse, anyway? At one end of the spectrum, spousal homicide was the most visible and intolerable example of family violence. At the other, mild physical rebuke by a husband would not have attracted attention or resulted in a fine. Somewhere in between these two extremes were conditions that required intervention because they involved bodily harm; but whether such circumstances always constituted abuse could be debated, at least by the standards of eighteenth-century observers.

Most instances of domestic abuse involved common assault, although the line that divided a husband's legal authority from molestation was thin indeed. English common law permitted the use of moderate force to correct an errant wife who neglected her obligations.[8] Seventeenth-century Puritans, who were on the cutting edge of legal reform, abandoned this practice—on paper, at least—stipulating in the 1641 Massachusetts Body of Liberties that a husband could strike his wife only in his own defense. In 1650, legislators wrote a gender-neutral statute into the books, declaring that neither husbands nor wives could strike the other. It is difficult to say how much theory affected practice in the Bay Colony, but it is likely that local customs rather than legal guidelines defined the perimeters of appropriate behavior. Colonists struggled to replicate many aspects of the world they left behind, and the generations of patriarchal attitudes that cemented their world were hard to dismiss.

In seventeenth-century Massachusetts, colonists negotiated the level of violence—prohibitions notwithstanding. They interpreted the Body of Liberties and subsequent laws in light of their own experience, expectations, and yardsticks of permissible discipline. As a result, the degree to which a husband employed physical force had only a tangential connection to formal rules governing corporal punishment of a wife.[9] As Mary Beth Norton aptly put it, despite the early Massachusetts legislation modifying chastisement, prosecutions of men who defied the law "probably represented only the small tip of a very large iceberg of behavior, given men's expectation of dominating their spouses."[10] At the same time, Norton maintains that in the absence of legal intervention, neighborly intercession during a dispute not only mitigated the severity of a beating, but acted as a humiliating reminder—especially to a husband—that his household was not in order.

That seventeenth-century Massachusetts and eighteenth-century Rhode Island were kindred spirits as far as spousal abuse was concerned is nowhere

JUDGE THUMB.

Bulls   Publ. Nov. 27. 1782. by W Humphry No 227
Strand

or — Patent Sticks for Family Correction: Warranted Lawful!

FIGURE 5. Judge Thumb, or—Patent Sticks for Family Correction: Warranted Lawful! This satirical etching by James Gillray (1756–1815) was published in London by W. Humphry in 1782. Judge Sir Francis Buller walks in the foreground, carrying bundles of rods; in the background a man is about to strike a woman who is running from him. The judge says "Who wants a cure for a nasty Wife? Here's your nice Family Amusement for Winter Evenings! Who buys here?" The woman is crying "Help! Murder for God sake, Murder!" The man, presumably her husband, responds "Murder, hay? Its Law you Bitch: its not bigger than my Thumb!" British Cartoon Prints Collection, Library of Congress.

more egregiously demonstrated than in the case of Marke Quilter, his wife, Frances, and Rebecca Shatswell, three Essex County (Massachusetts) residents. In March 1664, Marke Quilter was presented to the Ipswich Quarterly Court on two counts. He struck his wife and he battered Rebecca, the wife of Richard Shatswell. Furthermore, the second count is our back door into the first. Richard Shatswell complained against Marke Quilter "for cruel misusing of . . . Shatswell's wife"—not Quilter's wife, even though Quilter's abuse of his own wife was a long-standing community problem. Once Quilter was in front of the court, however, his violence toward his own wife became inseparable from his assault on Rebecca Shatswell. Johanah Greene related how Frances Quilter "divers times" begged Greene's daughter "to goe over" to the Quilters' house "and sit and worke with hir to bare hir company." Greene's daughter refused, but Frances Quilter resisted being alone with her husband. "Goody Quilter begged very hard that day at my dafter [daughter] and Good wife brewer to go over thare and bare hir company that very day she was hirt."[11]

Marke Quilter received fines for striking his wife and Rebecca Shatswell, but the spousal abuse did not receive the same attention that Shatswell's beating did. In fact, Frances came to her husband's defense. Marke Quilter had warned Rebecca Shatswell "against coming to his house," and Frances testified "that if Goodwife Shatswell had gone when her husband told her to, he would not have used violence."

The outlines of this tale contain many of the same elements found in eighteenth-century accounts of family violence. The wife, Frances Quilter, was not the complaining party, and she did not summon authorities on her own behalf. Frances tried to avoid being alone with her husband, and confided in neighbors. Marke Quilter endeavored to prevent an alliance with townspeople by refusing them access to his home. Those same neighbors were ambivalent about intervening, even though they were aware of Frances's predicament. Frances tried to excuse her husband and place the blame for his behavior elsewhere. There is evidence that Quilter continued to batter his wife even after being admonished by the authorities to control his behavior.

The same patterns of spousal abuse extended into the 1700s and beyond the borders of Massachusetts, even if common law (as interpreted by William Blackstone) gave a husband less discretion to correct his wife than he formerly possessed. The conclusions are based primarily on eight Rhode Island domestic violence cases, which, taken together, span the entire eighteenth century.[12] Admittedly, eight cases are a small sample, but they are surprisingly redundant, and cumulatively they reinforce each other. They have been chosen because of the number or quality of documents contained in the case files and the wealth of information those documents provide. All involve the battering of wives by husbands. Four men were eventually prosecuted for homicide, while four others appear to have been restrained from further aggression against their wives by the efforts of family, neighbors, and (in rare cases) local authorities.

In every case where records have been preserved, friends, servants, neighbors, and family played prominent and preventive roles, the nature of which varied from situation to situation. Neighborly intervention was often marked by a swift and supportive response, although people closest to the scene of violence occasionally showed reluctance and ambivalence about their intrusion into a volatile situation. Moreover, although authorities seemed to be aware of the more vicious long-term cases via the rumor mill, neighbors often appeared unwilling to encourage official involvement until it was too late. Yet, ironically, it is precisely these same members of the community—neighbors, friends, servants, even physicians—who ultimately determined the fate of an abusive husband after the death of his spouse.

There was nothing in the profile of three eighteenth-century Rhode Island tradesmen to suggest they were likely candidates for the hangman's noose. A Salem native, Jeremiah Meecum was a fortyish family man who earned his living as a weaver on wool-rich Aquidneck Island. What little is known about his family hints at the ordinary: on any given day, if Meecum had been looking for his wife, he might have found her catering to the needs of their two children or gossiping with her sister, Content Garsy. Otherwise she might have been passing time with Jeremiah's sister Jane, either at the Meecum house or at Jane's. Since Newport was a relatively small town at the beginning of the eighteenth century—something over twenty-five hundred people by 1720—Meecum might have crossed paths with another local artisan, William Dyre.

The Dyres were among Rhode Island's oldest and most distinguished Quaker families, although there was nothing particularly distinguished about William himself. In fact, his most distinctive claim was that his lineage included the martyred Mary Dyre, who was hanged for her Quaker beliefs. Eventually William and Mary would have more in common than an allusion to a royal pair, their family name, and Quaker roots. Large landholders and merchants were among William Dyre's contemporary kin; he himself was a respectable joiner and house carpenter. He had married well: his wife, Hannah Briggs, also descended from one of the founding families. A husband and father, a man with a large extended family, Dyre enjoyed good relationships with his brother Samuel and Samuel's wife, who lived nearby. In truth, he took considerable interest in his sister-in-law, Desire, whose very name

evoked thoughts best left unspoken. But townspeople talked nonetheless—
and apparently with good reason.[13]

Nathaniel Alcock, whose moment of ignominy came at midcentury, was
not a contemporary of Meecum or Dyre, but he, too, was a middle-class
Newporter with a wife and children to provide for. Admitted to the colony
as a freeman in 1739, Alcock was a cordwainer (shoemaker) who added to his
income by moonlighting as a cooper when the need or opportunity arose. His
family worshipped at Trinity Church, the gathering place of those committed to the Church of England. Given these unexceptional portraits, the usual
records would not have drawn Alcock or the others to our attention under
ordinary circumstances. But their circumstances became extraordinary in one
outburst of passion, thus setting these seemingly typical men apart from other
members of the community. All three were convicted of murdering their
wives. Meecum and Dyre were hanged. A royal pardon spared Alcock.

Not all batterers killed their wives. John Hammett, Nicholas Barber,
Emanuel Rouse, and Jeremiah Brown, also of Rhode Island, beat and threatened their wives, but surviving records indicate that their abuse stopped short
of homicide. Hammett confided to a friend that he had indeed intended to
kill his spouse, but a night in the cooler apparently chilled his rage. The same
is true for Brown, to the extent that neighbors, family, and servants consistently restrained him until the authorities granted his wife, Mary, a divorce.
Furthermore, spousal violence was not limited to men; women assaulted
their husbands from time to time as well. And what female attacks lacked
in quantity they made up in creativity: a poison plot involving adultery and
conspiracy was every bit as brutal, if not as bloody, a crime as those perpetrated by Meecum, Dyre, and Alcock. Moreover, women were more likely
than men to be accused of infanticide.[14]

No one actually saw William Dyre or Nathaniel Alcock kill their wives,
although the prosecution did not depend on firsthand accounts: circumstantial evidence stood in nicely for eyewitnesses in Rhode Island (unlike other
New England communities).[15] So did hearsay. Thus, colony officials wasted
no time arresting William Dyre on February 14, 1718/19, the day after
his wife, Hannah, died "very Sudenly," since "noe person but her husband
[was] with her." If the Dyres had lived in some remote location, Hannah's
husband might not have come under immediate suspicion, but because William Dyre's penchant for abusing his wife was a matter of public gossip, the
governor's assistants feared that he "had used Some means to make away with
his . . . wife." According to concurring medical opinions, the means was a
broken neck, and William Dyre sat out the rest of Valentine's Day in prison.
He remained there in irons until his murder trial at the end of March.[16]

Elizabeth Alcock's precarious circumstances were also a matter of common knowledge and collective memory. Thus, when the ambiguous nature of her death created enough uncertainty for her husband to escape prosecution, "sundry persons" in the know stepped in to prevent that outcome. "Applying" to justice of the peace Henry Bull on January 27, 1745/46, the day after Elizabeth's death, these anonymous "persons" shared their doubts and fears "wheither the wife of the said Nathaniel . . . did not come to her End by some abuse offered & don to her." They never mentioned Nathaniel by name. But persuaded of the possibilities of foul play, Bull summoned an inquest jury. Revelations by John Wilson and Esther Humphreys established with reasonable certainty that Elizabeth Alcock had been the victim of previous assaults by her husband. The jury itself viewed Elizabeth Alcock's remains and discovered "evident marks of Violence on many parts of her body." And after hearing that the physician and surgeon who examined Alcock's corpse found a dislocated neck in addition to "Sundry Large Contusions," the all-male inquest panel concluded that her broken vertebra was "the immediate occasion of her Death." Other medical practitioners were called in a day later, but their examination of Elizabeth's body resulted in the same findings. No one specifically implicated Elizabeth's husband, but sometime during that twenty-four-hour period Nathaniel Alcock was arrested and held for trial.[17] Thus, in both of these cases, friends and neighbors sought justice for the deceased women after the fact by revealing information about prior abuse that eventually resulted in murder convictions.

Female victims of abuse who ultimately died at the hands of their husbands were unlikely to seek help from town officials, preferring, for personal reasons, to mediate the situation themselves through friends, neighbors, and family. Since all the documents in these homicide cases are dated after the victim's demise—thus precluding any direct testimony from the victim herself—it is difficult to know why each woman chose a less public confrontation. Evaluating her choices, she might have feared that the sheriff, judge, or other town officials would put a family dispute on the back burner, leaving her to struggle with a husband who would have been even angrier at his wife's defection and his public denunciation.

If authorities hesitated to prosecute genial and upright citizens who happened to be wife beaters, it was not because they were oblivious to the disorderly households in their midst. New England communities were too small and rumors too rampant for local officials to remain in the dark for long. In Dyre's case, authorities had been aware of his misconduct "for many yeares past," although such information apparently reached them through indirect sources. "We by Reports did heare" that Dyre's wife "made Complaints of his abusing her." It had been "above two years" since they had been "in-formed" that Hannah Dyre "had said she was afraid he would do her some mischief." At some undisclosed moment in time, however, matters reached a point at which authorities could no longer ignore the gossip. Since Nathan-iel Coddington and Weston Clarke were, as they admitted, "in power and authority," they somewhat belatedly decided to inquire into the "Reports as was spread about."

A visit to the Dyre home confirmed that Hannah feared "to live with him or be in the house alone with him." Summoned to appear before Coddington and Clarke shortly thereafter, the couple responded to questions about their relationship as husband and wife. The papers do not reveal whether they were interrogated together or separately, but in either case, Hannah reiterated her fear that her husband "would doe her Some Mischief." When confronted, Dyre "made very light" of the accusations, at which point Coddington and Clarke threatened to jail him. Both William and Hannah protested—William for obvious reasons, Hannah in the futile hope that her husband "would be more kind and Considerate for the time to come." Whether she really believed he would reform or whether she was concerned that his ab-sence would jeopardize her economic viability is a moot point. Either way, the authorities agreed to "desist" and apparently faded into the background, indicating in their postmortem testimony that they "suppose[d]" her "Neere Nighbours" could "give an account" of Hannah's "troubles . . . since that time."[18] Without quite saying so, Coddington and Clarke acknowledged the role that neighbors played in such cases.

If battered wives were often reluctant to make their complaints official, and town officials in the know acted slowly even by eighteenth-century standards, how did women respond to the woeful circumstances in which they found themselves? Some must have suffered in silence, fearing embar-rassment or an escalation of abuse if they went public. Others surrounded themselves with a protective circle of friends, neighbors, family, and servants in whom they confided. Hannah Dyre told Mary Sanford "sundry times" that her husband had "often Threatened her Life." While being examined in connection with William Dyre's trial for the murder of his wife, Sanford disclosed that "one time . . . William Dyre's wife came to my House and Showed me her head, which she said her Husband had broke with a stick of wood." Having observed the wound, Sanford reported that "the blood Trickled Downe to her Heals."[19] But even being privy to this information, what could or would Mary Sanford do to protect her friend?

After Elizabeth Alcock's death, John Wilson disclosed that he, too, had been the confidant of a battered wife. In his deposition, Wilson claimed that when he came upon Elizabeth Alcock standing in the doorway of her husband's shop a week before she died, Alcock "complained that her husband had abused her . . . and that he Swore he would kill her . . . before morning."[20] Hannah Dyre had received a warning—or, more accurately, a death threat—as well. And she, too, passed that menacing comment on to a neighbor. Five weeks before Hannah's death, Virtue Records recollected, she spent the day at Dyre's house. In the course of conversation, Hannah confided to Records that her husband told her that "if he could conveniently meet with her, alone, he would do her business"—that is, he would kill her.[21] Neither Wilson nor Records revealed her response to this startling information, nor did they disclose any immediate effort on their part to prevent Nathaniel Alcock and William Dyre from carrying out their threats.

But Hannah Dyre did what she could to avoid being alone with her husband. She confessed to Mary Partridge that "she was not afraid of her Husband when any body was there, but that . . . her Husband would . . . privately . . . kill her." Thus, when Nathaniel Coddington and Weston Clarke paid an unexpected visit to the Dyre home and found "some people there," it was possible the gathering had been orchestrated by Hannah Dyre in an effort to protect herself. Yet daytime companionship was only a partial safeguard. What about the dark hours? Joseph Cooke testified at William Dyre's trial that Hannah "had spoake to his [Cooke's] son that when he was in Town he would come and lodge in her house Every night because she was afraid her husband would do her mischief."[22] Hannah Dyre, like other women who believed themselves in jeopardy, attempted to draw in others who would encircle her and act as a buffer between a violent husband and a vulnerable wife. She hoped, no doubt, that the company of family, friends, servants, and neighbors on a regular basis would act as a deterrent to a savage spouse.

Less than a month after William Dyre's arrest for the murder of his wife, Elizabeth Barber sought safety at the home of her father, John Rogers, complaining of "hard usages, outrages, and abuses" committed by her husband, Nicholas.[23] Rogers took her in. Since neither Elizabeth nor the authorities ever charged Nicholas Barber with assault, history is able to eavesdrop on the strife in the Barber household only because Nicholas sued his father-in-law for "entertaining, keeping, and Employing" Elizabeth contrary to law. The disgruntled husband demanded five hundred pounds in damages because Rogers had kept his daughter "against the will and consent of her husband." Publicly humiliated at her departure, Nicholas Barber claimed he lost "not only the comfort and enjoyment of her company but sustained great loss in his household affairs and family not being taken care of." Weston Clarke (whose memory of Hannah Dyre was still raw) was not willing to let history repeat itself. He and a fellow justice, Samuel Cranston, accepted the defense that Elizabeth Barber lived "in fear and hazard of her life," and ordered her to remain with her father until further notice. And in a compromise agreement, Elizabeth received custody of her youngest child, along with the household goods she had brought to marriage, while Nicholas retained charge of the couple's eldest child, possibly his namesake, born in 1713. In all but name, Elizabeth and Nicholas were divorced.[24] How the children responded to the dissolution of their family can only be conjectured.

Word of the Dyre trial must have spread rapidly, because Elizabeth Barber was not the only woman who was roused to action on the heels of Hannah Dyre's death. The same court that heard Dyre's case entertained a separation petition from a fearful Sarah Rouse, who was "afraid her . . . Husband would Take away her Life." Sarah had been a widow with five children when she married thirty-eight-year-old Emanuel Rouse in 1711. Even though Rouse was a financially successful landholder, he failed at marriage—at least according to Sarah.[25] The written record shares few of the sordid details, but after examining Sarah, the court granted her request for separation, although their concern for her well-being fell short of immediate financial assistance. The judges allowed her to "live separately" but stipulated that she should do so "without any charge to her Husband," a cooper. She would be on her own until the pair could "mutually agree between themselves or receive further Order from Lawfull Authority." Assuming, however, that Sarah would be taken in by family or friends, the court added a layer of protection by forbidding her husband from bringing action "in any court" against "any person that shall Entertain her."[26] In short, Emanuel Rouse was barred from the legal route taken by Nicholas Barber.

The Barber and Rouse cases confirm that spousal abuse (short of homicide) usually remained below the legal radar screen unless some peripheral matter brought the situation to light, or heightened fear prompted a woman to complain. Even in homicide cases, unless the case file includes depositions from witnesses, it is difficult to reconstruct the background or circumstances of the incident. Only one official document survives to tell the tale of Mary Flack's murder by her husband in 1771, although in this instance a newspaper account contributes other details.[27] The official report indicates that in late November of that year, Conrad Flack, a Newport baker, threw a pair of iron tongs at his wife, which struck her on the side of her head. She "languished and lived" for two days but finally succumbed to her "mortal wound." How often Mary Flack had been on the receiving end of her husband's temper, how she attempted to protect herself, whether neighbors were involved—all this is irretrievable from the court record.

The *Providence Gazette* provided its readers with a fuller—and more graphic—account of the incident. It appears that late on the evening of Friday, November 22, Flack and his wife engaged in "a high quarrel." As Flack's apprentice, Abiathar Wilson, looked on, Mary Flack called her husband "many hard names, struck him, and threw a plate at him." Conrad Flack responded by flinging the tongs at her "with such force, that one end entered her right temple, and stuck fast in her head." Flack took off, but Wilson, "seeing his mistress fall, flew to her." Observing the tongs "sticking in her head, he ran out after his master . . . and begged he would not run off and leave him." They both returned to the house, and after attending to Mary's wound as best they could, Conrad sought a doctor. Learning that there was "no probability" of his wife's recovery, Flack told Wilson "he was afraid he should be brought into trouble." When Flack realized that Wilson was the only witness, he tried to buy Wilson's silence by offering to release the apprentice from his indentures and furnish him "with money for his expences if he would go off, that he might not be an evidence against him." Wilson agreed, boarded a packet, and was about to flee when the vessel "was hailed by the Sheriff." Flack and Wilson "were committed to close jail after they were examined."[28] Shortly thereafter, the Reverend Ezra Stiles, minister of Newport's Second Congregational Church, took an interest in the case. Visiting "the criminal" in prison, Stiles learned something of Flack's background. "He tells me he was a Calvinist in Germany, and a Communicant at the Lords Table."[29]

That the tongs were iron should have sealed Flack's fate, since any iron implement used as a weapon proved intent to kill.[30] Yet, because "the case appeared so clear to the Jury that he had no premeditated design of murder, they gave in their verdict *Manslaughter,* without leaving their seats." The entire proceedings had taken "an hour and half," according to Ezra Stiles, who attended the trial.[31] And by pleading benefit of clergy, Flack was merely "burnt in the left hand." To be sure, his "Goods and Chattels" were forfeit as well, but all things considered, Flack got away with tong in cheek.[32] If the testimony about Mary hurling a plate at her husband predisposed the all-male jury to favor Flack, such information is lost to history. Nevertheless, the verdict and sentence suggest that whatever the circumstances, the jurors decided Flack did not deserve a death sentence.

The ongoing abuses suffered by Elizabeth Barber, Sarah Rouse, and Mary Flack are beyond recall, but the unusual number of file papers in Mary Brown's case reveals her unhappy circumstances in painful detail. The extensive record also shows that she confronted her situation more aggressively than women earlier in the century. Brown not only relied on the presence of other people to create distance between herself and a mentally disturbed husband, but she continued to press for a formal divorce even after her initial attempt had been rejected. In her first divorce petition to the court at Providence, in 1783, Mary Brown asserted that her husband, Jeremiah, had "manifested Such a Hatred towards her that she hath not Dared to be alone with him." To protect herself, Mary had taken up residence with her father-in-law, who, by taking her in, incurred his son's ire.

Mary's initial petition did not convince the panel of judges that her situation was as alarming as she represented, because a year later she was back in court, this time appealing to justices now sitting in Bristol, Rhode Island. And this time she came armed with corroborating evidence as she pleaded that her life was at stake. In this second divorce proceeding, a hired woman, Olive Walker, substantiated Mary's claim that Jeremiah had "repeated his abuses to her," and Mary was afraid "he would kill her." As a safety measure, Mary "constantly slept in the same Bed" with Walker, a move that put Walker in some danger—as she learned when Jeremiah stormed the chamber brandishing "a large stick in one of his hands, and an open Penknife in the other." To better provide for the safety of his household, Elisha Brown, Jeremiah's father, kept "a large strong Negro in the House, in order to defend him" from his son's rampages.[33] Further testimony about Jeremiah Brown's "shocking behavior," which included an eyewitness report that Mary's husband "had bitten a Piece off from one of her Fingers," finally convinced the court that a divorce would be in everyone's best interest.[34]

Sarah Hogan also petitioned for a divorce from an abusive husband in 1784. She asserted that during her five-year marriage her husband had not only denied her "the necessaries and comforts of life" but was guilty of "beating and threatening her and putting her in great Fear of Bodily Hurt if not of Life." He threw her out of doors, she complained, thus forcing her to rely on the charity of others. Sarah Hogan's petition was granted—leaving her to fend for herself, since the charity of friends was, no doubt, a temporary solution to a moment of crisis.[35]

The records indicate that a number of desperate wives, fearing for their safety, were forced to flee their homes. Occasionally alone, often with their frightened and bewildered children, they would throw themselves on the mercy of neighbors and beg to be taken in. "Many times," asserted Thomas Olney, "Jeremiah's wife Mary [Brown] hath come to my house late in the night in a Great Fright for Fear that her Husband would kill her, and requested me to let her continue in my house, and be locked up until Morning, which was accordingly done." Olive Walker confirmed as much when she admitted that bed sharing "did not always make her [Mary Brown] safe, for his Threats of Violence to her were so great . . . that She was often obliged to leave the House in the Night and go to one of the Neighbours to lodge."[36]

But if Mary Brown was comforted by the thought of supportive friends, not all women were as fortunate. It was not that the legal niceties governing family conduct prevented women from leaving an abusive husband; it was more that their options were, at best, limited. Esther Humphreys assumed that Elizabeth Alcock was free to desert her husband; she asked Alcock outright "why she lived with him." Alcock undoubtedly spoke for many ill-treated women when she responded "where Should She go she had no friend."[37] Presumably, she had no family to call on, either.

For those neighbors and friends willing to accommodate a female in distress, sympathy and ambivalence went hand in hand. The gesture might be seen as taking sides, with repercussions to follow if an enraged husband felt his friends were either abandoning or ganging up on him. One of the most revealing episodes bearing on this point rests on a single extraordinary document, a statement by John James describing events involving his friend John Hammett on the night of August 15, c. 1718 or 1719.[38] Thirty-seven-year-old John Hammett, esquire, a seemingly well-respected Rhode Island freeman, wore several public hats as schoolmaster, clerk of the assembly, clerk of the town council, clerk of the probate court, and attorney general.[39] He was also a wife beater, a matter that must have generated some interest, since his wife, Sarah, was the daughter of former Rhode Island governor Caleb Carr. The couple had at least five children: John, born on October 10, 1705, exactly nine months to the day after his parents' wedding, Mary (1711), Thomas (1712), Sarah (1714), Elizabeth (1716), and James (1718). Sarah was about a year older than her husband.[40]

On that late summer night Hammett "strocke Catharine Cook on the head with A shovel and wounded her very bad and he . . . kickt his wife on the Breast." Hammett's wife (who may have been pregnant) swooped up her children and fled to the house of John Clarke.[41] Clarke received them, but with little enthusiasm. Leaving his uninvited guests—perhaps in the care of his family—Clarke sought the advice of a friend, John James. "What shall we do with Hammett," Clarke ruminated, and then responding to his own question, he also revealed his deeper concerns. "I would not have you go to bed," Clarke told James, "for I will go Look for A Constable for I do not Care to go to bed while his wife and children are att my house for I Should Expect him About the house in the Night if they are there." In other words, Clarke was reluctant to return to his own dwelling so long as a visit by an irate John Hammett was a possibility. Accompanied by the constable, John Bennett, the men went to Hammett's dwelling, where they found "James

Peckham Persuading Hammett to be still and go to bed." Hammett refused, at which point the four men carried the resisting Hammett before Justice Lawton, who committed him to prison for the night.

The next morning, Hammett appeared at the shop of what must have been a very weary and wary John James. Hammett berated James for his part the night before, at which point James responded that "what we Did was against our will for we Did not want to hurt [you]." Moreover, Clarke's concerns the night before appear to have been justified. Hammett "seemed to be very angry with John Clarke." As James relates it, "I told him that his wife and children being there was the Reason that Clarke could not be Easey and was not to blame . . . for he Could Expect . . . to be Disturbed in the Night." James reminded Hammett that Clarke had been a good friend to him. Somewhat mollified by these remarks, Hammett began to "Reflect much upon himself and signified how wonderfull or Strange it was that he had come of [f] so well," since "to be sure" he "intended to kill her." So much for the allegedly gentler nature of the Quaker family.[42]

From the substance of the conversations recorded by John James, it appears as though he, Hammett, Bennett, Clarke, and Peckham were not strangers to each other. All of them were almost certainly Quakers whose social links extended from family to livelihood and beyond. The Society of Friends reported the death of John James in 1766, noting he was "advanced in life," which would make him a contemporary of John Hammett. Marriage cemented the relationship between the Bennetts and Peckhams, a bond that eventually included John James after he married Lydia Peckham in 1728. In 1725, Bennett, a fellmonger (dealer in hides) and tanner, and Peckham, a house carpenter, might have been partners in a shady deal involving the theft of hides. Indeed, they could have been discussing the details of their conspiracy on the same day that John James ran into them at the tanyard.[43] Since many Quaker families lived within an easy walk of their meetinghouse, they were probably neighbors at the time the Hammett incident took place. John Clarke, a mariner, owned a home at the corner of Charles Street and Washington Square, and it may have been this house to which Sarah Hammett fled.[44]

What to make of this narrative? It reveals a slice of life that is usually shielded from prying historians: an early eighteenth-century male friendship network, an attempt to help an abused wife, a fear of reprisal, the role of the constable and judge, and the response of the errant husband. "What we did was against our wills," James insisted. Yet even if James was acting as mediator, the tone of the statement suggests a greater concern with Hammett's well-being than with his wife's. Presumably, if Hammett had gone to bed as James Peckham recommended, all would have been forgiven, if not forgotten. The Quaker connection makes the sequence of events following Hammett's assault more comprehensible, but their willingness to subject Hammett to the authority of Justice Lawton is mildly surprising, given the propensity of Friends to handle such incidents privately. Alas, this chapter in the Hammett family saga ends here, although the record books do catch up with the Hammetts in later years. John Jr. seems to have become a respected Elder, while Thomas appears to have been a chip off the old block.[45] One suspects that John James's testimony made its way into the official record in deference to Sarah Carr Hammett's father, a hint that the community paid somewhat more attention to abused women with rank.

Women who eschewed legal remedies left no documentary trail, no quantitative evidence of the dimensions of spousal abuse. Yet those who sought immediate or long-range assistance from family or friends (and eventually died) inadvertently recorded the violence for future use in trial testimony and revealed the spontaneity and eagerness (or lack thereof) with which others responded to their plight. In her testimony at William Dyre's trial, Hannah Akins asserted that she "Lived att the house of William Dyre . . . about or between Seven and Eight Years and was well knowing To the affairs of that family." Time and again, Akins heard William Dyre threaten his wife and strike her, "which made the blood Run down to her heels"—a graphic description corroborated by Mary Sanford in exactly the same words, thus raising the possibility of testimonial collusion or, at the very least, a common worldview in which that phrase resonated powerfully.[46] Hannah Akins slept in a bed "In the Same Room as dyre and his wife," which not only provided an unparalleled opportunity to view Dyre's assaults firsthand, but put Akins on the front line, should Dyre's rage turn in another direction. Yet, for reasons that Akins never articulated, she remained in the Dyre household, and her presence appears to have stayed William Dyre's hand, at least temporarily. On one occasion, when William Dyre struck his wife with a stick, Akins told Dyre "To Leave of[f] or Else [she] would Cry out murder whearupon he answered and said Damn ye, will you and went out of the house."[47]

Responses by neighbors varied. One night shortly before Elizabeth Alcock died, Lydia Townsend, who lived in "one part of Nathaniel Alcock's house," heard Elizabeth "crying out" as her husband meted out "several blows." And although Townsend decided to listen rather than intervene, others were swift to act, even though they could not have known how much danger to their own persons lay behind the closed door. Remaining ensconced in her room, Townsend heard "Some persons opening the door [of Alcock's quarters] and coming in," at which point Alcock's wife said "she was glad they were come to See her murdered." Townsend asserted that "she often before . . . hear'd . . . Alcock's wife cry out murder," but succumbed to fears for her own safety rather than jump into the fracas.[48]

To react or not to react, that was the question. When Jeremiah Brown's daughter raced to Thomas Olney "in a Great Fright," crying that her father was about "to kill the Family," Olney "ran there immediately," only to see Brown waving an ax and threatening to split his wife's "Damned Brains Out." Fortunately, Brown dropped the ax at Olney's approach, but the matter could have turned out badly, not only for Mary Brown, but for the Good Samaritan as well.[49] Late one night in February 1784, Diademia Hubbard and Samuel Giles heard Mary Brown "Scream for help," and "all of us in the House ran up, expecting that Jeremiah had murdered his wife." That Diademia belies the eighteenth-century stereotype of a timid woman is beside the point. Here, both men and women instantly "ran up," not knowing what they would find, although fully expecting to be confronted with an armed and violent assailant. Brown, "perceiving" the group en route, "quited his wife, and ran to the Chamber Door, and held it shut," to prevent any intervention. Samuel Giles forced the door, and finding a bloodied—but living—Mary Brown, asked Jeremiah Brown "why he had abused his wife in such a manner."[50]

Ezra Hubbard, who had been "at some Distance" from the house in which Mary Brown was living when Jeremiah attacked her, "heard a dreadful Out Cry," and concluding that Mary was being "attacked" by Jeremiah, "ran with all possible haste to the Chamber where she was, being apprehensive, that he would murder her before [he] could Rescue her from him." Hubbard could not have known that "all our Family and the persons in the House" had already rushed into the chamber, yet he appears to have been willing to combat Brown alone if necessary.[51]

It is difficult to say whether there were more Lydia Townsends or Diademia Hubbards in the violent world of eighteenth-century domestic abuse. Discretion was certainly in the interest of self-preservation, and a thoughtful person might hesitate before becoming involved in what could turn out to be a deadly confrontation. The records suggest, however, that many people reacted instantaneously. When Patience Meecum and her sister resisted Jeremiah Meecum's attack, their screams attracted the attention of Stephen Essen (or Hassen), who tried to prevent the murders. But "coming to them he [was] also dangerously wounded" by the ax. Meecum then set his house on fire and "leap'd out of the Chamber Window Headlong among the People that were endeavouring to lay hold on him." According to the newspaper account, Meecum "tryed to murder himself by cutting his own Throat before he . . . was taken." Essen seems to have survived, but surely he must have realized how risky it was to thrust himself between Meecum and the two terrified women.[52]

Not everyone responded as quickly. Only when Samuel Pike received a second summons in the middle of the night did he reluctantly make his way to William Dyre's house, even though his "Indian woman" had informed him that someone was "Calling out for help" there.[53] Yet, if Pike paused, others were almost foolishly fearless in their haste, before and after the crime, to confront a potential murderer. The day after Hannah Dyre's death, Mary Partridge and Mary Almy examined the corpse in the presence of the new widower, William Dyre. Seeing the bruises on Hannah's head and neck, Partridge stated emphatically that "she was murdered and that her Husband she believed had murdered her." According to Partridge's later testimony, "William Dyre, standing then in the Same Roome by the fire, gave her an Ugly Looke, which caused her to Draw to the Doare." Dyre followed her and "shut the Dore against her." If Partridge's testimony was not exaggerated (to add fuel to the case against Dyre), it was lucky that she escaped with no more than an "Ugly Looke."[54]

There is, of course, the possibility that witnesses embellished their accounts after the fact. They did all they could, most of the deponents implied, but it was not enough. They tried to be good neighbors, but in the end they could not prevent several of these brutal men from killing their wives. Nevertheless, even if the testimony was self-serving, it still suggests that both men and women sought to curb unruly husbands and shield imperiled wives, notwithstanding the ongoing debate between permissible correction and excessive cruelty. Men and women might differ over where the former ended and the latter began, but both could be counted on to subdue a husband who was clearly out of control. Over the years, women who suffered from abusive husbands usually sought out other women as confidantes, although depositions suggest they trusted sympathetic male acquaintances with intimate information as well.

Hannah Dyre took Mary Partridge, Rebecca Proud, Mary Sanford, and Virtue Records into her confidence. She expressed her fears and spoke of threats and weapons; she exhibited her bruises and wounds. Yet she was just as outspoken with Joseph Cooke, whose son she asked to "lodge in her house." Hannah told Cooke that her husband admitted "he should not value the loss of his house soe She was burnt in it." That she intended to shock him (and elicit his sympathy) with the extravagant nature of her husband's plans for her demise is probably a stretch, but it is curious that Hannah Dyre never described this scenario in economic terms to her female friends. Or if she did, they did not repeat it for the record.[55]

Elizabeth Alcock's women friends were aware of her distress, but so also was John Wilson, who listened while Elizabeth complained "that her husband had abused her." Both William Dyre and Nathaniel Alcock must have known that their wives complained of their behavior, yet on the occasion of their wives' deaths, both men sought the assistance of the same women who had been privy to their cruelty. Dyre called for Mary Sanford, and Nathaniel Alcock sent for Ann Fisher and other nearby women, even though all of them had observed previous acts of violence and would be immediately suspicious of the cause of death.[56] They were also potential witnesses in any legal proceeding, something that seems to have eluded the consciousness of the men.

Far from being humiliated by the involvement of neighbors, these vicious spouses showed no reluctance about intimidating and abusing their wives in front of others, as long as nothing they did could be construed as lethal. Loud voices pierced walls; boarders in various rooms consistently testified to threats, blows, and screams. Within earshot of Joseph Cooke, William Dyre whispered to his wife "that he would kill Her." Hannah Akins saw William Dyre sling a stick over his wife's head and threaten "to beat out her brans." Lydia Townsend heard Elizabeth Alcock plead with her husband "don't kill me by Inches but kill me out right." Within Townsend's hearing, Nathaniel Alcock replied "that was what he Intended to do."[57]

John Hammett, William Dyre, Nicholas Barber, Nathaniel Alcock, and Jeremiah Brown were confident they could browbeat their wives with impunity. The drama, as it was played out, called for neighbors to restrain violent husbands and protect wives as best they could, but an abusive husband could be fairly certain that neither his wife nor those same neighbors would seek the assistance of constables, sheriffs, or judges. Patriarchal attitudes may have discouraged wives from initiating legal remedies to begin with; women may also have feared that their lives could become immeasurably worse if the authorities were summoned. Given eighteenth-century assumptions about household government, what if men in official positions simply brushed them off? If the threshold for brutality was high, and if local authorities assumed that they should look the other way until pressed to act, it would explain why so few incidents of family violence appear in the official records. Men who beat up other men, single women, or other men's wives were more likely to find themselves prosecuted than men who attacked their own wives.

Such an interpretation would also explain John Hammett's anger at John Clarke's surprising betrayal of their friendship, as well as John James's remark that "what we Did was Against our wills for we Did not want to hurt him." In other words, once Hammett's wife was out of immediate danger, the script did not call for a constable (much less a judge), and the "hurt" James alluded to was one Hammett's reputation would suffer once he was exposed to the legal process. In this sense it was a private matter, not subject to the scrutiny of public officials—even though the entire community must have known of Hammett's ill temper toward his wife. It was only because Hammett refused to "be still" and allow his wife to "come home" that the men took him before the judge.[58]

The belief that family matters were best resolved by self-help or extralegal remedies also meant that husbands could threaten their wives and strike them without directing blows to body parts covered by clothing. It was not even necessary to whisper, as Dyre allegedly did. Concealment was superfluous because it was unlikely that a husband would be called to account for his deeds—unless he tripped over the line between permissible and impermissible behavior. A spouse's demise was certain to raise questions, forcing Dyre, Alcock, and Flack to construct plausible explanations that would exonerate them from any crime. Even before his wife's death, Nathaniel Alcock was thinking ahead: Elizabeth "had taken poison," he told Esther Humphreys, who had stepped in to inquire about Elizabeth's head pain and "fits" (caused by Alcock's blows).[59] And after she died, Alcock explained the dislocation of his wife's neck by insisting that Elizabeth rose up "to take the Chamber pot" and "pitcht over the child which lay in the bed & fell with her head upon the floor." Dyre's defense was similar to Alcock's. Hannah's neck became "Dislocated & Broken," he explained, when she reached "for the pott to spit in . . . or by getting out of bed"—all the result of a bad cough.[60] Even before he was taken into custody, Conrad Flack told the doctor "his wife had fell with her head against the tongs." Flack's immediate arrest may be an indication of the physician's skepticism, as well as to his role as witness in the case.[61]

Existing evidence implies that the sex of the neighbor, servant, or family member had little influence on the part that person would play during an assault.[62] At the same time, a careful reading of the statements hints that gender became more nuanced and gender roles more defined as subsequent events unfolded. If gender guided community behavior only peripherally prior to the death of a battered wife, sex roles became more pronounced in the postmortem hours and days. Women sat and watched over a nearly dead woman. Women closed her eyes and laid out her body. Men began the legal process to determine the cause of death by summoning an inquest jury. Presumably, the "Sundry persons" whose suspicions led to an inquest in Elizabeth Alcock's case included both women and men. Nevertheless, the circumstances surrounding the inquest juries called to inquire into the deaths of Meecum's and Dyre's wives show that great anxiety attended the different roles that men and women would play in the legal process, once it became an official public matter.

Jeremiah Meecum killed his wife and sister-in-law with an ax on March 22, 1715/16. Only two legal documents survive as verification of this incident—the report of the inquest jury, which was summoned the following day, and Meecum's indictment. Most of the inquest report is formulaic: the jury viewed the body and agreed on the cause of death—"several larg woonds In thare heads which . . . ware maid by an axs or axses."[63] What is unusual about this twenty-four-member jury is that it was composed of twelve men and twelve women, their names neatly separated by sex in two long columns. All of the twelve men were literate; that is, each signed his name individually. Only half of the women inscribed their names by themselves; each of the remaining six scratched in "hur marcke" with a symbol peculiar to herself.

If the participation of women on Meecum's inquest jury raised no eyebrows, the inquest proceedings in William Dyre's case are replete with gender issues. Indeed, Hannah's death on February 13, 1718/19 required two inquest panels to resolve questions relating to her demise. Although no document survives from the original panel, subsequent file papers indicate that the first inquest jury was composed solely of women. A swift burial followed the inquest report, but three days later the case took an extraordinary turn. In a warrant issued to Major James Brown and the rest of the assistants and justices of the town of Newport, Governor Samuel Cranston directed that Hannah Dyre's body be "taken out of the Earth" for a second examination. This highly unusual step was necessary because "there is a generall Dissatisfaction of the people of the Towne that theire was not a jury of men as well as women upon the Body of Hannah Dyre, and further Serch and Inquiry Made." Cranston ordered Brown (who was also the coroner) to impanel "twelve or more well Quallified men" who would "view and Inspect" Hannah Dyre's body in order to judge how "she came by her Death." Moreover, Governor Cranston demanded the recall of the doctors who had "already made Some Inspection"—an order that highlights the role physicians played in abuse cases.[64]

That same day, four clearly exasperated surgeons "Being summonsed the second time to Revew & inspect the body of Hannah Dyer" made a more thorough examination of the disinterred woman only to conclude that their "first Judgment" had been sound. Furthermore, the doctors specifically noted that this time the "Jewrey . . . did see for themselves" the injury to Hannah's neck, thus implying that the first inquest panel did not have a close look at the damaged vertebra.[65] Without commenting on the reason for the dislocation of Hannah's "uppermost vertibra," the physicians presented their findings to the newly constituted, all-male inquest panel.

Why had there been "Dissattisfaction" with the original all-female jury? Was it merely a gender issue—an unwillingness to allow women to determine the fate of a man in circumstances that might lead to his execution? This seems doubtful, even if the first report did lead to Dyre's immediate arrest. Or was it commonly expected that a full inquest would include both men and women—as in the Meecum case? If so, it is curious that a woman's name has surfaced on only one other Rhode Island inquest jury.[66] More likely, Dyre and his lawyer (assuming he had one), used gender as a means to an end. The wording of the documents, the explicit comment that the second time around Hannah's neck had been "Open to Publick vew," suggests that Dyre had been looking for a way to discredit the first panel in order to assemble a different body that might be more sympathetic to him. The warrant to exhume Hannah Dyre's body implied that the dissatisfaction arose from the cursory examination made by the first jury—one that happened to be all female. They should have made "further Serch and Inquiry." It was possible, therefore, that Dyre was employing this defense strategy in the hope that an all-male jury would examine his wife's body more thoroughly and conclude that her death could be explained in a benign fashion. The greater danger to Dyre, however, was not merely the composition of the first jury; it was that these particular women were probably connected to a grapevine fully aware of William Dyre's savage proclivities. Hannah had not made a paper trail, but she had left a record of abuse nonetheless. That record, no doubt, colored the conversation as the first inquest panel deliberated behind closed doors.

Who first expressed dissatisfaction, or whether Dyre encouraged a male inquest panel, must remain in the realm of conjecture. Nevertheless, William Dyre had reason to hope that the second panel would give him the benefit of the doubt. Men might give more credence to his explanations, or at least express ambivalence about the way Hannah's neck had become dislocated. The jurors chosen for this round were clearly William Dyre's peers, if not his drinking partners. Of the nine men on the inquest jury whose occupations can be identified, eight were middle-class tradesmen or artisans, including three joiners or house carpenters who may have worked with Dyre on various projects. Two tailors, one cordwainer, a blacksmith, a yeoman, and a vintner made up the rest. Dyre's hopes for a more sympathetic hearing from the men he rubbed elbows with were dashed, however, with the decisive nature of the report, submitted on February 16. With no irresolution at all, the jury seconded the determination of its predecessor: "Our opinion in generall is that she Came to a Violent Death by the Breaking of her Neck." Twenty men signed the inquest report, an indication that coroner Brown had taken his assignment as an order to summon "more" than twelve men.[67]

Elizabeth Alcock also died by a broken neck. And the assessment of the cause of death by physicians, one or more of whom may have treated her at other times, again demonstrates the impact of the local medical community in such tense situations. Yet this time, the ambiguities in language, the absence of a collective statement signed by these consultants, and the disagreement among the physicians (evidenced by their unwillingness to make an unconditional finding) ultimately paved the way to a royal pardon for Nathaniel Alcock. The twelve male inquest jurors, sitting on January 27, 1745/46, initially summoned two doctors, Norbert Wigneron and Henry Hooper, to view Elizabeth Alcock's remains. Their sworn statement (of the same day) was succinct: they found "not only Sundry Large Contutions but the Second Vertebra of her neck Dislocated." How any of this might have come about was left to the imagination.[68] Despite the brevity and nonaccusative nature of these findings, the inquest jury reshaped the doctors' words in its report to imply human agency. "They [the doctors? jurors?] found evident marks of Violence on many part [sic] of her body as her breast on both sides much bruised her Sholders and Sundry other Parts much bruised and the Second Vertebra of her neck dislocated which we believe to be the immediate occasion of her Death." Without quite saying so, the inquest report conveyed the message that Elizabeth Alcock had been beaten, and that her death was the result of a broken neck. Whether the two were connected was omitted from the written record.[69]

The following day (and without explanation), three additional physicians were called in to further "Inspect the body of Elizabeth Alcock," who was "now lying dead & Suspected to have had violence us'd upon her." In addition to Hooper and Wigneron, doctors Clarke Rodman, John Brett, and Thomas Moffatt were asked for their opinions. Only Moffatt discovered "diverse and various marks of violence upon [Alcock's] body and that the second Joint of her neck was buscated forwards." The reports of the other two doctors were more ambiguous in tone. Rodman found Alcock's "brest brused & Several Scratches & bruses in her face and the Second Vertebras of her neck Dislocated." John Brett concurred with the dislocated vertebra and noted "Several marks on her face and one on her left Breast which . . . appeared to be a Contusion but from what Cause . . . this Deponent could not learn." In short, neither Rodman nor Brett subscribed to a finding of violence, which meant they were unwilling to point their collective fingers at Alcock. "Further" these deponents "saith not," but on January 28, all five physicians agreed to give evidence at Nathaniel Alcock's trial "the last Tuesday of March next."[70]

The "Sundry persons" who approached Justice of the Peace Henry Bull in the belief that Elizabeth Alcock came "to her end by some abuse offered and done to her, in her lifetime" initiated a chain of events that included the summoning of an inquest jury and the subsequent involvement of five medical practitioners whose evidence showed signs of equivocation. Nevertheless, testimony by witnesses to the abuse Nathaniel Alcock heaped upon his wife (as well as to the inconsistencies in his defense) eventually led to Alcock's conviction and sentence of execution. But the story does not end with Alcock swinging from the hangman's noose on June 6, 1746. Nor does community involvement in this case cease with the jury's seemingly unanimous decision. In a statement dated April 22, 1746 (a few weeks after Alcock's trial), Dr. Thomas Moffatt thought it "incumbent" upon himself to clarify "an Error prevalent with persons of every Rank." Contrary to what people might think, a broken neck did not lead to "instant or immediate death." It was an "absurdity" to think so, added Moffatt, implying that Elizabeth Alcock might have fallen—just as her husband insisted—incurring an injury that subsequently led to her death. Somewhat belatedly, Moffatt was

FIGURE 6. Colony House, Newport, Rhode Island. Designed by Richard Munday and built in 1739, Colony House is a splendid example of public architecture and the scene of many high-profile trials, including that of Nathaniel Alcock. Engraving by G. Wall, c. 1830. No. 2004.13.53. Courtesy Newport Historical Society.

raising reasonable doubt, even though his prior testimony had been the most damaging to Alcock's case.

Even before Moffat's gratuitous clarification, however, Nathaniel Alcock had petitioned the Rhode Island General Assembly for permission to apply for "the Kings Clemency."[71] This petition is a stunning moment in eighteenth-century legal history because it takes the reader into the jury room and reveals, in no uncertain terms, the way in which the court pressured the jury to reach a decision. It also reveals the partisan positions jurors took as deliberations proceeded. Alcock asked for mercy because he learned that "all the . . . Jurors (Except Three) were for Clearing your petitioner But were forced to Complye to the obstinate opinion of the said three Jurors who Declared were they to stay and Starve they would find your Petitioner Guilty."[72] Protesting his innocence, Alcock reiterated that the majority favored acquittal, but "by means of . . . Threats and Obstinacy" they succumbed to the will of three unyielding jurors. Moreover, Alcock asserted, the prosecution had not met the burden of proof because there was no evidence to "prove" the murder. In fact, Alcock insisted, he had "severall Materiall Witnesses who were by some means omitted to be Produced— who Could and would have made [Alcock's] Innocence [plain] appear." This last was a ploy, perhaps, a way to neutralize those jurors who knew the Alcocks, were aware of Nathaniel's violent tendencies, and had believed the worst. Pleading for "a Pardon, a Reprieve, a New Tryall or Such other act of Goodness," Alcock signed the petition in a bold hand.

Under Alcock's signature was another petition, initially signed by three jurors who declared that "each and every one of us at the time of giving in the verdict against said Allcock, then were and still are of Oppinion that he ought not to be found guilty of the murder of his Wife, upon the Evidence then Produced in Court against him, and that we and Each of us Insisted on Quitting him,[73] and used all the means and Persuasions that in our power Lay to Dissuade the said Jurors before mentioned from finding him Guilty, But to no Effect tho' we and each of us withstood their obstinate opinion for above the space of 24 hours and should have withstood them Longer had not our health been much Impaired for want of food." Hunger overcame justice, these petitioners claimed, and they were "obliged . . . to find him Guilty tho' very Contrary to our Inclinations." The signers urged the General Assembly to grant Alcock a new trial so that they "May Rest Easy in their minds (which otherwise they may not Doe) they thinking within themselves that they might be the unlawfull occasion of . . . Allcock's death." Shortly thereafter, four additional jurors signed a supplement to this petition, which repeated the earlier statement in nearly the same words.

That the fate of Nathaniel Alcock preyed on the mind of the jury, that some panelists rejected the circumstantial evidence against him, that several men appear to have been looking for a way to save him from the gallows is clear. Yet if the allegations in the petition are true, and three-quarters of the jury were ready to acquit Alcock, it is puzzling why they did not inform the court of their inability to reach a verdict. One can only assume that the bench would not have been sympathetic to an acquittal and would have sent them back for further deliberation. How conflicted they actually were is borne out most dramatically by one juror who, on subsequent days, had a change of heart for the second time. Matthew Borden, the foreman of the jury, appealed to the legislature to blot his name from the petition "that it may be no more read by the Considerable part of Mankind." This left six men to press the General Assembly for some "act of goodness" to mitigate Alcock's conviction and sentence. But what provoked Matthew Borden's second crisis of conscience?

Borden was "Heartily Sorry" that he had added his name to the petition. He subscribed to it, he said, at a time when he was "Strictly reflecting upon [his] Conduct as one of those Jurors occasioned by the [Clammers] of many People." Many people? To whom or what was Borden alluding? In awkward phrasing, Borden seems to be implying that he was a pawn of popular agitation. It was during a moment of self-doubt that the petition was "press'd" upon him, he admitted, and he "inconsiderately" signed it. Further reflection convinced him of his error, and he was now "steadily of the same Mind" as he was when he "gave the verdict." In other words, he was convinced of Nathaniel Alcock's guilt.

These extraordinary documents indicate that the community was divided and ambivalent about Nathaniel Alcock. Strong circumstantial evidence, accumulating from the testimony of various witnesses, convinced many jurors of Alcock's guilt. It is also possible that rumors and gossip, circulating among the townspeople, influenced their decision as well. Yet after the verdict, half the jurors claimed they were uneasy about putting a man to death on the basis of the evidence presented to them. Since no one had been brought up on wife-beating charges in the town's memory, and no husband had been executed for spousal homicide in more than a quarter century, perhaps the jury believed that Alcock, even if convicted, would get off with a whipping. Once the judges pronounced the death sentence, however, some of them may have felt that even if Alcock was responsible for Elizabeth's death, his culpability did not demand one broken neck for another. Their petition to the General Assembly suggests they believed the legislative branch of government (and particularly the lower house) would be more receptive to their appeal.

To bring this story to a close, the Assembly agreed to Alcock's request, his execution was stayed for twelve months, and with Richard Partridge, the colony's agent, acting as a go-between, Alcock obtained a royal pardon.[74] His reprieve may have been due to the posttrial wavering of jurors, the doctors' ambivalence, or it may have been for reasons the surviving records do not reveal. In the end, despite all the evidence against Alcock, the royal hand trumped a host of witnesses who knew how and why Elizabeth Alcock had died.[75]

William Dyre and Jeremiah Meecum spent considerably less time in Newport after their trials. Punishment was usually swift and certain in the eighteenth century, and the two were hanged shortly after their convictions—both of them in the month of April (albeit several years apart), just as the apple blossoms confirmed the arrival of spring. Just before his execution, Meecum repented and made the obligatory gallows speech before "a great Multitude of People" who had gathered to watch the hanging. Among other words of advice, he "Cautioned Married Persons to Guard against Strife and Contention in their Families," and specifically "forgave his neighbors," presumably for some transgressions against him.[76] Perhaps they had borne witness to Meecum's treatment of his wife.

Dyre, too, unburdened himself. In an extraordinary confession on the night before his execution, the doomed man revealed what might have been his motive for the abuse and murder of his wife, Hannah. At the request of Dyre's brother, Samuel, a committee of two (John Wanton and Thomas Rodman) accompanied Samuel and his wife, Desire, to the prison with the "Expectation" that William, in his last hours, "would have Cleared her [Desire] of the scandalous Reports that was spread abroad Concerning her." At first, William "seemed to be very Desierous To Do it." But as the unhappy man shifted and turned, he "seemed Loath to tell a positive Lye." After a while, Dyre admitted to his astonished listeners that "the storyes concerning her were true and that he had Layn with her many a time as often as oppertunity presented." Dyre apologized to his brother, but in a rush of words insisted that "he had rather been Ript open for he Loved her as his own Life," adding (somewhat gratuitously, under the circumstances) that "it would not Doe to Deny the truth then." Horrified, no doubt, at this unexpected confession, Desire "by her appearance and actions" gave Wanton and Rodman "sufficient grounds to believe that what he sayed concerning her uncleanness was true."[77] Hannah, it seems, had cast a shadow between William and his heart's Desire.

Neighbors, friends, family, and servants of both Dyre and Meecum could witness the public execution if they chose to do so, but only Meecum was left to the gaze of the community after his death. Although the authorities did not permit Dyre to be interred "in the burial place" of his "Ancestors" or "in the Common Burial Place," they did allow immediate interment on his brother Samuel's land, where his parents, both of whom survived him, could mourn their son. As for Meecum, so "barbarous" was his crime that the court decreed a punishment to fit it—one that required the community to bear witness. After his execution, Meecum's body was conveyed to the top of a nearby hill, where his corpse hung "in Irons on the Jibbet" until his body was "Consumed as a Capitall Criminall." This was part of the ritual that Dyre, presumably because of his family's status, avoided: Meecum's corpse, now carrion, would be booty for the scavengers of the sky.[78]

If adults took center stage in these domestic dramas, children were never far from the scene. And if youngsters were frightened spectators most of the time, occasionally they were called from the wings to play a more direct and decisive role. John Hammett's wife fled with her children in tow. Whether they witnessed the assault upon their mother is unknown, but clearly Sarah Hammett was concerned for their safety. Two nights prior to Elizabeth Alcock's death, her nine-year-old daughter, Elizabeth, "came up" to Ann Fisher (who lived in the Alcock house) and "begg'd" Fisher to "come down & help" her mother, who had "fallen out of bed."[79] Their "Young Child in the Cradle" (three-year-old Nathaniel, perhaps) was present the night of Elizabeth Alcock's death. The six-year-old twins must have been within hearing distance as well.[80]

In William Dyre's case, his wife had placed one child in the bed she and her husband shared, but two other "Little Children" were "in a truttle bed" in the same room, fearfully observing the events around them. It was these two children whom William Dyre told "to Run & See or Hasten Mrs. Sanford." In an attempt to comfort her mother, "when one of the children a girl came backe She Kneeled downe by the bead, and Looked in her Mothers face and said She was acoming." Although none of Dyre's children testified against him, the admissibility of hearsay evidence (in this case his children's conversation) proved damaging to Dyre. Virtue Records testified that Hannah Dyre told her "She heard Some of her Children Say one to the other, did not you Heard Father Say he would Kill mother when he could or Should get her alone."[81] Whether Dyre's children would have come forward independently is debatable, but they must have known that his conviction in a court of law would orphan them. Was a bad father better than no father at all?[82]

No one had to tell Jeremiah Brown's daughter to seek help when Brown went on a rampage. As Thomas Olney described it, "one of the Daughters of

Jeremiah Brown who lived with her Mother . . . came in a Great Fright and crying desired me to run immediately to her Grandfathers, for her Father . . . was going to kill the Family." It was bad enough for this girl to witness an assault on her mother; it must have been even more terrifying to think that her father might kill her as well. Nathaniel Alcock also threatened "the life of his own child," as well as "the negro child" who was part of the Alcock household.[83]

In the end, William Dyre's children were orphaned. So, too, were Jeremiah Meecum's offspring. Nathaniel Alcock received a royal pardon, so technically his children were not bereft of both parents. Whether they were returned to Alcock is unknown, although it is fairly certain that all the children bore considerable emotional scars into adulthood, even if they grew up in another household. In two cases (Meecum and Hammett) the document trail extends into the future. After Meecum's execution, the Rhode Island General Assembly ordered the sale of his estate at public auction, stipulating that if any surplus remained after all accounts were settled, the money would be turned over "to Major Bliss, for the support of . . . Meecum's children."[84] Bliss was the children's grandfather, but his custody was short-lived. Meecum's two children were "Desirous [of going] with their Uncle," and since rumor had it that the children had not been "soundly dealt [with]," the town council gave James Meecum ("a sober man") guardianship of his brother's children.[85]

If John Hammett's sons grew to adulthood in a household marked by strife between their father and mother, such persistent conflict might explain why Thomas, who was six or seven at the time of the incident recorded by John James, became a violent felon as an adult. In 1732, Thomas, now twenty, was convicted of murdering Katharine Cooke, the wife of William Cooke. The court sentenced Hammett to hang, although he escaped from the badly secured prison disguised in his wife's cloak before the sentence could be carried out.[86] What the relationship was between Hammett and the Cookes is unknown, although it is remotely possible that as a laborer, Thomas boarded at the Cookes' house, which was located on Newport harbor.[87] Thomas's father lived until 1773, refusing to give up life until he was ninety-three. He did so as a Baptist, having abandoned the Society of Friends after a dispute in 1740. Hammett was laid to rest in the Common Burying Ground near his wife, Sarah, who had died eight years earlier in her eighty-fourth year. They had been married for six decades.[88]

Most husbands and wives in New England surely bickered occasionally, as elsewhere, but under normal conditions such disagreements were, no doubt, contained and resolved. Excessively aggressive households were the exception, not the rule. At the same time, there is little doubt that some New

England husbands could and did inflict serious injury on their wives. Spousal violence may have been unacceptable in theory, but depositions from case after case suggest that the threshold for physical abuse was high, that spousal maltreatment was of long duration, and that husbands could assault their wives for a variety of reasons without fear of being brought up on charges. Neighbors might try to deter a menacing husband, but they could not always prevent a sudden blow, nor, it seems, could they always thwart a death stroke. The records indicate that abusive husbands whose ages can be determined were between thirty and forty-five years old.

In eighteenth-century Rhode Island very few spousal abuse cases short of homicide appear in the records. Occasionally, a related or peripheral matter catapulted domestic violence to center stage, but suits for loss of companionship or divorce proceedings are also small in number. Nevertheless, numbers can be deceiving, and the cases that do surface are suggestive of a larger picture. Even if only the worst offenders were charged as criminals, the details of such cases fill in blanks that would otherwise remain empty. Civil cases enrich our understanding of family disorder as well: Nicholas Barber was never hauled to court to explain why he beat up his wife, but his temper was inscribed in the written record when he peevishly sued for his wife's return.

Moreover, domestic dramas played in open air outside the courtroom when the formal legal system sputtered or halted. Community intervention—in this venue no longer spontaneous—became street theater in the form of "rough music" or skimmingtons, during which an incensed mob imposed physical punishment on an abusive husband. The clanging of pots and pans, ringing of bells, and the beating of drums summoned an audience to witness this ritual, which had its roots in England and the continent. Rarely seen before the 1730s in the colonies, skimmingtons were, perhaps, an alternative to a justice system that only hesitatingly responded to battered wives.[89] Especially in the early years of the practice's appearance on this side of the Atlantic, women were as likely as men to inflict punishment on an offender.

The most thorough study of skimmingtons focuses on the middle colonies, where incidents of rough music were reported in areas settled by transplanted New Englanders.[90] Few examples appear in New England newspapers, although it is difficult to know whether the absence of journalistic evidence is reflective of their rate of occurrence. One incident just over the Rhode Island border in Massachusetts did catch the attention of the *Newport Mercury* in 1764, however.[91] Under the byline "Boston," the article described the uproar over Jonathan Sheppardson of Attleborough, who "for some Time" had been the subject of neighborhood rumors that he "had been guilty of some bad Family Conduct." According to the report, "it was determined he should be punished by a certain Law, by the Vulgar called *Skimmington*, of which the most unruly Part of the Community set judges." Presumably sentenced by such a group, Sheppardson found himself "surrounded by 20 or 30 Men intirely disguised and armed with Clubs." In the melee that followed, Sheppardson killed a man and wounded others, which suggests that the violence could escalate beyond the intention of the skimmington's sponsors.

More interesting, perhaps, is the letter from Taunton, Massachusetts, that appeared in the *Mercury* some days later.[92] Responding to the frequency of such "lawless and outrageous Proceedings" (an indication that some incidents went unreported), the author asserted that "it is the grossest Violation of civil Society to punish any Person unheard." Due process aside, "if those Persons whose Indignation is so kindled, would take half the Pains to observe their Neighbours bad Conduct, as they do to punish it, at the Expence of public Peace, they might furnish the Authority with sufficient Evidence for Conviction, by which they would serve the Public, gratify their own Resentments, and at the same Time be free from the fatal Disasters and legal Punishments that attend *Skimmington Rioters.*"

The phrase "punished by a certain law" in the first account of Sheppardson's assault by a mob is intriguing. In context, it appears to be a reminder that the dividing line between legal and extralegal authority was thin indeed. Apparently, the shared beliefs that formed the governing principles of eighteenth-century New England society could be expressed by statute or through action. Thus, the author of this piece seems to be implying that some laws were class based, an observation that all but obliterated the distinction between legal and extralegal. Skimmingtons were a folk remedy for bad behavior—but as a disorderly response from the "Vulgar" sort, they were ill advised. Imprudent or not, rough music was part of a legal tradition: common law, after all, derived from customs that existed from time immemorial and were not only ancient, but frequently unwritten.

If we cannot determine the extent of domestic violence from the small number of cases that survive, what can we conclude from the information they provide? First (and this seems almost paradoxical), it is clear that knowledge about abusive husbands—or wives—permeated the community. We may be in the dark; they were not. As James Terett acknowledged during a 1774 divorce action between Ann and Asa Seten: "it was the common Report and the Generel Voice of the People Near them that ware well knowing that . . . Seten was a Very bad Husband and treated his wife Very Ill."[93] Particularly in the towns, houses were clustered together, with family, servants, apprentices, and boarders parading through chambers, stairways, and halls.

Walls were too thin and privacy too elusive for anyone to be out of earshot for very long. Battered wives bared their bruises to neighbors; neighbors gossiped; gossip reached town officials—and paused there. Physicians may have treated the worst cases, although the Hippocratic oath should have bound the medical profession to silence and confidentiality. Inquest jurors and/or trial jurors added to a widening circle of people drawn into domestic disputes.

Whether the constant proximity of husband and wife in an urban setting was an additional source of friction is also beyond the reach of historical investigation. But because home and production for income occupied the same space, it may not be entirely coincidental that all four homicides discussed here took place during colder months when people were more likely to share close quarters for longer periods of time. Mary Brown's brush with death took place in February. Three of the four homicides occurred on weekends, all during the late evening or night. Moreover, the heavy use of alcohol in early America probably exacerbated the tendency toward violence, although there are only glimpses of the connection between drinking and abuse. After one such episode, Esther Humphreys asked Elizabeth Alcock "wether her husband was in drink and she nodded her head by which the deponent understood that he was."[94]

There is little in these scenarios to suggest that the public household of colonial America (compared with the present-day private family) offered a wider safety net for women with abusive husbands.[95] The cases herein described hint that in this patriarchal society, the state and husband were allies, the former tolerating the actions of the latter as head of household, and seemingly reluctant to brake a husband who used intemperate force. That same common understanding about gender roles deterred individual neighbors, friends, family—even the victim—from seeking redress through the legal system. In short, husbands were given considerable leeway to treat their wives within identifiable—albeit broad—limits.

Spotty church records confirm that members and congregants occasionally attempted to resolve domestic disputes in that venue as well, but the few existing references to spousal abuse suggest that women could not count on a strong response from the sisters and brethren who worshipped together. In 1733, a Cambridge, Massachusetts, church accepted Eleazer Parker's "publick acknowledgment" that he "tried to kill his wife"—and let it go at that. And in 1771, the Rhode Island monthly meeting of the Society of Friends accepted the missive from John Borden who had "sent lines signifying sorrow for laying hands on his son John's wife in an angry spirit."[96]

Susan Juster's analysis of church discipline between 1740 and 1780 confirms that domestic violence was of far less concern to church members than contempt of authority, quarrels among members, or speech crimes. Of the 389 offenses in her study, only nine were "sins against family/household," a category that included spousal or child abuse and disobedience toward parents or masters. Of these nine accusations, two were against men and seven against women, although even in this group it appears that few involved actual physical abuse.[97]

Yet the willingness of neighbors to intervene in explosive situations is nothing short of remarkable, given the risks that they faced. No one mentioned firearms in any of the depositions, but axes, shovels, tongs, penknives, and sticks could be every bit as lethal in homicidal hands. Nevertheless, the involvement of members of the community may have spared women for whom no documents exist to tell the tale.[98] Ultimately, however, neighbors could do just so much. Their gossip, used as a means of social control, was limited in effect. If the goal was humiliation, the cases discussed here provide strong evidence that shame was a weak deterrent. How humiliated could a man be if he continued to assault his wife in front of others?[99]

Neighbors could protest a husband's use of his wife, reason or plead with him, even restrain him or take in his wife on a temporary basis, but as the extant records indicate, they could not save Patience Meecum, Hannah Dyre, Elizabeth Alcock, or Mary Flack. Timely intervention by authorities in the know might have averted the death of these women, but an eighteenth-century worldview precluded their involvement until it was too late. If friends and family had been able to rely on officials to intervene when summoned, they might have sought help earlier and more often. Yet how forcibly did the authorities act when called upon? They might imprison a batterer for a short time, but he would return to his wife in short order—perhaps more hostile than before. This was probably in Hannah Dyre's mind when she resisted the opportunity to jail her husband. With such a communal outlook and understanding, abusive husbands probably knew how much they could get away with. Under most circumstances, neither their wives nor witnesses were likely to summon town officials or commence legal proceedings. And even if Nathaniel Alcock was convicted of homicide, he was soon reabsorbed into the life of the town after his pardon. There was no need to relocate to avoid community censure; customers continued to purchase shoes, and he still earned a taxable income more than a decade later. His chances for remarriage, however, were slim.[100]

In the absence of a police force, community members interacted to patrol behavior in early American towns and villages. Yet surely there must have been boundaries between official (if weak) policing by a sheriff or constable, and that of individual inhabitants. Where did responsibility for keeping the peace lie? Was the informal dividing line consensual? Resolved on a case-by-case basis? Decided spontaneously? Moreover, if the intervention of neighbors was a common occurrence, the timing of that intercession becomes a central issue. At what point and for what reasons did outsiders inject themselves into a marital spat in order to mediate violence? How much abuse was too much? Did neighbors and friends negotiate the permissible level of violence among themselves before deciding what form that intrusion should take? Was there a point at which neighbors might have encouraged a wife to leave her abusive spouse? And if she refused, would they have continued to impose themselves between husband and wife?

Although the evidence is slim, it does appear that women who could turn to alternative patriarchal figures lived to tell the tale. Elizabeth Barber sought refuge with her father, Mary Brown with her father-in-law. Sarah Hammett flew to John Clarke's house. But "where Should She go?" queried Elizabeth Alcock when a female friend suggested that she leave her abusive husband. She admitted that she was friendless; in all probability she had no adult male family member to rescue her either. Her story turned out badly.

It is curious that prosecutions for spousal abuse appear to have declined in the eighteenth century from seventeenth-century levels. Rhode Island is probably a poor example of this trend, since so few cases arise to begin with, but Massachusetts and Connecticut files indicate that fewer cases were presented in those jurisdictions over time, and that women were viewed less sympathetically by the courts in cases of cruelty.[101] One might reason that a decrease in domestic violence accounts for the change, but the long-range trajectory of household violence in the United States militates against such an interpretation.[102] Conversely, if spousal abuse remained a pervasive part of New England culture, the reduction in eighteenth-century prosecutions would parallel the deteriorating position of women in other arenas: economic, religious, and legal. Furthermore, if intrafamily violence was abating only in terms of prosecutions, the rise of the companionate marriage, one marked by affection, respect, and heightened expectations, becomes not only a paradox, but somewhat suspect.

Albeit an alternative with an uncertain outcome, divorce was an option for Rhode Island women throughout the colonial era. Prior to the Revolution, however, petitioners seldom claimed cruelty, since they were well aware that adultery, desertion, and lack of economic support were the only grounds that courts were likely to entertain. Rarely, a woman might describe the physical abuse she suffered, but always in tandem with adultery or desertion. Thus, in 1764 Priscilla Pate claimed that her husband frequented a "house of ill fame," and added that several times he tried "to make way with her and her life had been frequently in danger." In 1774, Susanna Man described how "threats and menaces" by her husband "drove her out of doors," but her case rested on accusations of adultery and his unwillingness to support her.[103]

Divorce became a more viable remedy in the post-revolutionary decades as women turned to the state for assistance and the state more readily acceded to their petitions. Although the number of divorce cases remained relatively small (under fifty for Newport County between 1780 and 1800), a divorce provided a way out for a wife who decided she could no longer remain a dutiful consort to a man who assaulted her. A successful petition still coupled violence with adultery or the unwillingness of a spouse to provide the necessities of life, but the majority of petitions did not mention physical abuse at all.[104] Finally, in 1798, Rhode Island added "extreme cruelty" and "gross misbehavior and wickedness" to the grounds for divorce that already existed. But in Newport County, prior to 1800 no female petitioner requested a divorce on the basis of cruelty alone.[105] By opting for divorce, some women chose the certainty of even greater economic dislocation over the uncertainty of a dislocated neck. A court could demand financial support from an abusive husband in the wake of a separation or divorce, but compelling payment was another matter altogether. Women knew they faced cruel choices, and what proportion chose to end a marriage to an abusive spouse is something the records do not disclose—any more than they reveal the pervasiveness of ill-treatment in the pre-revolutionary decades. But given the hints in the few surviving documents, it has become increasingly clear that harmony and conflict coexisted in what we once believed were the peaceable kingdoms of early America. And although it is difficult to compensate for a lack of records, it is nonetheless true that evidentiary whispers can be as meaningful as the most explicit set of papers.

Violence against women took many forms, some of which were exaggerated in a patriarchal society where the legal culture favored men. Accusations of witchcraft and spousal abuse are only two corners where gender and malice intersected in early America. Another is rape or attempted rape, both of which are crimes that are less sexual matters than they are incidents involving masculine power and domination. Attempted rape is central to the following chapter, but race compounds the story, since it takes place in what would become the most important slave-trading port in early America.

CHAPTER 4

Cold Comfort

Race and Rape in Rhode Island

The warmly dressed widow seen boarding the ferry at Bristol was the only person seeking passage to Portsmouth in the late afternoon of December 23, 1742. With the sun only "one hour high," daylight would soon give way to dusk and a cold winter evening.[1] Despite her outer wrap, however, Comfort Dennis Taylor was already chilled by the ride over "some miles of stony, unequall road" en route to the wharf. Yet even if time and temperature argued for haste, she might have paused at Durfee's ferry house for a penny's worth of rum before climbing into the sailboat for the short ride. Her fare was a few pence more.[2]

Approaching the age of forty, Comfort was old enough to have borne six children and young enough to bear still more, should remarriage await her in the future.[3] As a longtime resident of Little Compton, Massachusetts, with an extended Dennis family in Portsmouth and Newport, Rhode Island, Comfort had no doubt crisscrossed this narrow alley in Narragansett Bay many times in the past. And since this was an established ferry route, she would have recognized the vessel's pilot, Cuff, an enslaved man belonging to the ferry owner, Thomas Borden.

What little we know about Cuff can be inferred only from the immediate circumstances. It is possible he was African-born, since Rhode Island did not import slaves in any number until the mid-1720s, and "Cuff" is an African name.[4] If so, Cuff must have lived in the colony long enough to learn English and acquire piloting skills. Alternatively, he might have come to Rhode Island as a captive who acquired basic navigational skills aboard a Spanish privateer.[5] Whatever his origins, as a ferry operator he would have been familiar with water depths, local currents, tides, shoals, and rocks. Indeed, by the time he was allowed to navigate the ferry by himself, he would have become familiar with wind patterns, as well as the geography of the mainland and islands. Moreover, Cuff would have been in his prime—somewhere on the lower side of thirty—since it required strength and agility to steer a thirty-foot wind-driven boat as large as a ferry.[6]

Most important, Cuff was invested with responsibility. As a ferry captain, he was also a gatekeeper. Locally, he could alert authorities to potential passengers with a contagious disease; with his eyes on the horizon, he could observe foreign ships as they headed toward Providence Bay. Cuff was integral to the water-dependent community he served, although we cannot know whether he felt an affinity to that community. While on the water, however, he assumed the power and authority he lacked on land. His navigational role put him in charge of the vessel and inverted the usual relationship between slave and free people. As captain of the ferry Cuff gave orders; he did not take them.

Furthermore, he would have been trusted by both his owner and the passengers he carried across this patch of Narragansett Bay, especially if his

VIEW of BRISTOL   NECK from TRIPS's in RHODE ISLAND *September 1765.*

FIGURE 7.   View of the ferry house at Bristol in 1765 as seen from Portsmouth, Rhode Island. Ink on paper. Courtesy the Rhode Island Historical Society—RHi X3 8152.

skills incidentally offered both means and opportunity for an escape from bondage.[7] Borden's reliance on Cuff, therefore, is testimony to his confidence in his slave's loyalty. And that loyalty, as offensive as it may have been to Cuff, was in Cuff's interest. Power to remove Cuff as ferry master always remained with the slave master. Whether Cuff risked Borden's displeasure by covertly ferrying undocumented slaves across Narragansett Bay is something only he and his passengers would have known—as long as they weren't caught.[8] Finally, Comfort Taylor's willingness to board the ferry in the absence of other passengers suggests a lack of concern for her safety—not to mention reputation. In short, this should have been a swift and uneventful run. But it wasn't, because race and sex trumped the routine. White woman, black man: Comfort accused Cuff of attempted rape.

Comfort's Story

The salacious details that accompanied Comfort's December 24 account of the alleged assault on the previous day give no hint of what transpired during the first forty-five minutes of the sail. Initially, it must have been a fairly calm passage, because Comfort was "Standing by the Cuddy of the Boat," a reference to a small cabin that would have been used for shelter or even light meals.[9] She chose to be outside, a hint that Mother Nature was in a good mood. Suddenly, however, the "Negro Cuff came in a felonas manner and put his hand or arm round my Neck and kissed me upon which I said I would Cry murder upon which he sd do not make such a damned noise for I swear I will Choak you And swore that he would fucke me upon which I Cryed out murder murder several times then he taking voilent hold of me dragged me to the after part of the ferry Boat and fell down upon me and sate a straddle of me and placed one of his hands to my throat Endeavouring to Choake me and with the other hand Indeavouring to pull up my Coats and did Likewise Run his hand up under my Coats as far as the Bottom of my Stayes in which action he Bruesed my body verry much and in which time the ferry boat drove a Ground on hog Island."[10]

Four men were in or near Thomas Durfee's house and wharf on the Bristol shore when Comfort and Cuff set out for Portsmouth that afternoon: Durfee (a Bristol ferryman and a Quaker), James Strange and William Cory, who were local laborers, and John Grinnill, an Indian.[11] After Cuff and Comfort "had been Gone one hour," or "Long Enough to goe over and Come back again," Strange, who had been outside the house, heard Comfort shout "murder murder for God sake help If you love a woman." Alarmed by this dramatic cry for assistance, Strange hastened to Durfee's house, where he repeated what he had heard. At this point William Cory went outside to see and hear for himself. The ferryboat, Cory later reported, was "Lying near the shore of hog island," and from where he stood Cory "heard a woman Cry for help" from "a board of the boat with the Negro Cuff."[12]

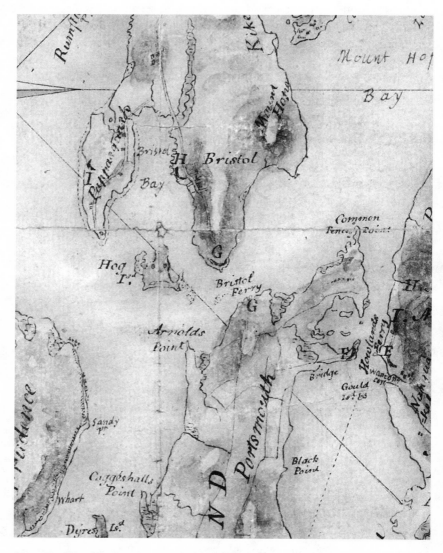

FIGURE 8.   Map of Narragansett Bay, Rhode Island (detail). Charles Blaskowitz, 1777. This section of the map shows the Bristol ferry and the narrow stretch of water between Bristol and Portsmouth. Pen, ink, and watercolor. Library of Congress Maps of North America, 1750–89.

Outside again, Strange saw "the Negro Cuff and the sd Comfort [] Scuf-fling in the boat." Clearly disturbed by what they perceived was happening, Strange and Grinnill immediately borrowed Durfee's boat and sped toward Hog Island. Neither man recorded what took place when they reached the stranded ferry, other than to say that they fetched Comfort "and her beast" and brought her back to Thomas Durfee's house.[13] Strange's December 29 account confirmed what Comfort had told the authorities several days ear-lier: that he and Grinnill "came to us in another Boat and took me and my beast into their Boat and Carried me back again to Thomas Durfies wharf which I believe prevented him the sd Cuff from having his voilant desire upon me."[14] The use of the word "beast" is curious, the more so because the peculiar phrase was uttered by both Comfort and Strange.

Once safely inside Durfee's house, Comfort related her harrowing experi-ence to the people gathered there. As Durfee later recounted, "She told me that the Negro cuff had tried to kiss her and had bruesed her very much and had throwed her down in the boat and she shewed me Several bruises upon her."[15]

It is unclear whether Strange and Grinnill transported Comfort and Cuff together, or whether they left Cuff to bring Thomas Borden's ferry back from Hog Island by himself. The accounts given by Strange and Taylor have everyone together in one boat, but the language of Cory's examination is ambiguous, as is Durfee's. Cory stated that the men went to "fetch" Com-fort "away from" Cuff, and he spoke of events "after the sd Cuff came ashore to Durfee's." Durfee reported that Strange and Grinnill "brought Comfort Taler from aboard of the ferry Boat from the Negro Cuff." Yet leaving Cuff on his own would have been irresponsible, given the severity of the accusations, especially since he had the motivation and ability to disap-pear into the night. But whether he returned voluntarily or not, Cuff ended up at Bristol Ferry, where William Cory overheard angry words between Cuff and Durfee: "I heard the Negro Swear by God that he would knock anny mans Branes out that whent to touch him and I whent to the dore and I see the Negro have a Cord wood Stick in his hand."[16] At some point Thomas Borden, Cuff's owner, must have been fetched from Portsmouth, because shortly thereafter, Major Thomas Green "assisted Thomas Burden In Carrying his negro fellow called Cuff to Justice Faleses house in Bristol."[17]

Cuff's Story

Given the nature of the accusation against Cuff, Comfort Taylor had the advantage, if not the game. Even if racial stereotypes about the alleged sexual proclivities of black males had not been firmly embedded by the mid-eighteenth century, she would have been far more credible than Cuff no matter how admirable his reputation.[18] She was, after all, a respectable white woman from an affluent family whose property was derived from both inherited wealth and a profitable tanning business. Cuff was an enslaved laborer, the property of another financially solid citizen, Thomas Borden. Borden's initial reaction to the incident indicates an almost knee-jerk acceptance of Comfort's account, and his immediate response on the night of December 23 was that "he would make her any Satisfaction that any Reasonable person should think proper." In addition, "his negro should be punished to her satisfaction." Borden offered to send Cuff "out of the country as soon as possible." Taking matters into his own hands, he then "carried his Negro to Gaol himself without any initiative from any authority." Thomas Borden, culturally programmed to believe in his slave's guilt, wanted to make this entire matter disappear as quickly as possible. Comfort appeared agreeable to his proposal.[19]

To Borden, a man familiar with Quaker teaching, private negotiation would be a customary solution to his problem. And since Comfort Taylor's birth family was saturated with members of the Society of Friends as well, she too would find such an arrangement reasonable. Furthermore, the negotiations between Borden and Taylor suggest that members of the community could informally consider (and inflict) an appropriate punishment in a criminal proceeding without consultation with or intervention from the authorities. That Cuff was a slave makes this particular scenario less surprising than it might have been if only free whites were involved. Nevertheless, their ability to circumvent the formal judicial system speaks to a legal culture where, in the absence of a relevant criminal statute, sanctions could be agreed upon—and imposed—by the parties involved.[20] Notwithstanding these private machinations, however, their actions hint at a paradox: on the one hand, the substance of their discussion implies that both Taylor and Borden were aware that Rhode Island law did not address *attempted* rape. Yet it also reflects a civility and respect for the judicial system—a system that extended its protection to Cuff. Consider the alternative: once the gossip network went into action, an outraged mob could have vindicated Comfort by rope rather than reason.

If the alacrity with which Thomas Borden offered to compensate Comfort implies an assumption of Cuff's guilt, so too does the tenor of the "the examination of a Negro man Cuff touching his felonas assalting Comfort Talor in the ferry Boat on the twenty third of this Instant."[21] By Christmas Day Cuff had been transported from Bristol (then part of Massachusetts) to "some of the authority" in Rhode Island, where Daniel Howland and William Anthony Jr. (the former an assistant to the governor, the latter a justice and deputy to the General Assembly) examined him.[22] Taken in the form of questions and answers, Cuff's interrogation on Saturday, December 25, is one of the few surviving documents where a slave's voice reaches the twenty-first century, even if it was mediated by a scribe. Furthermore, the transcript indicates that Cuff understood and spoke English. The examination took place at Captain Abiel Tripp's house in Portsmouth. Cuff's first response related to a question about time and indicates that for him as well as for others the sun was the official timekeeper. Cuff confirmed the time Comfort boarded the ferry ("wont above a quarter an our by the Sun") and that subsequently he and Comfort had been aboard the boat "about one hour."[23]

Having settled this point, Howland and Anthony turned to the alleged incident:

Q—How Came you to Goe back again
A—becaues the tide of Ebb Runn so strong I went to goe up in the Edy[24]
Q—how Com you to Goe ashore at hog Island
A—the boat was not ashore but only touched with her stern as I was seting by
Q—how Come you to Drive down the River so far
A—the tide drove me down so far that [turned] to go into the other Edy

Cuff's responses to the first set of questions indicate he had suffered grave navigational difficulties. He was specific in his answers, clarifying some points, refuting or correcting others.

The second set of questions dealt with Comfort's allegations, and as the men proceeded in their inquiry, the interrogation took a decidedly accusatory tone, which may be explained in part by the fact that the Howlands were related to the Dennis family.[25]

Q—how Com thee to Lay a voilant hand on Comfort[26]
A—I did not
Q—What was the Reason of Comfort Crying out murder
A—I did not here no Such thing
Q—how Came thee to Lay voilant hands on Comfort and drage her to the after part of the Boat
A—I did not

Q—how Come thee to place thy hand upon her throat and Endeavour
   to pul up her Coats with the other hand
A—I did not touch her

Cuff unequivocally denied the charges against him in plain but firm language. "I did not touch her."

Thomas Borden's Story

The rights to Bristol Ferry had been in the Borden family for some time before Thomas's stewardship. Before the turn of the eighteenth century, John Borden, Thomas's father, already held a license to operate a craft between Portsmouth and Bristol. And when he died in 1716, he left his estate in Portsmouth to Thomas, who inherited the ferry rights along with the property. These rights included an exemption from jury duty—no small perk in this litigious society.[27] At the time of his father's death Thomas was a thirty-four-year-old Quaker bachelor with substantial property holdings.

Although conflicting genealogical records preclude a verifiable timeline, the most likely sequence includes a marriage to the twenty-nine-year-old Catherine Hull in April 1717. Her death in February 1717/18 may have been childbirth related, but whatever the cause, Thomas Borden remained a widower for a decade after her decease. In 1727, at age forty-five, he wooed and won Mary Briggs, a young woman who had not yet reached her twentieth birthday. Their first child was born several months earlier than their nuptials, a matter that "aggitated" the Friends meeting, and a "Dishonour" for which Borden took full "blame and shame" when he apologized in 1728.[28] The Society accepted his admission of guilt, and Borden remained a member in good standing while Mary proceeded to bear Thomas children on a more-or-less regular basis: 1729, 1731, 1733, 1738, 1741 (three sons and two daughters). In 1738, however, Borden was at odds with the Society again, and this time he was "set from under" their care. For unknown reasons he had refused to abide by an arbitrator's decision concerning a dispute with another member, William Anthony Jr., over the placement of a fence between their properties on Hog Island.[29] Thus, at the time of the alleged rape attempt, Thomas Borden was a propertied family man with five young children, at least one slave, and a reputation for obstinacy and sharp business dealings.[30] His sometime antagonist, William Anthony Jr., was now in a position that could help or hurt him.

Borden's immediate reaction to Comfort Taylor's accusation was to placate Taylor as best he could under the circumstances. All the witnesses who were present on the evening of December 23 agreed that Borden told Taylor "he would make her any satisfaction that any Reasonable person should think proper." Borden offered to "send him out of the country"—presumably after a sale that would compensate Borden for the loss of Cuff's services. He would have Cuff "whipt as many stripes as she should order," and he would make her "Reasonable satisfaction," a reference, no doubt, to monetary damages. For her part, Taylor "neither Desired the black Beast to be whipt or hanged," since the former "might hurt his sale" and the latter render moot any financial advantage a sale would bring. "All her Desire was that he should be sent out of the Country that she might never se him no more." After making his offer "sundry times," Borden persuaded Comfort to settle instead of prosecuting Cuff. She agreed "she would not sware a gainst him" and instead would "take up Borden's offer."[31]

The next morning, December 24, Comfort reneged. She "said she was sorry she could not comply with his proposals for that she was advised to the contrary by her friends and said they told her she could not save her creditt and Reputation without Prosecuting said negro." Surprised and dismayed by her change of heart, Borden "Replyed . . . that what he proposed was as much as could be done if she prosecuted the affair and if she did not comply he thought it was only to get money out of his pocket."[32] Apparently Borden was trying to convince Taylor that she had nothing to gain by legal action.

It was on the following day—Christmas—that Cuff declared his innocence. This was not unusual; Sharon Block has noted that most slaves pleaded not guilty in similar circumstances, but in this case it is possible that Comfort's about-face influenced the sequence of events.[33] Despite his willingness to believe the worst of his slave, Borden (or the lawyer Borden hired to defend Cuff) may have mandated a not-guilty plea in the hope that such a countermove would compromise Comfort's position and force her to back off. Yet even if monetary considerations polarized Borden and Taylor, it is also possible that Cuff was acting on his own by refusing to plead guilty to a crime he did not commit. But if the plea was a ploy by Borden, it failed. Comfort opted for a trial rather than a settlement. With a private accommodation between Borden and Taylor all but dead, Cuff became a defendant in both criminal and civil cases that dragged on for over a year. Yet if Cuff had been turned into a pawn in this chess game, he was a pawn with a civil rights package that included warrant, indictment, jury, trials, and lawyers.

Rape and Other Matters

Portsmouth may have been Anne Hutchinson's pride in 1638, but Newport soon eclipsed the older town at the northern end of Aquidneck Island in both population and taxable wealth. The Portsmouth in which Thomas Borden and Cuff lived claimed fewer than 800 whites, something around 120 blacks, and no more than three score Indians—if the census figures are anywhere near accurate.[34] As ferry owner and helmsman, Thomas Borden and Cuff would have rubbed elbows with an assortment of people from Massachusetts, Rhode Island, and points south. Still, their immediate community was small and, as far as the white population was concerned, bound together by intermarriage. Familial ties should not be confused with familial harmony, however, and the reigning discord meant that the people of Portsmouth were no strangers to litigation. Yet Cuff's entrée into the world of crime, claims, charges, and courts was his first bout with the law. He had no record, no claims against him, no previous arrests, no history of violence.[35] Nevertheless, there was no reason to believe that his character would work in his favor.

Colonists on the eastern seaboard only slowly developed an indigenous American common law. Consummated rape was a capital crime everywhere prior to the Revolution, Rhode Island being among the first to enact such a statute in 1647. At the same time, specific laws governing *attempted* rape were conspicuously absent from the law books, even though the crime itself was hardly unknown.[36] At a special court of trials in Rhode Island in 1671, the jurors found an Indian, Quashcombe, guilty of abusing Martha Lay "by throwinge her downe in the highway way and actinge as if he would Ravish her." While the court was "fully satisfied" that Quashcombe deserved hanging, the judges could not quite bring themselves to impose such a sentence "because neither the Bill did accuse him of Rape nor the Jurrys verdict declare him to be guilty thereof."

Despite the "heinousness" of his action, Quashcombe had been convicted only of attempted rape, and in the absence of a statutory penalty for the lesser crime, the judges were in a quandary. What to do with Quashcombe? With few apparent alternatives, the court turned to the General Assembly for advice. That body "satt long" and finally dissolved without reaching a solution, having become "almost tired" of the mental challenge. The court, still unable to resolve the sentence, returned Quashcombe to prison, where he was ordered to remain chained until the next General Assembly, presumably refreshed, could consider their options. Quashcombe then disappears from the records. More than three decades later "Peter An Indian" pleaded not guilty to a charge of attempted rape on Grace Lambert, "A Young Woman." Convicted after a jury trial, Peter was sentenced by the court to be "burnt on ye brane of his thumbe on ye right hand with the Letter R & sold out of ye Cuntry." Given these incidents, it is curious that the General Assembly did not consider a law penalizing attempted rape.[37] In Rhode Island as elsewhere, attempted rapists continued to be sentenced on an ad hoc basis.

Notwithstanding this widespread statutory vacuum and the inconsistency with which sex crimes were punished, some colonies began to racialize attempted rape at the beginning of the eighteenth century. Legislatures passed specific laws aimed at slaves or free blacks whose objects of sexual assault were white women. Although New England, unlike its neighbors to the south, did not hold special courts to try free or enslaved African Americans, it is still true that black men faced more serious sexual charges than whites and were far more likely to be tried for rape. And since whites assumed that any sexual advance by a black man toward a white woman would be unwelcome, a black defendant faced a presumption of guilt before the trial even began. Following the usual guilty verdict, draconian punishment (often the gallows) awaited a black man convicted of attempting to rape a white woman. Indeed, as in Cuff's case, if the matter was handled by a higher tribunal rather than a court of general sessions or any lower criminal court, a stiffer sentence was the more likely outcome. And, as Sharon Block has demonstrated, courts were ready to convict black men even when the evidence (or lack thereof) demanded an acquittal.[38] Such was the daunting legal challenge facing Cuff when his trial began in the Superior Court of Rhode Island on March 29, 1743.

Cuff spent the short days and long nights between December 1742 and March 1743 in jail. More likely than not he awaited his criminal trial in the prison on Marlborough Street in Newport. If his cell faced the street he could time the passing hours by the sun as it swept from east to west, sinking—albeit temporarily—in the harbor between the sloops and schooners. When evening chased away the last light of day, Cuff would have heard laughter, even song, from the White Horse Tavern across the street as tipplers chased one rum with another. And as darkness shrouded his small space, Cuff's jailer might have brought the prisoner a candle so that he could eat his evening meal by its flickering light. The jailor's kindness (abetted by the clink of coin) might have extended to firewood.

Although attempted rape was not the same as consummated rape as far as the law was concerned, it was considered serious enough to be prosecuted in Rhode Island's Superior Court of Judicature rather than the lower Court of General Sessions. Cuff probably did not care that the trial would be held in the newly completed Colony House designed by Richard Munday, a structure said to be one of the more striking public buildings in America. Yet having been an unwilling guest of the town for three months, Cuff's anxiety must have been tempered by relief when he took the short walk from the jail to the imposing brick edifice at the head of the parade on March 29, 1743.

By the time Cuff's criminal trial began, he may have made another journey—a surprising one under the circumstances—into the folds of the church. On March 3, 1742/43, the United Congregational Church of Little Compton baptized and admitted one "Cuff," who was described as "col," presumably a reference to race rather than to a military title. With no other Cuff emerging from these extensive Rhode Island vital records, it is possible that this Cuff was indeed the enslaved man charged with attempted rape. If so, perhaps the Great Awakening had stirred him, or savvy lawyers had prodded him toward a religious epiphany. A jury or judge might show a little sympathy (or even leniency) to a convert who had taken the language of the revival to heart—even if the timing was a bit suspicious. It might be mere coincidence that Comfort Taylor lived in Little Compton and that Abigail Taylor (her daughter?) was a private member of the United Congregational Church in 1743. Yet it could also mean that the Taylors and Cuff were acquainted prior to the ferry incident.[39]

Even if Newport still lacked a local newspaper in 1743, reports of the incident had quickly spread beyond Rhode Island, through Boston and then on to the middle colonies courtesy of the Philadelphia press. Under the dateline "Newport, December 31," the *Boston Evening Post* of January 3 reported that "on Monday was committed to Goal here, a Negro Man who used to tend *Bristol* Ferry, for attempting to commit a Rape on a Woman that was passing the ferry with him in the Evening."[40] Given racial preconceptions, it was unnecessary to add that the woman was white.

Because of the incendiary nature of the incident, the criminal proceedings against Cuff would not remain a local matter. Furthermore, the twelve jurors who would hear Cuff's case had been collected from various corners of Rhode Island. Three men represented Newport, one or possibly two were from Portsmouth, and a single juror sat from each of the towns of Providence, Jamestown, East Greenwich, and Westerly. Three jurors remain unidentified by residence, although two of them had very Newport-sounding names. Positions of authority would not have disqualified any of the jurors; Ebenezer Richardson was a "Justice" from Newport in 1740 and 1743, John Martin had been a deputy to the Rhode Island General Assembly in 1741, and one of the three possible William Arnolds was a justice of the peace in 1742. Cuff's enslaved status and the nature of the crime precluded judgment by a jury of peers. The outcome would be determined by some of the more substantial freemen of Rhode Island.[41] How well his lawyers, Daniel Updike and John Andrew, represented him is beyond historical reach. Nevertheless, even though criminal trials of slaves were common enough, there is an irony to the very concept of a jury trial for an enslaved person—considering the nature of slavery as an institution and the limitations it placed on human freedom. That his owner, Thomas Borden, was willing to pay for attorneys, or that Rhode Island provided Cuff with two lawyers, is just as remarkable.

Yet if Rhode Island extended the protection of a trial to a slave, that gesture was accompanied by the costs of prosecution—charges that in this case were passed to an indigent defendant. Within two days of the alleged incident, Caleb Bennett had submitted a bill "for apprehending Cuff . . . and for fetching him from Bristol." His incidentals included charges for court attendance and for committing the "Beast" to jail. Daniel Howland and William Anthony Jr. also expected to collect for the "time and trouble" involved in "apprehending Cuff and examining him and Recognizing of Comfort Taylor and the evidences to Superior Court." Benjamin Hicks claimed expenses for serving a summons and "going to Hog Island." Comfort Taylor, her uncle Joseph Dennis, and Gideon Durfie provided two hundred pounds' worth of monetary assurance for their appearance at the criminal trial.[42] Once Comfort decided to press charges, the incident was transformed from a private to a public affair, instantly becoming an event that claimed an ever-wider circle of people. At the same time, money changed hands, and the not-so-deep pockets of both citizen and state were tapped to move the case forward.

According to the grand jury indictment, "Cuff did beat, wound and evilly intreat, and the throat of the said Comfort did seize, threatening and attempting at said Time and Place to have the carnal knowledge of the Body of the said Comfort by Force, And then and there in the Prosecution of that wicked Purpose, the Body of the said Comfort did greatly bruise, So that her life it was Despaired."[43] This last clause (even as boilerplate language) was something of an exaggeration, since testimony shortly after the incident confirms that neither Comfort nor anyone else despaired of her life. On December 29, Thomas Durfee swore that when Comfort "came into my house" after the alleged attack on December 23, she told him that Cuff had tried to kiss her "and had bruesed her very much."[44] She was mobile and conversational, hardly a woman poised to step through death's door. Clearly the charge was a formulaic legal strategy meant to incite the jury. But if this was the plan it had only a limited effect. The twelve male jurors took very little time to find Cuff guilty, but the court's sentence was surprisingly moderate, considering the charge and the profile of the defendant.[45] The court imposed a twenty-pound fine plus fees payable to the Crown, which was not an insignificant amount of money, but was surely preferable to hanging. Cuff was remanded to the custody of the sheriff (that is, jail) until he, his owner, or some benefactor came up with the money for the fine.[46] No one did.

Because the criminal court penalty failed to restore her reputation or line her pocketbook, Comfort immediately turned to the civil court for redress and sued Cuff in that venue for trespass.[47] On March 30, one day after Cuff's criminal trial, a warrant was issued for his arrest to answer the civil complaint, notwithstanding—as Sheriff Thomas Potter pointed out—that Cuff was already back in his cell. Cuff had been served and rearrested while behind bars.[48]

Since the original description of the attack failed to move the Superior Court beyond a twenty-pound fine destined for the local treasury, the revised wording of the complaint in the new civil case heightened the drama in the hope that it would bring about compensation more in keeping with Comfort's suffering. This time Cuff allegedly seized Comfort's throat "violently" and "the carnal knowledge of her Body to her great Terror did violently attempt." Once again "her life it was despaired." Notwithstanding these seemingly desperate circumstances, by the time Comfort made her first appearance in civil court at the end of May, she had made a remarkable recovery.[49]

If the relatively mild sentence in the criminal action against Cuff revealed a possible weakness in her case, Comfort responded to what must have seemed like a rebuff with a countermove designed to make the judges of the Inferior Court of Common Pleas sit up and take notice. Comfort Taylor sued Cuff Borden in civil court for one thousand pounds. Rhode Island being the sort of place it was, gossip about this exorbitant suit probably raced from courtroom to tavern, where the locals could debate the merits of the case. What may have escaped notice, however, was the irony of the situation. As a person with agency and as an inhabitant of Rhode Island, Cuff had already been granted a criminal trial with all the legal perquisites. And no one in authority appeared to question Cuff's ability, as a person, to be sued and to respond to a suit in civil court. Yet as property, Cuff could be sold to satisfy a judgment in the civil case if his owner refused to pay on his behalf. As a result of this paradox Cuff was both subject and object of the Crown. His body was collateral in a way that differed from that of a free person.[50] If this strange ambivalence was the result of a growing Quaker uneasiness with slavery, no one seemed to notice.[51] And whether or not Cuff considered his ambiguous position, no matter. He once again denied his guilt through his attorney, Matthew Robinson.[52]

If Daniel Howland, who had been intimately involved with the case (as Cuff's interrogator) from its inception, was informed about its progress, he did not share that information with his diary. More interested in recording weather patterns than the details of the current civil litigation that was heating up table talk, Howland noted for posterity that the winter of 1742–43 had been "exceedingly moderate," with little frost covering the ground. The meadows hosted grasshoppers in abundance, and Rhode Islanders enjoyed "fine pleasant weather," even "summer-like days," a stark contrast to the devastating winter of the year before. Avoiding any mention of the trial that surely consumed public attention in the spring of 1743, Howland merely commented that black worms were "remarkably plenty" and did "great damage to the meadows."[53]

The Court of Common Pleas took up the most volatile case on its calendar shortly after convening on Tuesday, May 31, 1743. The clerk issued summonses to William Anthony and Joseph Dennis to appear before them to give evidence on June 6, and to James Strange and William Cory to assure their presence on June 7.[54] Between June 1 and June 6, the judges read testimony from two other witnesses who had submitted statements in lieu of their appearance. In his deposition, taken in Bristol on May 30, Thomas Green spelled out in considerable detail the sequence of events to which he had been privy on the evening of December 23, 1742. Describing how he had carried the "Negro fellow called Cuff to Justice Faleses house" in Bristol, Green then related the conversation between Borden and Taylor as they negotiated a potential compensation package. Green indicated that both parties were satisfied with the arrangements they devised. Green was also present the following morning at Abiel Tripp's house in Rhode Island, where Borden repeated his offer to have Cuff publicly whipped to Comfort's order after the sentence was "Proclaimed by the Beat of Drum" (presumably to assure a wide audience). Borden also reiterated his willingness to "make any Reasonable satisfaction" and to send Cuff "out of the Countrey." According to Green, Borden repeated the offer to Taylor "sundry times" before Comfort's surprising declaration that Borden's offer was not acceptable after all. Green said nothing about Comfort's physical appearance either on the night of December 23 or on the following day, but his testimony implies that Comfort was lucid, showed no sign of shock, and that she did not demand substantial monetary compensation.[55]

Althea Fales, the other deponent, was the wife of Justice Timothy Fales of Bristol, Massachusetts. It was to the Faleses' house that Thomas Green brought Cuff on December 23, and it was there that Althea overheard the conversation described in detail by Green. In her deposition on May 30, she confirmed all that Green asserted in his own account. Fales had nothing to say about Comfort's injuries either.[56]

Two of the four witnesses whose presence was demanded on June 6 and 7 were repeat performers. Strange and Cory had issued statements on December 29, a few days after the incident, but had only given an account of the events preceding, during, and following the rescue. William Anthony and Joseph Dennis were apparently testifying for the first time on June 6, and as they did so they recalled Comfort's accusation and condition on December 24. Anthony stated for the record—and Dennis concurred—that Comfort charged Cuff with "Endeavouring to Commit a Rape on her."[57] As to Comfort's condition when she complained to Anthony the day after Cuff's alleged attempt, Taylor "appeared . . . to be very much abused for she walked Lame and was bruised on the side of her neck and on one of her shoulders & on one of her knees she likewise Complained of her Stomack & side being very much hurt and that she cou'd hardly lift up one of her hands to her head." That Comfort had been hurt was clear. It was also evident that her injuries were consistent with a fall to the ground during which she landed on one side. Anthony's description made it appear as though Comfort had been seriously injured by Borden's slave, although whether she had been actually "abused" (in a sexual sense) was a matter for the court to decide.

For his part, Cuff "made default," which meant that neither he nor his lawyer appeared in court to respond to the suit.[58] That being the case, and after considering the evidence, the court awarded Comfort one hundred pounds—one-tenth of what she had demanded—plus the costs of the suit. Since Cuff couldn't pay anything and Thomas Borden showed no willingness to cut his losses by paying Comfort off, Cuff, "having the Liberty of an Appeal," took it. The irony of a slave having the "Liberty" of anything was probably lost on those familiar with the case, and only Daniel Howland could say whether the black worms trespassing on the meadow was a subliminal metaphor.

Thomas Borden was, no doubt, making the decisions at this point. Why he continued to pursue the case is something the records do not reveal. For undisclosed reasons, therefore, Cuff, through his attorney Matthew Robinson, asked the Superior Court of Judicature to reverse the decision of the Court of Common Pleas. There was "no cause of action," he argued, and "with what more may be offered in Court," Cuff had little doubt of a reversal.[59] Even if Cuff (or Borden) really believed the standard language, it made little difference. The Superior Court, with no explanation, affirmed Comfort's one-hundred-pound award. Undaunted, Cuff appealed to the next Court of Equity.[60]

Until 1741, Cuff's appeal from Superior Court would have been heard by the Rhode Island General Assembly sitting in its capacity as a Court of Equity. The General Assembly mixed legislative and judicial functions as it sorted out facts and handed down equitable decisions based on the merits of each case. In the popular mind, this "court" of last resort dispensed justice—as the legislators saw it—not necessarily according to law, but according to the need for modifications of decisions from the courts below. Whether both parties to the disputes considered the results "equitable" is another matter altogether.

By 1741, the dual role of the General Assembly as both legislative and judicial oracle had become burdensome and subject to abuse. As a result, in 1741 the assembly lessened its workload by creating a special Court of Equity that would hear the appeals formerly considered by the legislature. Not willing to relinquish its power altogether, the General Assembly reserved the right to appoint the five sitting judges on the new Court of Equity on an annual basis. The judges who heard Cuff's appeal represented five different Rhode Island counties, and one of them, William Anthony Jr., was already familiar with the case.[61] It is doubtful that any of these justices had legal training, an educational abyss that would have bothered no one in 1743.

The leaves were displaying their rich fall colors by the time the Court of Equity met on the second Tuesday of October 1743 to hear Cuff's appeal. During its deliberations the court considered the testimony of two witnesses who had seen Taylor close to the time of the alleged assault.[62] The first, Patience Hall, was present at Thomas Borden's house in Portsmouth on December 29, six days after the incident.[63] In her testimony, she noted that Comfort Taylor was there as well, which was curious, given the heated words between Borden and Taylor days earlier. Thomas Borden took no part in the conversation between Hall, Taylor, and Borden's wife, Mary, that day, and it is easy to imagine that Comfort sought out Mary for a tête-à-tête in the hope that she would persuade her husband to settle, thus avoiding a public spat. Whatever Comfort's motivation, talk eventually turned to the allegations against Cuff, at which point Hall recounted that she "heard Mary Borden ask . . . Comfort to Lett her and [Hall] see where Negro Cuff had hurt . . . Comfort." Quite receptive to a public viewing, "Comfort showed her neck and Elbow." Hall told the court "she did not perceive it was much hurt then . . . Comfort Replyed she had no other hurt But what was Inwardly." Whether this woeful comment meant bruised ribs or a bruised self-image was unclear. According to Hall, Taylor also went on to say that "she smelt of Negro Cuff breath to see if he smelt of Rum" but allowed he "did not smell of Rum." Up and about (and traveling) less than a week after the alleged assault, Comfort did not appear to be badly hurt—at least according to Hall.

Thomas Durfee, the ferryman on the Bristol side of the passage, complemented and even reinforced Hall's statement. Durfee had been examined once before. In his first account, taken on December 29, Durfee explained that he had seen Taylor immediately after the incident when Strange and Grinnill brought her to his house. In his subsequent statement to the Equity Court on October 10, 1743, Durfee confirmed that on the previous December 23, Taylor had said "she was abused by Bordens Negro." He explained in detail how Taylor had elaborated on her injuries that evening: she claimed that "Cuff had hurt her knee and she shewed it to me and I saw that it was something hurt for the skin was of [f] and she said that her Elbo was Something bruised."[64] Something had happened to Comfort just before Thomas Durfee saw her on December 23, but Durfee's description of her injuries do not place her in a life-threatening situation.

Despite this testimony, however, the Court of Equity showed more sympathy to Comfort than she had received from either of the lower courts. Even though Comfort, as appellee, had only asked the Equity Court to affirm the "just and right" decision of the Superior Court, the Equity Court decided to act on its own. It reversed the judgment of the Superior Court, declared it null and void, and doubled Comfort's award, allowing her two hundred pounds plus costs. With no ability to pay one hundred pounds (much less two hundred), Cuff found himself back in jail, with an order to remain there "safely secure" until his debt was discharged.[65] What role William Anthony Jr. played in the court's decision against Thomas Borden's interests is unknown.

Taylor and Borden (not to mention Cuff) were at an impasse. Under ordinary circumstances, the loser's assets would be seized to pay the judgment, but Cuff was a slave and apparently had no assets.[66] As a result, the court's award was good only so far as Borden was ready and able to pay on Cuff's behalf, and he was clearly unwilling or incapable of doing so. How could Comfort collect? Her response shows not only her resourcefulness and her knowledge of Borden's legal obligations, but reveals, as few documents do, the ambiguous dichotomy between a slave as a person and as a chattel.

Shortly after the Court of Equity awarded Comfort two hundred pounds plus costs, she petitioned the General Assembly to allow the sheriff to sell Cuff to satisfy the debt. The problem appeared to be whether the sheriff was empowered to sell a person in lieu of goods. Comfort's phraseology betrays the quandary: "it is not Clear that the Sheriff can dispose of Him, which She apprehends He ought to have the power to do, Because said negro is not

Free, but a private Property; and therefore prayed That the said Sheriff might be empowered to sell Him, as other Personal Estate, taken by Execution, to satisfy Debts." Hoping that the General Assembly would grant her request, she topped her first supplication with a second plea: "considering the great abuse she has suffered, and the charge that will come out of [the value of] said Negro, for prison fees, she desired that the Fine of £20 against said Negro Cuff might be remitted, otherwise she should get Nothing for all the hardships she has endured."[67]

The General Assembly responded to Comfort's petition by declaring that the sheriff was "fully empowered to sell [the] Negro Cuff as other Personal estate." Nevertheless, the legislature refused to remit the twenty-pound fine and ordered it paid into the "General Treasury." Once "all other Charges" were deducted from the sale, Comfort would receive the remainder. Having received this mandate, the sheriff, John Potter, sold Cuff "at publick auction for one hundred pounds," the upper end of prices for adult male slaves in 1743.[68] Exactly how much Taylor eventually received is unrecorded.

What stands out in this entire sequence of events are the laws to which Comfort turned as each situation dictated. She knew—or was apprised by an attorney—that "in all Cases of Assault and Battery, the Person assaulted or battered shall have an action at Common Law, against the Persons committing such Assault or Battery, and shall recover his Damages received thereby."[69] For this purpose, Cuff was a "Person" under the law. But once Comfort prevailed in court, it no longer served her purpose to define Cuff as a person. In order to receive the proceeds of the monetary judgment, it became necessary to transform Cuff into property. Comfort succeeded in eating her cake and having it too.

She also succeeded in making law. In August 1743, before Comfort's bout with the General Assembly, that body passed legislation that could only have been a result of her confrontation with Cuff. Its enactment made Rhode Island the only New England colony with a law dealing with attempted rape by a black man.[70] Implying that there were multiple instances of "Negroes attempting to commit Rapes on white Women," the legislature decreed that any person "lawfully convicted" of such a crime hereafter would be branded on both cheeks with the letter R and would receive a public whipping at the discretion of the Superior Court. Within thirty days of judgment, the convicted felon would be sold by the sheriff to "any person" willing to transport him out of the colony forever. At any time during the six months following the sale, the "injured Woman" could request a "Special Action" in which she could demand proceeds from the sale to compensate her for damages. If any money remained after the woman collected her damages and the costs of the suit had been recovered, the balance would "be restored to the Person who was the Proprietor or Claimer of such Negro when he was prosecuted."[71]

The "hereafter" in the legislation signaled that the statute did not apply to Taylor—a disappointment, no doubt, and one that forced her to try another route. It also suggests that Thomas Borden received no compensation for the loss of his slave. Moreover, in a move that tilted power toward the state, the legislature disallowed any informal arrangement in the future between private citizens who found themselves in similar circumstances.

The location of the public auction at which Sheriff Potter sold Cuff is unclear, as is the attitude of potential buyers. Given the gossip surrounding the case, there must have been considerable public interest, particularly if there were lingering doubts about Cuff's guilt. Moreover, an auction with competitive bidding might also account for the high price Cuff commanded. Yet Comfort's accusation paired with Cuff's criminal conviction and subsequent civil liability should have made bidders a little more wary than they seem to have been. Why would anyone buy a slave scorched with such accusations—and at a premium, no less? The fact that Cuff did not flee the scene of the incident may have swayed public opinion in his favor. What William Blackstone would dub as reasonable doubt in rape cases in 1769 had been part of the collective consciousness for considerable time: the credibility of the alleged victim depended on whether "the party accused fled for it."[72]

Comfort's initial demand that Cuff "should be sent out of the Contrey that she might never Se him no more" had no legal standing.[73] As a result, Cuff's new master was a local Newporter. Evan Malbone, a member of Newport's distinguished merchant elite, bought the man described by several people as a "black beast."[74] Malbone, who in his mid-thirties was no stranger to the slave-trading schemes of his very rich Newport kinsman Godfrey Malbone, may have been skeptical of the charges against Cuff. If so, perhaps he put this skilled navigator to work aboard one of the Malbone ships. Or, Evan may have needed an extra hand at one of the several rum distilleries that, thanks to slave labor, earned its owner a fine return. Either way, Cuff retained a presence in Newport. He may have even been an attic or cellar resident in one of the Malbone mansions that faced the harbor on upper Thames Street.[75]

Nevertheless, Cuff's presence in Newport was short-lived. Humiliated by the charges and demoted from ferry operator to ordinary laborer, Cuff decided to take matters into his own hands. On the night of May 16, 1744, not quite seven months after Malbone purchased him, Cuff stole away wearing "a speckled Shirt and an Ozenbrig Frock and Trowzers . . . and Leather

Breeches." His trousers, "pretty much tarred," hint that he had worked at some maritime trade. Cuff planned to be away for the indefinite future. Even though it was mid-May, he "took with him a blue great Coat," presumably for future use in cooler weather or a more northern climate. Perhaps he intended to sell it, although an expensive article of clothing such as a greatcoat could shape identity by transforming a fugitive into a free man—at least at first glance.[76] According to the runaway notice, Cuff was "a stout, lusty fellow," a physical description suggesting strength and vigor. He was "aged about thirty years," and Malbone was willing to pay five pounds for his return, the going reward rate for runaway slaves.[77]

Cuff had one other feature to distinguish him from other runaways: "He has but one Testicle." This was an unusual addendum to a notice, with no further explanation about the source of this particular physical defect. One can only recoil at the possibility that it occurred as a result of mutilation by human hands. Castration for rape or attempted rape was hardly unknown in early America, but it did not occur with any frequency as a legal punishment until after the second half of the eighteenth century.[78] At the same time, dissatisfaction over the relatively light sentence Cuff received might have provoked an extralegal, albeit barbaric, response by someone close to Comfort Taylor. But why sever only one testicle?

The alternative is that Cuff was born with an undescended testicle. Yet only 3–4 percent of modern full-term male infants are born with this physical abnormality. Since the testicle usually descends into its proper place in the scrotum by the time a male child reaches one year of age, the percentage of modern adult males with undescended testicles is less than 1 percent. There

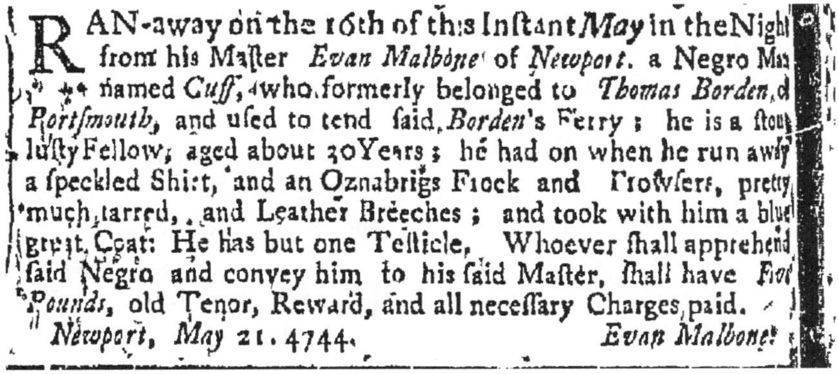

RAN-away on the 16th of this Instant *May* in the Night from his Master *Evan Malbone* of *Newport*. a Negro Man named *Cuff*, who formerly belonged to *Thomas Borden* of *Portsmouth*, and used to tend said *Borden*'s Ferry ; he is a stout, lusty Fellow; aged about 30 Years ; he had on when he run away a speckled Shirt, and an Oznabrigs Frock and Trowsers, pretty much tarred, and Leather Breeches ; and took with him a blue great Coat: He has but one Testicle, Whoever shall apprehend said Negro and convey him to his said Master, shall have Five Pounds, old Tenor, Reward, and all necessary Charges paid.
Newport, May 21. 4744.   *Evan Malbone*

FIGURE 9. Runaway notice for Cuff. This advertisement appeared in the *Boston Post-Boy*, June 18, 1744. Archive of Americana, Early American Newspapers, Series 1–5, 1690–1922.

is no way of knowing how Cuff became physically disfigured in this manner, but brutality cannot be ruled out and, in fact, may have given him extra
incentive to flee.[79]

Cuff must have planned his stealthy escape well in advance. No spur-
of-the-moment decision held hope of success, and even careful preparation
contained risk. To fly from a sleeping household meant that Cuff would not
be immediately missed, and a full moon that night would have guided him
to the harbor.[80] Safety required a speedy departure from Aquidneck Island,
where he was well known, and flight by water would have entailed knowledge of outbound vessels, information casually obtained from anyone working on the wharves. Many of those laborers would have been either enslaved
or free blacks, and Cuff would have easily melted into the group—at least
for a short time.[81]

Secrecy was essential, and Cuff had good reason to share his plans with
no one. A Rhode Island law required all subjects to turn in slaves traveling
without a certificate signed by the slave's master. Without such a document, Cuff ran the risk of exposure by anyone aware of his plans. Ironically, this legislation fell heaviest on ferrymen, who would be fined if they
transported unauthorized slaves across water.[82] It is difficult to gauge how
this legislation affected behavior and the subsequent recapture of slaves, but
there is little doubt that if people made laws, laws made people. If Rhode
Islanders were not His Majesty's most law-abiding citizens, their behavior
was still determined, at least in part, by statute and folk law. Under the
circumstances, there would have been colonists ready to turn Cuff in—
although there probably were at least a few radical Quakers willing to abet
his escape.[83]

Even fellow slaves could not be counted on. A year earlier, as an imprisoned Cuff awaited trial, another Newport slave "betray'd" a plot by "a
great Number of Spanish and other Prize Negroes to run away with one
of the Privateer Sloops in the Harbour."[84] Yet the variety and profusion of
boats bobbing on the water worked in Cuff's favor. During the war years,
Newport hosted a number of privateers, as well as the usual merchant vessels,
and Cuff, a trained sailor, would have had little trouble finding work aboard
a prize-seeking ship or one sailing on the morning tide for Europe, London,
or Africa. Jeffrey Bolster puts it very well: "ships . . . became both a means
to escape and an end in themselves for black men on the lam"—especially
during the war years when captains often lacked able-bodied seamen.[85] If all
else failed, Cuff could always stow away—wrapped up in a blue greatcoat to
ward off the chilly night air during the passage to who knows where. Since
the same runaway notice appeared weekly until the end of June in the Boston

newspapers, Cuff seems to have eluded his pursuers for over five weeks. No records speak of his return.

Rashomon Revisited

Very little in this saga makes sense. Comfort and Cuff offer competing narratives, with only a few bits of evidence favoring one side or the other. Even a historian who specializes in speculation is unable to subdue the surviving documents and force them to confess. Truth is illusory, of course, but surely there must be some way to make order out of this muddle of conflicting statements. "What if" and "but then" persist despite multiple readings, leaving only Rashomon-like story lines instead of one, rational conclusion based on solid historical detritus.[86] Either Comfort or Cuff was lying.

Let us assume for the moment that something happened on the ferryboat as Cuff steered it toward the Portsmouth shore. If Cuff attempted to rape Comfort, he did so against all common sense. He was an enslaved man, but even so, his position as a ferry operator upgraded his status and gave him a sense of liberty unknown to most other slaves. To risk certain, and perhaps deadly, reprisal for acting on a sudden impulse defies rational behavior. Cuff would surely have known the brutal punishment that awaited him for attempted rape. Furthermore, he had little ability to flee the scene, since authorities would have given chase, and an abandoned ferry would have led them sooner or later to his whereabouts. But Cuff didn't take flight even after Strange and Grinnill rescued Comfort. He returned to Bristol, possibly (even probably) alone in the ferry. By all accounts, Cuff was physically powerful, leaving one to wonder why he didn't consummate the rape, if that was his intention. If Comfort is to be believed, Cuff, an experienced pilot, must have left the ferry to the mercy of a strong current while he used both hands to choke and bruise her. Both could have drowned.

It is possible that Cuff's navigational troubles arose from a drop in the wind. If so, the sudden calm would explain why the ferry became a captive of the currents. In these conditions, why didn't he drop an anchor to stabilize the vessel and prevent it from being trapped by the tide?[87] On the other hand, without a wind to propel their boat, how would James Strange and John Grinnill have reached Comfort and brought her back to shore?

Let us assume again that something happened on the ferry. Comfort's charge was very serious, and it is difficult to believe she would fabricate such an incident. She insisted that during the alleged attack she screamed, and although Cuff maintained he "did not here no such Thing," James Strange and William Cory insisted the water carried the voice of a woman pleading for help.[88] It is reasonable to think the two men heard something, or else why would they have sped in a second boat toward the ferry? Comfort returned to Bristol injured and shaken. No one questioned her account or her strangely poetic exclamation, "if you love a woman."[89]

Comfort's actions during and after the alleged incident closely conformed to what the law required of a woman who was charging an assailant with attempted rape. In order to confirm resistance, she was expected to scream for help. Her credibility also rested on the speed with which she reported the assault. And Comfort strengthened her case by showing the bruises she incurred during a struggle.[90]

Yet to envision the sequence of events and the advance of darkness raises perplexing questions about sight as well as sound. If the sun was about "one hour high" when Cuff "whent to Carry over Comfort Taylor to Portsmouth," it would have been about 4 p.m. when they left Durfee's wharf. Strange recorded that it was "after they had been Gone one hour I heard her cry help." According to his testimony, then, it was about 5 p.m. when he saw "the Negro Cuff and the sd Comfort Scuffling in the boat."[91] But with sunset a few minutes after 5 o'clock that evening, and only a quarter moon hovering over a restless Narragansett Bay, could Strange and Cory actually see Comfort and Cuff thrashing about on the deck of a ferry a mile distant? Or did their imagination invoke evil images of a white woman and a black man alone on a boat after the two "had been Gone Longe [] Enough to Goe over and Come back again"?[92] Besides, if Strange could see Comfort and Cuff in the ferry, it is likely Cuff would have been able to spot the two men steering toward him a short time later. It hardly makes sense for Cuff to have remained vulnerable to capture if he had attacked Comfort.

And then there are questions about time, place, and clothing. All things considered, it was really imprudent to attempt a rape in late December in an open boat. It was cold, and Comfort was wearing layers of clothing. Presumably, Cuff was dressed for the weather as well. If he really attempted to rape her, he had to remove not only her clothing, but some of his buttoned apparel as well. How does Cuff accomplish this disrobing feat with both his hands occupied as she described?

Another assumption, another story—or two. Let's assume this time that Cuff was among the very small number of men who grew to adulthood with one undescended testicle. A side effect of such a condition is lower testosterone production, diminished sexual desire, and fewer aggressive tendencies. This profile does not sit comfortably with the man accused of an attempted rape on Comfort Taylor—unless, of course, he felt an overwhelming and uncontrollable urge to prove his virility because of a physical deformity that humiliated and emasculated him psychologically. Given the scrutiny that slaves faced in preparation for a sale, Cuff's physical features were, no doubt, common knowledge and a source of shame.

But what if (I said there would be "what ifs") the absence of a testicle was the result of human butchery subsequent to the alleged attack on Comfort? Not a lawful remedy; castration would have been legally impermissible at that time and place, but rather an angry folk law response to the light sentence he received as a result of his criminal trial. With all his parts in place prior to the alleged incident on December 23, 1742, Cuff would have fit the stereotype of the overly sexualized Caliban, prone to rape. Perhaps he was guilty after all. If so, Cuff's later religious conversion could be interpreted as the sign of a man who had become a repentant sinner.

Comfort Taylor may not have been familiar with Shakespeare's plot about a slave who repays kindness and trust with an attempt at sexual violation and murder, but she was surely aware of the alleged plot that had been "uncovered" in New York in the spring of 1741.[93] According to hysterical reports, a conspiracy to burn down the city and murder its inhabitants had been thwarted. After accusations, confessions, recantations, and trials, vengeance triumphed. While both blacks and whites were implicated, it was the slave population that suffered the harshest reprisals: thirteen blacks were burned at the stake, sixteen were hanged, and nearly four score were banished from the continent.[94] Unfortunately, a dearth of contemporary newspaper accounts, as well as extensive government censorship in New York City, frustrates the information trail; it is difficult to know what and when people along the eastern seaboard learned about the foiled (or nonexistent) conspiracy, although by July 1741 Boston newspapers carried abbreviated details of both plot and executions.[95] Rumors and gossip surely reached Rhode Island at the same time, if not before.

Several themes were woven into the testimony of the alleged conspirators. "Comfort's Jack" (a reference to a slave belonging to Geradus Comfort) asserted that once the fires had spread through "all the houses . . . in the town . . . they would kill all the white men, and have their wives for themselves." Sarah, "Burk's negro wench," confirmed the objective: the slaves "would kill the white men, and have the white women for their wives." And a little more than two weeks later, Mary Burton, John Hughson's indentured servant, swore she overheard the same plan: "they agreed . . . to kill their masters and take the white women for wives."[96] Trials continued into the spring of 1742, and even by summer it was impossible to still "Fears and Apprehensions . . . that the Enemy is still at work within our Bowels." Moreover, the New-York Weekly Journal published a warning from the lieutenant governor, George Clarke, that "from the many undoubted Informations I have received from divers Parts of the Country, the Insolence of the Negroes is as great, if not greater than ever . . . tho' we have felled the Tree, I fear it is not entirely rooted up."[97] It is impossible to know whether this charged atmosphere affected Comfort's actions—or reactions—on December 23, 1742, but surely the racial and sexual implications of the plot would not have been lost on her. Fantasy and an overactive imagination might have overwhelmed common sense that night.

If news of the New York conspiracy had reached Comfort's ears, does this explain how the phrase "black beast" permeated her consciousness? The words were not in common use—at least among surviving eighteenth-century documents—and although Daniel Horsmanden's journal of the proceedings in New York include an allusion to ungrateful slaves as "Beasts of the People," that record was not published until 1744, more than a year after Taylor's confrontation with Cuff.[98] Winthrop Jordan notes that as far back as the sixteenth century, writers connected Africans with "a beastly kind of life," while Englishmen did not hesitate to describe Africans as "beastly."[99] Yet even if, as Daniel Cohen argues, the image of a black man as a sexual predator was fixed in English crime literature by the beginning of the seventeenth century, the "black beast" stereotype was rarely used, particularly before 1800.[100] Thus, in the context of this case, the words stand out not only as an ugly commentary, but as an odd and unexpected choice of language.

Comfort used the word "beast" twice in reference to Cuff: once in her complaint when she described her experience and explained that Strange and Grinnell "took me and my beast into their boat." She also uttered it on the evening of December 23 when Thomas Green and Althea Fales confirmed that Comfort agreed to send "the Black beast" away. Comfort's use of the word "beast" was echoed by other witnesses to the events of Dec. 23 as well. James Strange testified on December 29 that he and Grinnell took Comfort "and her beast" to Thomas Durfee's house. Caleb Bennett, the town sergeant, spoke of taking the "Beast" to jail on December 23.[101] It appears, then, that Comfort first uttered the phrase on December 23, and others—all present and within hearing distance at some point during the evening—subsequently repeated the unusual pair of words. More peculiar, however, is the way in which Cuff was personalized. Comfort referred to Cuff possessively as "my beast." And James Strange speaks of "Comfort and her beast." Was it simply the incident that linked them in the minds of Taylor and Strange, or was there some prior, unrevealed—even consensual—relationship between Comfort and Cuff? What if?

On the other hand, there is another possible explanation. Comfort's husband had left his widow a "Riding Beast," along with a saddle.[102] Given that Comfort had to make her way to the ferry wharf and then proceed somehow once she reached her destination on the other shore, it is not impossible that the beast taken from the ferry was actually a horse. Both Comfort and the men who rescued her refer to "her" beast, a possessive that makes sense if they were actually speaking of an animal that belonged to Comfort. Yet it is also clear that both witnesses and the town sergeant referred to Cuff as a "black beast." "*The*" beast was Cuff; "*her*" beast was a horse. No one seemed puzzled by this conflation of Cuff and an animal, and no one protested it.

Whatever happened on the ferry that evening, Comfort ended up somewhat battered. Speculation (impossible to resist) invites an innocent explanation—one in which the ferry lurched and Comfort fell. Conjecture furthers the narrative: as Cuff helped her up, Comfort misinterpreted his intentions and began to scream. To cover her embarrassment, she concocted an elaborate story. It was only later, perhaps, that she realized that her embarrassment might be assuaged by extracting a considerable sum of money from Thomas Borden. This would have been all to the good, since Comfort's cordwainer husband, Philip Taylor, had left his "Luving wife" little independent income when he died in 1739.[103]

Philip Taylor's will enabled Comfort to sustain herself and her children in the 1740s, but with each passing year she would lose more and more control over the family assets. Philip gave Comfort the "use and Improvement" of his land and the structures on it until his sons reached twenty-one—"that is to say" as long as Comfort remained his widow. The eldest son, Joseph, belatedly born after three of his sisters arrived, would not reach that age until 1752, but in the meantime Comfort was financially hobbled by Philip's distribution of his "moveable Estate of Every Sort." His will assured each of his four daughters one-quarter of that property upon reaching eighteen. Susannah had already celebrated her eighteenth birthday in the spring of 1742, at which time Abigail was two years short of that goal. Deborah would receive her share in 1747. Remarriage would completely sever Comfort from these moveables, but time had already removed much of it from her management.

Yet in lieu of dower Philip did leave Comfort with a roof over her head, or at least the "use and Improvement" of "the Best Roome" in their Little Compton house for the duration of her widowhood. He also gave her ("free and clear") "the Best Bed," as well as his "Riding Beast" and "side saddle." As a result of these limitations, Comfort, in company with many eighteenth-century widows, would become increasingly dependent on the goodwill of her children, as time placed family assets in their hands. A quick settlement with Thomas Borden would have provided her with money of her own. Subsequent success in the courts would have meant one thousand pounds of pocket money, for her use alone. Far-fetched? Perhaps, but Comfort's remarriage to Lieutenant George Brownell in 1745 suggests that in her mind the benefits of abandoning widowhood outweighed her rights as Philip Taylor's relict.[104]

Comfort could not fall back on any inheritance from her parents either. There was nothing unusual about the wills they left, but with the law of coverture hindering her on one hand, and a litter of siblings squeezing her on the other, Comfort could not count on enough income from her parents' estates to support herself and her children. When Comfort's father died in 1730 he left tanyard equipment ("leather, hides, and bark") to Comfort and Philip jointly, which meant that Philip could dispose of everything as he chose. Comfort received thirty pounds from her father, presumably for her private use. Comfort's mother died in 1744, leaving her unmarried daughters temporary rights in the family homestead, as well as the service of Newport, a "negro man." Once Comfort's sisters wed, Newport was to be sold and the proceeds divided among each of the brides. The "outlands" in Tiverton belonging to Susanna Dennis, Comfort's mother, were to be shared by the eight sisters, a distribution that added little to Comfort's real property holdings. It is mildly interesting that both parents left slaves to various children—but not to Comfort.[105] There were, no doubt, several reasons for Comfort Taylor's marriage to Lieutenant Brownell, a man eighteen years her senior, but it is hardly a stretch to think that Comfort's financial well-being was among them.[106]

Comfort and George Brownell produced a daughter, Mary, in 1747, but the marriage lasted only until George's death in 1756. No record confirms how long Comfort Dennis Taylor Brownell survived her second husband, but she did so comfortably at their home near Westport Harbour, Massachusetts. Not to be outdone by Comfort's first husband, George also left his widow a horse and saddle (along with his "red chest").[107] Thomas Borden died the year Comfort and George married, but not before becoming the subject of a scathing postscript to a letter from Sir William Pepperell to the governor of Rhode Island. "I am this day informed that one John Wood, who deserted from Boston, out of Capt. Chaplin's company, and sent here by Capt. Thomas Burden, never was landed here, but carried off by said Burden. I hope you will call him to account for this, otherwise, this place will be lost by such vile actions." The governor, Gideon Wanton, vigorously denied the charge of "harboring and countenancing deserters" but was probably unable to reprimand Borden, since the latter's death must have intervened.[108] Nevertheless, one can only wonder whether this incident says something about Borden's character and whether some monetary inducement precipitated his willingness to spirit John Wood away.

If pounds and shillings close out this story—or at least that part of the narrative for which there is evidence—it is only to emphasize that monetary issues dot the story line throughout. Comfort Taylor's first response to the alleged assault was that she did not want Cuff whipped or hanged, since the former would devalue his worth and the latter preclude any sale. Thomas Borden was eager to resolve the matter privately by selling Cuff and compensating Comfort with part of the proceeds. His instincts were good; Borden knew that if Comfort pressed charges and prevailed, he stood to lose a valuable piece of property. Comfort decided to risk a trial in the hope that she would be rewarded with a restitution befitting her outrage. As it turned out, however, Comfort's court-determined award exceeded the price at which Cuff was sold, and was further diminished by court costs, Cuff's fine, and prison fees. Thus, by rebuffing Borden's offer and going public, Comfort had probably reduced her financial advantage. She might have salvaged her reputation, but as far as Comfort's benefiting from monetary damages, her "friends" had advised her badly. Similarly, Thomas Borden, forced to relinquish the proceeds from Evan Malbone's purchase, gained nothing from the sale of Cuff. Indeed, Borden lost his claim to Cuff because the *person* part of his property was held responsible for the crime perpetrated on Comfort.

The Narrator's Story

On one level, the confrontation between Comfort and Cuff became public the minute James Strange and John Grinnill "rescued" Comfort from the ferry. The dozen or so people who were immediately concerned with the alleged rape attempt increased later that evening with Comfort's inclusion of friends from whom she sought advice. The records do not reveal their identity, but it is likely that they spread information about the shocking incident—sooner rather than later. Each retelling of the event and every decision made by the protagonists extended the circle of people involved in the case and became embedded in the legal culture. If gossip remained local, court proceedings and newspapers did not. By the spring of 1744, nearly a year and a half after Comfort's initial accusation, the number of people involved in the legal action, or who had heard of the case or even had an opinion about the case, must have escalated to the high hundreds and more.

Comfort's family would have become aware of the episode immediately, although the abbreviated details that were shared with her children are beyond the reach of investigation. Moreover, the extended (and intermarried) Dennis, Taylor, Borden, Durfee, and Howland families, not to mention their subsidiaries, would have learned of the event within hours as well. How they processed the information, whether they took sides, and if the matter produced family schisms can only be imagined, but Comfort's charges surely consumed most of the table talk at Christmas dinner.

News travels. Within weeks, reports of the incident had escaped the boundaries of Rhode Island and Massachusetts and had reached the Philadelphia press. The circulation of the *American Weekly Mercury* meant that hundreds of readers and listeners would have absorbed slanted information about the case. The *Mercury* convicted Cuff with its report about the "Negro Man" who attempted "to commit a Rape on a Woman," an interpretation of events that reinforced the stereotype of the predatory black male.[109]

Once Comfort decided to go public, once she determined to "sware a gainst him," the number of people adumbrated by the shadow of the law increased exponentially.[110] The main characters, judges, jury, witnesses, clerks, lawyers, and eventually the Rhode Island General Assembly are only a small percentage of the people exposed to the case. Courtroom spectators, and the community of Newporters to whom they, in turn, reported the day's events added to the ripple effect and its impact on legal culture. Cuff's sale, in the fall of 1743, and his subsequent flight the following spring kept this volatile case alive—not only in Newport with its five thousand–plus people, but in Boston as well.[111]

Public discussion of the case influenced reputation. Cuff, who was a trusted slave at one time, must have been shamed, stigmatized, and humiliated by the accusations. As a ferry captain, he came into contact with the very people who would judge him. Although some might be convinced of his guilt, others would have had their doubts. He was a convicted felon who received a mild sentence and subsequently commanded top dollar at a local sheriff's sale. Under the circumstances, Evan Malbone must have felt betrayed by Cuff's escape, a maneuver that allowed skeptics to say I-told-you-so.[112] For some, Cuff's flight was an admission of guilt, thus perpetuating the belief that black men preyed on white women. Whether Comfort reestablished her reputation by her legal maneuverings was another matter, as was the restoration of her "creditt" (that is to say, her credibility).[113] Thomas Borden's ill-fated resolve to see the case all the way up to the Court of Equity must have affected his reputation in the court of public opinion as well. His unyielding stand may also confirm a stubbornness that surfaced a few years earlier when Borden refused to comply with an arbitrator's ruling, a position that cost him membership in the Society of Friends and the loss of William Anthony Jr.'s respect. His intransigence in 1743, as reflected by his refusal to pay Cuff's fine or settle with Comfort, may reveal a character trait that worked to his disadvantage. William Anthony sat on the Equity Court that doubled Comfort's award. He was also a member of the General Assembly that voted to allow the sheriff to sell Cuff for Comfort's benefit.

Once Comfort turned to the law and sought a public remedy to redress her grievances, legal culture influenced behavior and determined how this case would play out. Laws governing coverture and widowhood left Comfort Taylor financially unstable, yet those same laws offered her legal remedies and enabled her to institute proceedings against Cuff. Common-law requirements holding masters responsible for the actions of their slaves played a role in this narrative, as did the 1714 statute prohibiting the transportation of unauthorized slaves and requiring Rhode Islanders to apprehend and return runaways.[114] In the larger picture, laws governing blacks engaged in maritime activities affected Cuff. According to Jeffrey Bolster, whites feared blacks who traveled, learned white ways, met other blacks and helped them to escape. Finally, Comfort's decision to prosecute Cuff resulted in new law, a virulently racist statute that was among the earliest colonial laws addressing attempted rape. What began as an incident involving two people metastasized into a colony-wide affair that fed on and propagated a legal culture based on long-standing ideas about race and rape.[115]

From one perspective, the story of Comfort and Cuff is about reputation and honor. Comfort's friends advised her that her reputation would be salvaged only by a public trial in which Cuff would be portrayed as an assailant. Cuff's reputation was similarly at stake, and he had far more to lose unless he was acquitted, which was an unlikely outcome given time and place. Thomas Borden's intransigence jeopardized his own community standing as well.

Reputation continues to play a pivotal role in a Chaucer-like story that casts Samuel Banister as the protagonist in The Debtor's Tale. Always trying to better himself, often unable to make ends meet, Banister was usually on the wrong side of suits for recovery of debt. Because of the public nature of such cases, townspeople were well aware of his financial distress. Finally, in an effort to avoid eviction, Banister irreparably destroyed what little remained of his reputation by shooting one of the sheriff's party who had come to oust him from his home.

CHAPTER 5

He Would "Shoot him upon the Spott"

The Eviction of Samuel Banister

Samuel Banister refused to vacate the house. The sheriff, Peleg Brown, sent Martin Howard to reason with him, but Howard's arguments only infuriated Banister. Walter Cranston had purchased the dwelling at auction on November 19, 1744; two months later Banister still retained possession, angrily insisting he would not quit the premises. "Deliver up" the house "peaceably," pressed Howard, or else the sheriff "as sure as he was alive wou'd actually come with Sufficient aid and Dispossess him." Banister retorted that he had "Endeavoured to git a house but twas not in his power in no Respect." He had even persuaded a respectable distiller, John Belitho, to promise punctual payment of rent "if a house Could have been hired any where." There was nothing more "in the power of him to do," Banister asserted, and "he would not have his wife and family Sacraficed to be Turn'd out in the Snow." And whoever attempted to force him, "twas upon his peril."

As the argument escalated, Howard became more insistent and Banister grew more incensed. He announced that "the first man that offered to Break into the house upon him he would Immediately Shoot him upon the Spott." Howard left, but not without warning Banister that three days hence—on January 22, 1744/45—he would be forcibly evicted from the premises. On Monday, January 21, in a last-ditch effort to resolve the matter peaceably, Martin Howard (a lawyer by profession) sought out Banister "wonce more" and "using all the Arguments that [he] was Master of" tried to "prevail with him." It was to "no purpose." Banister repeated his earlier threats, "swearing and Declaring so sure as he was then a Live . . . he would kill or Shoot the first man that should attempt to Break in upon him to take possession of his house." *His* house, Banister stated unequivocally—a claim that presumed ownership by a tenant rather than by the actual owner, Walter Cranston, who had recently paid £540 for the residence. Howard "Endeavoured Streneously to Diswade him" and left.[1]

Sheriff Peleg Brown did not wait until January 22 to evict Samuel Banister from the house at the northern end of the town of Newport. Whether he concluded that Banister was beyond persuasion, or whether he was counting on the element of surprise is unclear. Whatever the reason, Brown and his deputies, William Dyre and Job Bennett, chose the darkening afternoon of January 21 to force the issue. When Dyre knocked at the front door of the house, Banister appeared at a window at the west end of the dwelling, opened it, and asked what the men wanted.[2] "We are come to take the possession of this house to give it to Mr. Cranston," replied Brown. Samuel Banister "made answer that we should not come in" and threatened to shoot "any man" who "offered to Enter the door." Brown ordered Dyre to break open the door, which Dyre unsuccessfully "endeavoured to do" with his feet. Seizing a fence rail, Dyre and Brown forced open the upper half of the double front door. They paused there as Banister rushed through the hallway "with a Gun in his Hand . . . and Swore by his Maker that if any Man presumed to come in he would shoot him." He railed at the men, waving the weapon at Dyre, Brown, and Bennett. Annoyed at the impasse, Dyre suggested to Bennett that he "run in for he durst not shoot." Although Dyre's reluctance to move forward himself indicates some ambivalence about Banister's actual intentions, Bennett obeyed and advanced toward Banister, at which point Banister threatened to shoot Bennett. Bennett hesitated.

The stalemate continued "for the space of Six or Seven Minutes," at which time John Brown and Captain John Griffith appeared on the scene. Griffith's apprentice, James Osborne, was already there, having followed Peleg Brown to the house as his "assistant."[3] John Brown told Banister "he would come in," and Banister "swore if he did he would shoot him." Momentarily distracted by the conversation and the movement of the men toward him, Banister thrust the muzzle of the gun outward over the fastened lower half of the double door. Captain Griffith grabbed the gun barrel, shoved it aside, and "sliped into the house," followed by John Brown, William Dyre, Peleg Brown, and Job Bennett. James Osborne was among those "pushing forward to get into [the] House." The gun, still in Banister's hands according to Dyre and Brown, "was fired off," and James Osborne fell either to the ground or "between the Steps which were much broke." The young man "had received a large wound in his Thigh" and was losing blood rapidly. Recognizing Osborne's need for immediate medical attention, the men brought him to Captain Griffith's house, where doctors frantically tried to save his life. Banister "was carried to the Gole [jail]" unmolested, but his victim, "the unhappy youth," died the following morning.[4]

Since Samuel Banister had been born into one of Boston's more affluent and respectable merchant families, this bizarre and tragic incident appears at best out of character, at worst inexplicable. Yet Samuel's family background, upbringing, financial difficulties, and subsequent behavior make this seemingly unpredictable event slightly more predictable. Born in Massachusetts in 1711 or 1712 (shortly before or after the great Boston fire of 1711), Samuel was in his early thirties during the winter of 1745; his brother John was several years older. Another brother (Chamberlain) and a sister (Frances) were the other surviving children of Thomas and Frances Banister, although the whereabouts of these siblings at the time of this incident are unknown. Their father, Thomas, a Boston merchant who had been a member of the Harvard class of 1700, was long gone by 1745: he had died in a shipwreck off the coast of England in 1716.[5] Young Samuel had hardly known his father, and he could have had but few memories of him later in life.

Samuel's mother, Frances Banister, was left to care for four young sons (Thomas, ten years old, John, nine, Samuel, five, and Chamberlain, three) and

FIGURE 10. British Queen Anne flintlock pistol. This is one of the more common eighteenth-century firearms and was probably similar to the weapon Samuel Banister used to shoot James Osborne. Courtesy nramuseum.com.

one daughter, her namesake, Frances, who at fourteen probably lorded it over her brothers while she had the chance. Frances Banister, senior, asked her late husband's brother, Samuel (after whom her son was named), to administer her husband's estate. Her deceased husband had benefited from the major part of that estate for only seven years, having inherited it from his father (also Thomas) in 1709. It was somewhat distant from the compact part of Boston; the property was not far from the western cove and faced the Common. The house itself was at the juncture of what would be Beacon, Walnut, and Spruce streets. Banister's Gardens, part of the estate, enjoyed some reputation, and it is not hard to imagine the children frolicking or playing hide-and-seek there while their mother ambled about.[6]

Who actually lived on that Boston estate for the next two or three decades is a matter of some speculation, since Frances's brother-in-law Samuel senior, and her son, Samuel junior, were indiscriminately named in various town records without enough details to set them apart. Yet whether they resided together or not, there was considerable interaction among the family members. In the absence of a father, Uncle Samuel seems to have set up his eldest nephew, John, in business, an unsurprising turn of events given the background of this old mercantile family. The flyleaf of Samuel Banister senior's daybook dating between 1728 and 1731 indicates that it was "A Blotter Belonging to Mr. Saml and John Banister." In 1728, John would have been twenty-one, a good time for a young man to get his feet wet in the shipping trade. The firm, Minot and Banister, conducted business locally or between Marblehead, Boston, and the Cape. They dealt in modestly priced goods: cordage, fishing gear, bread, pork, iron products, and fabric such as duck, kersey, flannel, and broadcloth. John's brother Samuel, now a youth in his mid-teens, attired himself with merchandise from the family store: a pair of hose for fourteen shillings, and a hat for one pound, five shillings.[7]

One of the two Samuels seems to have run into trouble with the Boston Selectmen in August 1736 when he dug up the Common and took "Stones for his own Use, Contrary to a Law." The Banister involved in this incident subsequently acknowledged "his Fault" and "was directed . . . to remove the Stones which he had already dug up, And to fill up the holes." He agreed to do so, but "had not fulfill'd his Promise" by December, at which time further testimony described how Samuel Banister and several laborers had collected the stones. There is no sure way of determining which of the two Samuel Banisters ran afoul of the law this time, but Uncle Samuel would have been close to fifty years of age, his nephew twenty-five or so.[8] Digging up stones is a young man's job.

Although the younger Samuel might have thought of the stone-stealing episode as nothing more than a lark, it is also possible that the incident hints at a deeper disregard for the law. Banister's actions suggest a cavalier posture toward community ordinances, which could be broken or ignored at will. Moreover, even if the authorities caught up with him—which they did—there were ways to avoid serious penalties. Early on he learned the tactic of promise and delay: promise to make amends and delay doing so. This is a pattern that Samuel Banister repeats later in life. What is curious is that his father treated the law just as casually. In 1710, the Boston Selectmen gave Thomas Banister permission to lay a cellar drain at a depth no less than five feet. Banister ignored the restriction. Two years later permission was again granted, as long as Banister was "attending the law." Ordered to remove the earth that he deposited in the highway in front of his house in Newbury Street, he delayed doing so despite the threat of prosecution.[9]

Samuel had not even been born yet when Thomas Banister was installing the drain contrary to the selectmen's orders. Yet that may be a moot point: such indifferent attitudes about legal responsibilities may have extended beyond the Banister family to the larger community. Thus, although Thomas Banister was absent for his son's formative years, Samuel may have grown up in a society that showed some ambivalence about the law. Moreover, Samuel's mother and uncle probably spoke of Thomas Banister to his young son and may even have recounted tales that made a lingering impression on the youth.

Such family lore might even have included Thomas's confrontations with the law, which in retrospect became humorous anecdotes. Young Samuel could have learned that his father was involved in "Debaucheries" at a Boston tavern in 1708, when he was a married man in his mid-twenties. As a result of this carousing, he was fined for "Lying," cursing, and for engaging in a "Breach of the peace for throwing the pots and Seale-box at the maid." Six years later, Thomas Banister once again contributed to "Disorders" at a south-end tavern where excessive drinking and toasts to the Queen's health were the source of the disturbance. Samuel Sewall, called in to restore peace, threatened the unruly group and finally "address'd . . . Mr. Banister," suggesting that since "he had been longest an Inhabitant and Freeholder . . . he should set a good Example in departing." Thomas Banister responded by inviting the merrymakers "to his own House"—presumably to continue their alcoholic expression of devotion to the Queen.[10] Thomas Banister must have turned thirty by this time, and the house to which he invited the revelers contained several children, including his son Samuel, a toddler of two or three years.

But this unseemly conduct was a thing of the past, and even if Samuel was aware of his father's escapades, there is no concrete evidence that it affected his own behavior decades later. Besides, Thomas Banister had been a well-respected merchant, young as he was. He might have enjoyed his brew, punch, and spirits, but he took his business affairs seriously—seriously enough to publish a pamphlet about "the principal branches" of New England's trade in 1715, barely a year after his rowdy behavior in Wallis's tavern. The pamphlet, in the form of a letter, was not only an exposé about the commerce of New England, but a prescient hint that the imposition of "great duties" might unite the colonies against the Crown.[11]

Whatever the posthumous influence of Thomas Banister on his son, however, there are hints from time to time that all was not well in the Banister household, and that fault lines had developed among the various family members. Thomas, the older brother of Samuel and John, had died in 1726, also the victim of an angry sea. He left a young widow and a civil suit against his uncle Samuel, the action involving a bequest from Thomas's grandparents.[12] Chamberlain, however, was partial to Uncle Samuel. In fact, on January 24, 1732/33, he petitioned as a nineteen-year-old minor to have Samuel become his guardian. Chamberlain's mother, Frances, was still very much alive, and his reasons for this move are a mystery, but clearly something was awry. Indeed, there are reasons to believe he was part of a troubled, if not dysfunctional, family.

Chamberlain's brother Samuel, now a twenty-one-year-old "merchant," appears to have assaulted their brother John the previous December. The matter was serious enough to have attracted the attention of the court, which released Samuel on his own recognizance but required him to appear before the next general sessions on January 3, 1732/3. He, his mother, and one Joseph Weldon acted as sureties for his appearance, and the court warned Samuel that "in the meantime" he was to be "of good behavior to all of his Majesty's Leage People [and] more Especially to John Banister."[13] The directive embedded in the language suggests that Samuel had not exhibited signs of brotherly love toward his sibling.

Frances may have requested her brother-in-law Samuel to administer her late husband's estate, but that relationship also deteriorated over time. Two years after her son Chamberlain sought refuge with his uncle Samuel, Frances petitioned the Massachusetts legislature for a stay against an arbitration award in Samuel's favor. Frances claimed that she had "had many disputes in the Law with her Brother in Law Mr Samuel Banister," that she had already paid a considerable part of the sum in question, and needed time to confirm what had been a transatlantic transaction. She added that although the sum should have been credited to her account, she "supposes it went to pay his [Samuel's] Debts."[14] This was the first inkling that Samuel senior was in any kind of financial distress.

Given the contentious behavior of his nearest and dearest, it can hardly be coincidental that John, brother to one Samuel and nephew to another, chose this moment to relocate to Newport, Rhode Island. By the spring of 1736 he had purchased real estate on the harbor from Edward Pelham, and in November of the following year he married Pelham's nineteen-year-old daughter, Hermione, "an agreeable young Gentlewoman."[15] John's wife was also a descendant of Governor Benedict Arnold of Rhode Island. Through this marriage John Banister would eventually inherit some of Newport's most valuable real estate. His mercantile business, first established in Boston, expanded quickly and prosperously with his new contacts. His European trade flourished. In 1739 John's privateering ventures showed great profits. In a short time John Banister had become one of Newport's most important merchants. His customers demanded luxury goods in addition to the usual staples, and the inventory at his store on Pelham's wharf now included mantua silks, worsteds, damask table linens, gold and silver lace, and Persian rugs.[16] Whether John's success (not to mention his connections) influenced his brother and uncle is unclear. Nevertheless, the two Samuels in John's life decided to follow him to Newport.

When exactly they determined to pull up stakes cannot be determined with any precision. In the early fall of 1739, Samuel Banister senior was still living "in Beacon Street [Boston] at the lower part of the Common." In addition to his other pursuits, he was engaged in the "Brewing Business." Yet Samuel's business involvement with his nephew John followed the latter's move to Newport. Before departing for Great Britain on business in 1737, John solicited settlement of accounts "in Company with his Uncle Samuel Banister in their Business late at Marblehead." A 1739 controversy between the Pelhams and Samuel Banister senior over a contested real estate title may have strained relations between John and his new in-laws, but in the end Uncle Samuel prevailed and advertised the farm at Cambridge in Middlesex County for sale. It is not known whether this dispute played a role in the dissolution of the partnership between Samuel senior and John, but the records indicate that by this year Uncle Samuel had formed his own firm, Samuel Banister and Company. Family squabbles did not intrude on business, however, since John Banister's ledger books show transactions with his uncle beginning in 1739, and with his brother Samuel, from 1741.[17]

Whenever it was that Samuel Banister junior arrived in Newport, he was accompanied by a wife and children. Unlike his brother, however, Samuel had not married into money or gentility. His wife, Mary Wheeler Porter, was eight or nine years Samuel's senior and had been previously married to one William Porter, by whom she had two daughters, Mary and Elizabeth. The Porters were a Connecticut family, and William's father was a blacksmith. Under these circumstances it is hard to imagine the Banisters welcoming Mary and her daughters into their family with any enthusiasm, even if Samuel and Mary subsequently added a third daughter to the clan, whom they named Susanna.[18] Samuel's personal assets may have been limited at the time, but that did not prevent him from living in style in Newport. He (and presumably his family) took up residence at the home of Newport's most affluent merchant-aristocrat, Captain Godfrey Malbone, where Banister (now in his late twenties) served Malbone as his "Bookeeper & to Negotiate his business." For "Upwards of Two Years" (1739–40?), Banister enjoyed the finest accommodations colonial America offered. Malbone, whose fortune derived from the slave trade, was determined that his home reflect his wealth. He did so in a blinding show of opulence by gilding his "great Room and the spout heads" with twenty-five hundred leaves of gold. His grounds were surrounded by a wall and wrought-iron gates into which Malbone's initials were woven. Inside the mansion, circular stairs invited access to the richly appointed upper floors. Paneled walls and marble mantels added to the lavishness of the interior, while a balcony, dormers, and a roof balustrade testified to the architectural splendor of the exterior. While the Banisters were in residence, Malbone was also building his legendary three-story pink sandstone country seat, magnificently finished with Caribbean mahogany.[19]

The records do not disclose exactly when—or why—Banister departed from Malbone's house, but subsequent evidence places the Banister family in John Allen's house for a short period (possibly during the spring of 1740). It was not until the late summer of 1740 that Samuel Banister, his wife, and daughters took up residence in the modest house that became the source of so much controversy. A head count suggests that the dwelling, which sat on an eighty-square-foot lot, was bursting at the beams, with five Banisters, two black servants or slaves (Tom and Sambo), and two other women (Margaret Parker and Ann Vroom) sharing what must have been close quarters. Clearly, this was a comedown for the Banisters, who had already relocated twice since their initial move to Newport.

Furthermore, no documents exist to reveal when or why Banister, a tenant himself, began to take in boarders. Presumably, he needed the income to make ends meet. The arrangement, more akin to a sublet of space than the ordinary owner-tenant relationship, may not have been unusual in an eighteenth-century urban environment, but in effect it created a tenancy tier, privileging the person who had initially let the entire house, and giving him or her fiduciary responsibility for collecting rent from the subtenants. This scheme also allowed Samuel Banister to think of himself as a landlord, a perception that was inscribed in Banister's account book when he billed Leonard Bazin for board "at my House"—and subsequently went to court to collect the rent from the dilatory lessee.[20]

Despite his efforts as a landlord and as a "merchant alias bookkeeper," Samuel Banister junior saw his fortunes decline at the same time his brother's were on the rise. Indeed, Samuel's future appeared shaky as his debts mounted and the months passed. From 1741 on he was forced to defend himself in one case of debt after another. Banister could not or would not pay his bills, and his creditors dragged him to court to compel him to do so. Law, the legal system, the courtroom, his adversaries, the expectations of the people with whom Banister did business—all of this pervaded and shaped Banister's life. It was not any particular judicial decision that made such an impact, but the collective outlook of those with whom Banister dealt. In short, it was not just the court judging him, but rather a community whose ethical standards about repayment of debt had been breached. In the mid-eighteenth century, debt had not quite made the transition in the public mind from moral failure to economic misfortune, and the old-fashioned outlook would have persuaded Banister's creditors to judge him harshly. Besides, as Bruce Mann points out, book debts merely recorded transactions; the promise of repayment was implicit rather than explicit, something that debtors might use to justify delays in settlement.[21]

The records leave no trace of Banister's defense in the actions against him, but each time he lost a case he either ignored the judgment against him or appealed to a higher court. He, like many of his contemporaries in the same situation, knew how to work the system. These stalling tactics bought him time and perhaps staved off insolvency. Nevertheless, the pounds mounted up, as each appeal confirmed the judgment of the lower court against Banister. In and out of the courthouse during this period as his creditors lined up against him, Banister only rarely secured a recovery in his favor. He was in debt to ordinary workers and tradespeople in Newport, as well as to merchant-gentlemen in Boston: Rhodes the distiller; Mumford and Bazin, mariners; Allyne and the Hills, merchants; Langley the joiner; and Carpenter the shopkeeper.[22] The sums ranged from eight pounds to eighty-three pounds, but the one clear verdict in Banister's favor was a mere five pounds, nineteen shillings. Even after the court rendered judgment against him, Banister delayed payment.

Samuel Banister's reputation must have suffered from these financial set-backs. In a community where people could be undone by gossip, Banister's inability (or even unwillingness) to honor his obligations must have been fodder for the rumor mill. Who would do business with him? Who would offer him credit? Even though debt litigation was a common feature of mid-eighteenth-century life, Banister (on the cusp of his thirtieth birthday) stood out as the antithesis of the model businessman. Indeed, compared to his brother John, he was a failure. Samuel Banister surely knew this.

At the same time that these cases were wending their way through Common Pleas, the Superior Court of Judicature, and the short-lived Court of Equity, Samuel Banister was also engaged in a controversy with his former physician, Dr. John Brett, over payment for services rendered by Brett between 1740 and 1741.[23] Unable to collect his fees amicably, Dr. Brett took his onetime patient—and friend—to court, where accusations, depositions, and appeals reveal a Samuel Banister who had learned to negotiate the legal system in order to evade his financial responsibilities.

According to John Brett, the Banister family frequently called upon him between August 1740 and August 1741 after Samuel Banister "discharged" Dr. Robinson. Brett's account books, produced as evidence, show constant visits to the Banister house during which Brett administered purges and vomits, prescribed various medications, and generally saw to the well-being of the Banister family. When Samuel Banister took sick in church, he summoned Dr. Brett. When Elizabeth Porter "fell out of a Window and hurt her self," it was John Brett who bled her. When "a Negro Boy" needed his "Kibed Heels" dressed with "hot Chamber lye," Dr. Brett attended to it. When Mrs. Banister "was taken with the Colick," Brett "prescribed several things . . . from Mr. Tweedy's," the apothecary. Banister's wife spoke of her ill health to Sarah Collingwood, admitting that "her disorders were such that she was constantly taking some stuff or other" from Dr. Brett, including one remedy "so that she should be with Child." If his treatment resulted in a pregnancy, "she should think that she could never do enough for him." In 1740–41 Mary Banister would have been in her late thirties and was probably hoping to present her husband with his first son before reaching the end of her childbearing years.

Margaret Parker and Ann Vroom, who "dwelt in the same House with Mr. Samll Banister," testified to Mrs. Banister's disabilities between October 1740 and June 1741, and that Brett came to the house in his capacity as a physician. Vroom was particularly taken with the pills Dr. Brett prescribed, noting that they were "wrapt up in leaf gold." Brett even tried to raise "Negro Tom" from the dead, saying "Tom don't be sullen, you have got a good Master," specious reasoning that was apparently unpersuasive. "Tom be dead," Brett finally admitted.[24]

When John Brett presented a bill for his services, Samuel Banister declined to pay. Forced into court by a physician who had lost patience with his patient, Banister claimed that Brett had come to his home as a friend, and that his daily visits were social rather than professional. In one deposition after another Banister's family denied they were sickly. And for whatever reasons, a few neighbors and friends confirmed Banister's position. The Banisters were generally "in Good Health," the Eccles asserted. Brett and the Banisters discussed "the news of the Town," and Samuel Banister made Dr. Brett "welcome with a part of a Bowl of Punch," from which, the Eccles couple assured the court, Samuel Banister never imbibed. Beriah [Whitham], a spinster who was in and out of the Banister house, assumed Brett "came only as a Friend to see Mr. Banister." Martha Thomas, a spinster who worked and lodged in the Banisters' house in the winter of 1740, thought so too. Brett and the Banisters "talked only of indifferent Matters," and his "transient" visits were "as a Friend." Sarah Allen concurred. She saw "Dr Brett Two or three times in a Day . . . when to her certain knowledge there was no sickness in the Family."[25] The records do not indicate whether the future wages of Whitham and Thomas were dependent on favorable testimony, but there is little doubt that they were drawn into legal quicksand as a result of their employer's malfeasance.

Banister's resistance forced Dr. Brett to sue for "medicines, Attendance, and Advice." The sum in question was fifty-five pounds, four shillings, and sixpence, although Brett claimed he had been damaged by Banister's foot-dragging to the extent of one hundred pounds. Brett filed his complaint in the Court of Common Pleas (the lower court for civil litigation) in October 1741, at which time the court ordered the sheriff to arrest Samuel Banister "merchant alias Bookkeeper" or "to attach his Goods and Chattles" until he gave "sufficient Bond" to answer Brett's complaint. Both Samuel and John Banister acknowledged the writ, although Samuel continued to insist that "he oweth the Plaintiff nothing." The documents do not reveal whether John refused to act as surety for his brother (and in so doing put his own property in jeopardy) or whether Samuel was reluctant to accept help, but in the end no one paid the bond imposed on Samuel, and he found himself "in the Custody of the Sheriff."[26] Since Samuel could make himself as comfortable as finances permitted in the lockup, and since the wheels of justice turned faster than they do in the twenty-first century, he and his family might not have been overly discouraged by this turn of events. Incarcerated debtors frequently came from Newport's finest families. However, the

Court of Common Pleas was about to hear Joseph St. Lawrence's suit against Banister in the same session, and a similar writ—to arrest Banister or seize his property—had been issued as a result of St. Lawrence's claim. As the Boston merchant noted in his papers of October 1741, Samuel Banister was already "in the custody of the sheriff."[27]

Custody notwithstanding, colonial Rhode Island showed ambivalence about incarceration for debt. The colony's 1647 code acknowledged that debts could be recovered by legal action, but envisioned imprisonment only as a last resort. The code provided for seizure of the debtor's property—if he or she possessed enough to discharge the debt—but in the absence of tangible assets, the legislation called for a committee composed of local officials and "able townsmen" to devise "a course between Creditor and Debtor" for repayment. The same legislation took a strong stand against imprisonment: no insolvent debtor should be "sent to prison, there to lye languishing to no man's advantage, unless he refuse to appeare or stand to their order" ("their" referring to the committee). Whether the creditor and debtor also took an active role in what appears to be a process akin to arbitration is unclear. Yet the framers surely understood that imprisonment for debt served little purpose. Only if an insolvent debtor refused to appear or abide by the binding resolution of the committee would he or she be removed from circulation.[28]

Over time Rhode Island retreated from its flirtation with common sense, and by the time Samuel Banister's financial problems arose, the Rhode Island General Assembly had overcome its sympathy for deadbeats. As Peter Coleman points out, by the early eighteenth century, insolvent debtors were often jailed for failure to settle their accounts. To compensate the town for maintaining such prisoners, and to enable imprisoned debtors to support themselves, in 1718 the General Assembly required prosecuting creditors to pay sixpence per day toward the maintenance of jailbirds and to provide work for debtors while incarcerated.[29] By the end of the 1730s, it "often" happened that insolvent debtors were "committed to Goal by their Creditors," where they "languished, to the Destruction of themselves and Families"—precisely the situation that legislators had attempted to circumvent in 1647. A 1739 statute repealed all previous legislation regarding the "Allowance" for insolvent debtors but did not consider the basic issue of incarceration. Instead, it raised the maintenance rate: in the future "the Party at whose Suit the Action is commenced, shall be obliged to pay the Goal Keeper *Six Shillings per Week* for the Support and Maintenance of such Debtor." This was the state of affairs when Samuel Banister was carted off to jail in 1741, and since both John Brett and Joseph St. Lawrence had sued him, they were able to split his six-shilling maintenance charge.[30]

On November 17, 1741, as he was whiling away the time behind bars, Samuel Banister received a double dose of bad news. In both cases, juries ruled against him, awarding Dr. John Brett fifty-five pounds plus costs of four pounds, and Joseph St. Lawrence four pounds, along with costs amounting to almost five pounds. Banister immediately appealed to the Superior Court of Judicature, which would hear both actions the following spring. Since "the last Tuesday in March" was over four months away, an extended jail residency must have seemed unappealing. This time someone put up bond, and Samuel Banister returned home. On March 30, 1742, Banister learned that the Superior Court had confirmed the decision of Common Pleas in the Brett case. To make matters worse, the court ordered Banister to pay the "further Costs" of litigation. St. Lawrence also prevailed against Banister, although the appellate court reduced the earlier verdict.[31] Banister wasted no time and appealed to the next sitting of the Court of Equity, to be held in May 1742.

In this round, Samuel Banister took advantage of a court that had only been recently established in Rhode Island and would outlive his case by less than a year. Until 1741 the Rhode Island General Assembly, sitting as a court of last resort, heard appeals from the Superior Court of Judicature. The litigants saw some benefit from this arrangement since the assembly claimed some members with legal training, which, oddly enough, was not a requirement for service on the Superior Court of Judicature. The General Assembly statute of May 1741 creating the Court of Equity was designed to reduce the workload of a body that had rendered judgments even during its busy legislative sessions. It was not intended that the new court handle matters any differently than the assembly had in the past. It would be business as usual, with money awards determined by the five judges who sat on the bench. But if the General Assembly had the power to give, it also could take away, and so it did in February 1743/44 in response to a petition enumerating the Equity Court's legal errors and faults. In a short time, the Court of Equity had become a "great grievance" to the colony's inhabitants, and it was disbanded.[32]

In his appeal to that body during its short-lived existence, Banister claimed that the judgments of the lower courts were wrong and that there was "No Foundation or Grounds" for Brett "to recover such a Sum of Him." Given the detailed written accounts that John Brett presented in evidence, the Court of Equity decided otherwise and during the summer session of 1742 affirmed Brett's judgment, "deducting therefrom the Sum of Ten Pounds" and awarding the doctor over forty-five pounds plus the costs of the suit— more than three pounds. Banister fared better in his controversy with Joseph

St. Lawrence. In one of his few successes between 1741 and 1745, the Equity Court reversed the judgment of the Superior Court, awarding St. Lawrence only twenty-six shillings and a small part of the costs, and allowing Banister to recover the heftier portion of the costs, which amounted to over twelve pounds. Litigation was expensive.[33]

The spring and fall of 1742 were even less kind to Banister than the summer had been. John and Thomas Hill, Boston merchants, caught up with Banister and "Mary his Wife" in Newport and won a verdict against them in Common Pleas for nearly thirty-five pounds plus costs, which was affirmed on appeal in March 1742. To add to Banister's problems, the Superior Court made Banister liable for five pounds more in additional costs. In September, Samuel Banister learned that another Boston associate, Samuel Allyne, had prevailed against him on appeal for a hefty sum as well. Between 1743 and 1745 Samuel Banister and Leonard Bazin, a mariner (and sometime tenant), were at odds over sums ranging anywhere from twenty-four pounds to one hundred twenty pounds plus costs—no small matter.

In a controversy that swallowed most of 1744, Banister sued Bazin for one hundred twenty pounds in costs and damages for boarding Bazin and his wife "and for washing[,] Firewood and Candles . . . for the Defts [defendant's] wife at the Defts request Cash lent her & for one pair of shoes and Ribbond" from October 6, 1743, through May 1, 1744. In addition, Mary Bazin had become "dangerously ill" at some point during their residency and needed "Extra wood[,] Candles etc. all night for Seven weeks" while she recovered under the care of Dr. Hooper. Compassion notwithstanding, Banister charged all these extras to Bazin's account. As Mary's husband, Leonard was legally responsible for the costs, but his concern for his wife's health may have waned in proportion to the mounting expense. A year earlier Mary had "elop'd" from Leonard "and run him in Debt Sundry very considerable Sums almost to his ruin." Reconsidering, she abandoned her plans and returned home at some point, for reasons unrecorded.

In any case, Bazin refused to settle with Banister, claiming that the numerous purchases Banister had made from Bazin completely offset Bazin's debt. For a man whose purse was growing lighter by the moment, Banister still enjoyed the good life. Charged against Banister—and overdue according to Bazin—were fine fabrics, a feather bed and chest, "chaneyware," wineglasses, "a looking glass," tablecloths, and "a Pistol."[34] Whether or not this was the weapon that fatally wounded James Osborne, the purchase suggests that Banister was no stranger to firearms. All these items added up to £120—which, conveniently, was precisely what Bazin owed Banister. Bazin defaulted in November 1744, the court awarded Banister sixty-two pounds, and Bazin appealed. The records pause at this point, which may mean that the parties settled—or that more pressing matters intruded.

Leonard Bazin was not the only tenant whom Banister sued for back rent. Benjamin Perkins, a stay maker, was also delinquent, but died before Banister could collect from him. Banister and the court looked to his estate for relief, but in March 1744 Perkins's administrators asserted they did not have the assets to compensate Banister. Banister pursued his claim between May and October 1744, prevailing twice but with little hope of recovery. Poor Samuel: even when he won, he lost.[35]

In March 1745, Banister suffered defeat in another appeal involving Leonard Bazin, this time in a case where Banister had initially received a favorable judgment for fifty-eight pounds. This was a cruel disappointment as well as an additional setback. To make matters worse, the court awarded Jabez Carpenter more than eighty-three pounds plus costs of over four pounds from Banister at the same time. Banister's financial worries may not have been his greatest concern in March 1745, however, since the same court that ruled in the debt cases would shortly turn its attention to the murder charges against him. One can only wonder whether Banister realized the bright side of the picture: a conviction in this capital case would end his financial problems once and for all.

Collectively, Banister appears to have owed his creditors somewhere between £160 and £200. This was the amount due to the men who sought to recover funds through litigation, although it is likely that Banister had other outstanding claims against him as well. In terms of value, if the sums in question were not exorbitant, neither were they meaningless. Converted into consumables, such pounds and shillings contributed to the good life. In the early to mid 1740s, Banister kept winter at bay with a greatcoat that would have cost him about eight pounds, and a pair of boots just under six pounds. Should he have wanted to surprise his wife with a pair of "Silver Shue Buckells," he would have parted with three pounds, nine shillings. His everyday vest and breeches would have set him back only two pounds, but a wig would have been priced at six times that figure. The cost of whatever house Banister rented depended on size and location. The tailoress Abigail Barker, who earned eight shillings per day, was able to secure a small lodging for twelve pounds per year, while the merchant and baker Isaac Stelle lived on a grander scale, paying sixty pounds annually for rent. Banister's live-in servant might have earned ten shillings per week. If Banister attended the funeral of Sueton Grant in September 1744, he might have partaken of some wine for which Grant's widow had paid thirty pounds for a quarter cask. All things considered, two hundred pounds could mean a great deal to a family such as the Banisters.[36]

If Samuel Banister was stalling his own creditors after 1741, he was, at the same time, helping his brother recoup money from his past employer, Godfrey Malbone. Samuel was not exactly disinterested in the outcome of the latter effort: these were funds that John had lent to Samuel, presumably at Malbone's behest.[37] According to Samuel, in January or February 1741, when he was still working for Malbone, his employer announced an impending trip to Boston. Concerned about his cash flow in Malbone's absence, Banister requested twenty pounds from Malbone to tide him over. Short of cash himself, Malbone replied that "he had no money even to Carry him down to Boston" but that he would return in a few days, presumably with cash to spare—or at least to share. As Samuel Banister later recalled, Malbone agreed that if his Boston sojourn exceeded a week, his bookkeeper could borrow from John Banister in Malbone's name. "Malbone readily answered Yes" to this proposal, insisted Banister. Two or three weeks later, when Malbone had still not returned, Samuel sought his brother's assistance, offering a receipt that clearly stated the terms of the loan. John, in turn, noted in his ledger (under Malbone's account) that on March 5, 1741/2, he had paid "Your Bookkeeper" twenty pounds. To all appearances, it was a routine transaction.

On his arrival back in Newport, however, Malbone declined to honor the debt. Why Malbone refused to reimburse John Banister, and why the issue precipitated litigation from Common Pleas to the Court of Equity is not recorded. Other merchants with whom Malbone did business testified to Malbone's willingness to have Samuel Banister sign for him for goods and services. Nevertheless, Malbone's attitude toward the brace of Banisters and the contested loan was unequivocal: "he owes the Plaintiff [John Banister] Nothing." John Banister offered to submit Samuel's testimony to the sequence of events "as Evidence," a move the court rejected on the grounds that Samuel was "a Person that would either get or Loose by the Event of the Cause." In other words, if John Banister lost the case—and the twenty pounds—he might try to wring the money out of his brother. It must have been to Samuel's relief, then, when his brother not only won the skirmish but the war as the matter traveled from Common Pleas in May 1743 to Superior Court in September/October 1743, and finally to Equity some months later. Whether the beginning of this dispute precipitated the rupture between Samuel Banister and Malbone is unknown, but by the time John Banister initiated his suit in May 1743, Samuel was clearly Malbone's "late" bookkeeper. Family solidarity notwithstanding, if John thought this tedious and time-consuming litigation would be his last day in court on his brother's behalf, he was sadly mistaken.

A year after the Equity bench found in Dr. Brett's favor, Banister was back in court, apparently having made peace with his former physician. This time Banister was neither plaintiff nor defendant, but rather a witness eager to establish a point in Brett's favor—a point on which the case hinged. The controversy was between Brett and a local butcher, Thomas Huxham, over purchases and prescriptions dating back to 1740. According to Huxham, Brett had "run in Dept Some thing Considerable" for meat he had acquired from Huxham. As Brett eyed the meat in his shop, Huxham said, the physician advised the butcher that he looked "porely." Obviously distressed by this gratuitous medical evaluation, Huxham "Lett him prescribe Something." Unaware that Brett intended to barter his services for Huxham's goods, the butcher only later realized he had been duped, calling Brett a "rogue" who submitted "Doctrs Bills to pay a Butcher Bill." Such an exchange did not sit well with Huxham, who had never inquired into the price of the expensive elixir that Brett prescribed. Moreover, deposed Huxham, Brett "never come to my house to visit me as a Sick man but rather Com to make me a Drunkan man for I often with his Chat yousily make punch more than there was need of."[38] This was precisely the argument Samuel Banister had used to defend himself against Brett's bills: the doctor's visits were social rather than professional. This time, however, the objective of Banister's testimony was reversed.

Banister's account was designed to help Brett, if only tangentially.[39] In 1740, Brett and Banister "used to go to Each others houses," Samuel Banister affirmed. One day, Banister recalled, he ran into Brett on the street and the doctor "ask'd him [to] go to his House." En route, Brett stopped at Huxham's shop and "ask'd him for a small bitt of Meat to make Gravey Sauce." Huxham "cut him off" a piece, and the two men departed. In the ensuing conversation, Banister learned that Brett "never was at a loss for gravey sauce for it was but going to Huxhams and saying Tom: I want a Bitt of Beef Mutton etc to make sauce & I always have it." Banister interpreted this remark to mean that "Huxham never made any Charge for what he had to make his Sauce." In short, Banister swore that Brett owed Huxham nothing, leaving the butcher with a stack of doctors' bills, a contested charge for a hogshead of rum, and no medical insurance.[40] Of no relevance here, but of some interest nonetheless, is the possibility that the newly married Brett had assumed the role of family chef. More to the point, however, is that Samuel Banister was constantly involved in litigation as plaintiff, defendant, or witness. As he would later remind the authorities who came to oust him from his house, "he knew something of the Law."[41]

Samuel Banister's legal problems were never far removed from local and foreign events of the 1740s. His financial difficulties kept pace with the runaway inflation that coursed through New England during that decade. Pegged to the pound sterling (as well as to the currency of Massachusetts), £100 sterling soared from £550 in local currency during the summer of 1741 to £600 in January 1744/45 as Banister was about to be evicted. With debt contracted at the old rate, angry British merchants leaned on their American customers, who dunned their local clients. As the price of the British pound spiraled upward, delay in payment became increasingly beneficial to debtors such as Banister, and all the more damaging to his creditors who had contracted with him at an exchange rate more favorable to them at the time.[42] Thus, inflation may have been behind the demands by several plaintiffs for judgments in excess of what Banister originally owed them.

International events also had an impact on Banister and his family. The European wars that raged during the early 1740s and spilled over into the Atlantic made some American merchants rich and others poor. Samuel Banister was not a player on the high seas at this time, but his brother John tried his luck at privateering, perhaps in response to recently disappointing ventures in hardware and textiles. By October 1740, John Banister had interest in half of the six privateers that sailed from Newport. A number of his privateering schemes were successful, but after losing his ship the *Virgin Queen* to impressments, suffering financial double-dealing by his captain, and becoming involved in prize litigation, John hedged his bets by turning some of his ships into letters of marque rather than privateers—which meant that they pursued profit both by trading and privateering, as the opportunity warranted. Yet privateering continued to lure him, despite the risks: while Samuel Banister was assisting his brother in court against Godfrey Malbone in the fall of 1743, John and two other merchants were fitting out the *Prince William* as a privateer in the hope of a large return on their investment.[43]

If the stress level of the Banisters was already high during the period 1743–44, they could hardly have escaped the additional anxiety produced by the religious revivals sweeping New England during the Great Awakening. In the summer of 1744, the traveler and diarist Dr. Alexander Hamilton stopped at Newport, noting at the time "two Presbyterian meetings, one large Quaker meeting, one Anabaptist, and one Church of England." He fell short of a few splinter groups and made no mention of the "enthusiastic discourse" raging through the rest of the Northeast, but he did observe that

Newporters were not "so strait laced in religion . . . as in other parts of New England."[44] Attitude aside, both Providence and Newport played host to the great revival preacher George Whitefield in the spring of 1745, a short time after Banister's murder trial. Yet the spiritual fires of the Great Awakening were sputtering, according to one observer: "Small numbers attend [Whitefield] now to what did some years ago. There is a change somewhere, in him or them."[45] That may have been true, but the Great Awakening was not quite spent in Newport, inspiring as it did polarization and splits among various Baptist denominations. Even Quakers were caught up in the movement, exhibiting greater zeal in their attempt at reform.[46] Mounting debt, rampant inflation, lingering war, religious fervor: this was the setting for the confrontation between Samuel Banister and the authorities who came to evict him.

When Martin Howard told Banister that "to keep possession" of the house was "Impossible," Banister retorted that "he knew something of the Law and that he Dared the Sheriff or any man upon his peril to offer to come there to Turn him out of Possession." At first glance this threat seems no more than the swaggering braggadocio of a desperate man determined to retain his home. Yet Samuel Banister did know something of the law. He had been a constant presence in Rhode Island courtrooms for years, and in addition to his firsthand experience, he may even have dug into his pocket for the revised law codes published at the direction of the General Assembly just as his eviction proceedings were heating up and his debt cases had reached the high court. Since the printer, Ann Franklin, had defied the General Assembly's order to limit the edition to five hundred volumes, Banister might have taken advantage of the sales war between the legislature and the lady to purchase a copy.[47] In any case, the publishing controversy seems to indicate that there was a market for law books.

Although most of Banister's battles with the legal system concerned debt litigation, Banister hinted that he had already collided with the authorities over this particular piece of residential property on a previous occasion. According to Martin Howard, an agitated Banister reminded him that "he had Been already wonce Turned out (and his family) by said Sheriff and the Possession given to Capt. John Griffith and afterwards he the said Banister Said he was admitted into the Possession again and therefore twas not in their power to turn him out again but Said the Sheriff [mought] Bring a writt of Error against him if he pleased." There is no reason to disbelieve Banister. The sequence of events probably took place as described, although Howard's deposition attached no date to the incident. At the same time, John Griffith does not appear in the chain of title for the property during this controversial period, and it is puzzling why Banister would have been dispossessed in favor of Griffith, unless Griffith had somehow become the primary lessee. Title notwithstanding, Griffith's presence on the day Banister was evicted could only have infuriated Banister still more.[48]

Furthermore, the multiple and unusual transfers of title to this property during Banister's tenancy may have left room for confusion over rights to the premises. John Cane originally owned the property, but a 1743 debt dispute between Cane and John Gidley was resolved in Gidley's favor, forcing Martin Howard, deputy sheriff, to attach and sell the house in order to generate funds to satisfy the judgment against Cane. Before the auction took place, however, Gidley's legal vindication blew up in his face—literally—when a gunpowder explosion in the fall of 1744 took the lives of several Newport merchants, Gidley among them. In the aftermath of this disaster, Gidley's widow sought to obtain her share of the proceeds of the Cane property when it was sold at auction on November 19, 1744, to Walter Cranston, "the highest bidder." William Dyre, deputy sheriff, conducted the sale on the premises, while an irate Samuel Banister probably observed the event from a nearby spot. Unfortunately, this transaction was prelude to a spell of legal chaos since the sheriff, Thomas Potter, inconvenienced everyone by dying after the sale but before composing and signing the deed.[49] Subsequently, all of Potter's papers were deposited with a committee that had little substantive knowledge of any of the unresolved proceedings, but was directed to receive and forward all relevant documents to the newly named sheriff, Peleg Brown.[50]

To complicate matters, Gidley's widow, Elizabeth, and Peleg Brown had joined forces as administrators of John Gidley's estate. Wearing his hat as administrator, therefore, Brown had an interest in seeing that Cane's property was sold in a timely manner and delivered without delay to the purchaser so that Gidley's widow could collect her proceeds. At the same time, Brown's role as the sheriff who signed off on the deed transferring Cane's property to Cranston enabled Brown to speed up the process as well. While legal, these dual roles suggest a potential conflict of interest, which did not work in Banister's favor and surely did not escape Banister's notice.[51]

This much we know: Banister had been ousted from this house once, he had been reinstated, and because he sought and won repossession, he stubbornly dismissed the legality of a second eviction. It is difficult to understand what law or laws Banister relied upon, unless his initial tenancy provided for a long-term lease that survived the death of or sale by the owner. According to common law, if a "lessee for years" was unlawfully expelled from the property, he or she could obtain repossession by a judgment of the justice of the peace. Cane was neither dead nor the willing seller of the house in which Banister and his family lived. As a result, conflicting opinions about the meaning of ancient statutes governing forcible entry and repossession made any interpretation ambiguous, and it is possible that Banister and the authorities were relying on different readings of the law.[52] Nevertheless, the deed that Peleg Brown eventually delivered to Walter Cranston for Cane's property gave Cranston the right to "Occupy" the premises. Unfortunately for Banister, Cranston was also "Discharged of & from all . . . Manner of former . . . gifts grants Bargains Sales Leases . . . and Incumbrances whatso-ever" on the property. The deed was signed on January 21, giving Banister no time at all to challenge its legality. Indeed, the ink was barely dry before Brown and his deputies sought to oust Banister from the house.

Given the web of details spun by witnesses following James Osborne's death, it is surprising that no one mentioned the use of firearms by the sheriff or his deputies. By the time the authorities attempted to evict Banister, they were well aware of his violent threats, and yet none of the depositions hint that any member of this small brigade came prepared to deal with a man who had ill feelings toward William Dyre and had threatened "to blow his brains out."[53] That the sheriff and deputies were entitled to carry weapons in performance of their duties is clear; that even a distraught Banister might have retreated if faced with personal injury or even death is possible. Banister might have been a debtor, but for all his bellicosity there is no reason to think he was a killer. Whether it was a conscious decision to forgo weapons, or simply bad judgment on the part of Brown, Dyre, and Bennett, their miscal-culation cost dearly.

Within a week, news of the bizarre incident at Newport had spread. For all its wealth and gentility, however, Newport still had no newspaper of its own, and it was left to the Boston pundits to report the incident. The *Boston Evening-Post* scooped its rivals on January 28 with a six-line report from Newport about a struggle between Mr. Samuel Banister and an officer who had come to dispossess him. As he resisted, Banister "unhappily discharged a loaded musket, whereby a young Man was mortally wounded in the Thigh, and died the next morning." By the time the story appeared in the *Boston Gazette* a day later, the printer had assembled more of the pertinent details. The paper referred to Peleg Brown and James Osborne by name and quoted Banister's threat to "shoot the first Person that should enter" the house. Yet where the *Boston Evening-Post* placed the blame for Osborne's death squarely on Banister, the language of the *Boston Gazette* hinted at mitigating circum-stances. As the men rushed in "to disarm" Banister, the paper reported, "the Gun was discharged of a brace of balls." Exactly how this had happened read-ers could discern for themselves. It was left for the *Boston Weekly News-Letter* to embellish what by January 31 must have become stale news. Banister's declaration was now made "in a solemn manner," and "all Reasonings with him were found ineffectual." In an attempt to substitute dramatic effect for timely reporting, however, the *News-Letter* added that the shot "narrowly" missed "one of the Deputy Sheriffs." But this journal, too, used passive language to ascribe responsibility for the shooting. Rather than point a finger, the article repeated the vague claim that "the Gun was discharged of a Brace of Balls." New Yorkers read of the tragedy in their own newspaper on February 18, and Philadelphians learned of the incident a few days later.[54]

The journalistic discretion reflected in the *Gazette* and *News-Letter* implies that the editors may have heard rumors about the findings of the inquest jury that viewed Osborne's body, which had been "lying dead at the house of the widow Arnold." Eighteen men had been summoned to determine Osborne's cause of death, among whom was Walter Cranston, whose involvement as the recent purchaser of the house in dispute suggests that perhaps the coroner might have made a more judicious choice of jurors. In any case, all the members of the inquest jury agreed they could not "tell who fired the gun off."[55] While they and the reading public gossiped about the matter, Samuel Banister once again sat in jail, this time to await his trial for murder.

The Superior Court of Judicature heard Samuel Banister's case at the end of their March 1745 term. His indictment was standard, although the case record referred to his weapon as a "Hand Gun (commonly called a small Arm)," rather than a musket as reported in the Boston newspaper. Whatever the weapon, Banister insisted the gun went off accidentally when Captain Griffith charged him, and, not surprisingly, he pleaded not guilty.[56] Banister went to trial before twelve of his fellow townsmen—some of whom had probably brushed shoulders with him at one time or another, and all of whom had certainly heard about the incident. The prosecution relied on witnesses who described Banister's volatile and aggressive behavior in the days prior to the shooting. In the face of Banister's intransigence, Martin Howard had warned Banister that the sheriff could command "50 or 500 men," or even "the whole County" to dispossess him, to which Banister rejoined that "he had a gun Charg'd" and would use it against anyone entering his house. Howard tried "to Diswade said Banister . . . telling him the Danger of such Rash attempts and that if he Should in his passion Kill a man the Consequence would be Desperate." Banister refused to listen.[57]

Brice Eccles, who had testified for Banister during the Brett dispute, deposed that the bad blood between Banister and William Dyre was both deep and of some duration. In mid-January, after Eccles offered Banister "all the Service" he could in one of Banister's nonstop torrent of civil cases (this one involving Nathanael Langley), Banister "Begun to talk of ye ill Triatment that he Received of Mr. Dyer & further said that his gun was then loaded with a brace of balls In order to blow his brains out." Eccles "Expostolated with him about ye haineousness of the Crime what a barbarous thing it was in its nature." In an effort to minimize Banister's aggressive tendencies, perhaps, Eccles concluded by saying that Banister "was well satisfied" with Eccles's "Discourse," and the two men parted.[58]

There may indeed have been long-standing hostility between Dyre and Banister, which only exacerbated the tension in the fading daylight of January 21, 1744/45. Dyre's testimony, sworn to on January 23, differs from Peleg Brown's in a small but significant way and suggests that Dyre wanted Banister held accountable for Osborne's death. Brown's version of the events that day states that "The Gun that said Banister had in his Hand was fired off upon which the said James Osborne immediately fell between the Steps which were much broke." Dyre, however, testified only that Osborne "immediately fell." This small discrepancy might have been overlooked if Dyre had not deleted the rest of the sentence he originally dictated. Although difficult to read through the quill marks designed to obliterate his words, Dyre's account appears to have initially confirmed Brown's statement about Osborne falling through the steps, a mishap that could have contributed to his death.[59]

The jury was left to decide by what means Osborne died. Did Banister deliberately fire his weapon, or did the gun discharge accidentally in the scuffle? Did the bullet wound in Osborne's upper left thigh cause him to bleed to death, or was his lacerated leg the result of his fall "between the Steps"? Despite the ambiguities—or perhaps because of them—Banister's lawyers prevailed, and the jury acquitted Banister. The court discharged the defendant, requiring him to pay the "Charges of Prosecution and all lawful fees."[60] Given his past reluctance to obey court orders, it is unlikely Banister ever did so.

Indeed, all the hefty costs of Samuel Banister's trial appear to have borne by his brother John.[61] Lawyers' fees took the lion's share of the expenses: "for Pleading his Case at his Tryale" Mr. Read of Boston (possibly John Read) charged £150, a staggering sum by eighteenth-century standards but no doubt compatible with this lawyer's reputation. At least one pretrial meeting with Read took place in the attorney's hometown, a trip that cost John Banister over six pounds to hire a horse and send one Harrison "to Boston to Consult Mr. Read." Read apparently took advantage of a travel allowance as well, and John Banister covered "Mr Read's Expenses etc at the ferry," which amounted to three pounds, thirteen shillings. John Banister may even have hosted Read in Newport while the latter pleaded his brother's case. John's ledger includes six pounds for "family expenses for 1 Doz. French Wine when Mr. Read was here at S. Banister's tryal," as well as eight shillings "for a quarter of lamb." John's ability—and willingness—to purchase French wine during the struggles between England, France, and Spain in the early 1740s only confirms that a well-stocked wine cellar took priority over the risks of privateering.

A later entry in John Banister's ledger suggests that Read was not Samuel's only lawyer. According to his cash book, in September 1745 John Banister paid fifty pounds for "expenses of S. Banister's Prosecution per Thomas Ward, Esq. for discount with Major Martin in full of his fee for pleading the Case etc." But attorneys' fees were only part of the cost of prosecution. Samuel's "prison fees" came to fifty-two pounds, a sum indicating the degree of comfort Banister enjoyed while imprisoned. Indeed, John may even have sent over some special delicacies to celebrate the birth of his second son and namesake, who was baptized in Trinity Church on March 18, 1744/45.[62]

What role the fifty-nine-year-old Samuel Banister senior played during his nephew's trial—or what he thought of his nephew's behavior during the early 1740s—is unknown. That he was in financial distress himself is clear from John Banister's ledgers, but the elder Banister's death somewhere on or about March 29, 1744/45, must have unsettled Samuel junior and John, coming as it did scarcely weeks after John junior's birth and in the midst of Samuel's trial. His funeral expenses, paid by John, came to ten pounds, a sum that included the mandatory gloves distributed as souvenirs to the attendees. In 1750, after considerable difficulty, John was granted administration of his uncle's estate, which, for all the delay, amounted to very little.[63]

After his acquittal, Samuel Banister, still in his early thirties, decided to make a new life for himself and his family in Connecticut. With the help of his brother, he acquired land in Stonington, just west of the Rhode Island border, and removed there sometime after his trial. He continued to conduct business with John, who remained in Newport, although distance did not improve their relationship. What information precipitated John's angry letter of May 26, 1748, is unknown, but whatever Samuel revealed in his own letter of May 21 set John off. "You have meet with the fate all men of your ungreatfull Principles ought to doe," John responded to his brother. "What I have to add is in few words namely that I wont directly or Indirectly Act or assist many affairs with you until you Execute the Instrument Draughted of John Read Esq . . . further if this affair [is not] finish'd so as to Commence a Suit at the next Inferior Court I will accommodate matters with those in Possession . . . let me have an [answere] emeadiatly."[64] A less contentious document connecting John and Samuel is John's memorandum of "Books Rec'd from Stonington December 11, 1753." Among the historical, literary, and religious works that had been, presumably, in Samuel's library was a volume titled *Bookkeeping Methodized,* a sign that Samuel had taken his onetime profession seriously.[65]

Samuel Banister seems to have died in Stonington sometime during the spring of 1755. Not surprisingly, John administered his brother's estate, such as it was. Indeed, the notice posted by John Banister in a Boston newspaper may have been ordinary in tone, but it was a fitting sequel to Samuel's life: "Those who have just Demands . . . against the Estate of Samuel Banister, late of Stonington . . . are desired to send in such their Demands to John Banister of . . . Newport." And with a nod to legal niceties (albeit with a shrug to reality) he added, "Those indebted are also desired to pay the same."[66]

In 1767, when John composed a lengthy will distributing his own very substantial and valuable estate between his two sons—except for "two Negro Slaves," who were to be set free three months after his death—he left only a token to his niece "Susannah Banister, Daughter of my brother Samuel Banister." If Susannah lived ten years after John's decease, she would inherit "£5 Lawfull Money." To put this sum in perspective, his son Thomas would receive fifteen hundred pounds sterling (as well as extensive property and slaves), and his housekeeper fifteen pounds—the latter bequest to take place six months after his death.[67] Susannah did, in fact, live long enough to collect that munificent sum from her uncle, who died in the late fall of 1767. She was admitted to the First Congregational Church in Stonington in 1764 and was married there in 1783 to John Jones, when she must have been in her mid-forties.[68]

While Samuel Banister used the law to further his own ends, the law took over Samuel Banister's life. As it did so, the system drew more and more people into Banister's circle, shaping relationships and creating dynamics among relatives, friends, employees, and business associates. The mentalité of this seaport community provided the script for this merchant's tale, and these same governing principles—collectively speaking, Newport's legal culture—sped the story to its denouement.

On the most elementary level, Banister's legal problems concerned his unpaid debts. He was constantly involved in litigation after his arrival in Newport, almost always because he refused or was unable to meet his obligations. Between 1741 and 1744 his overlapping cases traveled the entire length of the judicial system. At each stop Banister's debt increased as the court tacked the costs of litigation onto the amount in controversy. Yet the simplicity of the underlying disputes was deceptive. The notion—the expectation—that debts should be repaid and that creditors were entitled to demand satisfaction from a recalcitrant debtor in a court of law propelled a sequence of events that ended in tragedy. Banister's frustrations were surely intensified by the mounting pressures of his legal losses.

Samuel Banister's troubles were also closely connected to the growing literacy of New England. In the seventeenth century, transactions were often made informally and sealed with a handshake. By the middle of the eighteenth century, however, people were more likely to rely on an assortment of daybooks, cash books, account books, and ledgers rather than a sometimes shaky memory. And a page covered with names and numbers was more persuasive than an unreliable memory or unprovable assertions in court, leading, no doubt, to a larger number of plaintiffs' verdicts. Time and time again book evidence determined the outcome of a case. Truth in lending—indeed the very concept of a bargain—changed with every stroke of the quill.

But the written record did not resolve one of the more thorny issues of debt litigation. How long was too long when a person did not pay his or her bills? How long should Dr. Brett have been expected to carry Samuel Banister "on the books?" How long should the butcher, baker, or candlestick maker have allowed a customer to charge merchandise without payment? A year? Two years? And was the interval a generally recognized community decision? Or did it vary from situation to situation? John Brett and Samuel Banister were friends in addition to their doctor-patient relationship. Because of their social connection, Brett must have allowed Banister considerable leeway before going to law to settle their differences. Banister's resistance, which ultimately forced Brett to resort to the legal system to obtain payment, strained their friendship. It was apparently repaired when Banister subsequently testified on Brett's behalf in another case, but the sequence of events testifies to the way in which litigation damaged long-standing associations.

Samuel Banister's reputation suffered, no doubt, as a result of his failure to conform to community expectations. The legal judgments against him, along with his defaults, would have made it increasingly difficult to obtain credit and conduct business. And if people spoke of Banister disparagingly—as a man from whom payment was difficult to extract—such negative perceptions would have put his personal life in jeopardy as well. He was unable to find a home to let, a problem made not out of a housing shortage, but rather because his track record made him an undesirable tenant.

Furthermore, by forcing Banister's eviction, the sheriff and his deputies were, at the same time, attacking his masculinity. Banister was a head of household, an eighteenth-century patriarch, and as such he was expected and obligated to provide for his family's welfare. By compelling him to abandon the premises in the absence of another dwelling to which he could relocate his wife and children, the authorities effectively emasculated Samuel Banister. He resisted them to the end, declaring "he would not have his wife and family Sacraficed to be Turn'd out in the Snow."[69] In this context, Banister, as a husband and father, must have seen himself as a failure. The jailhouse shielded him from the elements but offered no shelter for Mary and his three daughters. Under what roof they spent the remaining weeks of winter is unknown.

Perhaps John Banister took his sister-in-law and nieces into his own home. Such a step, even if done with ill grace, would have been in character, since John had constantly thrown his brother lifelines in the past. After Samuel's arrival in Newport, John had given him credit, lent him money, put up bail, and paid his legal fees. In another sense, then, the law dictated and mediated the relationship between these two brothers. There can be little doubt that Samuel would have liked to emulate John's lifestyle as an independently successful merchant. Instead, as a debtor, Samuel lost his independence, a reversal that made him indebted to and dependent on his older brother.

Could John Banister have looked the other way? Probably not. His reputation was also at stake in this community of something under fifty-five hundred people, and it is likely that he would have been expected to lend assistance to a brother whose fortunes had ebbed.[70] Indeed, apart from the murder trial, Samuel Banister's story must have been repeated time and again in countless families as debt litigation drew in tangible and intangible resources from extended families. Not every household could count on a John Banister, but most families must have had someone to shell out a month's rent or make a mortgage payment, or pay a bill so that a sister, father, aunt, son, or daughter could avoid the humiliation and expense of a courtroom appearance. This familial support system was also a product of the community's legal culture, and an example of how the governing principles of that society created a ripple effect that made an impact on the lives of so many people.

Samuel Banister's debts are an integral part of a society on the cusp of the modern era. The conversion from indentured servitude to wage labor had begun by the 1740s, as had the transition from an economy based on barter and landed wealth to one rooted in cash and paper assets. Because of this evolution, property transactions and issues related to inheritance became more complex, especially when the potential heirs were illegitimate children, as they are in the following chapter.

Thomas Harris wrote a will before his death in 1791, but his brother James, who was the executor, did not carry out its provisions. Thomas Harris's ghost followed the sequence of events and prodded his old friend, William Briggs, to intervene on behalf of Harris's children. That a ghost would take an interest in a property dispute sets him apart from seventeenth-century spirits whose expertise was murder and mayhem. At the same time, it confirms that modern ghosts were well tuned into the economic needs of the late eighteenth and early nineteenth centuries, and that the public still found them useful as legal tools.

CHAPTER 6

A Ghost Story

This is a ghost story. And because ghosts evolve along with the society in which they appear, the apparition in this tale of lechery and greed reflects the eighteenth rather than the seventeenth century. The spirit does not return to avenge a bloody murder, nor is he a night prowler. More aggressive than Casper, less terrifying than Banquo, this ghost is persistent but nonthreatening. He appeals to reason, reminds of promises, and persuades with assurance. His goal is the settlement of a 1796–97 civil suit that involved former lovers, four illegitimate children, and the proceeds from an estate. And if the waning years of the eighteenth century are remarkably late for a ghost to involve himself in mundane legal affairs, it is no less true that his testimony was central to the resolution of a case that aroused considerable gossip in Queen Anne's County, Maryland.

To be sure, there was little that set Queen Anne's apart from the counties that bordered it to the north, east, and south, and nothing at all that might encourage a traveler—human or otherwise—to pause there. Indeed, there was no particular reason for a roving apparition to appear in Queen Anne's County other than to resolve the local dispute that had caused a disturbance on the Eastern Shore of Chesapeake Bay. All things considered, however, the arrival of a ghost would have stirred more interest than disbelief in the 1790s, given the intellectual climate of that decade. Queen Anne's County might have been a rural backwater, but it could claim its share of cultured, educated, and wealthy people.[1] The new county seat, Centreville, may not have been London or New York, but it was within striking distance of Annapolis, Baltimore, and Philadelphia. The town may not have had a library, but contemporary literary trends were too popular to have bypassed Queen Anne's County altogether. In general, the American reading public had acquired a taste for sentimental novels, and an appetite for sinister tales of ghosts and villains. It would have been surprising, therefore, if the spirit of Thomas Harris had not been received with as much conviction as doubt by the local inhabitants. Furthermore, the less literate, as well as those attuned to the best sellers of the day, would have been drawn to this legal scenario, as the supernatural emerged from the book page to become the stuff of backdoor rumors.

During his lifetime, Thomas Harris, a middling (albeit undistinguished) farmer, appears to have had an ongoing affair with Ann Goldsborough, a woman related by birth or marriage to one of the most prominent and wealthy families on the Eastern Shore of Maryland. Although her precise identity remains obscure, their illicit relationship continued throughout the 1780s and resulted in the birth of three sons and a daughter. Harris died in 1791, just short of his fortieth birthday, and left a will bequeathing his property to his "Four Children begotten of ann gouldsbrough." The will designated Thomas's younger brother James as executor and instructed him to sell Thomas's "lands goods and Chattels" in order to support Thomas and Ann's children until they "Come to the age of Seven years old." According to the will, any additional proceeds from Thomas's estate were to be equally divided among the four youngsters. Thomas and Ann's behavior may have been scandalous—even salacious—by eighteenth-century standards, but Thomas tried to do right by his children, if not his paramour, who was conspicuously absent from his bequests.[2]

A narrative of the case indicates that the designated executor, James Harris, attempted to sell his deceased brother's property as required by the will but was shocked to learn that the seventy-five-acre estate, "Tom's Fancy Enlarged," was entailed, a turn of events that would have made James (as the next male in line) the sole legitimate legatee. Although in theory property confined by entail to a family chain could not be sold in fee simple, James's buyer was willing to slither through the legal crevices, and by spring 1793 James had pocketed the £230 proceeds originally destined for Thomas's children.[3] In the meantime, Thomas Harris's ghost (au courant and unhappy), had already begun his campaign to ensure that his children, rather than his brother, would inherit the profits from the sale.

Ghosts were fairly picky about the people with whom they struck up conversations, and in this instance Thomas Harris chose his longtime friend,

William Briggs, to set things right. Armed with intimate information di-vulged by Thomas Harris's ghost, Briggs approached James Harris and ca-joled him into divesting himself of the proceeds in favor of his nephews and niece. Alas, James (still in his thirties) died intestate later in 1793, before actu-ally transferring the funds.[4] Moreover, his widow, Mary, was not inclined to restore her brother-in-law's estate to his children, despite the alleged wishes of her deceased spouse. Mary Harris was still resistant after more than two years, forcing the state of Maryland, which had taken over guardianship of the children, to sue Mary Harris on their behalf in 1796. The case was post-poned a year, and finally tried in the spring of 1797, with four of the most renowned members of the Maryland bar acting as counsel for opposing sides. William Briggs testified in exquisite detail to a rapt audience about his conversations with Thomas Harris's ghost, and although the brevity of the surviving legal record makes the resolution ambiguous, it appears that the parties eventually reached a settlement.

In an immediate context, the legal issues in this bizarre case affected sev-eral families and dozens of people. It was, no doubt, the talk of the town in 1796 and 1797. More than that, it resisted historical obscurity, appearing in print as a judicial curiosity now and again over the course of the nineteenth century. A closer look at the record, however, reveals more than a "Remark-able Trial." It is a case filled with contradictions, legal ambiguities, incom-petent (or corrupt) lawyers, and the shadow of national political conflict. In short, it was embedded in the legal culture of early national Maryland.

The promise of testimony by a ghost (albeit through his conduit, Wil-liam Briggs) must have packed the new Queen Anne's County Courthouse in 1796 and 1797, and one can picture small groups of people gossiping on the green in front of the handsome Centreville building during breaks in the trial. It is surprising, then, that no contemporary newspaper account of the May 1797 case has surfaced.[5] In fact, the only immediate record of the case appears in a judicial docket book, which briefly notes the name, date, and possible disposition of the case.[6] Sad to say, minutes, depositions, and a judgment record are missing from the archives.

For reasons that are not immediately obvious, however, George Keatinge, a Baltimore printer and bookseller, took an interest in the story a decade later and published a remarkable pamphlet that described the case in great detail. According to the cover page, the account was constructed "from attested notes, taken in court at the time by one of the council."[7] At the time of the trial, in 1797, two distinguished jurists had represented the plaintiff (the state of Maryland): Robert Wright, who was governor of Maryland in 1807 when Keatinge's pamphlet appeared, and Joseph Hopper Nicholson, who had been appointed chief judge of the Sixth Judicial District of Maryland in 1806. In 1797, John Scott and Richard T. Earle, also prominent citizens, represented the defendant, Mary Harris. A decade later, Earle was active in politics and a member of the Governor's Council.[8] Which of these lawyers penned the notes that became the basis of the pamphlet is far from certain—and it is unclear how Keatinge obtained the notes in the first place. Indeed, since "Fryer and Rider" printed the pamphlet for Keatinge, they may have obtained the notes rather than Keatinge.

Still, by the early nineteenth century, George Keatinge had a reputation for printing (or republishing) Maryland laws or statutes and advertising them for sale in his shop. He stocked his shelves with almanacs and periodicals as well, and was occasionally drawn to "Marvellous . . . Unaccountable . . . Strange . . . Narratives." Eclectic in taste, Keatinge sold educational books for children and religious tracts for adults. Interspersed with treatises on Freemasonry were novels and advice literature. But it was the occult and sensational trials that captured his attention between 1804 and 1808, and it is in this context, no doubt, that he published the *Authentic Account* of the Harris case.[9]

Keatinge was also following literary trends. Puritan execution sermons had given way to a more secular literary genre that focused on crime narratives, a subject that eventually became eroticized later in the nineteenth century. Published in 1807, Keatinge's pamphlet treats fornicators, bastards, and lovers only by implication, although he takes a more candid approach to the central issue of the case—illegitimacy.[10]

The pamphlet outlined the case itself in a seemingly straightforward manner, although it tripped up on a few dates that should have been accurate in the original notes. Thomas Harris died in 1791, not 1790, James Harris met his maker in 1793, not two years later, and the case was brought in 1796, only to be held over until 1797 (not "tried in 1798 or 1799" as stated in the pamphlet.)[11] It is possible that the original notes were undated, although it would be surprising if Harris's date of death did not appear somewhere in the pages. In any case, the accuracy of the dates—or lack thereof—does not impeach the strange story itself.

Notwithstanding these fuzzy chronological details, Keatinge's account of the case is curious—even by eighteenth-century legal standards. "Before the jury was sworn in the case," according to the pamphlet, "it was agreed by the counsel on both sides, that nothing could be recovered in the action except the balance of the personal estate, because the land was entailed." Furthermore, the children suffered another disability: they were unable to inherit because they were illegitimate. Finally, even if the property had not been

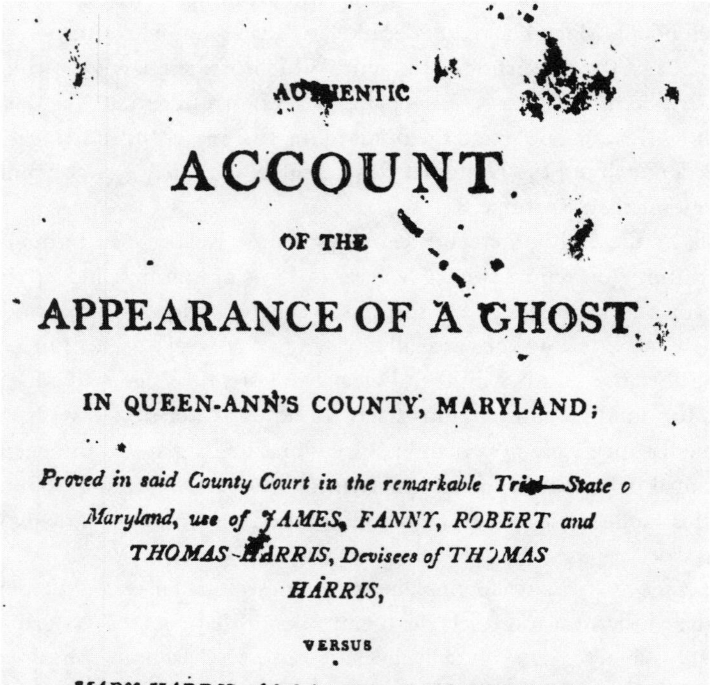

AUTHENTIC
ACCOUNT,
OF THE
APPEARANCE OF A GHOST,

IN QUEEN-ANN'S COUNTY, MARYLAND;

Proved in said County Court in the remarkable Trial—State o
Maryland, use of JAMES, FANNY, ROBERT and
THOMAS HARRIS, Devisees of THOMAS
HARRIS,

VERSUS

MARY HARRIS, Administratrix of JAMES HARRIS.

FROM ATTESTED NOTES, TAKEN IN COURT AT THE TIME BY ONE
OF THE COUNCIL.

BALTIMORE:
PRINTED FOR G. KEATINGE'S BOOK-STORE,
NO. 133, MARKET-STREET.

1807.

FIGURE 11. *Authentic Account of the Appearance of a Ghost.* Title page of George Keatinge's 1807 pamphlet about the Harris trial. Shaw and Shoemaker, Early American Imprints, second series 12018.

entailed, but rather held in fee simple, it could not devolve upon the children because "no person was appointed by the will to make sale of the land."[12] If the pamphlet's choice of words reflects the actual sequence of events, it appears that the attorneys had colluded and determined the outcome of the case before the jury was seated. Moreover, the assertions on which the case rested are questionable. First, there is no reason to believe that Thomas Harris's property was ever entailed. And as for the right of illegitimate children to inherit, William Blackstone made it clear that they could do so through a will. Taken together, the shaky foundations of these legal arguments suggest that counsel for both sides were creating obstacles in order to prevent the property from descending to Thomas Harris's children, as stipulated by his will.

In any case, entail should never even have been an issue in 1796, because Maryland abolished it in 1782, nearly a decade before Thomas Harris's death. "Any person . . . seized of any estate tail . . . shall have full power to grant, bargain, sell and convey, any lands . . . whereof he . . . shall be so seized . . . as any person seized of an estate in fee simple may."[13] It is inconceivable that all four eminent lawyers in this case were unaware of entail's demise.

Notwithstanding the elimination of entail in law, it is extremely unlikely that Thomas Harris's property had ever been entailed to begin with. Thomas's grandfather Thomas Baily (probably the person after whom young Thomas was named) had bought a slice of a parcel, "Tom's Fancy Enlarged," sometime in the past from one Fairclough Wright. Many owners held parts of this enormous tract, which did not appear to be governed by entail in any way. In 1753, Baily, "in consideration of his love and affection," gave half of his share to each of his two daughters, one of whom was Rebecca Harris, Thomas's mother.[14] Rebecca had been married to James Harris for seven years by this time, and there is no indication that the family resorted to any legal device giving her control of the property or the ability to devise it. Thus, "Tom's Fancy" was probably ruled by the usual common-law marital restrictions. Apart from any legal entanglements, however, Rebecca Baily Harris left no will, and no property by that name was mentioned in her husband's will. Interestingly, James (Rebecca's husband), left his second son and namesake (Thomas's younger brother) the family's "Dwelling Plantation," as well as the hundred-acre tract called "Crumps Chance." Although the siblings were to share equally in their father's personal estate, the only other mention of the eldest son, Thomas, was a peculiar notation at the bottom of his father's will: "Thomas the Heir at Law is now a minor, as is said!"[15] Thomas was twenty when his father died in 1772, brother James several years younger. Clearly, James was a minor as well.

We know very little about Thomas's children and even less about their mother, Ann (or Anna) Goldsborough. No document survives to explain when or how Anna and Thomas met or became lovers, why they did not marry, or when their children were born. We do not even know whether they lived together. James, Fanny, Robert, and Thomas ("Harris" in Keatinge's account; "Harris alias Goldsborough" on the judicial docket) were likely to have been born in the 1780s, since their father's 1791 will indicates that none of them had reached the age of seven by the time he died.[16] No one contested their status as illegitimate children, but how bastards inherited property from their father is another matter altogether.

According to William Blackstone, "the rights [of a bastard] are very few . . . for he can inherit nothing . . . he cannot be heir to anyone." At the same time, "all persons being seised in fee-simple (except feme-coverts, infants, idiots, and persons of nonsane memory) might by will and testament in writing devise to any other person" their landed property. Blackstone's magnum opus thus allowed illegitimate children to receive by will what they could not inherit from an intestate.[17] In other words, if a father left no will, his illegitimate son or daughter would be barred from inheriting, but a written will would trump this prohibition and allow a father to bequeath property to his progeny. It is likely that Harris knew this. Alas, for unknown reasons, none of the lawyers made any attempt to interpret Blackstone in such a way as to carry out Thomas Harris's last wishes.

Moreover, the argument that Thomas "did not . . . appoint any person to make sale" of his land is specious at best. True, the will did not say in so many words that his brother James should sell "Tom's Fancy," but Thomas did appoint James Harris as his executor, and the will did specify that Thomas's "lands goods and Chattels" were to be sold at auction. A reasonable person might conclude that Thomas expected James to arrange the sale. At the time of the trial in 1797, the lawyers on both sides seem to have gone out of their way to be unreasonable. Besides, "this understanding of the council was known only to themselves," a bond of confidentiality among the lawyers that prevented pertinent information from reaching the litigants.[18] Obviously, Thomas Harris had to return from the grave to take matters in hand.

After reducing the case to its essential elements in the pamphlet's prologue, Keatinge moved on to the trial testimony itself—evidence that had been a matter of great curiosity a decade earlier. According to the narrative, "the public were anxious to hear" more of "the extraordinary reports" that had been "circulated out of doors" about the apparition's conversations with William Briggs. The forty-three-year-old Briggs, a former Revolutionary War soldier, was allegedly "a man of character, of firm, undaunted spirit."

Maybe so, but his statement that he was "perfectly disinterested between, and unconnected with the parties" leaves room for doubt. William Briggs and Thomas Harris were lifelong friends and Queen Anne's County farmers.[19] Briggs's testimony, as related in the pamphlet, is too rich to be abridged or paraphrased. Thus, after identifying himself and beginning his sworn testimony with information about Thomas Harris's date of death, he offered the following account:

> In the March following [Thomas Harris's death] he [Briggs] was riding near the place where Thomas Harris was buried, on a horse which formerly had belonged to Thomas Harris; after crossing a small branch, his horse began to walk on very fast—it was between the hours of 8 and 9 o'clock in the morning; he was alone; it was a clear day; he entered a lane adjoining to the field where Thomas Harris was buried; his horse suddenly wheeled in a panel of the fence, looked over the fence into the field where Thomas Harris was buried toward the graveyard and neighed very loud; witness then saw Thomas Harris coming towards him in the same apparel as he had last seen him in his lifetime; he had on a sky blue coat; just before he came to the fence, he varied to the right and vanished; his horse immediately took the road—T. Harris came within two pannels of the fence to him—he did not see his features, nor did he speak to him. He was acquainted with Thomas Harris when a boy and there had always been a great intimacy between them. He thinks the horse knew Thomas Harris, because of his neighing, pricking up his ears and looking over the fence.
>
> About the 1st of June following he was ploughing in his own field, about three miles from where Thomas Harris was buried; about dusk, Thomas Harris came alongside of him and walked with him about two hundred yards; he was dressed as when first seen; he made a halt about two steps from him; John Baily who was plowing with him came driving up and he lost sight of the ghost—he was much alarmed; not a word was spoken; the young man, Baily, did not see him—he did not tell Baily of it; there was no motion of any particular part; he vanished; it preyed upon his mind so as to effect his health. He was with Thomas Harris when he died, but had no particular conversations with him. Sometime after as he was laying in bed, about eleven or twelve o'clock at night, he heard Thomas Harris groan; it was like the groan he gave a few minutes before he expired; Mrs. Briggs, his wife, heard the groan—she got up and searched the house; he did not, because he knew the groan to be from Thomas Harris. Some time after, when in

bed, and a great fire light in the room, he saw a shadow on the wall, at the same time he felt great weight upon him. Some time after when in bed and asleep, he felt a stroke between his eyes, which blackened them both; his wife was in bed with him and two young men were in the room: the blow awakened him and all in the room were asleep; is certain no person in the room struck him; the blow swelled his nose. About the middle of August he was alone, coming from Dicky Collins's, after dark, about one hour in the night, Thomas Harris appeared, dressed as he had seen him when he was going down the meeting-house branch, three miles and a half from the grave-yard of T. Harris. It was star-light; he extended his arms over his shoulders; does not know how long he remained in this situation; he was much alarmed; T. H. disappeared; nothing was said; he felt no weight on his shoulders; he went back to colonel Linsi, and got a young man to go home with him; after he got home he mentioned it to the young man; he before this time told James Harris that he had seen his brother's ghost.

In October, about twilight in the morning, he saw T. Harris about one hundred yards from the house of the witness: his head was leant on one side; same apparel as before; his face was towards him; he walked fast and disappeared; there was nothing between them to obstruct the view; he was about fifty yards from him and alone; he had no conception why T. H. appeared to him.—On the same day, about 8 o'clock in the morning, he was handing up blades to John Baily, who was stacking them; he saw T. H. coming along the garden fence, dressed as before; he vanished; and always to the east; was within fifteen feet of him; Baily did not see him; about one hour and a half afterwards, in same place, he again appeared coming as before; came up to the fence, leaned on it within ten feet of the witness, who called to Baily to look there, (pointing towards T. H.) Baily asked what was there; don't you see [T.] Harris?—does not recollect what Baily said; witness advanced towards T. Harris; one or the other spoke as witness got over the fence, on the same panel that T. H. was leaning on. They walked off together about five hundred yards; a conversation took place as they walked on; he has not the conversation on his memory; he could not understand T. H. his voice was so low; he asked T. H. a question, and he forbid him; witness then asked why not go to your brother instead of me? T. H. said, ask me no questions; witness told him his will was doubted; T. H. told him to ask his brother if he did not remember the conversation which passed between them on the east side of the wheat stacks, the day he was taken with his death sickness; that he then declared that he wished all his property should be kept together by James Harris until his children arrived at age, then the whole should be sold and divided among the children, and should not be immediately sold, as expressed in his will; that he thought the property would be most wanting to his children while minors, therefore he had changed his will, and said that witness should see him again; he then told witness to turn, and disappeared; he did not speak with the same voice as in his lifetime; sometimes could not understand him; he was not daunted while with T. H. but much so afterwards. Witness then went to J. Harris, and told him he had seen his brother three times that day, and related the conversation he had with him; asked James Harris if he remembered the conversation between him and his brother at the wheat stacks: he said he did, and told him what had passed; said he would fulfil his brother's will; he was satisfied that witness had seen his brother, for that no other person knew that conversation. On the same evening, returning home about an hour before sun-set, T. H. appeared to him; came along side of him; witness told him that his brother said he would fulfil his will; no more conversation on THIS subject; he disappeared. He had further conversation with T. H. but not on this subject; he was always dressed in the same manner; he has never related to any person the last conversation, and never would.

At this point, Baily took the stand, corroborated Briggs's narrative, and confirmed that he, Baily, had seen no one.[20] Following Baily's testimony, the lawyers prodded Briggs to reveal his remaining conversation with the ghost. Briggs zealously refused, and the lawyers countered with the argument "that as a religious man, he was bound to disclose the whole truth." Briggs appeared agitated and "declared nothing short of loss of life should make him reveal the whole conversation, and claimed the protection of the court, that he had disclosed all he knew relative to the case." The court overruled the attorneys and did not force Briggs to divulge any further discussion with Harris. So ended the testimony (and the pamphlet), except for a list of personnel: Hon. James Tilghman, judge; Robert Wright and Joseph H. Nicholson, counsel for the plaintiff; John Scott and Richard T. Earle, counsel for the defendant.

There is no indication that the case went to the jury. Instead, it may have been settled shortly after Briggs's testimony, according to the terse entry in the docket: "Trial Friday 12th May Judgt. Agreeable to Terms filed. [Rept] filed."[21] Just what those terms were is lost to history, but in the absence of an appeal by the state, it is likely that Briggs's testimony affected the terms

FIGURE 12. Queen Anne's County Court House, Centreville, Maryland, where the Harris trial took place. The original building was constructed between 1791 and 1794. Courtesy Maryland Historical Society.

of settlement in favor of Harris's four children. Nevertheless, there are curious aspects to Briggs's testimony that suggest it was a carefully orchestrated device designed to bring about that end—leaving the question of the apparition's honesty ambiguous. It is impossible to know whether Briggs saw a ghost, thought he saw a ghost, or made up the entire tale in order to secure a predetermined outcome. It is equally impossible to know how much of this strange narrative the judge, jury, lawyers—or anyone else—believed.

In some ways, Thomas Harris was a perfectly ordinary ghost. He appeared to one person rather than a group of people; he confronted someone he knew rather than a stranger. Only the person he sought had the ability to see him. The apparition had a purpose in mind, and once his mission was accomplished he did not linger to socialize. Notwithstanding the similarities of this narrative to others of the same genre, however, Briggs's account lacks spontaneity. Rather, it signals that Briggs had put considerable thought and effort into its construction.

In order to achieve his purpose and establish credibility, Briggs knew that Thomas Harris's identity had to be firmly established. Thus, Briggs relates that not only did he recognize Harris, but so, too, did Harris's former horse. Briggs verifies the clarity of the environment—his vision was unimpaired. Most of the visitations took place during daylight hours, but even at the one nighttime meeting the stars shone. Nothing obstructed Briggs's view, and the ghost's proximity to Briggs left no doubt in Briggs's mind as to his identity. Furthermore, Harris could be recognized by his clothing. On six occasions the ghost appeared in the same apparel that Harris had worn in his lifetime (which seems to confirm that this ghost did not attempt to dazzle with a sartorial display). But whether, as one subsequent editor disdainfully noted, the ghost had "very bad taste" is rather beside the point.[22] Briggs clearly believed that the apparition was Thomas Harris.

At the same time, Briggs planted tiny seeds of doubt. It was his word alone, and he admitted he did not see Harris's features. The ghost spoke in a low voice—so low, in fact, that Briggs could hardly hear him. Indeed, Harris did not speak with the same voice as he did during his lifetime, and sometimes Briggs could not understand him. Yet, it is not surprising that Briggs opened the possibility of mistaken identification. Perjury was a serious crime, and if challenged in court, Briggs could claim mistaken identity rather than deliberate deceit.

In some ways, Briggs was appealing to communal memory and a time when oral testimony was unconditionally accepted into evidence. Before early American courts were flooded with documents written by an increasingly literate population, before rules about hearsay triumphed over conversations between family and neighbors, before the "rock" near the "oak tree" was measured by metes and bounds, juries solved property disputes by relying on what witnesses had seen and heard in the past. It was no longer the seventeenth century—indeed, it was nearly the dawn of the 1800s, but William Briggs was trying to convince the court that words between brothers—words that he, Briggs, was not initially privy to—should supersede a written will. By spring 1797, Briggs could not turn back the clock; the property had been sold and recorded. But he could appeal to Mary Harris, through her brother-in-law the ghost, to do the right thing.

From a modern perspective, however, the most interesting aspect of the narrative is the way Briggs built tension into the story, in much the same way that Alfred Hitchcock captured an audience in his films. Thomas Harris was silent at first. He said nothing during his first appearances. Briggs was much "alarmed," and troubled. He was attacked by an invisible assailant at night at home and manhandled outside at dusk. Imagine what Briggs's audience visualized: shadows from the fireplace dancing on the wall in the depth of night. (That it was June in Maryland and Briggs was unlikely to have kept

a fire going into the night hardly detracts from the tale.) Surely the spectators in the crowded courtroom were spellbound. What would happen next?
When would the ghost speak? What would the spirit reveal? What was the
mysterious conversation that Briggs ultimately refused to disclose?

Harris's apparition finally spoke to Briggs after six silent approaches, but
Briggs, oddly enough, maintained he did not remember the substance of
that initial conversation. Harris forbade Briggs from asking questions. Finally, Harris's purpose became clear: he wanted to change his will. To that
end, the ghost related an earlier conversation he had with his brother James
(during his lifetime), in which Thomas declared that instead of immediately
selling his property, as stipulated in his will, he wanted his brother to maintain it whole after Thomas's death, until his children came of age. Exactly
when Thomas Harris (or his conduit, William Briggs) began to regret the
sale of the property cannot be determined. Nevertheless, since the estate
had already been sold years before the trial, this change of heart was a moot
point—except that it confirmed Thomas Harris's ongoing concern with his
children's welfare from beyond the grave. Besides, enforcement of such a
postmortem codicil would have been a legal stretch despite the murky law
that seems to have governed this case.

It was enough that James Harris, apparently convinced that Briggs had
actually conversed with the ghost of his dead brother, agreed to carry out
the provisions of his brother's will, which presumably meant returning the
proceeds of the estate to Thomas's children. Yet James's actual intentions,
in words paraphrased by William Briggs, are somewhat ambiguous—if not
deceptive. James told Briggs "he would fulfil his brother's will," and Briggs
in turn relayed that information to Thomas Harris's ghost: "James would
fulfil his will." But what exactly were those words meant to convey? Did
James mean "will" in the sense of his brother's recent revocation and retraction (and that he would do his brother's bidding), or "will" as in Thomas's
original last will and testament? Would James turn over the money or
not?

If James actually intended to return the proceeds of the estate to Thomas's
children, his willingness to do so presumably arose from a profound sense of
guilt, a fear of community disapproval, or his belief that no one knew of the
1791 conversation between brothers except the two men themselves. And
since that conversation purportedly occurred on the day Thomas died, the
timing closed a loophole in Briggs's testimony. Should any skeptics suggest
that Thomas had revealed to Briggs the substance of that tête-à-tête with
his brother, Briggs could remind them of his sworn testimony that he "had
no particular conversation" with Thomas on his deathbed.[23] During Harris's

last visit as an apparition, Briggs told him that James had agreed to comply with his deceased brother's wishes, but being a ghost, Thomas Harris probably knew that already.

That Briggs controlled the carefully crafted narrative is not to be doubted. He, after all, decided what the ghost would say and when he would speak. Yet there was little precedent for Briggs to follow: in the past, ghosts specialized in criminal, rather than civil, cases. Yet late eighteenth-century ghosts had matured, and with that maturity came responsibilities congruent with post-revolutionary American society. By 1797, William Briggs knew that apparitions now intervened in civil as well as criminal matters, and his testimony reflected that awareness. Exactly when supernatural duties underwent a change is unclear, but before the nineteenth century was well under way it was understood that ghosts were commissioned to oversee "the restitution of money unjustly withheld from an orphan or widow."[24] It must have been plain to all concerned that ghosts were keeping pace with the changing nature of the American economy.

With this transformation in mind, the timeline—the several appearances of the ghost—must be understood in the context of Thomas Harris's death (August ? 1791) and the sale of his property by James Harris in January 1793. Thomas Harris's ghost first sought out William Briggs in March 1792, approximately seven months after Thomas's death. During that interval, Harris's will had been probated and his estate inventory registered. Between March and mid-August 1792, Harris's ghost had visited Briggs three times, and at some point during this same period, Briggs told James Harris that he had seen his brother's ghost.

It is likely that by this time James Harris had learned that his brother's property was allegedly entailed, but despite this legal roadblock, he entered negotiations for the sale of the estate. Accordingly, it was in the midst of these negotiations that Thomas Harris's ghost intervened in October 1792 and appeared to Briggs four times on a single day. Harris-as-ghost finally clarified his position: he did not want the property sold. The sale was consummated nonetheless, and the indenture, signed January 5, 1793, was recorded the following May. If Briggs, according to probable "instructions" from his deceased friend, Thomas, relayed the contents of that October 1792 conversation to James, James had ignored his deceased brother's request to keep the estate whole. Exactly when James had second thoughts, precisely when guilt overcame him and he determined to return the proceeds to his orphaned nephews and niece, is unknown. But James's death in the fall of 1793 put an end to the potential restitution and left the decision in the hands of his widow. Her resistance created the need for Thomas Harris's spirit to intervene through the testimony of William Briggs, although Briggs never revealed his reasons for interceding.

The substance of Briggs's testimony was reflected two decades later in an 1816 article entitled "Remarks on Ghosts," the content of which suggests that the cultural reworking of a spirit's actions, attitudes, and apparel may have been entrenched in American thought well before Briggs designed his script. According to this nineteenth-century treatise, "some audacious spirits" were known to appear "even by daylight," and current literature provided examples of "ghosts striking violent blows." Central to Briggs's constructed narrative was Harris's clothing, a point substantiated by the 1816 "Remarks": "ghosts appear in the same dress which they usually wore whilst living." Consistent with the rules—and confirmed by Briggs's testimony—"a ghost has not the power of speaking until it has been addressed," and "during the narration of its business, a ghost must by no means be interrupted by questions of any kind"—were admonitions Briggs either forgot or ignored.

More important, "Remarks on Ghosts" verified that ghosts did not deal directly with people who were most likely to redress a particular situation. Thus, in murder cases a ghost would not appear to a sheriff, but rather to a third party who lacked authority. Similarly, "the same circuitous mode is pursued with regard to the redressing of widows and orphans; in which cases it seems that the shortest and most certain way would be to go to the person guilty of the injustice, and haunt him continually until he be terrified into restitution. Or they might communicate with one of the worshipful judges of the orphan's court." In short, it would have been more sensible (and direct) for Thomas Harris's ghost to haunt James Harris and, after his death, James's wife, Mary. Indeed, the author of this provocative piece seems to have been aware of the Harris case, because in an interesting footnote, the editor thanked "some one of his friends, on the Eastern shore of Maryland, for an account of a ghost, whose testimony was produced in one of the county courts, some years ago."[25]

What ties this intriguing article even more directly to the Harris case is the way in which ghosts certified their credibility. To do so, they "communicate . . . some secret, known only to the parties concerned and themselves." In Briggs's reconstruction, Thomas Harris's ghost did exactly that: he revealed to Briggs the contents of a private conversation he had with his brother James just prior to his death. Moreover, late eighteenth-century apparitions were more refined and mindful of their manners than their predecessors: "they return their thanks to the agent, and sometimes reward him by communicating some secret relative to himself, which nothing will ever induce him to reveal." As William Briggs asserted, "He has never related to any person the last conversation, and never would."[26] As the author of the drama, Briggs presented the culturally defined plot with precision and played his role adroitly.

The cast of characters in what can only be described as great theater ranges from the obscure to the most prominent. Thomas Harris, the oldest son of James and Rebecca Harris, was born in St. Luke's Parish, Queen Anne's County, in 1752.[27] His siblings included two younger brothers (James and Nathan) and five sisters, only one of whom (Esther), was older than Thomas. James Sr. died in 1772, leaving a widow and several young children. Two years later only three of the eight children (Esther, Thomas, and Rebecca) had reached their majority, which was sixteen for females, twenty-one for males. By this time, Esther had married William McCosh and had left the Harris household to live with her husband.

James Sr. had willed the homestead, "Crump's Chance," not to Thomas, but to his second-oldest son, James, and it appears that some or all of the remaining family continued to live on the property, at least through the 1776 Maryland census. That tally lists James (albeit still a minor) as head of household, presumably because it was *his* property in law. How he could inherit as a minor and Thomas, the "heir in law," could not is a puzzle. The 1776 census indicates one male over twenty-one as residing in the Harris household, which was probably Thomas, since his name does not appear elsewhere in the census.[28] In any case, there are eight Harrises accounted for, which could have been mother Rebecca and her seven unmarried children.

In 1776, the family of William Bridges lived in next-door Talbot County, but it is impossible to say whether this is "our" William Briggs, even if Briggs and Bridges were used interchangeably. Nevertheless, there was an Elizabeth Briggs in St. Luke's Parish, Queen Anne's County, in the mid-1740s, and it is more likely that William was related to her and whatever family she had.[29] If so, it would explain the long-term friendship between William Briggs and Thomas Harris, since the Harris family belonged to St. Luke's Parish as well.[30]

Thomas and James Harris, William Briggs, and Robert Wright were army buddies months before the Continental Congress declared independence, serving as Minutemen from Queen Anne's County in February 1776 under the command of Captain James Kent.[31] All four were among the privates who marched from Centreville, Maryland, to the Northampton, Virginia, courthouse in early February 1776 to thwart the military plot concocted by the royalist governor, Lord Dunmore. Deprivation accompanied the trek south, however, setting off strong words of protest from the local Committee of Correspondence. "We find there is no . . . cooking utensils . . . no person . . . to pay the men their wages . . . many of the poor young men are barefooted." Equally frustrating, the men were ordered "to stay six weeks longer than they enlisted for."[32] This apparently did not sit well with Thomas Harris.

Although two Thomas Harrises took up the rebel cause, they can be differentiated by rank. *Captain* Thomas Harris led a company of soldiers; *Private* Thomas Harris remained at that lowly grade throughout the war. Captain Harris was wounded in 1778; Private Harris seems to have temporarily abandoned the war effort that year. Although Private Harris received an honorable discharge from the Continental army in 1783, his military record is nothing short of erratic. Documents suggest a cycle of enlistments, desertions, and reenlistments, showing him in and out of the Maryland line during the war years. His name appears on a 1780 list of recruits and substitutes for Queen Anne's County, indicating that he—and a brother—signed up with the Continental army as substitutes for a three-year term. His comrade in arms, William Briggs, appears as a private for a shorter period and was discharged in 1779 from the Seventh Regiment with "Twenty eight Pounds, ten shillings in Cloathing."[33]

The identity of Ann (or Anna) Goldsborough remains a mystery. A variety of women with that name appear in various genealogical and biographical sources, but it is impossible to pin down Thomas Harris's ladylove. More than a few Goldsboroughs named their daughters Ann, Anna, or Anna Maria, and of that group, several were born in the 1750s and 1760s. Some were sisters or sisters-in-law; others were cousins; a few were mothers and daughters. The genealogical data is unreliable, unless two or three Ann Goldsboroughs married the same man within a few years of each other.[34] To complicate matters still further, Goldsborough might be Ann's married name, in which case she would have been a fornicating widow or an adulteress when she took up with Thomas Harris. Since surviving records indicate she was never prosecuted for fornication, adultery, or bastardy, the exact statute she violated is probably irrelevant.

The most titillating, although undoubtedly *in*correct, option is Anna Maria Tilghman, who was born in Queen Anne's County, Maryland, in 1754, which would make her two years younger than Harris. This Anna was the daughter of Edward and Elizabeth Chew Tilghman, both of whom claimed descent from wealthy, well-established families.[35] Thomas Harris's will refers to the mother of his four children as Ann Goldsborough, a name that this Anna Tilghman took when she married Charles Goldsborough in July 1774. Anna Maria Tilghman Goldsborough would make the story much more melodramatic than it otherwise would be. Not only did she have freckles, but her husband died of an accidental gunshot wound shortly after their marriage.[36] On the other hand, although the timing of this particular Goldsborough-Tilghman match fits the story line quite neatly, it falls apart if this is the Anna Goldsborough who subsequently married the Reverend Robert Smith in 1782 or 1783 (without her father's approval). Unless she was an adulteress as well as a disobedient daughter, she was not the Ann Goldsborough whose attachment to Thomas Harris caused tongues to wag.[37]

Another appealing—and possibly more viable—option is the Ann Goldsborough who witnessed the 1792 inventory of one Robert Goldsborough of Queen Anne's County. The drama here is that twenty-five-year-old Robert died in a drowning accident in 1790 or 1791, thus ending the life of another young Goldsborough man under tragic circumstances. Since the law required close kin to attest to a decedent's estate inventory, the signature of "ann Goldsborough" at the bottom of this document suggests she was his sister, since he never married. If this is the Ann Goldsborough of the story, she lost a lover and a brother within the same twelve-month period. It would also mean that by 1788 she was the orphaned daughter of one of Queen Anne's County's most respected and influential men, and that she was alive in 1792.[38] Alas, certainty eludes us.

Once Thomas Harris, James Harris, and William Briggs were discharged from military service, they made their way back to Queen Anne's County and settled into a routine as farmers. Thomas now worked his seventy-five-acre holding, "Tom's Fancy," and James plowed the one-hundred-acre homestead, now referred to as "Crumpton." William Briggs tilled his own farm nearby. The Harris brothers held two of the less valuable parcels in the area, and in contrast to many of their neighbors, they owned no slaves.[39] Clearly, they were among the less prosperous farmers in a county where Tilghmans and Goldsboroughs possessed extensive estates and worked their plantations with slave labor. When and where Ann Goldsborough and Thomas Harris met, what the attraction was between the two, when they began an intimate relationship, and when their children were born can only be left to conjecture, although all of this must have transpired as the 1780s moved from beginning to end.

The really intriguing question, of course, is why Thomas and Ann never wed. Married couples were known to have "premature" infants, and it was no secret that many pregnant brides marched to the altar with their willing or not-so-willing grooms. Indeed, it appears that the late eighteenth century saw a greater share of pregnant brides in the Chesapeake than the years before or after.[40] Furthermore, it was quite unusual for a couple facing the birth of a child to ignore community expectations and eschew the marital state. In fact, it was probably unheard of for a couple to continue to flout the law and proceed to parent not one but four illegitimate children. Needless to say, fornication statutes frowned on such irresponsible and criminal behavior. The legal blows fell most heavily on women in Maryland, although, by the 1780s, sanctions did not include corporal punishment. Child support rather than morality was the defining issue, and the authorities demanded security from the mother unless she was willing to "discover" the father, in which case she was off the hook. If she revealed his identity, he became responsible for defraying the cost of raising a child or children born out of wedlock. The question of parental responsibility aside, no records have survived to suggest that any constable, armed with a warrant, hauled either Ann Goldsborough or Thomas Harris in front of a justice of the peace to offer security for their children's maintenance.[41] With so little evidence to assess, it is impossible to say whether this means that either one or both of them willingly accepted their financial burden according to the statute, or whether Ann's standing as a Goldsborough meant that someone close to the wheels of justice made the family scandal go away. This would not be surprising in the late eighteenth century, by which time the state was likely to leave matters involving familial disorder for the family patriarch to resolve.

The financial capacity of this couple to raise Thomas, Fanny, Robert, and James depends on which Ann Goldsborough was the culprit, how sympathetic or involved her natal family was, and whether the Harris clan helped out in any way. Whatever the circumstances were, however, the couple's status as fornicators—recidivist fornicators, to boot—gave the state opportunity to invade their lives with legal oversight that intruded upon their privacy despite the movement toward the privatization of the family. Why would Thomas and Ann accede to this? Something or someone prevented a marriage between these two people.

To say that perhaps either or both simply did not want to marry would be anachronistic, albeit not impossible. Yet in the context of postwar eighteenth-century Maryland, there is probably a better reason. No documents hint that Thomas Harris already had a wife, but Ann may have had a current or previous husband. If she were a widow with assets, only a prenuptial agreement would have permitted her to retain that property and prevent it from being controlled by a subsequent husband.

Maryland law prohibited marriage between any people "related within any of the degrees of kindred or affinity" listed in the statute—forty in all. Given the inbreeding at that time and place, it is a wonder any marriages took place at all. Or perhaps Marylanders winked at that statute too.[42] It is also possible that Ann Goldsborough was underage and her parents refused to give her permission to marry the gentleman of her choice. Without parental consent, no minister could "join" any male under twenty-one or any female under sixteen who had never been previously married. Since the two lovers continued to procreate over the years, it is likely that Ann eventually reached the statutory age—yet they still did not tie the knot. Both would have been in a position to ignore parental disapproval, an increasingly common occurrence in the late eighteenth-century Chesapeake.[43]

Perhaps instead, Ann Goldsborough was a servant, an intriguing if unrealistic possibility considering the status of the Goldsborough family. Yet no minister could marry a free person and a servant without "leave of the master or mistress of such servant." Would it have been ignominious—indeed, unthinkable—for a Goldsborough to have been a servant at that time and place? Probably so.

It is more likely that the affluence of the Goldsborough family holds the key to the story. Assuming that Ann, whoever she was, had assets from a deceased husband or potential assets from a doting father, her relationship with Thomas Harris could threaten her economic future. The Ann or Anna Goldsborough in question may not have needed parental approval to marry, or she may have been blessed with liberal eighteenth-century Chesapeake parents who were unlikely to interfere with their children's marital choices.[44] Yet a father's disapproval of a marriage partner had legal implications even if his daughter, under the law, was a free agent. He could disinherit her, a risk any Ann Goldsborough might not have been willing to take, since she could lose a share of a large estate. Her choice of a partner notwithstanding, the production of four illegitimate children was not likely to have endeared her to her natal family either. Either way, she was economically vulnerable.

No matter which way Ann turned, Maryland law boxed her in. Any dower interest in a former husband's estate would cease with her death, and as the mother of four illegitimate children by another man, the property would revert to her deceased husband's family. A will prepared by a former husband might have allowed her an income or property only as long as she remained single. In short, Ann's children by Thomas Harris would have no claim to anything from Ann's former marriage—should there have been a prior union. That issue aside, however, Ann would still have problems, since illegitimate children were unable to "inherit both real and personal estate from their mother" until 1820.[45] If she were Thomas Harris's wife, this legal prohibition would be a moot point, since the children would be legitimate. But marriage was risky: without a prenuptial agreement, coverture would prevent her from controlling her Goldsborough assets or composing a will that would allow her to bequeath those assets to whom she chose. Thus, if Ann was a wealthy widow or endowed with part of the Goldsborough fortune, she may have wanted to hedge her bets and retain her independence. Rather than exert time and energy in a prenuptial agreement that kept her assets out of Thomas's hands, she may have refused marriage to him altogether.

And what about the children? Since the state of Maryland eventually sued on their behalf, it is probably safe to assume that whatever branch of the Goldsborough tribe Ann belonged to, the family was less than eager to add the little bastards to their family circle. Nearly as invisible as their father's ghost, James, Thomas, Fanny, and Robert must have been quite young when their father died. Thomas's will indicates that none had reached the age of seven, which means that they were all born in the 1780s after Thomas returned from Revolutionary War service. The household goods listed in his 1791 estate inventory (two beds, a "Quantity" of pewter plate, some cutlery, a frying pan, an "old-pott & Tea Kettle," and a "Linen weel") hint at a possible female presence, but nothing material suggests that young children shared the rudely equipped dwelling. Yet Ann and his children might have been there nonetheless. A 1790 head count places two males over sixteen, two males under sixteen, and two females on the premises, despite the sparse furnishings. Such a group would account for all but the youngest boy, whose birth could have taken place a year later.[46] Their well-being depended on the success of his crops. The ninety-two-pound inventory of personal property places Harris above the least fortunate of Queen Anne's County farmers, but those assets, such as they were, consisted of harvested corn and wheat, farm animals, and farm equipment.[47]

Despite his unique circumstances as a parent, Thomas Harris showed enough concern for his children's welfare to provide for them in his will. After arranging for the sale of his property, Harris ordered a yearly payment to them of "twenty pounds Current money," until "thea come to the age of Seven years old," as well as an equal division of the remainder of the proceeds thereafter. It was not until 1796, five years after Harris's death, that the law compelled fathers of illegitimate children to maintain them at a rate "not exceeding 30 dollars per annum until the said child shall arrive to the age of 7 years." The language of the act suggests there must have been some common understanding prior to its passage of the amount necessary to raise a small child to that age. More interesting, the statute does not contemplate multiple out-of-wedlock births, as demonstrated by the ambiguity of the language: was it thirty dollars for each or all bastards born to one woman?[48]

Thomas Harris did not mention Ann Goldsborough in his will, other than to name her as the mother of his children. Indeed, no reference by anyone else exists to confirm her existence: not by William Briggs, nor James Harris, nor Harris's ghost. No surviving document indicates her date of birth or death, and it is even possible that she predeceased Harris. Since the state as well as the mother was authorized to bind out illegitimate children, it is possible Ann Goldsborough did not have custody of them. And if she was not their guardian or if she was already dead, it would explain why the plaintiff in the 1796–97 case was the state of Maryland. Yet no orphan or guardian records for the appropriate time period list any of the children.

Nevertheless, if the children were bound out, they would surely have been brought up with a different family model, once again allowing the state to define that relationship by choosing a specific family (with or without Ann's approval) and outlining the rights and duties of all parties. But then who would decide how Thomas Harris's assets would be allocated? Strangers? If this was the sequence of events, it would explain the ghost's change of heart when he "told" William Briggs that "he wished all his property should be kept together by James Harris" until his children became of age instead of selling it and immediately distributing the proceeds as originally stipulated in his will. It makes even more sense if the children were already living with James Harris by the time his brother's ghost made his appearance. But then James Harris died.

If illegitimate children generally took their mother's name, it is puzzling that the four children left no verifiable trace or record of their lives—given that genealogical information about the Goldsboroughs is bountiful.[49] Yet even if they called themselves Harris (as in the ambiguous case title: "Harris alias Goldsborough"), it is impossible to discern which of the many Harrises they might have been later in life.

James Harris died with considerably more property than his brother Thomas, and the differences are reflected by a more comfortable living style, as well as a female presence in the household. Among the items worth £268 were not only the usual bevy of horses, cows, and pigs, but a large quantity of flax and corn, the former suggesting that James raised a more profitable crop than his brother. This household contained not only more beds, but sheets and blankets as well. Tables and chairs, copper teakettles, a copper spice mortar, earthen jugs, wool and flax (for spinning or sale?), tinware, and a sugar box, taken together imply a higher standard of living than that enjoyed by James's brother. Moreover, James owned some books.[50]

It is surprising, therefore, that when Crumps Chance was valued at the time of Mary Harris's death in 1803, most of the structures were in such disrepair. Several log houses shared the 150-acre "plantation," one of which was "out of repair," another "almost rotten." A third was "only weather boarded . . . without doors or windows," while an "old log house" was also "much out of repair." This branch of the Harris family owned a "Negro boy," named Frise, "aged about sixteen years."[51] Given these deteriorating conditions, which were surely of some duration, it would have been in the widow's best interest to keep the proceeds from Thomas Harris's estate—and it may explain why she tried to do so. Besides, if the state of Maryland won the case, the profits would evaporate—as the orphans' court doled out money for the children's upkeep. Better to keep the proceeds in the family and let the state bear the cost of the children's support.

Four years after Mary Harris's death and ten years after this peculiar trial took place, George Keatinge published his *Authentic Account* of the case. The appearance of the pamphlet was less coincidental than timely, as were similar publications by the fourteen newspapers and one magazine that suddenly took a collective interest in the case in 1809—along with the monthly magazine that followed suit in 1810.[52] All these publications appeared in New England, New York, New Jersey, and Pennsylvania. No Maryland newspapers reprinted the story, nor, apparently, did any publication south of Maryland. Of the thirteen newspapers for which a tentative political leaning has been identified, ten were clearly in the Federalist camp.[53] Two were linked to the Republicans on the basis of article content and/or editors who had previously shown a Jeffersonian persuasion. One appeared partial to the Quids, a small group of men opposed to the policies of the Republican leadership.

Federalists and Republicans (or Democratic-Republicans or Jeffersonians) continued to snarl at each other throughout the first decade of the new century, even as the Federalist Party was on the wane. The war of words, accompanied by an occasional weapon, intensified over Jefferson's nonimportation, embargo, and enforcement acts that passed Congress between 1806 and 1809. In Maryland, as elsewhere, Federalists opposed the embargo. Initially Republicans were divided, although in the end Maryland Republicans stood against it too. While this played out, the parties were at each other's throats in 1808 and 1809. Federalists carried the state of Maryland in the 1808 election, ending up with a 43–37 majority in the House of Delegates. At the same time, Maryland's congressional delegation remained unchanged, with a 6–3 Republican majority and a slate of Republican electors.[54]

The connection between politics and poltergeist takes on greater clarity with the realization that three of the four attorneys—not to mention the judge—in the Harris case were, by 1807, prominent and highly placed Jeffersonian Republicans, and that one of them, Robert Wright, was governor of Maryland. They were all from Queen Anne's County and had social, political, and military ties going back two decades and more. The judge, James Tilghman, was a Goldsborough relation, a fact that probably raised eyebrows only slightly in 1797.[55] Yet how deliciously malicious to lampoon these Republican stalwarts by announcing to the world that they had been party to a "remarkable case," perhaps a scam, that had all the earmarks of corruption. Indeed, the title of Keatinge's 1807 pamphlet informed the reader that one of the attorneys provided the attested notes from which the published accounts of the trial were composed. A subsequent narrative, published late in the nineteenth century, identified Joseph Hopper Nicholson as that lawyer.[56]

It was former governor Wright, however, who would have been most tarnished by the cluster of publications in June and July of 1809. Wright had been forced to resign the governorship in disgrace after he pardoned eight rioters who had assaulted, beat, tarred, and feathered one Robert Beatty, a Baltimore shoemaker, "in revenge for his expressing an independent opinion"—as one disinterested pundit remarked. Governor Wright had taken a very different view of Beatty's anti-Jeffersonian opinion, however. According to the governor's pardon declaration, the Bermuda-born Beatty "abused the Americans, declaring them a set of rebels, the offspring of convicts, transported for thieving, murder or treason." Worse, Beatty's assailants were offended by his declaration that "the president and congress, were a set of French jacobites, that they supplied Bonaparte with money to carry on his war." In Wright's mind, such outrageous slander of Jefferson justified Beatty's beating, and the culprits deserved a reprieve.[57]

The uproar following the pardon was ferocious, with one high Federalist paper denouncing "the encouragement which the perpetrators of outrage received from the Chief Magistrate of the State."[58] Such was the context in which Federalist newspapers published accounts of the Harris trial. Determined to deprive Wright of further political opportunities and to make sure of the widest possible audience, six of the newspapers printed the story on page 1.[59] To this extent the Federalists were successful: Wright did not obtain the judicial appointment he ardently sought.

To connect the dots more directly, the *Connecticut Mirror,* a staunchly Federalist newspaper, prefaced its account of the Harris case with an editorial note that derided Wright:

We republish the following trial, as a curiosity in jurisprudence. How it has happened, that it should be published just at this time, is not explained. It may perhaps have some blind relation to the present circumstances of one of the counsel, lately his Excellency Robert Wright, who is well known to have passed through a scene within a few months, which may be called *civil death.* If so, the particulars of the case should be explained. In the meantime, it would be gratifying to the public to learn, whether His Excellency's horse, might not with some propriety neigh at the appearance of the ghost of a Governor.[60] Thus did a ghost enter national politics.

There is no way of measuring whether Marylanders took to heart—any more than other Americans—the late eighteenth-century enthusiasm for sentimental and seduction novels as well as gothic fiction, but the Harris-Goldsborough liaison must be seen through the lens of such literature.[61] Moreover, because our information about this couple is sparse, the temptation to speculate about their relationship against the background of late eighteenth- and early nineteenth-century fiction is overwhelming. Indeed, it is impossible to resist, even to the fringe of fiction itself. Was this a case of passion and/or seduction? Was Thomas Harris a seducer? Was Ann unable to control her emotions? Was he lustful? Was she? Thomas Harris may have been a rake, a roué, a scoundrel, but Ann Goldsborough may have been a willing participant rather than a coerced victim—unless, of course, he "ruined" her, and she had no place to go and/or no one to turn to. But with four illegitimate children, it is likely that from a post-revolutionary perspective, Ann contributed to her "downfall." Passion explained a great deal at that time, and in this case, passion ruled. Indeed, community sympathy for a passionate relationship might explain a reluctance to prosecute Harris or Goldsborough for fornication, just as a lack of parental intervention may have paved the way for the relationship to begin—and flourish.

Alas, speculation invites rebuttal. Even if familial behavior changed as the eighteenth century drew to a close, even if parents were less intrusive in their children's choice of mates (and Thomas had no father to intrude anyway), even if state intervention into family affairs had lapsed, such behavioral modifications reveal little about the effect of literature on people's lives. We know that Thomas Harris could sign his name, but we do not know whether he could scribble more than his signature or whether he could read. As for Ann Goldsborough, two documents with the signature of some Ann Goldsborough are filed among official papers, but they may have nothing to do with the woman who consorted with Thomas Harris.[62] There is no way of knowing whether Ann could read or write, or whether she had access to the romantic novels that captivated the American public. Furthermore, it is tricky business to aver that literature affected human behavior in any material way.

If adult sons and daughters in late eighteenth-century America were the beneficiaries of relaxed parenting, it is not likely to have been the result of literature's model parents, who were actually very involved in their children's lives. Clarissa's parents were meddlers, Pamela's overly solicitous. All of Emily Montague's relatives advised her about her marital prospects, Charlotte Temple came to ruin because she abandoned the moral tenets of her upbringing, and Maria Kittle's father and mother not only approved of her husband-designate but hastened the couple's nuptials.[63] Whatever Americans may have been thinking, however young adults interpreted independence, their actions do not appear to be reflective of fictional parent-child relationships. Fictive parents were involved parents.

Yet involvement cut two ways. If real-life parents were less likely than fictional parents to intrude on children making life choices—even the wrong ones—they might still have intervened at some later point as necessity arose. High-status families were well positioned to prevent the authorities from interfering in family affairs. With this in mind, the Goldsboroughs would have been able to salvage their reputation by keeping multiple fornication prosecutions off the dockets and thus away from public scrutiny. Once the appearance of Thomas Harris's ghost became a matter of public knowledge, however, it would have been impossible for even the Goldsboroughs to maintain a low profile. Moreover, the shift toward melodrama, romanticism, and sentimentality that marked theatrical performances at the time was no less responsible for giving a trial top billing where the star witness (as actor) engaged in dialogue with a ghost. The judge permitted Briggs's soliloquy in an official forum, and by entertaining (encouraging?) the lengthy testimony, the court lent its imprimatur to a melodrama that emphasized emotion, feelings, and intuition—in short, a theatrical moment. Whether Judge Tilghman (or any of the lawyers) believed in ghosts is another matter altogether. That many in the audience were believers is not to be doubted.

The judge and lawyers knew what they were getting themselves into, because even "before the trial of the cause, this case had made much noise, it having been said that the ghost of Thomas Harris had in the lifetime of his brother James Harris, frequently appeared to a man by the name of Briggs, and the reason why the ghost . . . had appeared was to compel James Harris . . . to return the proceeds of the sale of the land to the orphan's court."[64] As the plaintiff in this case, the state of Maryland (on behalf of the orphans' court and children) must have approached the proceedings with at least some degree of seriousness and would have been happy to have had the star witness on its side. The lawyers for both sides knew in advance what the testimony was composed of and took the case nonetheless. It would hardly have been in their interest to do so had they thought they would be ridiculed. In turn, the affiliation of such reputable attorneys would have authenticated Briggs's testimony. As a result, there is no indication that anyone objected to Briggs's statements on the grounds of hearsay or claimed that it was all a hoax. Besides, the ghost was rational: he did not prophesy, he did not predict dire consequences if the jury was not swayed by his story.

If, at the end of the eighteenth century, ghosts showed up on a less regular basis than they had during the Mathers' lifetime, their occasional appearances were still newsworthy. In 1796 and 1797 the American public was treated to at least two ghost-related stories, both of which emanated from Europe: *The Ghost-seer; or Apparitionist* and *The Ghost of John Young the Homicide* were published in New York at roughly the same time that the Harris case enthralled Queen Anne's County residents.[65] A year later, a Philadelphia magazine published an article on the different species of phobia, among which was "The Ghost Phobia." Although the writer indicated that servants and children were most likely to retain a belief in ghosts, the author indicated that he or she had "heard of a few instances of grown people, and of men of cultivated understandings, who have been afflicted with this species of phobia . . . witnesses who have convicted by their evidence—judges who have condemned by their influence."[66] Such interest in ghosts may also suggest a curiosity—not to mention an anxiety—about the afterlife and what it was like.

Ghost stories continued to roll off the English printing presses during the first decade of the nineteenth century, and several of them enjoyed popularity on both sides of the Atlantic. Apparitions starred in *The Three Ghosts of the Forest, News from the Invisible World, Tales of Terror!* and many more.[67] But the Harris trial and Briggs's narrative resonate most powerfully with aspects of the "gothic" novel, a genre that was critical of a commercial and individualistic culture and disapproving of the idea that men and women could govern their passions without external restraints. Ann Goldsborough and Thomas Harris succumbed to passion. If the gothic villain was greedy and materialistic, James Harris fit that bill. Central to the most popular gothic tales were property rights, disputed inheritance, legitimacy, female or orphaned victims, and the thrill of supernatural intervention. In one 1796 novel, ghosts intervened to prevent an aunt and cousin from defrauding orphaned children of their inheritance.[68] Jurors immersed in a literature that confused fact and fiction may have only dimly realized where the Harris trial ended and the gothic tale began.[69]

Indeed, it was unnecessary for townspeople, spectators, and jurors to believe in the supernatural in order to be swayed by Briggs's testimony. Fascinated by gothic novels that ensnared skeptics into believing the unbelievable—if only for the moment—Briggs's listeners could have easily succumbed to his gothic narrative of a ghost, orphans, and inheritance denied. Just as apparitions temporarily suspended rationality in Ann Radcliffe's

The Mysteries of Udolpho, so too could Thomas Harris's ghost beguile an audience conditioned to the literature of the 1790s. After all, "when the mind has once begun to yield to the weakness of superstition, trifles impress it with the force of conviction."[70] And if justice eventually prevailed in *Udolpho,* should not the Harris case end similarly?

In 1809, when newspapers reprinted the account of this "remarkable trial," most did so without editorial comment. At least one, however, showed some skepticism, although even this editor did not condemn the proceedings outright:

> There is so much of the marvelous in the following report of a trial before the Court of Judicature in Maryland, which, if it was not an occurrence of yesterday, and related with something like an official responsibility, would be entitled to just the same credit that attaches to the wonder moving stories of ghosts and goblins of the 16th century; but as it is, it becomes a matter of speculation, without much danger of alarming the faith of anyone.[71]

There is reason to believe, however, that interest in the spiritual world remained unabated in the early nineteenth century. The index to the *American Magazine of Wonders, and Marvellous Chronicle* (1809) lists nearly a dozen entries for "spirits and apparitions, proof of" or "apparitions, account of."[72] Included on the list of well over a thousand subscribers to this publication were members of some of the most elite families of Philadelphia, New York, and Baltimore. Among the less-well-known aficionados were a William Brigs and a Thomas Harris—not the originals, of course, but perhaps their sons and namesakes.

This case touches on so many facets of legal culture it is difficult to know where to begin or how to assess them. The events surrounding the story originate in a rural county on the Eastern Shore of Maryland. Over time, aspects of the case emerge on the state and national level, as one party claims it as a political tool. This in itself illustrates the way law is integrated into culture and society. Not surprisingly, a written public record and an increasingly literate population contributed to the speed of absorption and community involvement as well. People appear to have been informed about what the law demanded of them, as well as their rights under the legal system they devised and lived by. They were also aware of the ways they could circumvent the law and even ignore it, should they choose to do so. But there was a price to pay for violating community standards: Thomas Harris and Ann Goldsborough may have flouted the law, but in the end they were subject to its dictates.

If this trial was unusual to the extent that a ghost dominated the process, it was quite ordinary in terms of the number of legal matters touched by the litigation. Marriage and coverture, widowhood, inheritance, fornication, bastardy, evidence, guardianship, and child support are only a few of the thorny issues that were integral to the proceedings. At the same time, a commitment to established legal procedures or a circumvention of formal legalities alternated (or collided) on a daily basis, which only confirms that the participants used whatever means necessary to reach a desired result. And it was not only the litigants themselves who were caught up in the legal web. The extended Harris family (Thomas's children and his siblings), his brother James's widow and their children, anyone with the name Goldsborough, William Briggs, his spouse and offspring, the attorneys and judge, not to mention friends, neighbors, and curious spectators who converged on the Queen Anne's County Courthouse in the spring of 1797, were among the many people whose interests intersected with this litigation. Interest in the case propelled Thomas Harris's ghost into the next century with amended publications of Keatinge's pamphlet both in the United States and abroad. As one nineteenth-century editor concluded, "testimony as to the appearance of an actual ghost was . . . given, and solemnly received."[73] Without evidence to the contrary, one can only assume that the court took Briggs's narrative seriously.

The few surviving legal documents in this case reveal something about the people involved in the proceedings beyond the contested issues. Thomas Harris's will suggests he was committed to his children and concerned about their future welfare, knowing as he probably did that they were unlikely to inherit from their mother—her Goldsborough pedigree notwithstanding. He divided his property equally among his four children, showing no preference to his oldest son.[74]

But there is a glaring omission in Harris's will: he mentions Ann Goldsborough only in passing, as the mother of his children. Harris makes no provision for her, which he has no obligation to do, but which is surprising given their long-term relationship. The absence of a bequest to Ann Goldsborough hints that she is either dead by this time or (less likely) that she has abandoned the family. Perhaps she married someone else. It may simply be the case, however, that the law stepped in and required the state of Maryland to act as guardian for the children because they were either orphans or bastards (in this scenario both).[75] The state generally bound out such children as apprentices, but in this case no document confirms that this was the route taken. As a result, Thomas, James, Fanny, and Robert disappear from the records.

In some ways, Ann Goldsborough disappears as well. If she is conspicuously absent from Thomas Harris's will, she is even less visible in William Briggs's testimony or in George Keatinge's preface to that narrative. Indeed, she is not mentioned at all, even though the narrative would never have existed without her. This is a story overtly constructed from a male perspective, and Ann Goldsborough, as a dangerous post-revolutionary independent woman, is given no voice. Instead, the voices we "hear" are those of Thomas Harris, James Harris, William Briggs, John Baily, the lawyers who prod Briggs to reveal more of his conversation with the ghost, the judge, and George Keatinge.

Yet even if the surviving documents conceal the role women played in this drama, women are indispensable to the narrative. Ann Goldsborough, Thomas Harris's partner and the mother of four illegitimate children, sets the story in motion. But it is Mary Harris who steals the show. Her intransigence hurtles her to center stage as the defendant in the lawsuit brought by the state of Maryland. She could not have planned the sequence of events, but Mary Harris was an eighteenth-century woman who was everything her culture railed against. Her independent streak initiated the proceedings because—much to everyone's surprise, no doubt—she refused to credit Thomas's children with the assets from his estate. Why she resisted restoring their property is a question that cannot be answered, other than to speculate that her definition of immediate family was limited to her own children. We will never know whether outside forces prodded her to take the stand she did, but the lure of property ownership must have given a boost to whatever self-assertiveness and stubbornness she already possessed. For reasons that the records do not reveal, Mary may have felt that justice was on her side. Documents written by her husband and brother-in-law, testimony offered by William Briggs, and the pamphlet published by George Keatinge may have erased her voice, but the suit against her—which she forced—confirms they did not silence her.[76]

Furthermore, even if the narrative appears to exclude women's voices, it is important to remember that the involvement of other women was no less central to the legal culture of late eighteenth-century Maryland. Ann Goldsborough would not have delivered her infants alone; neighboring women would have surrounded her during labor and birth. The first time around they might have listened for Ann to disclose the identity of her partner, if such information was not already community knowledge. Legally responsible for the infant's upbringing, the father would be brought to the attention of the authorities by these "gossips." By the fourth time they were called to assist Ann through her labor, they, along with everyone else, must have been aware of Harris's paternity, and each of the infants was, by definition, a bastard—with all the legal disabilities that status implied. Whether social disabilities accompanied that status is a subject yet to be explored.

"Legitimate" and "illegitimate" were categories well defined in law. And since the right to property was at stake (whether it was Goldsborough or Harris property), keeping fornication, bastardy—or even, perhaps, adultery—charges out of court and out of the formal grasp of the law might have been worth the effort. Preventing prosecution would not change inheritance restrictions, but it might have alleviated the embarrassment to which the Goldsboroughs and Harrises were subjected. Dealing with this issue privately before it became a cause célèbre meant that the children would be less stigmatized, even if bereft of property from their mother's side.

This case thus illustrates the glaring differences between the way in which statutory (formal) law and community (informal) law operated. Fornication, the lesser of Ann and Thomas's "crimes," was a prosecutable offense, yet the authorities did not take either of them to court. Moreover, their immediate neighbors and townspeople looked the other way. Whether the Goldsborough name had clout or whether the community just did not care enough to make an issue about this romance, the fact remains that Ann Goldsborough and Thomas Harris went about their business without fear of prosecution, producing four illegitimate children in what might have been nearly a decade.

Legal issues aside, illegitimacy raises other interesting questions. Did an illegitimate child or children threaten the legitimacy of patriarchy? It is tempting to say no, because quite a few early American children were born out of wedlock, and the patriarchy showed no signs of collapsing. At the same time, whether such children were mulatto and enslaved or white and free, few white males went about proclaiming their pride at having fathered bastard children. Besides, if marriage was constructed to protect property, illegitimacy—and the concealment thereof—created difficulties for a patriarch with affection for an extramarital child who by virtue of law could not inherit. Thomas Harris was a landholder, a head of household with dependents, a defender of his country. But was he a patriarch? Was his ghost?[77]

Finally, William Briggs never explains why he needs the ghost of Thomas Harris to right a wrong. Perhaps, as Judith Richardson posits in her perceptive work on hauntings in the Hudson Valley, ghosts may symbolize those whose deaths leave guilt in their wake. Richardson's suggestion that ghosts represent contested space, conflicting ideas, and that they reflect social structures has a ring of truth as well. As for Briggs, he may not have fully appreciated the subliminal reasons that evoked his vision of Thomas Harris. Whatever those reasons might have been, Richardson is surely right that ghosts often signify the things that words alone cannot express.[78] In this case, Briggs's words became meaningful because they emanated from Thomas Harris's ghost—hearsay notwithstanding.

Epilogue

I wish I had said it first, but alas, Alexis de Tocqueville beat me to it. His insightful comments about "the shadow of the law" acknowledged Themis's power over America, a grip that caught Tocqueville's attention and captured his imagination because of its extent and depth.[1] The Greek goddess of law, order, and justice embraced America at its inception and never loosened her hold. Indeed, by 1775, the American enthusiasm for things legal had become the subject of discussion across the pond. "In no country perhaps in the world is the law so general a study . . . [A]ll who read, and most do read, endeavour to obtain some smattering in that science."[2] "Science" may have overstated the case, but Edmund Burke clearly recognized the magnetism of law.

As Themis hovered above early America and spun her magic, legal doctrines, woven across the Atlantic and tailored to meet local needs, accompanied post-revolutionary Americans as they moved west to new and fearsome territory. And as it had done previously, law offered security by making the strange familiar. Trans-Appalachian settlers could not surround themselves with all the coveted possessions left behind in the "civilized" world, but intangible legal precepts fit nicely into their mental baggage. Once resettled, emigrants tried to replicate the world they knew, just as English and Dutch colonists had done generations before. Far from their original homes, nineteenth-century Americans applied the rules and expectations that had formerly governed their lives to conditions on the frontier. As they did so, attitudes and assumptions they took for granted forged community dynamics and, on a more intimate level, individual lives. Law continued to shape life by framing and impinging on familial, social, and business relationships. Building on two centuries of colonial experience, western settlers were well positioned to define the "other"—outcasts, deviants, and villains. Having already allocated privilege by race, sex, and class, it was easy to empower some and marginalize others in new settings. Both formal and folk law worked together to integrate the past, shape the future, and establish a sense of stability in the present. Common values Americanized emigrants as they built new lives in the West.

If legal history—at least legal history as we interpret it—claims few sweeping narratives that carry early Americans into the nineteenth century and beyond, how do the six chapters in this book foreshadow the post-revolutionary United States? It is, perhaps, not too much to say that the deeply held values, as well as the themes that permeate and solder the chapters, such as property, power, family, race, and gender, are perpetuated in fresh surroundings. English colonists may not have said it as well—or as often—as the Dutch, but both groups firmly believed that justice was inseparable from order. Law was integral to both, which means that settlers integrated long-standing and deeply held beliefs about social relationships into the new western communities through the legal system. Said another way, the themes I have explored in each chapter, when extended forward, trace a continuum of small changes that nudge early Americans into the nineteenth century.

Slanderous words themselves needed no updating, even as the law of slander underwent revision. Although this is not the place to discuss such legislative or judicial changes in detail, it should be noted that sexual smears as they affected female reputation were still important components of many western legal agendas. Indeed, even before statehood, an 1813 Indiana statute permitted a cause of action for sexual slander.[3] It is noteworthy, however, that nineteenth-century slander legislation continued to link the reputation of women to their marketability as marriage partners. Accusations of sexual impropriety may have masked underlying anxieties, but the assumption persisted that "whore" was an insult that damaged marriage prospects. In legal theory, at least, sexual reputation (that is, chastity) mattered far more than the character of women as economic agents even as the economy underwent dramatic change.

Witches had largely disappeared by the nineteenth century, which meant that fewer of Satan's minions traveled along with the wagon trains as they made their way west. An 1801 opinion article in the *Vermont Gazette* indicated that when the author was a boy, "scarcely a week passed without hearing some notable tale of recent witchcraft," although "at this day we hardly hear such a tale once a month." Not everyone agreed that this was a positive development, however, since "the rising generation, having nothing to fear," would be only weakly governed. Some held increasing wisdom responsible for the demise of witchcraft, others pointed to "its decrease in the time of war."[4] Notwithstanding the possibility of enlightenment thought or warfare as factors contributing to witchcraft's decline, it is not impossible that by subjecting witches to the same legal procedures as everyone else the differences between witchcraft and run-of-the mill malevolence were demystified and minimized.

Yet if prosecutions for witchcraft decreased as the eighteenth century crept toward its close, so too did prosecutions for domestic violence. As the patriarchal culture that marked American society traveled to the frontier, domestic violence tagged along. Massachusetts banned spousal abuse at the beginning of the seventeenth century, yet those men—and it was almost always men—who perpetrated such violence in spite of the prohibition were rarely penalized for violations. Domestic assaults, prevalent in early America, were no less widespread in the nineteenth century, nor have they diminished in the twenty-first.

The story of the alleged attempted rape of Comfort Taylor by Cuff, an enslaved man of African descent, continued to resonate in nineteenth-century America as well. The Rhode Island legislation that furthered the racial chasm between white women and black men was merely a precursor to a growing racist ideology and contest over slavery that was finally played out in the territories and new western states. Colonies south of New England had passed racialized laws for attempted rape during the first half of the eighteenth century, but the isolated law that evolved from the 1742/43 incident between Comfort and Cuff was New England's only contribution to that early body of law that singled out black men. Other states would play catch-up in the post-revolutionary era, when more severe penalties for race-based sex crimes, including castration, were added to the books. As Sharon Block has noted, colonies, and then states, distinguished themselves by racializing and Americanizing British common law as it applied to rape and attempted rape. In the early republic, statute law included punishments for both black and white men convicted of sex crimes, but the punishments for white males were not as sadistic as those reserved for black men convicted of the same offense.[5]

Furthermore, if the 1743 Rhode Island law invalidated private responses to criminal actions and gave greater authority to the government to act on behalf of victims, one might speculate that a similar legal evolution took place on the frontier. In short, if during the initial phase of settlement frontier circumstances demanded frontier responses, it is likely that such informal legal devices eventually capitulated to statute law in the West as conditions stabilized. In other words, public safety may have relied on informal mechanisms of control in newly established communities before formal legislation codified the rules.

It wouldn't have done Samuel Banister much good to live another half century, since controversial laws providing relief for insolvent debtors came and went without establishing stable precedent. It is true that by 1800, when Congress passed a short-lived bankruptcy bill, Banister's moral failings would

have taken less blame for his unfortunate situation than the impersonal downward slide of the marketplace. But in terms of practical help, the ideological
shuffle did nothing to provide needed remedies, especially on the national
level. When western settlers encountered economic difficulties as they reck-
lessly rushed to gobble up land and securities or because the proliferation
of paper money was insufficient for their needs, an occasional state law, not
federal regulation, stood between them and disaster.[6]

Although most ghosts, like witches, fade into the background during the
nineteenth century, Thomas Harris's ghost has a longer shelf life. Created as
an agent to oversee the transmission of property in a changing postwar economy, the apparition ends up as a political tool. Nevertheless, the story is as
much about legal issues as it is about the spiritual world, although one is left
to wonder why so many high-powered men took an interest in a case with
so little at stake. Entail, a legal device to prevent the breakup of large landed
estates, had already been abolished in Maryland by the time the Harris case
reached the court. Even before the Maryland edict, revolutionary upheaval
had curtailed entail—albeit with some controversy—in Virginia and Georgia. Other states abolished both primogeniture and entail during or shortly
after the Revolution.[7] Why the issue arose at all in the Harris case is a mystery,
unless conservative forces in that state hoped to use an insignificant contested
inheritance case (not to mention one where entail was raised erroneously)
as a means of resurrecting a feudal institution that favored the rich. Given
the incremental efforts toward democratization in the revolutionary era and
beyond, this is an unlikely scenario, although the one person (or rather ghost)
who knows what happened refuses to confirm or deny.

More important for the thesis of this book, the western commitment to
the same values that governed the former English colonies glued succeeding
generations of emigrants to a common culture. The absence of a nationally
recognized religion may have motivated people—even subliminally—to co-
alesce under the banner of law. But whatever the reasons, ethical standards,
honed through decades of experience, were unpacked in legislatures all along
the frontier. Folk law, some of it violent, may have reached new destina-
tions first, but even so, formal judicial proceedings were never far behind.
In this way, law built communities, not from scratch but with the building
blocks of a shared ideology that bound, unified, and Americanized settlers.
That ideology had a downside, of course. Many of those who embraced it
made a distinction between people who could claim a European heritage and
those whose genetic chemistry marked them as "the other." Moreover, the
shared dedication to specific, long-standing principles included the right to

discriminate according to sex as well as to race, thus reserving the benefits of republican government, albeit temporarily, for adult white men.

During his American sojourn, Alexis de Tocqueville noted that in the United States everyone voted except slaves, servants, and paupers supported by the townships. Completely ignoring women, who were also excluded from choosing the representatives who would govern them, Tocqueville overlooked the inconvenient fact that majority rule didn't mean exactly what it implied. Nevertheless, despite Tocqueville's emphasis on male participation in the electoral process, his general statement about American commitment to law and the legal process undoubtedly applied to both men and women. "Every one," he asserted, "is personally interested in enforcing the obedience of the whole community to the law." A citizen in the minority on one issue could be in the majority on the next, thus prompting Americans to comply with each law, however "irksome" it might be. Every individual saw lawmaking as both "the work of the majority," and as "his own."[8] In such a way, Americans personalized the law.

Americans had taken this lesson to heart two centuries earlier. Satisfied with the way their legal system operated on an individual, local, and national level, western settlers in the 1800s sought comfort in a new life by replicating and extending the old. Their worldview, like a trusted wine, traveled well. As a result, the case can be made that legal history does, in fact, offer a general interpretation of the American experience.[9] More to the point, it is possible that this elusive sweeping narrative may be best demonstrated through a variety of microhistorical accounts that illustrate the dynamic intersection between people and the law. Indeed, such small stories may be among the most valuable expressions of the deeply embedded principles that were confirmed on a daily basis as settlers moved from east to west.

Notes

Introduction

1. Berthold Fernow, ed., *The Records of New Amsterdam from 1653 to 1674* [Minutes of the Court of Burgomasters and Schepens 1662–1663] (Baltimore: Genealogical Publishing Co., 1976), 4:3–6 (1662) (hereafter Fernow 1:, 2:, etc.). Legally speaking, proof of Teunis's sexual flings would have made her an adulteress, since she was the wife of Cornelis Jansen.

2. Richard D. Brown, "Microhistory and the Post-Modern Challenge," *Journal of the Early Republic* 23 (Spring 2003): 18, 19.

3. My previous book explores a single seventeenth-century incident. Elaine Forman Crane, *Killed Strangely: The Death of Rebecca Cornell* (Ithaca, N.Y.: Cornell University Press, 2002). Excellent examples of microhistory include Irene Q. Brown and Richard D. Brown, *The Hanging of Ephraim Wheeler* (Cambridge, Mass: Harvard University Press, 2003); Angela Burke, *The Burning of Bridget Cleary: A True Story* (New York: Viking, 2000); Patricia Cline Cohen, *The Murder of Helen Jewett: The Life and Death of a Prostitute in Nineteenth-Century New York* (New York: Vintage, 1999); Natalie Zemon Davis, *The Return of Martin Guerre* (Cambridge, Mass: Harvard University Press, 1983); John Demos, *The Unredeemed Captive: A Family Story from Early America* (New York: Vintage, 1995); Carlo Ginzburg, *The Cheese and the Worms: the Cosmos of a Sixteenth-Century Miller* (Baltimore: Johns Hopkins University Press, 1980); Michael Grossberg, *A Judgment for Solomon: The d'Hauteville Case and Legal Experience in Antebellum America* (Cambridge: Cambridge University Press, 1996); Cynthia B. Herrup, *A House in Gross Disorder: Sex, Law, and the 2nd Earl of Castlehaven* (New York: Oxford University Press, 1999); Donna Merwick, *Death of a Notary: Conquest and Change in Colonial New York* (Ithaca, N.Y., Cornell University Press, 1999); John Ruston Pagan, *Anne Orthwood's Bastard: Sex and Law in Early Virginia* (Oxford: Oxford University Press, 2003); James Sharpe, *The Bewitching of Anne Gunter: A Horrible and True Story of Deception, Witchcraft, Murder, and the King of England* (New York: Routledge, 2000); Simon Schama, *Dead Certainties (Unwarranted Speculations)* (New York: Vintage, 1992); Alfred F. Young, *The Shoemaker and the Tea Party: Memory and the American Revolution* (Boston: Beacon Press, 1999).

4. For a discussion of the connection between microhistory and legal history see the introduction to Christopher L. Tomlins and Bruce H. Mann, eds., *The Many Legalities of Early America* (Chapel Hill: University of North Carolina Press, 2001). In the introduction (p. 6), Tomlins considers Stanley Katz's criticism that microhistory did not result in a general interpretation of early American history. See Stanley N. Katz, "The Problem of a Colonial Legal History," in *Colonial British America:*

Essays in the New History of the Early Modern Era, ed. Jack P. Greene and J. R. Pole (Baltimore: Johns Hopkins University Press, 1984), 457–90.

5. One might argue that African Americans and Native Americans were also "bound" by these values. Nevertheless, most members of these groups did not consent to be bound by laws that codified such values. Perhaps a better way of clarifying the distinction would be to say that Euro-Americans "embraced" the values that bound them together.

6. An overview of seventeenth-century legal procedures will be found in Edgar J. McManus, *Law and Liberty in Early New England: Criminal Justice and Due Process, 1620–1692* (Amherst: University of Massachusetts Press, 1993).

7. Fernow 2:249–50 (1656–1658).

8. This was surely why Rebecca Cornell took it badly when her son, Thomas, warned her that "Her name did stinke about the Island or Country," a hint that even Rhode Islanders might suspect her of witchcraft. See Jane Fletcher Fiske, transcriber, *Rhode Island General Court of Trials, 1671–1704* (Boxford, Mass., 1998), 29–30.

9. David D. Hall, *Worlds of Wonder, Days of Judgment: Popular Religious Belief in Early New England* (New York: Knopf, 1989), 3.

1. In Dutch with the Neighbors

1. Arnold J. F. Van Laer, trans. and annotator, *New York Historical Manuscripts Dutch* [*Council Minutes, 1638–1649*] (Baltimore: Genealogical Publishing Co., 1974), 4:496–97, 360–61 (hereafter Laer 1:, 2:, etc.).

2. Evarts B. Greene and Virginia Harrington, *American Population before the Federal Census of 1790* (Baltimore: Genealogical Publishing Co., 1981), 88, 93n. Another estimate places the population of New Amsterdam at two thousand in 1643. If this is anywhere near accurate, it suggests that the Indian wars between 1641 and 1645 took a terrible toll. See Henry H. Kessler and Eugene Rachis, *Peter Stuyvesant and his New York* (New York: Random House, 1959), 17. A recently published study of New Netherland indicates that the population of New Amsterdam was approximately twenty-five hundred in 1664. Jaap Jacobs, *The Colony of New Netherland: A Dutch Settlement in Seventeenth-Century America* (Ithaca, N.Y.: Cornell University Press, 2009), 32. This is considerably more than the population estimated in a 1664 remonstrance to the director-general urging capitulation to the English. That document speaks of "about fifteen hundred innocent souls, only two hundred and fifty of whom are capable of bearing arms." E. B. O'Callaghan, ed., *Documents Relative to the Colonial History of the State of New York,* 15 vols. [Albany, N.Y.: Weed, Parsons and Co., 1853–87] (New York: AMS Press, 1969), 2:248.

3. Berthold Fernow, *The Records of New Amsterdam from 1653–1674* [*Minutes of the Court of Burgomasters and Schepens, 1653–1655*] (Baltimore: Genealogical Publishing Co., [1897] 1974), 1:31, 5 (hereafter Fernow 1:, 2:, etc.). Although some scholars who are fluent in Dutch have criticized Fernow's translation of these records, a check against the original manuscripts convinces me that the substance of the slander cases is accurate throughout. In the rare instance where a particular word has been mistranslated or is open to question, a correction has been made in a footnote. I am grateful to Virginie Adane for comparing the quotations from Fernow in this chapter against the original Dutch-language minutes.

4. Laer 4:34 (1638), 4:331–32 (1646); Fernow 3:23 (1659); 7:107 (1674).

5. Fernow 3:160 (1660); Fernow 7:9 (1673). As early as 1638, the council passed an ordinance that prohibited immorality, which included a provision against "calumny." *Laws and Ordinances of New Netherland, 1638–1674,* comp. and trans. E. B. O'Callaghan (Albany, N.Y.: Weed, Parsons and Co., 1868), 12. In the council minutes, "calumny" is translated from the Dutch as "slanderous language." See Laer 4:4(1638).

6. Hugo Grotius, *The Jurisprudence of Holland,* trans. R. W. Lee, (Oxford: Clarendon Press [1631], 1929), 481.

7. Fernow 4:1 (1662).

8. Laer 4:332 (1646); Fernow 4:234 (1663), 3:307 (1661), 7:238 (1659).

9. Fernow 1:10 (1648); Fernow 4:234 (1663); Laer 4:47.

10. Genesis, 18:29–32; William Blackstone, *Commentaries on the Laws of England* (Oxford: Clarendon Press, 1769; reprint, New York: Legal Classics Library, 1983), bk. 4, chap. 27, 352. As Voltaire explained, "'Tis much more Prudence to acquit two Persons, tho' actually guilty, than to pass sentence of Condemnation on one that is virtuous and innocent." *Zadig* (London: John Brindley, 1749), chap. 6, p. 53.

11. See Linda Biemer, "Criminal Law and Women in New Amsterdam and Early New York," for a more detailed explanation of Roman-Dutch law. This essay may be found in a collection entitled *A Beautiful and Fruitful Place: Selected Rensselaerwijck Seminar Papers,* which was published by the New Netherland Project in 1991. It is also online at www.nnp.org/nnp/publications/ABAFB/3.1.pdf, pp.73–82 (n.d.); See also Scott Christianson, "Criminal Punishment in New Netherland," www.nnp.org/nnp/publications/ABAFB/3.2.pdf, pp. 83–90.

12. These numbers were arrived at by counting cases in Laer, *New York Historical Manuscripts* (vols. 1, 2, and 4) and Fernow, *Records of New Amsterdam* (7 vols.) The total should be considered the bare minimum number of cases brought before the courts, since some were only peripherally and/or latently about injurious words. Cases that were continued on following days or weeks were considered part of the original action and were not added to the count. Although the records have been translated from Dutch into English, difficulties remain for non-Dutch-speaking historians who are familiar only with English or French documents. First, most people seem to have several names, all of which appear at various points in the records, and which are shortened or lengthened for unfathomable reasons. Second, women did not always take their husbands' names upon marriage, making it difficult to know who was married to whom, unless it was specifically noted. Sometimes married women were recorded by their married names; sometimes they were not. Since Dutch names were unfamiliar, only after a while did it become apparent to me that female names frequently ended in *je* or *ie.* I should add that the Dutch names in the sources, particularly those of women, not only take various forms but also contain erratic spellings. In order to remain faithful to the original text I have made no attempt to standardize any names, especially since the various scribes seem to have had a very casual attitude toward uniform spelling even within a single document. This lack of conformity is not to be confused with the seventeenth-century translation of Dutch into English equivalents once the English conquered New Amsterdam in 1664. For example, once the takeover was completed, Tomas Lourens would become Thomas Laurensen.

13. Maryland's population in 1650 was approximately forty-five hundred, and in 1660, eighty-four hundred. *Historical Statistics of the United States: Colonial Times to 1970* (Washington, D.C.: Bureau of the Census, 1975), 2:1168. Mary Beth Norton, "Gender and Defamation in Seventeenth-Century Maryland," *William and Mary Quarterly,* 3rd series, vol. 44, no. 1 (January 1987): 3–39.

14. Norton, "Gender and Defamation," 7–8; Greene and Harrington, *American Population,* 123. Although Maryland's population numbered in the hundreds in the early 1640s, by 1660 improving conditions permitted a consistent increase in the number of inhabitants.

15. My thanks to professor Karen Kupperman for this last insight.

16. Between 1641 and 1647, the authorities heard at least eight slander cases. Of the eight, two involved women. Seven concerned simple accusations of theft, while one of the women alleged the defendant called her a whore and thief. The remaining woman was accused of theft, and she, like the other female target, sued the male defamer directly.

17. It is also curious that slanders may have had a seasonal pattern. Women were never slandered in April or May between 1653 and 1674, and there is only one instance of a slander against a woman in July. In every other month, women were slandered between three and seven times. Women were most likely to be insulted in March (seven times) and in October (six times). Only one male was slandered in July and in December during these two decades. The highest incidence of slanders against men occurred in June (nine times) and October (ten times).

18. Fernow 6:39–40 (1666); 7:82 (1674), 4:263–64, 283–84 (1663). It is likely that the phrase "black pudding" was used as a racial slur, but it may have also meant a fool or idiot. The literal translation of *bloedt beulingh* is "blood sausage" (which has a dark cast to it). Similarly, although Fernow translated *wilden hont* (or *hondt*) as "Indian dog," the word *wilden* might also be translated as "heathen."

19. Moreover, in the Netherlands cases were more likely to consist of prosecution against people who made slanderous accusations of witchcraft. J. L. Price, *Holland and the Dutch Republic in the Seventeenth Century: The Politics of Particularism* (Oxford: Clarendon Press, 1994), 201.

20. Norton, "Gender and Defamation," 10.

21. Between 1638 and 1649 there were nine defamation cases where a woman was called whore. In eight of the cases, the defamer was male; in one, the woman proclaimed herself a whore. The plaintiff was female in four of the cases.

22. There are two recorded cases of sexual slanders against men before 1653 (in 1639 and 1645). In both cases the defamer was male. In one instance the target was a cuckold by implication; in the other a son of a bitch. See Laer 4:49 (1639); 277, 282, 283 (1645).

23. Fernow used the word "cuckold" as the translation for either *cournoede* or *hoorenbeest* (literally: horned beast). Fernow translates both *hoere kindt* (child of a whore) and *bastaard* as "bastard."

24. De Witt accused Kocks of abusing her husband "as a cuckold." Jan de Witt, Geertruyd's husband, submitted a written protest to the court in which he asked that the defendant "repair the injuries inflicted on him and his wife, honorably and profitably." Kocks denied having insulted Jan de Witt. The court's attention was directed toward the physical violence, particularly because Geertruyd de Witt was pregnant.

Nothing further came of the slander suit, and Kocks was fined for the assault. What is particularly interesting about this case is that de Witt, as a married woman, had standing to sue for an insult against her husband. Fernow 4:130, 134–35, 140, 146 (1662). Fernow's use of "lust" would be better translated as "desire" or "urge." Fernow 4:247–48 (1663).

25. Laer 2:34 (1642).

26. O'Callaghan, *Laws and Ordinances,* 12.

27. At least 26 cases out of 129 involved an assault.

28. Fernow 3:76 (1659).

29. My thanks to Paul Gilje, whose paper "To Swear Like a Sailor: Cursing in the American Age of Sail," presented at the McNeil Center for Early American Studies on May 15, 2009, alerted me to the multiple meanings of curses in early America.

30. Price, *Holland and the Dutch Republic,* 105, 107–8.

31. Firth Haring Fabend, "Sex and the City: Relations between Men and Women in New Netherland," in *Revisiting New Netherland,* ed. Joyce D. Goodfriend (Leiden: Brill, 2005), 265–66, 280–81. Nevertheless, as Fabend points out, a husband was the legal administrator of their joint estate and could alienate property without his wife's consent.

32. I would like to thank professor Susanah Shaw Romney for her insights about commercialism and sexual traffic in Amsterdam and New Amsterdam.

33. Lotte van de Pol, *Der Bürger und die Hure: Das sündige Gewerbe im Amsterdam der Frühen Neuzeit* (Frankfurt/Main 2006), 17, 14, 15. This book by van de Pol has not been translated into English, and I am grateful to my colleague Dr. Susan H. Ray for translating relevant sections from the German edition for my use. The book was originally written in Dutch and published as *De Burger en de Hoer: Prostitutie in Amsterdam* (Amsterdam: Wereldbibliotheek, 2003). Translated into English, the title is *The Citizen and the Whore: Amsterdam's Sinful Business in the Early Modern Period.*

34. Van de Pol, *Der Bürger und die Hure,* 55, 26.

35. Fernow occasionally translates Dutch words such as *cappelaarster* and *gerieff* as synonyms for "bawd."

36. Van de Pol, *Der Bürger und die Hure,* 55, 60.

37. This interpretation of Vermeer's work is drawn from a lecture by Walter Liedtke, *"The Milkmaid:* Discreet Object of Desire," at the Metropolitan Museum of Art, New York City, September 26, 2009.

38. I am grateful to Dr. Burton Blau, who talked me through these issues.

39. Wim Klooster, "The Place of the Netherlands in the West India Company's Grand Scheme," in Goodfriend, *Revisiting New Netherland,* 68, 69.

40. Dennis J. Maika, "Securing the Burgher Right in New Amsterdam: the Struggle for Municipal Citizenship in the Seventeenth-Century Atlantic World," in Goodfriend, *Revisiting New Netherland,* 108–12, 113–14.

41. Simon Middleton, "Joris Dopzen's Hog and Other Stories: Artisans and the Making of New Amsterdam," in Goodfriend, *Revisiting New Amsterdam,* 140–41n. See also Maika, "Securing the Burgher Right," 117, and Maika, "Commerce and Community: Manhattan Merchants in the Seventeenth Century," PhD diss., New York University, 1995, appendix.

42. Russell Shorto, *The Island at the Center of the World* (New York: Doubleday, 2004), 268; Fernow 2:346 (1658).

43. For information on the development of the fur trade see Oliver A. Rink, "The Growth of Dutch Commerce in the Lower Hudson River Valley," in *Dutch New York: The Roots of Hudson Valley Culture,* ed. Roger Panetta (New York: Fordham University Press, 2009), 7–34. Indeed, it may even have been those pelts that made their way to Europe and to Jan Vermeer's studio where his painting *Officer and Laughing Girl* (Frick Collection, New York) shows a magnificent fur hat worn by the male sitter. Vermeer painted this canvas at the height of the transatlantic fur trade (c. 1657).

44. I would like to thank Virginie Adane, a graduate student at École des Hautes Études en Sciences Sociales (Paris), for this last observation.

45. Van de Pol, *Der Bürger und die Hure,* 15, 55, 60.

46. O'Callaghan, *Documents Relative to the Colonial History of the State of New York,* 2:221. Fernow 4:247 (1663); 6:40, 57, 60 (1666, 1667). It should be noted that some allegations fall into a category different from the usual accusations of sexual misconduct, as when a man claimed reparation from a woman who charged him with "dishonorable proposals . . . to satisfy carnal lusts." Elsie Gerrits's husband, Abram Carpyn, was a small burgher as well.

47. The records for this case are to be found in Fernow 1:51, 53, 58, 59, 60, 61, 65, 67, 72, and 76 (1653). According to Jaap Jacobs, the original Dutch is more colorful than the weakened translation. Jacobs explains that d'Wys asked Goderis "for permission to 'fuck the plaintiff's wife,' since 'Allard Anthony does it.'" The Dutch word for fuck is *neuken,* which reveals the real meaning of the English expression "a little nookie." Jacobs, *Colony of New Netherland,* 240 and n83.

48. Joost Goderus was born about 1625 and married Jacomyntie Frans Walings in New Amsterdam in 1650. It may be of some importance that Anthony was not married at the time this alleged incident took place, since no one was implying that Anthony had committed adultery, a serious offense. Samuel S. Purple, ed., *Records of the Reformed Dutch Church in New Amsterdam and New York: Marriages from 11 December 1639 to 26 August 1801* (New York: New-York Genealogical and Biographical Society, 1890), 20.

49. What goes around comes around. In 1674 Isaack Bedloo's widow, Elizabeth de Potter, sued Gabriel Minvielle, complaining that Minvielle "grossly defames her late husband." O'Callaghan, *Documents Relative to the Colonial History of the State of New York,* 2:690. A *lettre de représaille* may also be translated as a letter of reproach.

50. Fernow 3:89 (1659).

51. Fernow 1:61 and 61n., 67 (1653).

52. Fernow 1:67 (1653).

53. In this and the following sections, I have replicated the arbitrary spelling of names that appear in the court records.

54. Fernow 1:328, 316, 319, 322 (1655).

55. Fernow 1:328 (1655).

56. Fernow 1:47 (1661), 370 (1655); 3:26–27, 42 (1659); 1:328 (1655); 2:60, 243 (1656).

57. Fernow 1:329 (1655).

58. Fernow 3:155 (1660).

59. It is unclear what Boot meant when she said Jansen "scolded" and "troubled" her. From her perspective, calling him "rogue" and "knave" was equivalent to having "scolded him." Fernow 3:160 (1660).

60. Fernow 3:160 (1660).

61. Fernow 3:172, 177, 195, 217 (1660).

62. Maika, diss. appendix, "Additional Small Burghers." Burgher rights included citizenship and trading privileges.

63. Fernow 2:335 (1658).

64. Ibid. The only Maria Joris from New Amsterdam who turns up in genealogical records was christened in 1631, which would make her twenty-seven at the time of these proceedings. Even so, it is possible that this is not the same Maria Joris, or the source of information is incorrect, since even in the first third of the seventeenth century twenty-seven would hardly be considered old. FamilySearch.org.

65. Fernow 2:374–75 (1658).

66. Fernow 4:304, 328 (1663).

67. A stiver was a small unit of currency. Fernow 2:335 (1658).

68. Fernow 3:260 (1661); 4:26 (1662), 195, 197 (1663).

69. Fernow 3:290–91, 299, 312, 430 (1661); 4:4, 19–20 (1662).

70. Fredrick Arentszen and Grietje Pieters were married in 1656. Purple, *Records of the Reformed Church,* 20.

71. Fernow 3:89 (1659).

72. Fernow 3:93, 100 (1659, 1660).

73. Fernow 3:228–29 (1660).

74. Fernow 3:207 (1660).

75. Fernow 3:215; Norton, "Gender and Defamation," 11.

76. As an interesting aside, on the same day that Pieters sued Ackermans concerning allegations of theft, Ackermans was also prosecuted for various business irregularities. Testimony in this case included evidence that Ackermans "scolded and abused" the schout and "applied even godless words to Dr. Megapolensis." Fernow 5:192–93, 196–97 (1665).

77. Fernow 5:194, 197 (1665).

78. Fernow 5:197, 246 (1665).

79. Fernow 5:246–47, 260, 265 (1665). At this point Grietje maintains she is accused of having stolen several beavers—not just one.

80. Fernow 5:272–73 (1665). Fernow erroneously referred to Josyn as a male and in some instances mistakenly translated "she" as "he." See Fernow 6:131 (1668), 293 (1671).

81. The Dutch surrendered to the English in 1664, at which time New Amsterdam became New York. Yet apart from changes of title (schout, burgomasters, and schepens were eliminated as of June 1665 and replaced by a mayor, aldermen, and sheriff), there appears to have been little alteration in the operation of the court. An order pertaining to jury trials was published in January 1666, although juries do not appear regularly in the records until 1667. Fernow 5:115–16, 128 (1660), 330 (1666).

82. Fernow 5:272–73 (1665).

83. The concern that women in New Amsterdam exhibit about accusations of theft appears to differ sharply from that shown by women in Maryland. See Norton, "Gender and Defamation," 10.

84. If Wolfert Gerritsz is Woúter Gerritszen, he married Marritje Hendricks in 1662. Purple, *Records of the Reformed Church,* 28.

85. This story is related by Oliver Rink in his article "Growth of Dutch Commerce," 23.

86. Fernow 5:134, 146 (1664).

87. Fernow 5:287 (1665).

88. For an update on slander as it pertains to the issues in this chapter see Andrew J. King, "Constructing Gender: Sexual Slander in Nineteenth-Century America," *Law and History Review* 13, no. 1 (Spring 1995): 63–110.

2. Bermuda Triangle

1. For the population estimate see *Calendar of State Papers: Colonial Series, 1574–1660,* ed. W. Noel Sainsbury (London: Longmans, Green, & Co. 1860), 13:449. The rest of the seventeenth century saw additional accusations and prosecutions on Bermuda. Altogether twenty-one witches were tried (four men), but no further executions took place after 1655.

2. This list includes Gardiner, Middleton, Stevenson, Moore, Bedwell, Bowen, Brangman, Franklin, and Cole. The status of Page and Hopkins is ambiguous, with the manuscript referring to them as "Mrs" (mistress), but not "Goody." For a profile of English witches see Malcolm Gaskill, "Witchcraft in Early Modern Kent: Stereotypes and the Background to Accusations," in *Witchcraft in Early Modern Europe: Studies in Culture and Belief,* ed. Jonathan Barry, Marianne Hester, and Gareth Roberts (Cambridge: Cambridge University Press, 1996), 258, 263–64. Alan Macfarlane and Keith Thomas maintain that accused witches rarely had living husbands; Gaskill argues that in Kent, female witches were likely to be married. See Alan Macfarlane, *Witchcraft in Tudor and Stuart England: A Regional and Comparative Study* (London: Routledge, 1970) and Keith Thomas, *Religion and the Decline of Magic: Studies in Popular Beliefs in Sixteenth and Seventeenth Century England* (London: Weidenfeld & Nicolson, 1971).

3. J. H. Lefroy, comp., *Memorials of the Discovery and Early Settlement of the Bermudas or Somers Islands, 1515–1685,* 2 vols. (London: Longmans, Green, and Co., 1877–79; Hamilton: Bermuda Historical Society; Bermuda National Trust, 1981), 2:609 (hereafter L1: or L2:); Examination of Margery Tucker, April 13, 1653, Examination of John Burch, April 13, 1653, Examination of Elizabeth Middleton, April 15, 1653, L2:606–7. Elizabeth Middleton had been accused of cursing Anthony White's six- (nine-?) month-old child. L2:603; A. C. Hollis Hallett, ed. and comp., *Bermuda under the Sommer Islands Company, 1612–1684, Civil Records,* 3 vols. (Bermuda: Juniperhill Press and Bermuda Maritime Museum Press, 2005), 1:336 (hereafter CR1:, 2:, or 3:).

4. CR1:336. Returning a bill marked *ignoramus* indicated a refusal to indict. In such cases the grand jury chooses to "ignore" the bill.

5. Examination of Thomas Hess and Michael Burrowes, May 4, 1653, L2:607.

6. Testimony of John Middleton, L2:608, 610.

7. L2:609.

8. L2:610.

9. According to Michael Dalton, a "presumption" of witchcraft exists "if they be given to usual cursing and bitter imprecations." See "The Discovery of Witches, compiled by Michael Dalton" in C. L'Estrange Ewen, ed., *Witch Hunting and Witch Trials: The Indictments for Witchcraft from the Records of 1373 Assizes Held for the Home*

Circuit, A.D. 1559–1736 (New York: Lincoln MacVeagh: Dial Press, 1929), appendix 2, 268. Yet Bermudians did not couple cursing and witchcraft, at least not legally. A 1652 gubernatorial proclamation lumped together all those who committed blasphemy, swearing, lying, and cursing and put them on notice that they would be prosecuted to the full extent of the law (CR1:332). On the other hand, Elizabeth Middleton was accused of using "many cursed speeches" against Anthony White's "young child," who subsequently "fell into strange fitts." According to the grand jury presentment, Elizabeth Middleton allegedly combined with the devil to use "that abominable Practice of witchcraft upon the body of the child." It is unclear whether the curse or combination with the devil caused the child's fits. (L2:603). It is also puzzling why Elizabeth Middleton would curse a six- or nine-month-old child, unless it had some connection to the inroads that proto-Baptists were making against infant baptism. In the absence of ecclesiastical courts, authorities considered this issue at the November 1650 assizes: "And for all those that were presented for not coming to church and [negligence of] the ordinances of Sacramental Baptism, they were discharged with admonition that in case they would not reform for time to come that the law should proceed against them to the uttermost." CR1:302.

10. CR II (pt. 1) (1647–61), 89 verso, Bermuda Archives, Hamilton, Bermuda. Neither Lefroy nor Hallett could bring themselves to transcribe this offensive admission accurately. Instead, they both substituted the phrase "crimen haud inter christianos nominandum" (the crime never named among Christians). L2:610; CR1:351. Many thanks to my colleagues professors Richard Gyug and Maryanne Kowaleski for translating the Latin.

11. CR1:99–100 (1627), 159 (1630), 258 (1639), 323 (1652).

12. L1:364.

13. CR1:27, 40–41, 46, 47. One Hugh Middleton was plaintiff in a debt case as early as 1617 (CR1:10), making the Middletons one of Bermuda's earliest families. John may have been a brother of Solomon Middleton (d. circa 1654) and thus an uncle to a chain of nephews and nieces, one of whom was also named John.

14. CR1:51, 123, 135.

15. CR3:77, 79; CR1:343.

16. CR1:324. A strip is a narrow piece of textile material or an ornamental article of attire, chiefly worn by women. A bandstring is a string for fastening bands, such as a neckband or collar. In the seventeenth century, it could be a ruff as well (*Oxford English Dictionary*). If these were actually trading goods belonging to Elizabeth Middleton, it might contextualize John Middleton's apology for "making awaie" his wife's estate.

17. L2:604, 33.

18. The following testimony by Makaraton and Middleton may be found in L2:604–5 and CR1:340–41.

19. Although Bermuda's estimated population only amounted to three thousand people in 1656, it was already a biracial society. There are no reliable figures for the slave population in the 1650s, but by the 1670s the ratio of whites to blacks was approximately 3:1 in a population of approximately six thousand people. L2:87; Virginia Bernhard, *Slaves and Slaveholders in Bermuda, 1616–1782* (Columbia: University of Missouri Press, 1999), 66.

20. L2:604–5.

21. Testimony of Alister Smith, L2:605.

22. John Murrin, "'Things Fearful to Name': Bestiality in Early America," in *American Sexual Histories,* ed. Elizabeth Reis (Oxford: Blackwell Publishers, 2001), 16–18.

23. "An Act Against Conjuration, Witchcraft and dealing with evil and wicked spirits 1604," I James 1c.12, in *Witchcraft and Society in England and America, 1550–1750,* ed. Marion Gibson (Ithaca, N.Y.: Cornell University Press, 2003), 6; L2:605. See also C. L'Estrange Ewen, *Witch Hunting and Witch Trials: The Indictments for Witchcraft from the Records of 1373 Assizes Held for the Home Circuit, A.D. 1559–1736* (London: Kegan Paul et al., 1929), 25. Dalton, "Discovery of Witches," in Ewen, *Witch Hunting and Witch Trials,* 268.

24. Examination of Elizabeth Middleton, April 15, 1653, L2:607.

25. Elizabeth Middleton remarried only months after her husband's execution. She refused to pay his debts, the governor complained to the Somers Company, and the company responded that all of John Middleton's goods were liable to satisfy his debts. CR1:371 (item 24). Thus to add to his troubles, John Middleton had been in financial difficulty. For instances of the forfeiture of property, see Ewen, *Witch Hunting and Witch Trials,* 25.

26. Examination of John Burch, April 13, 1653, CR II (pt. 1) (1647–61), p. 384 (80), Bermuda Archives, Hamilton, Bermuda; L2:606.

27. Examination of Margery Tucker, April [13,] 1653, CR II (pt. 1) (1647–61), Bermuda Archives, Hamilton, Bermuda. Lefroy and Hallett again disguised the sexual aspect of the testimony in Latin, this time by saying "inter anum et testem." 2:606; CR1:342; CR3:162.

28. L2:606; CR1:341–42. The six men were——Willis,——Bristow, Peter Lun, Robert Powell, Henery Paskere (or Paskow), and Thomas——.

29. Lefroy refused to transcribe Elizabeth Middleton's testimony in full, saying "Part of this abominable woman's evidence is grossly indecent," thus presumably unsuitable for the eyes of historians. See L2:607 and CR1:342. Although the newly published civil records of Bermuda include the excised portions of Elizabeth Middleton's testimony, the transcription contains errors. See the manuscript version of Elizabeth Middleton's testimony in CR II (pt. 1) (1647–61), p. 388 (82), Bermuda Archives, Hamilton, Bermuda.

30. L2:605. Symon appears to have been a servant of the governor. Suggesting that the governor put words in Symon's mouth in order to absolve Makaraton at Middleton's expense would be another way of interpreting this scenario. Even though Symon is referred to as a boy, his age remains speculative. Decades earlier (1617) another "Simon the Negro" was enslaved by the governor, and in 1646 and 1647 references are made to "old Symon" as well as to his son, George, and his daughter. It is likely that the "boy" in 1653 was either the son or grandson of "old Symon" and Sarah Simon, also held by the governor (1660). CR1:10, 489; CR3:89, 213.

31. Examination of Robert Priestley, April 17, 1653, L2:607.

32. A. C. Hollis Hallett, comp., *Early Bermuda Records, 1619–1826: A Guide to the Parish and Clergy Registers with Some Assessment Lists and Petitions* (Bermuda: Juniperhill Press, 1991), 39–40.

33. For details concerning the banishment of the Independents see CR1:283, 286, 291, 295. See also CR1:400; CR2:499 for details about Jonas Middleton.

34. L2:607 (MS 388 [82]).

35. L2:608–9.

36. L2:602, 617.

37. L2:609. The best explanation for this odd instruction is that crying "twang" will enable a sharp object to pierce through something hard. (*Oxford English Dictionary*, s.v. "twang.")

38. "In the mouth of Goody Gardiner there is a blewe spott wh. Being prickt close by it bled the which wee leave to the judgment of Phisitians. Mr. Hooper and the chirurgion being appointed to viewe that spott the daye that she was to come to her triall and it was fallen away and flat, and being prickt it bled and it was knowne to be there 18 yeares." L2:602–3.

39. L2:625. Although Lancaster, England, claimed witches as early as 1612, the reference was probably to the 1633/34 episode, which attracted considerable attention not only from the public but from playwrights as well. Records suggest that nineteen witches were condemned during the latter outbreak and sixty were under suspicion. James Sharpe, *Instruments of Darkness: Witchcraft in Early Modern England* (Philadelphia: University of Pennsylvania Press, 1997), 126.

40. On "pricking" see Keith Thomas, *Religion and the Decline of Magic: Studies in Popular Beliefs in Sixteenth and Seventeenth Century England* (London: Weidenfeld & Nicolson, 1971), 445. See also Peter Elmer, "'Saints or Sorcerers': Quakerism, Demonology and the Decline of Witchcraft in Seventeenth-Century England," in *Witchcraft in Early Modern Europe,* ed. Jonathan Barry et al., (Cambridge: Cambridge University Press, 1996), 152, and Wallace Notestein, *A History of Witchcraft in England from 1558 to 1718* (New York: Russell & Russell, 1965), 206–8. An interesting aside is that one Ralph Gardiner discussed the Lancaster episode in a pamphlet titled *England's Grievance Discovered in Relation to the Coal Trade* (London: R. Ibbitson, 1655). Jeane Gardiner, a convicted witch executed in Bermuda in 1651, was married to a Ralph Gardiner. The author of the pamphlet was born in 1625, making his relationship (if any) to Jeanne Gardiner something other than that of a husband.

41. Brian P. Levack, "State-Building and Witch Hunting in Early Modern Europe," in Barry et al., *Witchcraft in Early Modern Europe,* 106–7.

42. Michael Dalton, *The Countrey Justice* (London, 1655; reprint, New York: Legal Classics Library, 1996), 107, 207, 342.

43. L2:617, 602, 606. These abnormalities were likely to have been blue nevus or nevus of Ota. Blue nevus is a flat or dome-shaped, popular or nodular lesion found usually on the hands, face, or arms. These lesions appear early in life, grow slowly for a while, and remain stationary in size and color for years. Nevus of Ota may affect the eye, face, scalp, and buccal mucosa (mouth). The lesion is often present at birth, after which it may enlarge for a while and reach a stationary size. George M. Lewis, MD, and Clayton E. Wheeler Jr., MD, *Practical Dermatology* (Philadelphia: W. B. Saunders Co., 1967), 391, 393. I am indebted to James M. Cohen, MD, for this explanation and citation. Christian Stevenson explained that the marks "on the inside of her cheeks . . . came by reason of an Impostume of the one side. And the other came by a ragged Tooth on the other side, and this was about 5 yeares since."

L2:611. The blue spot in Jeane Gardiner's mouth "was knowne to be there 18 yeares." L2:603.

44. The only difference in her profile was that Christian Stevenson was married. English witches did not usually have living husbands.

45. L2:616–17.

46. L2:615.

47. L2:615.

48. L2:614; Macfarlane, *Witchcraft in Tudor and Stuart England,* 105. John Middleton had referred to Christian Stevenson as the wife of Thomas, although this is the only reference to a Thomas Stevenson in the records. It is possible that "Thomas" is an error, since Henry Bishop testified that in a dream a Stephen Stevenson "bewitched him," and it was thought that witchcraft followed family lines. (L2:616; CR1:345). (There is a transcription error in the CR edition. The published text refers to "Goody" Stevenson, but in the MS the word is "Stephen.") Unfortunately, this portion of the manuscript page no longer survives. (CR1:342; L2:607).

49. Sarah Murrill (Murrell) was born on November 2, 1652. Thomas and his wife, Sarah, had another daughter, born on November 13, 1653, whom they also named Sarah. The sequence of births and naming patterns suggests that the first Sarah had died in infancy and was the child referred to in Murrill's testimony. It also appears that Murrill's wife was pregnant at the time of Christian Stevenson's trial. Hallett, *Early Bermuda Records,* 11; C. F. E. Hollis Hallett, *Early Bermuda Wills, 1629–1835* (Bermuda: Juniperhill Press, c. 1993), 396.

50. Sharpe, *Instruments of Darkness,* 116; L2:611, 616.

51. L2:611–12.

52. Barry, *Witchcraft in Early Modern Europe* (introduction), 8–9; Gaskill, "Witchcraft in Early Modern Kent," in Barry, 259.

53. L2:611. A croseleth is a small cross (*Oxford English Dictionary*). It is unclear what Murrill meant by "tone." According to the *OED,* tone could be archaic for t'one, which was often paired with t'other. In that case, Murrill might have been saying that he wouldn't have anything to do with her one way or the other. Or he might have been noting that he wasn't willing to meddle with her tone of voice or attitude.

54. Thomas, *Religion and the Decline of Magic,* 544–45.

55. L2:615–16.

56. L2:614.

57. Barry, *Witchcraft in Early Modern Europe* (introduction), 38; *Oxford English Dictionary,* s.v. "plunder."

58. There is only a tenuous link between witchcraft and roses. According to occult lore, the Rose Queen (Dame Venus) hid the rose of Lucifer when it fell from heaven. This rose was the emerald upon Lucifer's brow or crown. Love potions routinely consist of rose petals, and it was well-known advice to put a rose under the pillow of one's intended to cast a spell. As incidental as all this appears to the Stevenson case, it would be stretching still further to attribute political motivation to her seemingly innocuous offer, since the white rose of York and the red of Lancaster had probably faded from public consciousness by this time.

59. L2:615.

60. Sharpe, *Instruments of Darkness,* 159.

61. L2:612–13.

62. L2:608.

63. See Richard Norwood's survey of Pembroke Tribe in L2, appendix 15, 677–84, and accompanying map.

64. CR1:413, 588.

65. CR1:354, 420; L2:611. An impostume is a swelling, cyst, or abscess (*Oxford English Dictionary*).

66. CR1:313, 318, 439. For examples of Ford's litigation history see CR1 passim.

67. CR:380, 418, 457, 609; L2:616, 617. Michael Jarvis asserts that Stephen was Christian's husband. See Michael Jarvis, "'In the Eye of All Trade,' Maritime Revolution and the Transformation of Bermudian Society, 1612–1800," PhD diss., College of William and Mary, 1998, 226.

68. Gaskill, "Witchcraft in Early Modern Kent," in Barry, *Witchcraft in Early Modern Europe,* 259; Barry, *Witchcraft in Early Modern Europe* (introduction), 11.

69. This is consistent with English prosecutions. See Barry, *Witchcraft in Early Modern Europe* (introduction), 13.

70. L2:622.

71. L2:621.

72. L2:618, 619, 629, 621, 622.

73. L2:621, 620, 622, 619.

74. L2:622. Thomas Turner was appointed governor in 1646.

75. L2:620, 622.

76. Although the witchcraft statute of James I (1604) prescribed a year's imprisonment for any person who destroyed, wasted, or impaired cattle and a death sentence only for recidivists, Moore was not convicted and executed under this provision. According to the indictment, Moore "did contract with the Devil," which demanded the death penalty. Witchcraft Act of 1604, 1 Jas. I, c. 12.

77. CR1:390–91.

78. L2:628–29.

79. L2:624.

80. L2:624–25.

81. Thomas, *Religion and the Decline of Magic,* 36; Ewen, *Witch Hunting and Witch Trials,* 240–42; Gaskill, "Witchcraft in Early Modern Kent," in Barry, *Witchcraft in Early Modern Europe,* 261.

82. L2:625.

83. William Shakespeare, *The Tragedy of Macbeth,* act 1, scene 3, lines 14–17 (New Haven, Conn.: Yale University Press, 1962), 6. It was not unusual for sailors to conflate Quakers with witchcraft. When the sailors aboard a vessel crossing from England to Cork encountered bad weather in 1655, they blamed a Quaker passenger, Barbara Blaugdone. "We had much foul weather, so that the Sea-men said, that I was the cause of it, because I was a *Quaker,* and they conspired to throw me over-board." Barbara Blaugdone, *An Account of the Travels, Sufferings and Persecution of Barbara Blaugdone* (Shoreditch, 1691), 21.

84. CR1:364. If Page and Hopkins were Quakers, their class status raises questions about the "quality" of people who joined the movement.

85. Charter agreement, August 2, 1654, CR3:539–40, 663.

86. L2:626, CR1:364.

87. L2:627.

88. L2:625.

89. The devil was known to promise revenge upon the enemies of a witch who covenanted with him. See testimony to this effect in James Sharpe, "The Devil in East Anglia: The Matthew Hopkins Trials Reconsidered," in Barry, *Witchcraft in Early Modern Europe,* 245–46.

90. L2:625–26. Thomas Cobson was probably the husband, brother, or father of Elizabeth Cobson, a previous witness.

91. Dalton, "The Discovery of Witches," in Ewen, *Witch Hunting and Witch Trials,* appendix 2, 267.

92. In his dissertation about Bermuda, Michael Jarvis interprets the testimony of Anthony Love to indicate a different scenario. Love's testimony begins "That Mrs Page her maide havig mist a bottle . . ." Jarvis translates this passage to mean that Elizabeth Page was Hopkins's maid, although the sentence is admittedly ambiguous. The syntax is common to the seventeenth century, and this phraseology often substitutes for the possessive. Since both Hopkins and Page are referred to independently as "passengers" aboard the *Mayflower,* it seems more likely to me that the "maide" was a woman who belonged to Page. Besides, given Page's uncanny ability to move a compass dial, she should have been able to conjure the bottle herself. Jarvis, "'In the Eye of All Trade,'" 230–31.

93. Examples of "witch bottles" and an explanation of their contents and use will be found at the Museum of Witchcraft in Boscastle, Cornwall, England. For further information, see www.museumofwitchcraft.com.

94. L2:626, CR1:364, Colonial records microfilm p. 432 [205, 206], Bermuda Archives, Hamilton, Bermuda. My thanks to Virginia Bernhard for lending me the microfilm.

95. Barry Reay, *The Quakers and the English Revolution* (London: Temple Smith, 1985), 9, 10, 11, 26, 67, 71, 77; Hugh Barbour, *The Quakers in Puritan England* (New Haven, Conn.: Yale University Press, 1964), 51, 55.

96. John Smolenski, "Friends and Strangers: Religion, Diversity, and the Ordering of Public Life in Colonial Pennsylvania, 1681–1764," diss., University of Pennsylvania, 2001, 52; Elmer, "'Saints or Sorcerers,'" in Barry, *Witchcraft in Early Modern Europe,* 145.

97. Arthur J. Worrall, *Quakers in the Colonial Northeast* (Hanover, N.H.: University Press of New England, 1980), 9; Carol Karlsen, *The Devil in the Shape of a Woman: Witchcraft in Colonial New England* (New York: Vintage, 1989), 122–23.

98. Barbour, *Quakers,* 60; Henry Wilkinson, *The Adventurers of Bermuda: A History of the Island from Its Discovery until . . . 1684* (London: Oxford University Press, 1933), 364.

99. Edward H. West, *History of Portsmouth [R.I.], 1638–1936* (Providence, R.I.: J. Green, 1936). Unpaginated.

100. Barbour, *Quakers,* 60.

101. CR1:294–95, 371; L2:3, 54, 56, 68, 99, 122.

102. CR1:529, 142; ER, 40; CR2:714, 107; CR1:283.

103. White appears as a Quaker in 1672. CR2:143–44.

104. Reay, *Quakers and the English Revolution,* 36–39.

105. CR1:325 (July 1652); See also Jarvis, "'In the Eye of All Trade,'" 173.

106. Barbour, *Quakers,* 163–65.

107. L2:609.

108. L2:612, 620.

109. L2:435.

110. Joseph Besse, *A Collection of Sufferings of the People Called Quakers . . . 1650–1689,* 2 vols. (London, 1753), 2:177–78; Smolenski, "Friends and Strangers," 50.

111. Elmer, "'Saints or Sorcerers,'" in Barry, *Witchcraft in Early Modern Europe,* 160–76.

112. L2:624.

113. Sharpe, *Instruments of Darkness,* 114.

114. Elmer, "'Saints or Sorcerers,'" 146; Reay, *Quakers and the English Revolution,* 69. See also Amelie Mott Gummere, *Witchcraft and Quakerism: A Study in Social History* (Philadelphia: Biddle Press, 1908), 31.

115. Audrey Sullivan, ed., *Joseph Besse's Collection of Quaker Sufferings, 1650–1689,* index to vols. 1 and 2 (Fort Lauderdale, Fla.: Genealogical Society of Broward County 1991), 52, 70–71, 112, 133, 141; CR1:260; CR3:85, 280, 500; Hallett, *Early Bermuda Records,* 30, 37. See also index to CR1–3.

116. Ewen, *Witch Hunting and Witch Trials,* 101–8, 110; Sharpe, *Instruments of Darkness,* 109.

117. See John P. Demos, *Entertaining Satan: Witchcraft and the Culture of Early New England* (New York: Oxford University Press, 1983), appendix, esp. 401–4, and Lyle Koehler, *A Search for Power: The "Weaker Sex" in Seventeenth-Century New England* (Urbana: University of Illinois Press, 1980), appendix 5.

118. I am indebted to Michael Jarvis, "'In the Eye of All Trade,'" 208–19, for the preceding synthesis. For the religious background of this period see also A. C. Hollis Hallett, *Chronicle of a Colonial Church* (Bermuda: Juniperhill Press, 1993), chaps. 1–5; L1 and 2, passim; Joan Kennedy, *Isle of Devils: Bermuda under the Somers Island Company, 1609–1685* (London: Collins, 1971), chap. 12; Walter Brownell Hayward, *Bermuda Past and Present: A Description and Historical Account of the Somers Islands* (New York: Dodd, Mead & Co., 1926), 28–31; Wilkinson, *Adventurers of Bermuda.*

119. For an interpretation that places Bermuda's witchcraft outbreak in a political context see Virginia Bernhard, "Religion, Politics, and Witchcraft in Bermuda, 1651–1655," *William and Mary Quarterly,* 3rd series, vol. 67 (October 2010): 677–708.

120. Hallett, *Chronicle of a Colonial Church,* 57.

121. CR1:324 (July 1652).

122. *Calendar of State Papers: Colonial Series, 1574–1660,* 370, 353, 378.

123. Wilkinson, *Adventurers of Bermuda,* 292–93; CR1:355, 356.

124. Jarvis, "'In the Eye of All Trade,'" 175, 190; See also Robert V. Wells, *Population of the British Colonies in America before 1776: A Survey of Census Data* (Princeton, N.J.: Princeton University Press, 1975), 177, and Elaine Forman Crane, "The Socioeconomics of a Female Majority in Eighteenth-Century Bermuda," *Signs* 15.2 (1990): 231–58.

125. *Calendar of State Papers: Colonial Series,* June 25, 1653, 404; Christian J. Koot, "A 'Dangerous Principle': Free Trade Discourses in Barbados and the English Leeward Islands, 1650–1689," *Early American Studies* 5, no. 1 (Spring 2007): 141.

126. Sharpe, *Instruments of Darkness,* 165–66.

127. L2:623–24, 628.

128. Gaskill, "Witchcraft in Early Modern Kent," in Barry, *Witchcraft in Early Modern Europe,* 259; Barry, *Witchcraft in Early Modern Europe* (introduction), 10–11; Sharpe, *Instruments of Darkness,* 155.

129. Richard Bernard, *A Guide to Grand-Jury Men* (London, 1627); Dalton, *Countrey Justice;* Notestein, *History of Witchcraft,* 151.

130. Deposition of Charles Hill (1667), *Records and Files of the Quarterly Courts of Essex County, Massachusetts* (Salem, Mass.: Essex Institute, 1913), 3:420.

131. *Records and Files of . . . Essex County,* 8:356.

132. Elaine Forman Crane, *Killed Strangely: The Death of Rebecca Cornell* (Ithaca, N.Y.: Cornell University Press, 2002), 45.

3. "Leave of[f] or Else I Would Cry Out Murder"

1. Berthold Fernow, *The Records of New Amsterdam from 1653–1674* [Minutes of the Court of Burgomasters and Schepens, 1656–1658] (Baltimore: Genealogical Publishing Co., 1974), 2:335.

2. Mary Beth Norton, *Founding Mothers and Fathers: Gendered Power and the Forming of American Society* (New York: Knopf, 1996), 77–81; Seventeenth-century Rhode Island court papers record only one prosecution for wife beating between 1641 and 1667. In 1644 John Hicks was accused of beating his wife, Harwood (Herod). He, in turn, asked for a divorce on the grounds of adultery, which he called "whordome." In 1668, Elizabeth Stevens declared that she stood "in feare of her life of her sayd Husband Henry Stevens" and desired "Releife" from the court. The court imposed a bond of twenty pounds from her husband to ensure his "good behavior." What connection his acquittal on an adultery charge earlier in the same session had to these proceedings went unrecorded, but the fact that Henry did not appear at the next session of the court, as required, may be indicative of his attitude. In 1678, Abraham Butterworth of Rhode Island was committed to prison "for Misbehavior in and towards his family," but on a promise to behave, he was released. Five years later, Ann Warner complained to the Rhode Island General Assembly that her husband had laid "violent hands on her," and petitioned for a divorce. Unwilling to grant one until the Court of Trials ruled on the case, the General Assembly (sitting as a court itself) issued a separation and maintenance agreement as well as a restraining order on John. In September 1683, when Ann's case came before the Court of Trials, she pleaded with the court not to release her husband from his bonds, insisting that she "still went in fear of her life." Presumably because he had not exhibited good behavior in the past, the court imposed an unusually high bond of fifty pounds. These proceedings do not appear to have injured Warner's reputation, since he was elected deputy to the General Assembly from Warwick both before and after the case. According to the records, the foregoing are the only spousal violence cases brought before Rhode Island courts in the seventeenth century. Furthermore, an examination of indictments from the Newport County Superior Court of Trials indicates that no husband was charged with assaulting his wife during the eighteenth century. I would like to thank my graduate assistant at Fordham University, Anthony Giattino, for his help on this last research point. "Aquidneck Quarter Court Records 1641–1646,"

in *Documentary History of Rhode Island, ed.* Howard M. Chapin (Providence, R.I.: Preston and Rounds Co., 1916), 151–52; *Rhode Island Court Records: Records of the Court of Trials of the Colony of Providence Plantations, 1647–1670,* 2 vols. (Providence: Rhode Island Historical Society, 1920–22), 2:72, 74, 77; John R. Bartlett, ed., *Records of the Colony of Rhode Island and Providence Plantations in New England* (Providence, R.I.: Knowles, Anthony and Co., 1858), 3:121 [1683], 124 [1683], 167 [1685]; Jane Fletcher Fiske, transcriber, *Rhode Island General Court of Trials, 1671–1704* (Boxford, Mass.: privately printed, 1998), 79, 121–22. For further information about Rhode Island cases see Lyle Koehler, *A Search for Power: The Weaker Sex in Seventeenth-Century New England* (Urbana: University of Illinois Press, 1980), 321.

3. Randolph A. Roth, "Spousal Murder in Northern New England, 1776–1865," in *Over the Threshold: Intimate Violence in Early America,* ed. Christine Daniels and Michael V. Kennedy (New York: Routledge, 1999), 65–93. See also the perceptive overview by Christine Daniels, "Intimate Violence, Now and Then," in *Over the Threshold,* 3–21, as well as G. S. Rowe and Jack Marietta, "Personal Violence in a Peaceable Kingdom: Pennsylvania 1682–1801," in the same volume, 22–44, esp. 25, 29, 30. Lyle Koehler's 1980 book is still the best source for a quantified study of spousal abuse. See Koehler, *Search for Power,* 137–65, 321. Merril Smith's work on eighteenth-century marital discord in Pennsylvania makes important observations and raises interesting questions. See Merril D. Smith, *Breaking the Bonds: Marital Discord in Pennsylvania, 1730–1830* (New York: New York University Press, 1991).

4. J. A. Sharpe, "Domestic Homicide in Early Modern England," *Historical Journal* 24 (1981): 24–48; Susan Dwyer Amussen, "'Being Stirred to Much Unquietness': Violence and Domestic Violence in Early Modern England," *Journal of Women's History* 6 (1994): 70–89; Randolph Roth, "Child Murder in New England," *Social Science History* 25 (2001): 104–14. Roth's transatlantic quantitative studies suggest that intrafamily violence in New England persisted at lower levels than in England, but his tentative conclusions are based on indictments and prosecutions, which do not take the threshold for violence into consideration. In short, at what point was abuse considered serious enough to prosecute? Did it differ from region to region? See Randolph Roth, "Family and Intimate Homicide in American History," paper presented at the Society for Historians of the Early American Republic conference, July 22, 2004.

5. Amussen, "'Being Stirred to Much Unquietness,'" 75, 78, 82. Amussen's conclusions differ from Margaret Hunt's. Hunt's description of family violence in early modern London more clearly resembles New England. See Margaret Hunt, "Wife Beating, Domesticity, and Women's Independence in Eighteenth-Century London," *Gender and History* 4, no. 1 (Spring 1992): 10–33. Laura Gowing, who has also written on family violence in early modern London, maintains that even though men were cautioned not to inflict bodily damage on their wives, divorce testimony by witnesses indicates that some women were badly beaten. See Laura Gowing, *Domestic Dangers: Women, Words, and Sex in Early Modern London* (Oxford: Clarendon Press, 1996), 207.

6. Helena Wall argues that the community—both neighbors and authorities—consistently intervened in the affairs of married couples throughout the colonies, but even she admits that patriarchy overwhelmed justice and compassion in cases of spousal abuse. Helena M. Wall, *Fierce Communion: Family and Community in Early America*

(Cambridge, Mass.: Harvard University Press, 1990), 54, 59, 77–78. For a concurring opinion see Elizabeth Pleck, *Domestic Tyranny: The Making of American Social Policy against Family Violence from Colonial Times to the Present* (New York: Oxford University Press, 1987), 30–31.

7. Hunt, "Wife Beating," 23.

8. The phrase "rule of thumb" was commonly used in the seventeenth century but mistakenly interpreted to mean that a husband could chastise his wife by beating her with a stick no thicker than his thumb. In 1782 an English cartoonist perpetuated this erroneous belief in the popular mind with a graphic that satirized what he thought was a 1782 judicial decision allowing such correction.

9. See Lena Amarosa, "House of Pain: Spousal Violence in Seventeenth-Century New England, 1641–1683," history honors thesis, Fordham University, 2003, p. 43 and passim.

10. Norton, *Founding Mothers and Fathers*, 72–73, 78–83.

11. George F. Dow, ed., *Records and Files of the Quarterly Courts of Essex County, Massachusetts* (Salem, Mass: Essex Institute, 1913), 3:140–41, 152, 192.

12. See William Blackstone, *Commentaries on the Laws of England* [1765–69], ed. Thomas Cooley (Chicago: Callaghan and Co., 1899), bk. 1, p. 445. The cases involve Jeremiah Meecum (1715), John Hammett [1718/19], William Dyre (1718/19), Nicholas Barber (1718/19), Sarah Rouse (1718/19), Nathaniel Alcock (1745/46), Conrad Flack (1772), Jeremiah Brown (1784). All the case files may be found at the Rhode Island Judicial Archives in Pawtucket, Rhode Island (hereafter RIJA). I am grateful to J. Stephen Grimes, public information officer, Rhode Island Supreme Court, for providing me with copies of the relevant documents. My thanks also to Bertram Lippincott, librarian and genealogist at the Newport Historical Society, for adding to the store of information on these families. It should be noted that the curious cluster of cases in 1718/19 also includes the murder of Freelove Dolliver by Reuben Hill, although this does not appear to be an intrafamily homicide. The case was on the September 1719 docket, and Hill was hanged for the crime.

13. Examination of William Dyre, February 28, 1718/19 (Dyre), RIJA. (Hereafter the name in parentheses refers to the case file.) The last part of Dyre's examination, which concerned a letter he had written to his brother's wife, was crossed out, presumably because it was immaterial to the proceedings at hand. It involved "Ill Reports" of his sister-in-law and "how much she was wronged by the Speech of people." Desire Slocum Dyre, born in 1691, married Samuel Dyre in 1710. He was twenty-four, she nineteen. Lelia Morse Wilson, comp., *Ten Generations from William and Mary Dyer, Pioneer Settlers in Newport, Rhode Island* (Putnam, Conn., 1949), 4. See also the will of Charles Dyre, in which his bequests are likely to have been in birth order. Jane Fletcher Fiske, *Gleanings from Newport Court Files, 1659–1783* (Boxford, Mass.: privately printed, 1998), no. 28.

14. In December 1738 Benedict Arnold charged that his wife, Mary, conspired with her lover to obtain her husband's estate by fraud, poison him, and then marry her partner-in-crime. The couple tried to enlist the aid of a surgeon, who refused their request for poison, but the pair apparently procured some elsewhere—a dose of which sickened, but did not kill, Arnold. Since Mary left her very ill husband "to Dally with her Irishman," Benedict decided his best course of action was divorce. Ar-

nold's divorce petition may be found in the Rhode Island petition collection (5:1) at the Rhode Island State Archives in Providence. On infanticide see Ann Jones, *Women Who Kill* (New York: Fawcett Columbine, 1980), 42–62, and Cornelia Hughes Dayton, *Women before the Bar: Gender, Law, and Society in Connecticut, 1639–1789* (Chapel Hill: University of North Carolina Press, 1995), 210–13.

15. Edgar J. McManus, *Law and Liberty in Early New England: Criminal Justice and Due Process, 1620–1692* (Amherst: University of Massachusetts Press, 1993), 35–36.

16. Arrest warrant (Dyre), February 14, 1718/19, RIJA.

17. Warrant to Impannel [*sic*] the Jury of Inquest, January 27, 1745/46; Report of Inquest Jury, January 27, 1745/46; Evidence of John Wilson and Hester Humphrey, January 27, 1745/46; Evidence of Doctors Hooper and Wigneron, January 27, 1745/46; Summons for Doctors Rodman, Brett, Moffatt, Hooper, and Wigneron, January 28, 1745/46; Evidence of Doctors Moffatt, Rodman, and Brett, January 28, 1745/46 (Alcock), RIJA.

18. Evidence of Nathaniel Coddington and Weston Clarke, March 30, 1719, docket 170 (Dyre), RIJA.

19. Examination of Mary Sanford of Newport, February 28, 1718/19 (Dyre), RIJA. This graphic description appears to be one common to early America. It is used again by another deponent here and, interestingly, was employed by Mary Rowlandson in her narrative of the Indian attack of 1675: "Thus we were butchered by those merciless Heathen, standing amazed, with the Blood running down to our Heels." "A True History of the Captivity and Restoration of Mrs. Mary Rowlandson," in *Colonial American Travel Narratives,* ed. Wendy Martin (New York: Penguin, 1994), 11. The same phrase is found in a 1748 newspaper account of spousal abuse: "The husband whipp'd her with Rods till the Blood run down her Heels." In this instance, such brutality caused the wife to prosecute her husband. He was sent to prison, "to which Place he was conducted thro' the Peltings, Hissings, and Blows of Two-thirds of the Women in the Town." The incident took place in Philadelphia and was reported in the *Boston Weekly News-Letter* of October 20, 1748.

20. Evidence of John Willson, January 27, 1745/46 (Alcock), RIJA.

21. Deposition of Virtue Records, March 24, 1718/19 (Dyre), RIJA.

22. Examination of Mary Partridge, February 28, 1718/19 (Dyre); Testimony of Joseph Cooke, April 6, 1719 (Dyre), RIJA.

23. The first generation of Barbers lived in Massachusetts. Two Barber brothers left the Bay Colony for Connecticut and Rhode Island around 1635, and it is from the Rhode Island branch that Nicholas must have descended. What makes his story particularly interesting is that a William Barber, presumably an ancestor, was admonished for beating his wife in Essex County, Massachusetts, in 1643. Presented for "assaulting his wives father . . . and abusinge his wife" in 1652, Barber was whipped, presumably for the former assault rather than the latter abuse. Lois J. Barber Schroeder, comp., *Moses Barber of South Kingston, Rhode Island and His Many Descendants, 1652–1984* (privately printed, 1984), 375. *Essex County Court Records* 1:57, 58, 258–59.

24. These events took place between March 3, 1718/19, and September 1721. Elizabeth Barber sought refuge with her father on the former date. Fiske, *Gleanings,* no. 132.

25. Richard G. Rouse, "Emmanuel Rouse of Rhode Island . . . and Some of His Descendants," *Rhode Island Roots* 19 (1993): 70–71.

26. Rhode Island Superior Court, March 1718/19, bk. A, p. 302, RIJA; Fiske, *Gleanings,* no. 123.

27. Rhode Island Superior Court, 1772, bk. F, p. 10, RIJA.

28. *Providence Gazette and Country Journal,* November 23–30, 1771, under the dateline Newport, November 25, 1771. The *Boston Evening Post* reprinted the same article on December 2, 1771.

29. Ezra Stiles, *The Literary Diary of Ezra Stiles,* ed. Franklin B. Dexter, 3 vols. (New York: Scribner's, 1901), 1:195 (November 24, 1771).

30. It is stipulated in Numbers 35:16 that a murderer who uses an iron implement shall be put to death. See Elaine Forman Crane, *Killed Strangely: the Death of Rebecca Cornell* (Ithaca, N.Y.: Cornell University Press, 2002), 56, for a discussion of this point.

31. The result of Flack's March 7 trial was reported in the *Providence Gazette and Country Journal,* March 14, 1772, under the dateline Newport, March 9. The implication of this statement is that even if eighteenth-century trials were swiftly conducted, juries usually left the courtroom for deliberations. Stiles, *Literary Diary,* 1:217 (March 7, 1772).

32. A little more than a decade earlier, a New Hampshire woman warned against leaving such potential weapons where a violent husband might seize them. Speaking specifically of men who abused alcohol as well as women, she asserted that "after teasing their Wives all Day, their voracious Appetites leads them to the Tavern, where they riot, and come home disguised; and at that Time 'tis dangerous for the Women to leave Tongs or Shovel in the way of these unthinking Wretches." *New Hampshire Gazette,* January 9, 1761.

33. Divorce petition of Mary Brown, third Monday in March 1783 (Brown); Deposition of Olive Walker, March 26, 1784 (Brown), RIJA.

34. Deposition of Olive Walker, March 26, 1784 (Brown); Deposition of Benjamin Hubbard (Brown), March 29, 1784, RIJA.

35. Divorce proceedings, *Sarah Hogan v. John Hogan,* Rhode Island Superior Court, September 1784, bk. F, p. 245, RIJA.

36. Testimony of Thomas Olney, April 13, 1784 (Brown), RIJA; Deposition of Olive Walker, March 26, 1784 (Brown), RIJA.

37. Deposition of Esther Humphreys, January 27, 1745/46 (Alcock), RIJA.

38. Testimony of John James, August 15, c. 1718 or 1719, RIJA. This document may be found among the William Dyre file papers, but it bears no relevance to that case.

39. John R. Bartlett, ed., *Records of the Colony of Rhode Island and Providence Plantations in New England* (Providence, R.I.: Knowles, Anthony and Co., 1859), 4:38 (1708); 4:120 (1711); 4:131 (1712); 4:145 (1712); 4:172 (1714); Fiske, *Gleanings,* nos. 29, 35, 30.

40. James N. Arnold, comp., *Vital Records of Rhode Island, 1636–1850,* 1st series (Providence, R.I.: Narragansett Historical Publishing Co., 1893), 4 (part 2): 35; Hammett family folder, Newport Historical Society, Newport, R.I. (hereafter NHS). It is not impossible that Sarah's pregnancy precipitated rather than followed the wedding. They were married by Governor Samuel Cranston in a civil ceremony.

41. According to Mary Partridge, Hannah Dyre told her that "her Husband was always worse in his carriage to her when She was with child." Examination of Mary Partridge, February 28, 1718/19 (Dyre), RIJA.

42. Hammett was a member of the Society of Friends. Hammett family file, NHS.

43. Arnold, *Vital Records of Rhode Island,* 4:22, 51, 65, 110, 7:5; Stephen F. Peckham, *Peckham Genealogy: The English Ancestors and American Descendants of John Peckham of Newport, Rhode Island, 1630* (New York: National Historical Co. [1921?]), 40, 221, 225. It should be noted that none of the James Peckhams listed in this genealogy was likely to have been the one referred to in the James document. Fiske, *Gleanings,* nos. 216 (1725) and 375 (1728).

44. Antoinette Downing and Vincent J. Scully Jr., *The Architectural Heritage of Newport, Rhode Island* (New York: Bramhall House, 1967), 449. Clarke sold the property in 1726, but it is likely he was the owner at the time of Hammett's attack.

45. Fiske, *Gleanings,* nos. 737 and 768; Rhode Island Superior Court, 1732, bk. B, p. 438, RIJA.

46. Deposition of Hannah Akins, April 2, 1719 (Dyre); Examination of Mary Sanford, February 28, 1718/19 (Dyre), RIJA.

47. Deposition of Hannah Akins, April 2, 1719 (Dyre), RIJA. Akins may have been an indentured servant, making it more difficult, but certainly not impossible, for her to leave the Dyre household.

48. Evidence of Lydia Townsend, February 7, 1745/46 (Alcock), RIJA.

49. Testimony of Thomas Olney, April 13, 1784 (Brown), RIJA.

50. Deposition of Diademia Hubbard, March 29, 1784 (Brown); Deposition of Samuel Giles, April 10, 1784 (Brown), RIJA.

51. Deposition of Benjamin [Ezra] Hubbard, March 29, 1784 (Brown), RIJA. This incident took place in February 1784.

52. "Memoranda from the Rev. William Cooper's Interleaved Almanacs," March 23, 1715, *New England Historical and Genealogical Register* 30 (1876): 435; *Boston News-Letter,* March 21–28, 1715, under the dateline Rhode Island, March 25.

53. Testimony of Samuel Pike, April 6, 1719 (Dyre), RIJA.

54. Examination of Mary Partridge, February 28, 1718/19 (Dyre), RIJA.

55. Examination of Mary Partridge, February 28, 1718/19 (Dyre); Examination of Rebecca Proud, February 28, 1718/19 (Dyre); Examination of Mary Sanford, February 28, 1718/19 (Dyre); Deposition of Vartue Records, March 24, 1718/19 (Dyre); Deposition of Joseph Cooke, April 6, 1719 (Dyre), RIJA.

56. Deposition of John Wilson, January 27, 1745/46 (Alcock); Examination of William Dyre, February 16, 1718/19 (Dyre); Examination of Mary Sanford, February 28, 1718/19 (Dyre); Examination of Ann Fisher, January 30, 1745/46 (Alcock); Examination of Nathaniel Alcock, January 28, 1745/46 (Alcock), RIJA.

57. Examination of Mary Sanford, February 28, 1718/19 (Dyre); Declaration of Hannah Akins, April 2, 1719 (Dyre); Evidence of Lydia Townsend, February 7, 1745/46 (Alcock), RIJA.

58. John James statement [c. 1718/19]. (This case involves John Hammett, but the statement is located in the Dyre case file, RIJA.)

59. Evidence of Esther Humphreys, January 27, 1745/46 (Alcock), RIJA.

60. Examination of Nathaniel Alcock, January 28, 1745/46 (Alcock); Examination of William Dyre, February 28, 1718/19 (Dyre), RIJA.

61. *Providence Gazette and Country Journal,* November 23–30, 1771.

62. This is not necessarily true of early modern London, where, according to Laura Gowing, women were more likely to intervene in an altercation between husband and wife. Gowing also maintains that women protested spousal abuse more often than men and acted as witnesses more frequently. "It was women to whom battered wives turned first." Men only belatedly became involved. Gowing, *Domestic Dangers,* 217–18.

63. Report of Inquest Jury (Meecum), March 23, 1715/16 (docket 114), RIJA. This document is erroneously filed as an indictment. The indictment may be found in bk. A, Superior Court Records of Newport County, p. 225, RIJA.

64. A warrant for tak[ing] up the Body of Hannah Dyre, February 16, 1718/19 (Dyre), RIJA.

65. Surgeon's Report for second inquest jury in case of Hannah Dyre, February 16, 1718/19 (Dyre), RIJA.

66. Elizabeth Hall's name was inserted later and by a different hand on a list of inquest jurors assembled to inquire into the death of Edward Thornes. The original list was composed of twelve men. Clarence S. Brigham, ed., *Early Records of the Town of Portsmouth* (Providence, R.I.: E. L. Freeman and Sons, 1901), 294 (March 5, 1684/5).

67. Return of the jury of Hannah Dyre when she was taken out of the Grave, February 16, 1718/19 (Dyre), RIJA.

68. Evidence of Doctors Hooper and Wigneron, January 27, 1745/46 (Alcock), RIJA.

69. The Jury Inquisition, January 27, 1745/46 (Alcock); Petition of Nathaniel Alcock, March 1747, RIJA.

70. Summons, January 28, 1745/46 (Alcock); Dr. Moffatt's Evidence, January 28, 1745/46 (Alcock); Doctor Rodman's Evidence, January 28, 1745/46 (Alcock); Dr. Brett's Evidence, January 28, 1745/46 (Alcock); Recognizances of Doctors John Brett, Thomas Moffatt, Clarke Rodman, Henry Hooper, and Norbert Wigneron, all dated January 28, 1745/46 (Alcock), RIJA.

71. Petition of Nathaniel Alcock for reprieve from sentence of murder May 1746, Petitions to the Rhode Island General Assembly 1743–48, vol. 6, p. 116, Rhode Island State Archives, Providence (hereafter RISA). My thanks to Kenneth S. Carlson for sending me these documents.

72. Conflicts between bench and jury were common in early America, and it was not unusual for judges to force a verdict by withholding food or denying a recess. See Crane, *Killed Strangely,* 148, and Thomas A. Green, *Verdict according to Conscience: Perspectives on the English Criminal Trial, 1200–1800* (Chicago: University of Chicago Press, 1985).

73. In modern language, "acquitting."

74. Petition of Nathaniel Alcock to the Superior Court of Judicature . . . of Rhode Island, March 1747, RIJA; "An Act for suspending the execution of Nathaniel Alcock," Bartlett, *Records of the Colony of Rhode Island,* 5:212n [1747]; Journal of the House of Deputies [R.I.] May 1746, RISA.

75. Statement by Thomas Moffatt, April 22, 1746 (Alcock), RIJA. In response to a question about how his wife's neck had become dislocated, Alcock had asserted that two days before her death, she had fallen out of bed on her head. Examination of Nathaniel Alcock, January 28, 1745/46 (Alcock), RIJA; Fiske, *Gleanings,* no. 903 (1758).

76. *Boston News-Letter,* April 11–18, 1715, dateline Rhode-Island, April 15.

77. "Desierous"? Was this a pun on the part of the scribe? Friends' Monthly Meeting, 30th of the 4th month 1719, Quaker Record Book no. 808, p. 166, vault A, NHS. Curiously, Dyre used similar language during his assaults on his wife. Hannah Dyre told Mary Partridge that her husband had threatened "to Ripe her open" with a penknife he had sharpened for the purpose. Examination of Mary Partridge, February 28, 1718/19 (Dyre), RIJA. Desire Dyre died September 3, 1760, at age sixty-nine. Her husband, Samuel, died seven years later on September 15, 1767, at age eighty. See Arnold, *Vital Records,* 4:99.

78. The court's sentencing for Meecum and Dyre is in Newport County Superior Court Records, bk. A, p. 225 (Meecum) and p. 301 (Dyre), RIJA.

79. Evidence of Ann Fisher, January 30, 1745/46 (Alcock), RIJA; "Trinity Church Baptisms," NHS.

80. Examination of Margaret Hasey, February 7, 1745/46 (Alcock), RIJA.

81. Examination of William Dyre, February 28, 1718/19 (Dyre); Testimony of Vartue Records, March 24, 1718/19 (Dyre), RIJA.

82. See Irene Q. Brown and Richard D. Brown, *The Hanging of Ephraim Wheeler: A Story of Rape, Incest, and Justice in Early America* (Cambridge, Mass.: Harvard University Press, 2003) for a discussion of the mental anguish faced by a daughter called upon to testify against her father.

83. Testimony of Thomas Olney, April 13, 1784 (Brown); Evidence of John Wilson, January 27, 1745/46 (Alcock), RIJA.

84. Bartlett, *Records of the Colony of Rhode Island,* 4:196 (1715).

85. Town Council Records, vol. 3 (1714–19), p. 32, NHS.

86. Carl Bridenbaugh, *Cities in the Wilderness: The First Century of Urban Life in America, 1625–1742* (New York: Oxford University Press, 1938), 385.

87. Rhode Island Superior Court, 1732, bk. B, pp. 438–39, RIJA; Fiske, *Gleanings,* no. 210. It is intriguing that the victim in this case bears the same name as the woman Thomas Hammett's father assaulted with a shovel years earlier.

88. Hammett family file, NHS.

89. See Steven J. Stewart, "Skimmington in the Middle and New England Colonies," in *Riot and Revelry in Early America,* ed. William Pencak, Matthew Dennis, and Simon P. Newman (University Park: Pennsylvania State University Press, 2002), 41–48.

90. Brendan McConville, "The Rise of Rough Music: Reflections on an Ancient New Custom in Eighteenth-Century New Jersey," in *Riot and Revelry,* ed. Pencak et al., 87–106.

91. *Newport Mercury,* November 8, 1764.

92. Ibid., November 12, 1764.

93. Deposition of James Terett, December 20, 1773, *Ann Setin [Seten] v. Asa Setin* (1774), bk. F, p. 91, RIJA. Asa Seten was, by his own admission, a bigamist, and it is unclear to which wife Terett referred in his comments.

94. Patience Meecum and Hannah Dyre died in March, Elizabeth Alcock in January, Mary Flack in November. Evidence of Esther Humphrey, January 27, 1745/46 (Alcock), RIJA. Dyre and Flack on Friday; Alcock on Sunday. The Meecum murders occurred on a Tuesday during the day. Hammett's assault took place the evening of August 15.

95. See Daniels, "Intimate Violence, Now and Then," 4 and passim.

96. Stephen P. Sharples, *Records of the Church of Christ at Cambridge in New England, 1632–1830* (Boston, 1906), 126; Records of the Minutes of the Rhode Island Monthly Meeting 1739–1773, p. 355, binder no. 809, NHS.

97. Table 1, "Discipline of Various Offenses in Baptist and Separate Churches, by Sex, 1740–1780," in Susan Juster, *Disorderly Women: Sexual Politics and Evangelicalism in Revolutionary New England* (Ithaca, N.Y.: Cornell University Press, 1994), 84–85, 98–100.

98. The amount of neighborly intervention at any given time has been a disputed question. Merril Smith's research on Pennsylvania suggests that the eighteenth century was a transition period where formal regulation of domestic disputes was supplanting informal mechanisms. She argues also that as expectations of marital affection increased, perceptions of what constituted wife abuse changed as well. As a result of heightened expectations about marriage, neighbors continued to assist battered wives despite the growing acceptance of family privacy. My hesitation with Smith's conclusions is that neighbors had intervened in the past when, theoretically at least, there was no expectation of a loving, respectful, companionate marriage, nor any expectation of family privacy. See Smith, *Breaking the Bonds,* 107, 114–15, 128, 137.

99. Although the extent of neighborly intervention in England was similar to that of the colonies, Laura Gowing admits that "such interventions were not necessarily effective." Gowing, *Domestic Dangers,* 216. Margaret Hunt sees shame as evolutionary, calling it an eighteenth-century means of dealing with abusive husbands. See Hunt, "Wife Beating," 25.

100. Newport Tax Assessment, 1760, RISA. Alcock's assessment of nine shillings was at the low end of the rate. Fiske, *Gleanings,* no. 903 (1758).

101. See Dayton, *Women before the Bar,* 105–8, 111, 130, 136–38; Roger Thompson, *Sex in Middlesex: Popular Mores in a Massachusetts County, 1649–1699* (Amherst: University of Massachusetts Press, 1986), 10–11.

102. Brendan McConville maintains that violence against wives increased during the eighteenth century. See McConville, "Rise of Rough Music," 94. Although McConville's study concentrates on the middle colonies, if his thesis has wider application, there may be reasons other than the ones he articulates. For example, the demographics of New England towns show more women than men in the eighteenth century, a reverse of the previous century. More adult women than men may have been seen as a threat—even a subliminal one—to some men and might even account not only for an increase in domestic violence, but for the decline in prosecutions for assault.

103. *Priscilla Pate v. Robert Pate* (1764), bk. E, p. 252, and file papers; *Susanna Man v. John Man* (1774), bk. F, p. 103, RIJA.

104. Post-revolutionary cases combining cruelty with other grounds include *Catherine Wight [White] v. Francis Wight* (1784), bk. F, p. 246; *Elizabeth Dernier v. Peter*

Dernier (1786), bk. F, pp. 271–72; *Sarah Browning v. George Browning* (1789); *Sarah Nichols v. John Nicholes* (1782), bk. F, p. 201; *Abigail Parker v. Nicholas Parker* (1785), bk. F, p. 260; *Lydia Belcher v. Joseph Belcher* (1784), bk. F, p. 236; *Sarah Taylor v. James Taylor* (1800), bk. G, p. 116; *Anna Read v. David Read* (1793), bk. G, 42–43; *Meribe Callahan v. Frederick William Callahan* (1797), file papers; *Hepzibah Barrington v. Roger Barrington* (1797), bk. G, p. 36; *Sarah Hogan v. John Hogan* (1784), bk. F, p. 245; *Lany Wendel v. Henry Wendel* (1791), bk. G, pp. 81–82, RIJA.

105. On divorce see, for example, Elaine Forman Crane, *Ebb Tide in New England* (Boston: Northeastern University Press, 1998), 192–95, Nancy F. Cott, "Divorce and the Changing Status of Women in Eighteenth-Century Massachusetts," *William and Mary Quarterly* 33 (1976): 586–614, Dayton, *Women before the Bar,* 107, 135–36, 156, and Sheldon S. Cohen, "The Broken Bond: Divorce in Providence County, 1749–1809," *Rhode Island History* 44 (1985): 67–79. Merril Smith maintains that women sought assistance from neighbors and friends more toward the end of the century than earlier, a move that would parallel the rising divorce rate, but it is difficult to know how this could be quantified. Smith, *Breaking the Bonds,* 118.

4. Cold Comfort

A special thanks to Wilton Tejada for his perceptive insights and willingness to discuss this case with me.

1. Examination of James Strange, December 29, 1742, file papers, folder March 1743, Rhode Island Judicial Archives, Pawtucket (hereafter RIJA). On December 23, 1742, the sun set at 5:05 p.m. Nathanael Ames, *An Astronomical Diary, or, An Almanack for . . . 1742* (Boston: John Draper, 1742).

2. Carl Bridenbaugh, *Gentleman's Progress: The Itinerarium of Dr. Alexander Hamilton, 1744* (Westport, Conn.: Greenwood Press, 1948), 103; in 1743 a gallon of New England rum was 2.35 shillings. "Average Annual Wholesale Prices of Selected Commodities 1720–1775," *Historical Statistics of the United States, Colonial Times to 1970* (Washington, D.C.: Bureau of the Census, 1975), 2:1197; "An Act for the Stating of Prices of Ferriage . . . in This Colony" (1743), *Acts and Laws of His Majesty's Colony of Rhode Island, and Providence Plantations in America* (Newport, R.I.: Widow Franklin, 1745), 265.

3. Comfort Dennis had married Philip Taylor in 1723. He died in 1739, leaving her with four daughters and two sons. In 1742 they ranged in age from five to eighteen. Elaine Dennis Young, *Some Descendants of Robert Dennis of Portsmouth, Rhode Island* (Norwalk, Ohio, 1957), 3.

4. Indeed, Jay Coughtry indicates that "there is no evidence that Rhode Island sold African slaves in Rhode Island until 1725." Jay Coughtry, *The Notorious Triangle: Rhode Island and the African Slave Trade, 1700–1807* (Philadelphia: Temple University Press, 1981), 167. This does not preclude sales by other traders, but it is still unlikely that Cuff was born in Rhode Island. It is remotely possible—although a leap—that Cuff arrived in Rhode Island on the *Charming Susanna* along with Venture Smith in 1739. Yet even if they arrived at different times, Cuff and Smith might very well have crossed paths in Newport in 1740 when Smith was living there with his owner's sister. See Smith's narrative of his life (1798) and articles about him in James Brewer

Stewart, ed., *Venture Smith and the Business of Slavery and Freedom* (Amherst: University of Massachusetts Press, 2010).

5. Great Britain and Spain had been engaged in what was known as the War of Jenkins' Ear (1739–42). The capture and impressment of slaves is discussed in Charles Foy, "Coerced Maritime Labor: Dark-Skinned Mariners as Prize Goods, 1739–1783," Columbia Seminar in Early American History and Culture, November 11, 2008.

6. Anna Augusta and Charles V. Chapin, *A History of Rhode Island Ferries, 1640–1923* (Providence, R.I.: Oxford Press, 1925), 60.

7. Skilled mariners, including ferrymen, were among those more likely to attempt an escape from slavery. See Gerald A. Mullin, *Flight and Rebellion: Slave Resistance in Eighteenth-Century Virginia* (London: Oxford University Press, 1972), 94, 95, 98. While Mullin's statistics relate to the southern experience, the same undoubtedly holds true for points north.

8. Such activity was strictly prohibited by a 1714 law. "An Act to prevent Slaves from Running Away from their Masters." *Acts and Laws of Rhode Island* (1745), 49–50.

9. Examination of Comfort Taylor, December 24, 1742, file papers, folder March 1743, RIJA; *Oxford English Dictionary,* s.v. "cuddy."

10. By "coats" Comfort meant petticoats, a garment that was akin to a skirt. Given the weather, her petticoat might have been quilted and backed with worsted. She would have worn a cloak to protect herself against the cold. And her reference to "stays" suggests a concession to warmth as well as to fashion, since this corset-like garment was frequently lined. Stays were an essential component of any Anglo-American female wardrobe in the eighteenth century. They shaped the body and helped maintain proper posture. For what it's worth, Comfort was probably not wearing "drawers." See C. Willett Cunnington and Phillis Cunnington, *Handbook of English Costume in the Eighteenth Century* (Boston: Plays Inc., 1972), 106, 150. See also Linda Baumgarten, *What Clothes Reveal: The Language of Clothing in Colonial and Federal America; The Colonial Williamsburg Collection* (Williamsburg, Va.: Colonial Williamsburg Foundation, and New Haven, Conn.: Yale University Press, 2002), 89, 121, 29.

11. James Strange was probably born between 1695 and 1698, putting him somewhere in his middle to late forties at the time of the incident. He was a married man with children and lived in Portsmouth. William Cory seems to have been the son of William and Mary (Earle) Cory. His father was a house carpenter, and it is possible that William junior followed that trade as well. See the *New England Historical and Genealogical Register* 19, no. 4 (October 1865): 324, and Harry Harmon Cory, ed., *The Cory Family: A Genealogy* (Minneapolis: Argus, 1941), 12.

12. Examination of James Strange, December 29, 1742, RIJA; Examination of William Cory, December 29, 1742, file papers, folder March 1743, RIJA.

13. As subsequent testimony shows, the word "beast" was a reference to Cuff if not here, then elsewhere.

14. Examination of James Strange, December 29, 1742, RIJA; Examination of Comfort Taylor, December 24, 1742, RIJA.

15. Examination of Thomas Durfee, December 29, 1742, file papers, folder March 1743, RIJA.

16. Examination of William Cory, December 29, 1742, file papers, folder March 1743, RIJA.

17. Examination of William Cory, December 29, 1742; Examination of Thomas Green, May 30, 1743, Equity Court file papers, October session 1743, vol. 6, p. 107, document 2, Rhode Island State Archives, Providence (hereafter RISA).

18. Sharon Block, *Rape and Sexual Power in Early America* (Chapel Hill: University of North Carolina Press, 2006), 170–73, 180–81.

19. Examination of Thomas Green, May 30, 1743, RISA. The jail was in Bristol, Massachusetts.

20. Rhode Island did not have a statute addressing attempted rape in 1742.

21. Examination of Cuff, December 25, 1742, file papers, folder March 1743, RIJA.

22. Bristol did not become part of Rhode Island until 1747. "To Caleb Bennit Sarjant of the town of Portsmouth or to Either of the Constables for the town," December 24, 1742, file papers, RIJA.

23. If, as previously noted, the sun was only "one hour high," and the official sunset was a few minutes after 5 p.m., Cuff's response confirms that Comfort boarded the ferry at roughly 3:45 p.m.

24. An ebb is a river bend at which the current flows backward; an eddy is a current running contrary to the main current, especially one moving circularly (as a whirlpool).

25. Furthermore, the Dennis family was also related by both blood and marriage to the Bordens, which makes this saga a complicated family quarrel.

26. In this question the word "you" is stricken out and replaced by "thee." Since "thee" is used throughout the rest of the questions, it leaves no doubt that the questioner was a Quaker. But both of Cuff's interrogators were members of the Society of Friends, making it difficult to know in which order Anthony and Howland questioned Cuff.

27. Chapin, *History of Rhode Island Ferries,* 178–79, 29.

28. Records of Rhode Island Monthly Meetings 1707–1739, bk. 808, p. 254; To the Monthly Meeting to be held in Portsmouth the 25th of the 4th mo. 1728, Friends Records Testimonies 1718–1827, bk. 821, no. 12, Newport Historical Society, Newport, R.I. (hereafter NHS).

29. Records of Rhode Island Monthly Meetings 1707–1739, bk. 808, pp. 360, 361, 362, 363, 364, NHS.

30. Hattie Borden Weld, *Historical and Genealogical Record . . . of Richard and Joan Borden* (Los Angeles: H. B. Weld, 1899; reprint, Bethany, Okla.: Richardson Reprints, 1985), 70–71. Reputation notwithstanding, Borden engaged in a series of inexplicable real estate transactions in 1739. On January 15, 1738/9, Borden sold nine lots of land on Hog Island to nine local men. Each lot contained ten acres, and each cost three hundred pounds current money of New England. Less than five months later, on June 4, 1739, Borden repurchased the same property from the same men at the same price. Although it is difficult to say who eventually came out ahead in financial terms, these multiple transactions may have had some connection to the emission of one hundred thousand pounds in bills of public credit by the Rhode Island General Assembly in December 1738. Through this "bank," paper money became available for a variety of purposes. Yet Rhode Island's paper currency had a tendency to

depreciate, so if Borden bought the property back at the same price he had sold it for five months earlier, he would actually be repurchasing for less money. If this is the case, a question arises about the willingness of Borden's buyers to resell at the original purchase price if the currency fluctuation worked against their interests. It is also possible that the transaction could have been a mortgage or loan. In other words, Borden might have needed cash, and the nine men formed a consortium in order to "lend" him the money. In such circumstances Borden would have "mortgaged" his property as security, and when he was able to pay it back he did. Yet there is no mention of interest charges, and it is difficult to understand why the nine "buyers" would have entered such an arrangement. Sydney V. James, *Colonial Rhode Island: A History* (New York: Scribner's, [1975]), 178, 180; Grantor Index, vol. 4, 149, 151–58, and Grantee Index, vol. 4, 232–33, Portsmouth Town Hall, Portsmouth, R.I.

31. Examination of Thomas Green, May 30, 1743; Examination of Althea Fales, May 30, 1743, Equity Court file papers, October session, 1743, vol. 6, p. 107, document 3, RISA; Deposition of Thomas Durfee, October 10, 1743, Equity Court file papers, October 1743, vol. 6, p. 107, document 4, RISA.

32. Examination of Thomas Green, May 30, 1743, RISA.

33. Block, *Rape and Sexual Power,* 180–81.

34. Rhode Island census of 1730 and 1748–49 in Evarts B. Greene and Virginia D. Harrington, *American Population before the Federal Census of 1790* (Baltimore: Genealogical Publishing Co., 1932, 1981), 66.

35. General Court of Trials and Gaol Delivery 1725–1730 and Judicature Court of Assize 1730–1741, Newport County, vol. 3; Rhode Island Superior Court of Judicature, bk. C, September 1741–September 1746, RIJA.

36. Block, *Rape and Sexual Power,* 142, 145–49.

37. Jane Fiske, *Rhode Island Court of Trials, 1671–1704* (Boxford, Mass: privately printed, 1998), 6, 7, 221. The *Oxford English Dictionary* is unclear as to where the "brane" of a thumb might be located.

38. Block, *Rape and Sexual Power,* 142, 145, 147, 170–73, 148, 187.

39. http://www.newenglandancestors.org, *Vital Records of Rhode Island,* town search, Little Compton, church records, United Congregational Church; *Confession of Faith and Covenant of the United Congregational Church in Little Compton* (Boston: John Putnam, 1846), 18.

40. *Boston Evening Post,* January 3, 1743, p. 2; *American Weekly Mercury* (Philadelphia), January 27–February 1, 1742/43, p. 3.

41. The identity of the jurors has been established through John Russell Bartlett, ed., *Records of the Colony of Rhode Island and Providence Plantations in New England* (Providence, R.I.: Knowles, Anthony and Co., 1860), vols. 4 and 5 (hereafter RICR), as well as from Ronald V. Jackson, "Rhode Island in 1742 and 1747," Accelerated Indexing System International, North Salt Lake, Utah, n.d. (Courtesy New Jersey State Library, Trenton).

42. See *Rex v. Cuff,* folder March 1743, RIJA.

43. Equity Court file papers, October session 1743, vol. 6, p. 107, fifth document, p. 1, RISA. *Rex v. Cuff,* indictment, folder March 1743, RIJA.

44. Examination of Thomas Durfee, December 29, 1742, RIJA.

45. Profiles of the judges give no hint as to why Cuff received such a light sentence. The governor and assistant governor along with nine assistants sat on the

bench at this session. All of them were designated as "Esq.," and taken together they were among Rhode Island's elite. Their church affiliations varied, although at least a third may have been members of Trinity Church, the Anglican church of Newport. Quakers are conspicuously absent from the list.

46. One reason for the relatively light sentence is that the charge was *attempted* rape, not *consummated* rape. But given the disparity of sentences between black and white defendants, twenty pounds was suspiciously low, nonetheless. A year later in Maryland, a white male defendant received a twenty-pound punishment for attempted rape. See Block, *Rape and Sexual Power,* 147. To determine the relative value of twenty pounds (£20), one might assess its purchasing power. In 1739 the Rhode Island General Assembly permitted a withdrawal of twenty pounds from the general treasury for the repair of a bridge. In the same year, Daniel Updike was allowed twenty pounds for writing up the points of a land dispute between Massachusetts and Rhode Island, and an outlay of twenty-five pounds was permitted for the purchase of a courthouse bell. Twenty pounds would purchase two cows. Although house rentals varied in price, eight pounds would rent an average house for a year between 1740 and 1746. A live-in Newport servant, Elizabeth Stafford, earned ten shillings per week in 1742–43, which was the equivalent of twenty-six pounds per year. Raisins sold for two shillings per pound weight in August 1743, while broadcloth could be bought for anywhere from twenty-five shillings to five pounds per yard at the same time. In 1743, a gallon of molasses cost 1.87 shillings, while the same amount of New England rum cost over 2 shillings. RICR, 4:553, 557, 566; *Acts and Laws of Rhode Island* (1745), 293; Thomas Richardson, petty account book, 1722–54, binder 487, NHS; *Boston Post-Boy,* August 15, 1743.

47. Trespass is an action charging unlawful interference with one's person, property, or rights.

48. Equity Court file papers, October session 1743, vol. 6, p. 106, document 1, p. 2, RISA.

49. Ibid., p. 4.

50. There is a rich literature on the ambiguities of a slave as both person and property. That literature, however, focuses primarily on the nineteenth century and the southern states. Such articles concentrate on the dual nature of slaves in the three-fifths clause of the Constitution, slaves accepted as judgment for debt, case histories of slaves as persons vis-à-vis property, questions of whether liberty or property prevailed in inheritance contests over slaves, the rights of slaves to sue for their freedom, the extent of power that a master had over a slave, contracts between masters and slaves, and the ability of the state to bring criminal charges against slaves. While this list is not exhaustive, I have not found works that discuss the existence of civil suits against slaves in the eighteenth-century northern colonies. The most complex study is Ariela Gross, *Double Character: Slavery and Mastery in the Antebellum Southern Courtroom* (Athens: University of Georgia Press, 2000), which investigates these issues in the Deep South. For studies of the upper South, most of which concentrate on Virginia, see J. Thomas Wren, "'A Two-Fold Character': The Slave as Person and Property in Virginia Court Cases 1800–1860," *Southern Studies* 24 (Winter 1985): 417–31; James H. Kettner, "Persons or Property? The Pleasants Slaves in the Virginia Courts, 1792–1799," in *Launching the "Extended Republic": The Federalist Era,* ed. Ronald Hoffman and Peter J. Albert (Charlottesville: University Press of

Virginia, 1996), 136–55; A. E. Keir Nash, "Fairness and Formalism in the Trials of Blacks in the State Supreme Courts of the Old South," *Virginia Law Review* 56, no. 1 (February 1970): 64–100; A. Leon Higginbotham and Barbara K. Kopytoff, "Property First, Humanity Second: The Recognition of the Slave's Human Nature in Virginia Civil Law," *Ohio State Law Journal* 50 (1989): 511–40; Malick W. Ghachem, "The Slave's Two Bodies: The Life of an American Legal Fiction," *William and Mary Quarterly,* 3rd series, vol. 60, no. 4 (October 2003): 809–42.

51. Rhode Island contained a considerable number of Quakers in the mid-eighteenth century, and although it is not possible to estimate the number of slaves in Rhode Island held by Quakers, there is little doubt that many Quakers, like Thomas Borden, were slaveholders. Pennsylvania Friends had already expressed discomfort about slave trading and slaveholding as early as the 1730s, but the situation in Rhode Island was more complicated, since Newport would shortly become the major slave-trading port of New England. See Arthur J. Worrall, *Quakers in the Colonial Northeast* (Hanover, N.H.: University Press of New England, 1980), 152–55; Jean R. Soderlund, *Quakers and Slavery: A Divided Spirit* (Princeton, N.J.: Princeton University Press, 1985), 118–20; A. Leon Higginbotham Jr., *In the Matter of Color: Race and the American Legal Process; The Colonial Period* (New York: Oxford University Press, 1978), 295.

52. Documents relating to the civil cases between Comfort Taylor and Cuff will be found in the Rhode Island State Archives in Providence (RISA) and the Rhode Island Judicial Archives in Pawtucket (RIJA).

53. Diary of Daniel Howland, February 19, 1743, and passim in microfilm of records in James Arnold's family notes. Town notes collection at the Knight Memorial Library, Providence, R.I. Filmed by Genealogical Society of Utah, 1992 (Salt Lake City), abstracts and indexes to diaries from Rhode Island and Massachusetts 1739–1865, no. 1839091, item 3.

54. Equity Court papers, October session 1743, vol. 6, p. 106, document 2, pp. 5, 6, RISA. Joseph Dennis was Comfort Taylor's uncle.

55. Deposition of Thomas Green, May 30, 1743, Equity Court file papers, vol. 6, p. 107, document 2, RISA.

56. Equity Court file papers, p. 107, document 3, RISA.

57. Statement of William Anthony Jr., June 6, 1743, Equity Court file papers, document 2, p. 7, RISA.

58. Equity Court file papers, October session 1743, vol. 6, p. 106, document 3, p. 10, RISA.

59. The first Tuesday of Sept. AD 1743, Equity Court file papers, vol. 6, p. 106, document 3, p. 9, RISA.

60. Equity Court file papers, vol. 6, p. 106, document 3, p. 10, RISA.

61. I have relied on Zechariah Chafee Jr., "Records of the Rhode Island Court of Equity 1741–1743," in Colonial Society of Massachusetts *Publications* 35 (Transactions 1942–1946): 91–118 (1951) for the information in the preceding two paragraphs. The judges who sat in October 1743 were Robert Hasard (South Kingston), Josiah Arnold (Jamestown), William Anthony (Portsmouth), Thomas Spenser (East Greenwich), and John Potter (Providence).

62. Today it would be highly unusual for an appellate court to review anything but the records from the lower court.

63. Testimony of Patience Hall, October 7, 1743, Equity Court file papers, October session, 1743, vol. 6, p. 107, document 1, RISA.

64. Deposition of Thomas Durfee, October 10, 1743, RISA.

65. Equity Court file papers, vol. 6, p. 107, document 5, RISA.

66. It is not impossible that Cuff earned a small income as ferry captain, but there is no evidence either way on this point.

67. Petition of Comfort Taylor to the General Assembly, October 1743, Rhode Island Colony Records (MS) 1729–45, RISA. At least two other versions of this petition exist. One is in the petition collection of RISA (vol. 5, p. 33); the other is in RICR 5:72–73. Subtle changes hint either at Comfort's (or her lawyer's) care in preparing the petition, or a secretary's use of alternative wording. Taylor either "desired," "prayed," or "humbly hoped" the General Assembly would remit the twenty-pound fine.

68. Elizabeth Donnan, *Documents Illustrative of the History of the Slave Trade to America* (Washington, D.C.: Carnegie Institution, 1930–35) 3:64, 65n. In Newport in 1743 the price of boys ranged from £75 to £105 and men from £50 to £105.

69. *Acts and Laws of Rhode Island* (1745), 118.

70. Block, *Rape and Sexual Power,* 148.

71. "An Act for the more effectual Punishment of *Negroes* that shall attempt to commit a *Rape* on any white Woman," (August session, 1743) *Acts and Laws of Rhode Island* (1745), 263–64.

72. William Blackstone, *Commentaries on the Laws of England* (Oxford: Clarendon Press, 1769), 4:213.

73. Deposition of Thomas Durfee, October 10, 1743, RISA.

74. Evan Malbone (1707–84) was a Virginian by birth. His brother, Francis Malbone, was his business partner. Thanks to Bert Lippincott, genealogist and reference librarian at the Newport Historical Society, for this information. For further information on the Malbones see the *Newport Historical Magazine* 3, no. 1 (July 1882): 119. Malbone's obituary may be found in the *Newport Mercury,* May 26, 1781, p. 3.

75. Antoinette Downing and Vincent Scully, *The Architectural Heritage of Newport, Rhode Island, 1640–1915,* 2nd ed. (New York: Bramhall House, 1952, 1967), 52, 39, 64, 98.

76. As a runaway advertisement in Virginia noted, a female slave absconded with clothing that "makes her appear more like a free woman." *Virginia Gazette* (Rind), October 26, 1769, quoted in Baumgarten, *What Clothes Reveal,* 139. A greatcoat would have been worth approximately eight pounds. Isaac Stelle ledger 1741–64 (1746) (no. 496), NHS.

77. Runaway notice in the *Boston Evening-Post,* June 4, 1744, p. 2, and June 11, 1744, p. 3. The notice also appeared on June 18, 1744, and June 25, 1744, in the *Boston Post-Boy.* For the use of the word "lusty" see an advertisement for "A Lusty Young Negro Man fit for any Work either in Town or Country," in the *New-York Weekly Journal,* December 6, 1742, p. 4.

78. According to Sharon Block, "no castrations appear to have been carried out in the mainland colonies as a rape or attempted rape sentence until close to the time of the American Revolution." Block, *Rape and Sexual Power,* 150–51. Winthrop Jordan maintains that castration as a legal punishment was limited to the early eighteenth century and was disallowed by Great Britain. Winthrop Jordan, *White over Black:*

American Attitudes toward the Negro, 1550–1812 (Chapel Hill: University of North Carolina Press, 1968), 154–58.

79. There are many websites on undescended testicles and the implications of such a condition. See, for example, http://www.nlm.nih.gov/medlineplus/ency/article/000973.htm and http://www.urologychannel.com/testosteronedeficiency/symptoms.shtm/. It is interesting that the runaway notice indicates that Cuff was "stout." Obesity is a symptom of low testosterone. See http://www.sciencedaily.com/releases/2008/06/080617124020.htm.

80. A full moon appeared on May 15 at six in the morning. Nathanael Ames, *An Astronomical Diary, or, An Almanack for . . . 1744* (Boston, 1743).

81. See Marcus Rediker, *Between the Devil and the Deep Blue Sea: Merchant Seamen, Pirates, and the Anglo-American Maritime World, 1700–1750* (Cambridge: Cambridge University Press, 1987), 29, 62, 67, 68, 112, for evidence of enslaved dockworkers in port cities.

82. "An Act to prevent Slaves from Running away from their Masters" (1714). *Acts and Laws of Rhode Island* (1745), 49–50.

83. By this time Quakers were agitating for an end to the slave trade, but there was no concerted effort to abolish slavery until the 1750s. See Higginbotham, *In the Matter of Color,* 295.

84. *Boston Evening Post,* February 7, 1743, p. 4.

85. See the *Boston Post-Boy,* April 30, 1744, p. 2, and May 14, 1744, p. 3, for prospective outward-bound ships from Rhode Island (Newport). Four black men served on the *Revenge* in 1741. W. Jeffrey Bolster, *Black Jacks: African American Seamen in the Age of Sail* (Cambridge, Mass.: Harvard University Press, 1997), 26, 29, 32. See also Lorenzo J. Greene, *The Negro in Colonial New England* (New York: Atheneum, 1969), 129–30, for evidence of slaves serving as crew members on New England vessels during the midcentury wars.

86. *Rashomon,* a Japanese short story written by Akutagawa Ryunosuke in 1915, takes place in ancient Japan and involves a woman who is raped and whose husband, a samurai, is murdered. Four different accounts of the crime are rendered: by the widow, the murderer, the victim, and a woodcutter who finds the body. The short story, and the 1950 movie directed by Akira Kurosawa, question the concept of "truth."

87. A wind would have prevented Cuff from being swept up by the current. My thanks to Rhode Islanders Richard and Joan Youngken for teaching this landlubber something every sailor knows. Bert Lippincott also pointed out that high and low tides (with water rushing in or out) affect currents as well. Tides are most extreme during the full and new moon, neither of which prevailed on December 23, 1742.

88. Examination of Cuff, December 25, 1742, file papers, RIJA.

89. As it turns out, the poet Nicholas Breton (1545–1626) used this phrase in his essay "The Praise of Vertuous Ladies and Gentlewomen." There is an edition of this essay published in London in 1599 by Thomas Creede, and the quote may be found on p. 174. The essay was republished a number of times in the seventeenth century, although it appears to have lost popularity by the eighteenth century.

90. Block, *Rape and Sexual Power,* 130–34.

91. Examination of James Strange, December 29, 1742, RIJA.

92. Examination of William Cory, December 29, 1742, RIJA.

93. The New York "plot" was only the most well-known of a series of alleged conspiracies and potential uprisings that attracted public attention between 1729 and the early 1740s.

94. Daniel Horsmanden, *The New York Conspiracy,* ed. Thomas J. Davis (Boston: Beacon Press, 1971), vii.

95. For the most recent and thorough examination of the so-called plot, see Jill Lepore, *New York Burning: Liberty, Slavery, and Conspiracy in Eighteenth-Century Manhattan* (New York: Knopf, 2005). Her assessment of surviving documents may be found on pp. 93–94. See also the *Boston Evening-Post,* July 6, 1741, p. 2, and the *Boston Weekly News-Letter,* July 23, 1741, p. 1.

96. Horsmanden, June 1, 1741, 118, 121; June 17, 1741, 180.

97. *New-York Weekly Journal,* August 9, 1742, p. 1.

98. Horsmanden, *New York Conspiracy,* 402.

99. Jordan, *White over Black,* 33–34, 28.

100. Cohen also alludes to the possibility of consensual relationships. See Daniel A. Cohen, "Social Injustice, Sexual Violence, Spiritual Transcendence: Constructions of Interracial Rape in Early American Crime Literature 1767–1817," *William and Mary Quarterly,* 3rd series, vol. 56, no. 3 (July 1999): 484, 489, 513.

101. Examination of Comfort Taylor, December 24, 1742, RIJA; Examinations of Thomas Green and Althea Fales, May 30, 1743, RISA; Examination of James Strange, December 29, 1742, RIJA; Account of Caleb Bennett, December 25, 1742, folder March 1743, RIJA.

102. Will of Philip Taylor, March 20, 1739, NHS.

103. Ibid. A cordwainer was a shoemaker, but Taylor also seems to have operated a tannery to process hides.

104. Comfort Taylor married George Brownell on April 19, 1745. See Young, *Some Descendants of Robert Dennis,* 3.

105. See Robert and Susanna Dennis's wills in Marie Ray Davis and Myrtle Dennis Lundberg, comps., *The Family of Robert Dennis and Sarah Howland* (Portland, Ore., 1969), 184.

106. "Family of Susanna Briggs and Robert Dennis," Pane-Joyce Genealogy, http://aleph0.clark.edu/~djoyce/gen/report/rr10/rr10_064.htm.

107. James N. Arnold, comp., *Vital Records of Rhode Island, 1636–1850* (Providence, R.I.: Narragansett Historical Publishing Co., 1891–), 4 (part 6) (Little Compton records); Pane-Joyce Genealogy; Benjamin Franklin Wilbour, comp., *Little Compton Families* (Little Compton, R.I.: Little Compton Historical Society, 1974), 90–91.

108. Thomas Borden died at the end of 1745. See his will dated October 14, 1745, on microfilm at the NHS. Sir William Pepperell to Governor Gideon Wanton, Louisbourg, September 13, 1745, and Governor Wanton to the agent of Rhode Island in London, Xber 20, 1745. RICR, 5:143, 147. Pepperell commanded the expedition against Louisbourg.

109. *American Weekly Mercury,* January 27–February 1, 1742/43, p. 3. Since the dateline of the story was December 31, it is likely that the *Mercury* picked it up from another paper—probably one published in Boston.

110. Deposition of Thomas Durfee, October 10, 1743, Equity Court records, RISA. Michael Grossberg's phrase, "shadow of the law," particularly applicable in this context, is meant to convey the way the law extends a lengthening shadow over people and proceedings. See Grossberg, *A Judgment for Solomon* (Cambridge: Cambridge University Press, 1996).

111. Greene and Harrington, *American Population,* 66. Cuff's runaway notice appeared in the *Boston Evening Post* June 4 and 11, 1744.

112. Malbone may have felt betrayed, but it was business as usual. In June 1744 Malbone, Thomas Wickham, and Jonathan Thurston outfitted the privateer sloop *Phoenix,* a venture that compensated its owners with the booty from two ships. Howard Chapin, *Rhode Island in King George's War, 1739–1748* (Providence: Rhode Island Historical Society, 1926), 122.

113. Examination of Thomas Green, May 30, 1743, RISA.

114. *Acts and Laws of Rhode Island* (1745), 49–50.

115. Bolster, *Black Jacks,* 24–25, 26, 36, 40, and passim.

5. He Would "Shoot him upon the Spott"

1. Deposition of Martin Howard, January 23, 1744/45. Samuel Banister papers, Rhode Island Judicial Archives, Pawtucket (hereafter RIJA); Notification of Sale, November 19, 1744, Banister papers, RIJA. At a ratio of 6:1, this would have been ninety pounds sterling. John J. McCusker, *Money and Exchange in Europe and America, 1660–1775* (Chapel Hill: University of North Carolina Press, 1978), 141.

2. Deposition of Job Bennett, January 23, 1744/45. Samuel Banister papers, RIJA.

3. Evidences of Peleg Brown, William Dyre, and Job Bennett, January 23, 1744/45, RIJA.

4. Evidence of Doctor Henry Hooper, n.d. but probably January 23, 1744/45, RIJA; *Boston Weekly News-Letter,* January 31, 1745.

5. "The Will of John Banister of Newport, Rhode Island," *New England Historical and Genealogical Register* 69 (October 1915): 351, 352. When word of the tragedy reached Boston, Samuel Sewall, the eminent Boston jurist, paid a condolence call on "Madam Banister," the former Frances Walker. Samuel Sewall, *The Diary of Samuel Sewall,* 2 vols., ed. M. Halsey Thomas (New York: Farrar, Straus and Giroux, 1973), 2:842. Frances Banister survived her husband by nearly two decades.

6. Samuel Barber, *Boston Common: A Diary of Notable Events, Incidents, and Neighboring Occurrences* (Boston: Christopher Publishing House, 1916), 115.

7. Samuel Banister Day Book 1728–1731, no. 562, p. 98ff., 20, Newport Historical Society, Newport, R.I. (hereafter NHS).

8. *Records Relating to the Early History of Boston,* vols. 1–27 (Boston: Rockwell and Churchill City Printers, 1876–90); vols. 28–38 (1898–1908) (Boston: Municipal Printing Office); 13 (1885): 315; 15 (1886): 14, 15, 200.

9. *Records Relating to the Early History of Boston,* 11(1884): 120, 165, 180, 216–17.

10. Sewall, *Diary,* 1:596, 2:741–43.

11. Thomas Banister, *Letter to the Right Honourable the Lords Commissioners of Trade and Plantations; or a Short Essay on the Principal Branches of the Trade of New-England:*

With the Difficulties They Labour Under, and Some Methods of Improvement (London, 1715).

12. *New England Historical and Genealogical Register,* 73:156.

13. Recognizance for Samuel Banister, Jr., January 3, 1732/3, Superior Judicial Court, Suffolk County, reel 719, document 165638, Massachusetts Archives, Boston. A year earlier Samuel had been required to post bond for his good behavior toward John Crosby of Boston, a peruke maker. Suffolk County General Sessions, April–July 1731, reel 718, document no. 165210, Massachusetts Archives, Boston.

14. *Acts and Resolves, Public and Private of the Province of Massachusetts Bay* (Boston: Wright and Potter, 1904), vol. 12 (Resolves, etc. 1734–41) [1734–35], 80, 117.

15. *Boston Gazette,* November 21, 1737. John's marriage to Hermione Pelham may have been his second, since Boston records also show an intention of marriage between John Banister and a Jane Sharp on April 13, 1732. Records Commissioners, Boston marriages 1700–51, 28:219. See also "Will of John Banister," 344.

16. Darius Baker, "The Newport Banisters," *Bulletin of the Newport Historical Society,* no. 43 (January 1923): 1–3; *Boston Gazette,* November 5, 1739.

17. *Records Relating to the Early History of Boston,* 15:200; *Boston Gazette,* February 14, 1737, March 5 and 12, 1739; Ledger Book of John Banister, 1739–46, no. 65A, NHS.

18. Mary Wheeler was born and baptized in June 1703. She married William Porter April 19, 1722. *Boston Transcript,* August 3, 1903 (response to query 447). Records Commissioners, 28:223. Marriage intentions of Samuel Banister and Mary Porter, April 5, 1735. See also Dr. John Brett's accounts with Samuel Banister: "to visit and purge Daughter Mary," as well as other references to Mary and Elizabeth Porter. Equity Court records 3:47:1–23 and 3:48. Equity Court records are found at the Rhode Island State Archives, Providence (hereafter RISA).

19. Equity Court records, 6:35, RISA; Antoinette Dowing and Vincent Scully Jr., *The Architectural Heritage of Newport, Rhode Island (1640–1915)* (New York: Bramhall House, 1952 [1967]), 39–40.

20. *Banister v. Bazin,* May 28, 1744, RIJA.

21. Bruce H. Mann, *Republic of Debtors: Bankruptcy in the Age of American Independence* (Cambridge, Mass.: Harvard University Press, 2002), 10.

22. These cases may be found in the Rhode Island Superior Court of Judicature records, bk. C (1741–46), pp. 22, 53, 58, 81, 105, 298, 313. See also the separate folder "March Term 1745," containing the case of *Carpenter v. Banister* and the papers involving Benjamin Kent's suit for debt against Samuel Banister. RIJA.

23. Brett's case, Equity Court records passim in RISA.

24. Depositions of Sarah Butler [and] Matthew Collingwood, April 14, 1742, Equity Court records, 3:47:16–18; Deposition of Elizabeth Chace, April 14, 1742, Equity Court records, 3:47:15–16; Deposition of Brice and Mary Eccles, [March 30], 1742, Equity Court records, 3:47:11–13; Deposition of Elizabeth Porter, March 30, 1742, Equity Court records, 3:47:8–10; Deposition of Beriah [Whitham], March 30, 1742, Equity Court records, 3:47:14; Deposition of Martha Thomas, March 30, 1742, Equity Court records, 3:47:14. Deposition of Sarah Allen, March 30, 1742, file folder March Term 1742, *Brett v. Banister,* RIJA; Depositions of Margaret Parker and Ann Vroom, April 14, 1742, Equity Court records, 3:47:18–19, RISA.

25. Deposition of Brice and Mary Eccles, March 30, 1742, Equity Court records, 3:47:11–13; Deposition of Martha Thomas, March 30, 1742, Equity Court records, 3:47:14, RISA.

26. Equity Court records, 3:47:1–3; 3:47:4, RISA.

27. Equity Court records, 3:50:1–3, RISA.

28. John R. Bartlett, ed., *Records of the Colony of Rhode Island and Providence Plantations in New England,* 10 vols. (Providence, R.I., 1856–65), 1:180–81.

29. Peter J. Coleman, *Debtors and Creditors in America: Insolvency, Imprisonment for Debt, and Bankruptcy, 1607–1900* (Madison: State Historical Society of Wisconsin, 1974), 86.

30. "An Act for the Maintenance of Insolvent Debtors in Goal; and for the Repealing the Several Acts heretofore made for that Purpose" (1739). *Acts and Laws of His Majesty's Colony of Rhode Island and Providence Plantations, in New England, in America* (Newport, R.I.: Widow Franklin, 1745), 223–24.

31. Equity Court records, 3:47:6–7; 3:50:5–6; 3:47:22–23; 3:50:7–9, RISA.

32. Zechariah Chafee Jr., "Records of the Rhode Island Court of Equity," *Publications of the Colonial Society of Massachusetts* [Transactions 1942–1946] (Boston: Colonial Society of Massachusetts, 1951), 35:91–118.

33. Equity Court records, 3:46; Equity Court file papers, July and August sessions, 1742, vol. 3, cases 17 and 18, RISA.

34. *Banister v. Bazin,* May 28, 1744, RIJA.

35. Folder marked "1744 Banister v. Grant," RIJA.

36. Isaac Stelle ledger 1741–64 ("Calf Skin Book"), binder 496, NHS; Thomas Richardson, petty account book, 1722–54, binder 487, NHS; Benjamin Greene account book, 1734–56, Massachusetts Historical Society, Boston.

37. The documents in this case may be found in Equity Court records, vol. 6:34:3–6, 6:35, and case 13, RISA.

38. Equity Court records, vol. 6, p. 7:1, RISA.

39. Ibid., p. 7:2.

40. Ibid., p. 7:3–4.

41. Deposition of Martin Howard, January 23, 1744/45, Samuel Banister papers, RIJA.

42. John J. McCusker, *Money and Exchange in Europe and America, 1600–1775* (Chapel Hill: University of North Carolina Press, 1978), 141, 126–30.

43. Newport was more heavily engaged in privateering (that is, private vessels in pursuit of enemy merchant ships) than any other colonial port. By the eighteenth century, letters of marque vessels were extremely rare. Carl E. Swanson, "American Privateering and Imperial Warfare, 1739–1748," William and Mary Quarterly 42 (1985): 359, 362, 363n. See also Sydney V. James, *Colonial Rhode Island: A History* (New York: Scribner's, 1975), 292; Howard M. Chapin, *Rhode Island Privateers in King George's War, 1739–1748* (Providence: Rhode Island Historical Society, 1926), 8, 26, 92, 201–2.

44. Alexander Hamilton, "The Itinerarium of Dr. Alexander Hamilton," in *Colonial American Travel Narratives,* ed. Wendy Martin (New York: Penguin, 1994), 252, 293.

45. James McSparran, *A Letter Book and Abstract of Out Services Written during the Years 1743–1751* (Boston: Merrymount Press, 1899), 25.

46. Sydney V. James, *The Colonial Metamorphoses in Rhode Island: A Study of Institutions in Change* (Hanover, N.H.: University Press of New England, 2000), 228–29.

47. In 1743 the Rhode Island General Assembly ordered the publication of five hundred copies of the revised law code. Each member of the assembly was to receive a copy gratis, and probably the clerk, governor, deputy governor, his ten assistants, the secretary, attorney general, and general treasurer would each receive one as well. Apparently, the General Assembly intended to recoup the cost of publication by selling the remaining volumes. In June 1745 the General Assembly got wind "that Ann Franklin has printed a number of colony law books for herself, over and above what she was employed to print for the colony, without the consent of the committee appointed to get the same printed. It is therefore resolved, that the said Ann Franklin, or any person in her behalf, do not sell any of said books within one year from the rising of the Assembly, upon the penalty of £5 for every book that shall be sold." It appears that Franklin had gone into competition with the General Assembly in the expectation that she could profit from the sale of law books. Bartlett, *Records of the Colony of Rhode Island,* 5:64, 70, 120.

48. Deposition of Martin Howard, January 23, 1744/45, RIJA.

49. John Cane's whereabouts were unknown at this point. Notification of Sale, November 19, 1744; Deed of Sale from Peleg Brown to Walter Cranston, January 21, 1744/5, Banister papers, RISA.

50. Act Enabling the Present Sheriff of Newport County to receive Executions not yet served & returned etc., March 1745, RIJA.

51. Letter of Administration, E. Gidley Peleg Brown on the Estate of J. Gidley, October/December 1744, Banister papers, RIJA.

52. Michael Dalton, *The Countrey Justice* (London, 1655; reprint, New York: Legal Classics Library, 1996), chap. 77, pp. 225–27. On leases see William Blackstone, *Commentaries on the Laws of England* (Oxford: Clarendon Press, 1766; reprint, New York: Legal Classics Library, 1983), 2:318ff.

53. Deposition of Brian Eccles, n.d. but after January 25, 1744/45, RIJA.

54. *Boston Evening-Post,* January 28, 1745, *Boston Gazette or Weekly Journal,* January 29, 1745, *Boston Weekly News-Letter,* January 31, 1745. The story also appeared in the *Boston Post-Boy,* January 28, 1745. See also the *New-York Evening Post,* February 18, 1745, and the Philadelphia *American Weekly Mercury,* February 20–26, 1745.

55. Jane Fiske, *Gleanings from Newport Court Files, 1659–1783* (Boxford, Mass.: privately printed, 1998), no. 770 (1745).

56. Supreme Court of Judicature, bk. C, March 1745, p. 316, RIJA; Fiske, *Gleanings,* no. 770 (1745).

57. Deposition of Martin Howard, January 23, 1744/45, Banister papers, RIJA.

58. Deposition of Brian Eccles, n.d. but after January 25, 1744/45, Banister papers, RIJA.

59. Deposition of William Dyre, January 23, 1744/45; Deposition of Peleg Brown, January 23, 1744/45, Banister papers, RIJA.

60. Superior Court of Judicature, bk. C, March 1745, p. 316, RIJA.

61. See the Cash Book of John Banister 1739–47 (no. 368), for March, April, May, and September 1745, pp. 98, 99, 100, 105, NHS.

62. "Will of John Banister," 353.

63. See the Cash Book of John Banister, 1739–1747 (no. 368), pp. 98, 99, NHS, for references to Samuel Banister Sr.'s funeral. See also "Will of John Banister," 351, for information about the administration of Samuel Banister Sr.'s estate.

64. John Banister to Samuel Banister, May 26, 1748, Letter Book of John Banister 1748–50 (no. 68), p. 18, NHS. See also p. 474 for a business letter from John, which starts out with the salutation "brother."

65. John Banister Memorandum Book (no. 92), p. 171, NHS.

66. *Boston Evening Post,* May 12, 19, 26, 1755.

67. "Will of John Banister," 345–50.

68. *History of the First Congregational Church (Road Church) Stonington, Connecticut, 1674–1974* (Stonington, Conn.: Road Church and Stonington Historical Society, 1974), 236, 259.

69. Deposition of Martin Howard, January 23, 1744/45, Samuel Banister papers, RIJA.

70. The population of Newport in 1748–49 was 5,529. Robert V. Wells, *The Population of the British Colonies in American before 1776* (Princeton, N.J.: Princeton University Press, 1975), 98.

6. A Ghost Story

1. The total population of Queen Anne's County, Maryland, in 1790 was 15,463, of which 8,171 were free whites, 6,674 enslaved, and 618 free "colored." *Heads of Families at the First Census of the United States Taken in the Year 1790* (Maryland) (Baltimore: Genealogical Publishing Co., 1998), 9.

2. Will of Thomas Harris, August 25, 1791, executed October 11, 1791. MdHR 18, 471–73 [C1496–24, 2/3/4/31], Maryland State Archives, Annapolis (henceforth MSA).

3. Sale of "Tom's Fancy Enlarged" from James Harris to James Newt (January 5, 1793), STW 2, pp. 388–90, MdHR 13, 848 [C1426–20, 2/1/1/20], MSA. To entail an estate was to designate a specific line of descent. Conversely, a fee-simple estate was one without limitations or conditions on descent or assignment.

4. Inventory of James Harris (November 1793), CD1, pp. 303–4, MdHR 16, 728 [MSA C1412–9, 2/2/4/36], MSA.

5. Maryland newspapers available at the time include the *Maryland Herald and Eastern Shore Advertiser* (Easton), *Maryland Gazette* (Annapolis), *Federal Gazette* (Baltimore), *Telegraphe* (Baltimore), *Maryland Herald* (Elizabethtown), *Bartgis's Federal Gazette* (Fredericktown), and *Rights of Man* (Fredericktown).

6. State for use of James, Fanny, Thomas & Robert Harris alias Goldsborough v. Mary Harris ad. Of James Harris, Imparlance Docket: May Term 1797, case no. 218, continued from May Term 1796, case no. 218, MSA.

7. *Authentic Account of the Appearance of a Ghost in Queen-Ann's County, Maryland, Proved in said county court in the remarkable Trial—State of Maryland, use of James, Fanny, Robert and Thomas Harris, Devisees of Thomas Harris, versus Mary Harris, Administratrix of James Harris, From Attested Notes, Taken in Court at the Time By One of the Council* (Baltimore: printed for C. [*sic*] Keatinge's book-store: Fryer and Rider, 1807). By "council" Keatinge meant "counsel" or "attorneys."

8. For information on these men and their careers see Frederic Emory, *Queen Anne's County, Maryland: Its Early History and Development* (Baltimore: Maryland Historical Society, 1950), passim.

9. In this Keatinge was following literary trends. Puritan execution sermons had given way to a more secular literary genre composed of trial transcripts. See Sharon Block, *Rape and Sexual Power in Early America* (Chapel Hill: University of North Carolina Press, 2006), 205. See also A. Rachel Minick, *A History of Printing in Maryland, 1791–1800* (Baltimore: Enoch Pratt Free Library, 1949) and Roger Pattrell Bristol, *Maryland Imprints, 1801–1810* (Charlottesville: Bibliographical Society of the University of Virginia, 1953) for Keatinge's contribution to the book trade.

10. For a succinct account of changes in pamphlet literature see Patricia Cline Cohen, *The Murder of Helen Jewett* (New York: Vintage, 1999), 26–27.

11. Keatinge, *Authentic Account,* 4, 5.

12. Ibid.

13. Thomas Herty, ed., *A Digest of the Laws of Maryland, Being An Abridgment, Alphabetically Arranged, of all the Public Acts of Assembly Now in Force, and of General Use From the First Settlement of the State, To the End of November Session 1797* . . . (Baltimore: printed for the Editor [Thomas Herty], 1799), 234.

14. R. Bernice Leonard, *Queen Anne's County Land Records,* bk. 4, 1743–55, vols. RTC and RTD (St. Michaels, Md., 1994), 70.

15. Queen Anne Register of Wills (Wills, Original), Will of James Harris (February 13, 1772) [C1404–14, C1496–10, 2/3/4/24], MSA.

16. Queen Anne Register of Wills (Wills, Original), Will of Thomas Harris (August 25, 1791), MdHR 18, 471–73 [C1496–24, 2/3/4/31], MSA.

17. William Blackstone, *Commentaries on the Laws of England* (Oxford: Clarendon Press, 1766; reprint, New York: Legal Classics Library, 1983), bk. 2, chap. 23, 247, 375; bk. 1, chap. 16, 447.

18. Keatinge, *Authentic Account,* 5.

19. Ibid.

20. It is possible that John Baily was related to Thomas and James's mother, Rebecca Baily Harris.

21. State for use of James, Fanny, Thomas & Robert Harris . . . Imparlance Docket, May Term, 1797, MSA.

22. John Hill Burton, *Narratives of Criminal Trials in Scotland,* 2 vols. (London: Chapman and Hall, 1852), 2:109.

23. Keatinge, *Authentic Account,* 7.

24. "Remarks on Ghosts," *The Port-Folio* (Philadelphia), 1:2 (February 1816), 131–38; quote on 131.

25. Ibid., 133, 134, 135, 136. This acknowledgment might also suggest that the author of "Remarks on Ghosts" drew on Briggs's testimony in order to compose his essay. If so, this would account for the similarities between Briggs's narrative and the 1816 article.

26. Ibid., 137; Keatinge, *Authentic Account,* 9.

27. F. Edward Wright, *Maryland Eastern Shore Vital Records, 1751–1775* (Silver Spring, Md.: Family Line Publications, 1984).

28. Bettie S. Carothers, *1776 Census of Maryland* (Lutherville, Md., [1976]), 150. Thomas was born in 1752, and two younger sisters separate him in age from James. Thus it is unlikely that James would have reached twenty-one by 1776.

29. One Esther Briggs married Samuel Munger in 1745. Robert Barnes, comp., *Maryland Marriages, 1634–1777* (Baltimore: Genealogical Publishing Co., 1975), 107.

30. Vol. 10 of *Index to American Genealogical, Biographical, and Local History Materials* (Middletown, Conn: Godfrey Memorial Library, 1952–c. 2000) indicates that the William Briggs listed in the 1790 Queen Anne's County, Maryland, census (indisputably "our" Briggs) was born in "175—?". If, as Briggs testified, he was forty-three in 1797, he would have been born in 1754, making him two years younger than Thomas Harris.

31. Emory, *Queen Anne's County,* 284.

32. Committee of Correspondence to the Maryland Council of Safety, February 19, 1776, Emory, *Queen Anne's County,* 284.

33. Archives of Maryland (online: http://archivesofmaryland.net/html/index. html), 18:122, 124, 302, 375, 416, 538; Emory, *Queen Anne's County,* 307; *Calendar of Maryland State Papers: The Red Books,* no. 4, pt. 2 (Annapolis: Hall of Records Commission, 1953), 25; *Calendar of Maryland State Papers, Executive Miscellanea,* no. 5 (Annapolis: Hall of Records Commission, 1958), 59; Archives of Maryland, 18:50, 190, 309, 645; 21:480.

34. Among the candidates (all Marylanders) are Anna Maria Tilghman, b. 1753 or 1754, who married Charles Goldsborough (d. 1774), Anne Goldsborough, b. circa 1767, who married John Singleton either in 1785 or 1790, and an Anna Goldsborough b. 1765. There is also an Anna Goldsborough whose name appears in the Queen Anne's County orphans' court records in 1798. She is referred to there as "Anna Goldsborough, now Caule." See Annie Walker Burns, comp., *Orphan Court Record: Guardian Reports,* bk. no. WHN 1, 1798–1803 (Chicago: Institute of American Genealogy, n.d.), 1. Another Ann Goldsborough (or was it one of the above?) witnessed a Queen Anne's County inventory in 1792 and inscribed her signature thereon. Inventory of Robert Goldsborough, May 3, 1792, Queen Anne's County Register of Wills, misc. papers, 1756–92 [C1452–1, 2/3/4/42], MSA. There were, no doubt, others, but I am unable to sort them out.

35. FamilySearch, http://www.familysearch.org. It is also possible that the online source of this information is incorrect.

36. Freckles were thought to be an unattractive female feature, and if this were a fictional narrative, I would create a scenario wherein a man ridiculed Anna Maria's freckles, her husband challenged him to a duel, and was subsequently killed in a lethal dawn contest. In fact, no record has surfaced thus far to indicate the precise nature of Charles Goldsborough's wound or how he received it. For the existing historical data, such as it is, see Charles Goldsborough to Edward Tilghman, [February 7] 1774, and Edward Tilghman to Charles Goldsborough, February 7, 1774, printed in "A Romance of 1774," in *Maryland Historical Magazine* 8 (1913): 193–94.

37. For the possible birth date and marriage(s) of Anna Maria Tilghman see FamilySearch (online). "My daughter Anna lately intermarried with the Revd. Robert Smith of CharlesTown . . . against my approbation." See the will of Edward Tilghman, Queen Anne's County Register of Wills (Wills, Original), 1785, MdHR 8877–12–93 [MSA C1496–19, 2/3/4/28], MSA.

38. The additional signature of "Sary Goldsborough" on the estate inventory reinforces this supposition, since this Robert Goldsborough, son of Robert (d. 1788) and Sarah Yerbury Goldsborough (d. 1787) had a sister named Sarah. The problem with this interpretation is that young Robert should have inherited property from his father by 1790–91, and yet his estate inventory shows a meager thirty-three pounds of property. Inventory of Robert Goldsborough, May 3, 1792, Queen Anne's County Register of Wills, misc. papers, 1756–92 [C1452–1 2/3/4/42], MSA.

39. General Assembly House of Delegates Assessment Record 1783, Queen Anne's Corsica District, p. 51, S1161–8–9 [S1161–80, 1/4/5/51]; Bettie S. Carothers, comp., *1778 Census of Maryland* (Lutherville, Md., n.d. but before 1977), 23–26.

40. Daniel Blake Smith, *Inside the Great House: Planter Family Life in Eighteenth-Century Chesapeake Society* (Ithaca, N.Y.: Cornell University Press, 1980), 139.

41. Herty, *Digest of the Laws,* 256–58. See also *Acts of Assembly of the Province of Maryland . . . 1749* (Annapolis: Jonas Green, printer, 1749), 15 ("An Act for taking off corporal Punishment inflicted on Females having base-born Children . . . ").

42. "Marriages," in Herty, *Digest of the Laws,* 350–52.

43. As noted above, one Ann Goldsborough, widowed in 1774, remarried Rev. Robert Smith in 1782 despite her father's disapproval, something he remarked on in his will. Will of Edward Tilghman, Queen Anne's County Register of Wills (Wills, Original), 1785, MdHR 8877–12–93 [MSA C1496–19, 2/3/4/28], MSA.

44. Smith, *Inside the Great House,* 144–45.

45. Clement Dorsey, *The General Public Statutory Law and Public Local Law of the State of Maryland from the Year 1692 to 1839 Inclusive* (Baltimore: J. D. Toy, 1840), in Archives of Maryland, 141:835. Maryland law did not bar dower on remarriage of a widow, and Charles Goldsborough had made no such provision to deny dower in his will.

46. *Heads of Families at the First Census,* 100.

47. Will of Thomas Harris, August 25, 1791; "An Account of Property of Thomas Harris," October 24, 1791, and October 28, 1791, CD1, pp. 124–25, MdHR 16, 728 [MSA C14:2–9, 2/2/4/36], MSA.

48. See "Fornication" in Herty, *Digest of the Laws,* 256–57.

49. Nancy Zey maintains that illegitimate children ordinarily took the mother's names. In addition, Christine Daniels explains that almost all illegitimate children in Maryland in the late eighteenth century were bound out as apprentices, but if Ann Goldsborough bound them out herself, it was likely to have been privately negotiated (comments at session 51, Omohundro Institute of Early American History and Culture conference, 2007).

50. Inventory of James Harris (November 1793), CD 1, pp. 303–4, MdHR 16, 728 [MSA C1412–9, 2/2/4/36], MSA.

51. Queen Anne's County Register of Wills (guardianship papers, 1779–1855) [C1404–14, 2/3/3/42], MSA.

52. Newspaper reprints of case: *Gazette* (Bedford, Pa.); *Carlisle Gazette* (Carlisle, Pa.), June 23, 1809, p. 4; *New-York Spectator,* June 28, 1809, p. 2; *Daily Advertiser* (Boston), July 3, 1809, p. 1; *New-Jersey Telescope* (Newark), July 4, 1809, p. 1; *Massachusetts Spy or Worcester Gazette* (Worcester), July 5, 1809, p. 2; *Norfolk Repository* (Dedham, Mass.), July 6, 1809, p. 2; *Connecticut Gazette and the Commercial*

Intelligencer (New London), July 12, 1809, p. 1; *The American* (Providence, R.I.), July 14, 1809, p. 1; *Connecticut Mirror* (Hartford), July 17, 1809, p. 4; *New-Hampshire Patriot* (Concord), July 25, 1809, p. 4; *Northern Whig* (Hudson, N.Y.), July 25, 1809, p. 1; *American Eagle* (Catskill, N.Y.), August 9, 1809, p. 1; *Freeman's Journal* (see *Massachusetts Spy* for reference). Magazine reprints of case: *Omnium Gatherum, A Monthly Magazine Recording Authentick Accounts of the Most Remarkable Productions, Events, and Occurences in Providence, Nature, and Art* (Boston: T. Kennard, 1810); *Lady's Weekly Miscellany* (New York), July 22, 1809, 9, 13. Pamphlets and miscellaneous: *Authentic Account of the Appearance of a Ghost in Queen-Ann's County, Maryland, Proved in said county court in the remarkable Trial—State of Maryland, use of James, Fanny, Robert and Thomas Harris, Devisees of Thomas Harris, versus Mary Harris, Administratrix of James Harris, From Attested Notes, Taken in Court at the Time By One of the Council* (Baltimore: printed for G. Keatinge's Book-Store, 1807); *Opera Glass, for peeping into the microcosm of the fine arts and more especially of the drama,* (London), February 3, 1827; *Notices Relative to The Bannatyne Club,* Instituted in February, 1823, including Critiques On Some Of Its Publications (Edinburgh: printed for private circulation, 1836, 191–97). Books and journals that have incorporated accounts of case: John Hill Burton, *Narratives of Criminal Trials in Scotland,* 2 vols. (London: Chapman and Hall, 1852), 2:107–10; Catherine Crowe, *The Night Side of Nature* (New York: Redfield, 1858), 257–61; Andrew Lang, *Cock Lane and Common-Sense* (London: Longmans, Green, and Co., 1894), 263–67; Kenneth L. Carroll, "The Court Inquires about a Ghost," *Maryland Historical Magazine* 55 (1960): 38–43; Oliver E. Carruth, "Famous Ghosts," *Miami Herald Record,* July 5, 1922, p. 9.

53. The Federalist newspapers were *Daily Advertiser, Massachusetts Spy, Connecticut Gazette, The American, Connecticut Mirror, New-Hampshire Patriot, New-York Spectator, New-Jersey Telescope, Northern Whig,* and *American Eagle.* The Republican papers were the *Norfolk Repository* and the *Carlisle Gazette.* The *Freeman's Journal* leaned toward the conservative Quids.

54. L. Marx Renzulli, *Maryland: The Federalist Years* (Rutherford, N.J.: Fairleigh Dickinson University Press, 1972), 249–51.

55. Two Goldsboroughs (at least) were Federalists (John and Robert), but what their relationship was to Ann and whether this affiliation made for a political confrontation that was played out in the courtroom in 1797 is unrecoverable.

56. Lang, *Cock Lane and Common-Sense,* 263–64. Nicholson had a penchant for submitting his writings to newspapers. See John Randolph to John Hopper Nicholson, February 4, 1800, and January 31, 1807, JHN papers, vol. 1, no. 1053, and vol. 3, p. 1374a, Library of Congress.

57. *New-York Gazette and General Advertiser,* February 3, 1809; *Connecticut Journal,* February 16, 1809; *Federal Republican & Commercial Gazette,* March 17, 1809; *Connecticut Mirror,* July 17, 1809; and *Vermont Centinel,* July 14, 1809.

58. *Federal Republican & Commercial Gazette,* March 17, 1809. For a detailed discussion of journalistic partisanship in the early republic see Eric Burns, *Infamous Scribblers: The Founding Fathers and the Rowdy Beginnings of American Journalism* (New York: Public Affairs, 2006).

59. The newspapers that printed the story on page 1 were the *Daily Advertiser, New-Jersey Telescope, Connecticut Gazette, The American, Northern Whig,* and *American Eagle.*

60. *Connecticut Mirror,* July 17, 1809.

61. See, for example, Ruth Bloch, "Changing Conceptions of Sexuality and Romance in Eighteenth-Century America," *William and Mary Quarterly,* 3rd series, vol. 60, no. 1 (January 2003): 13–42; Block, *Rape and Sexual Power;* Cathy Davidson, *Revolution and the Word: The Rise of the Novel in America* (New York: Oxford University Press, 1986). Male bonding and friendship was also a popular theme in the literature of the 1790s, and the fact that the "sighting" came from Harris's old friend Briggs may have been of interest to audiences of the time.

62. For the signatures of Ann(a) Goldsborough see Inventory of Robert Goldsborough, May 3, 1792, Queen Anne's County Register of Wills, misc. papers, 1756–92 [C1452–1, 2/3/4/42]; Queen Anne's County Register of Wills (Wills, Original), Will of Charles Goldsborough, 1774, MdHR 8877–5–77 [MSA C1496–8, 2/3/4/23], MSA.

63. Samuel Richardson, *Clarissa: or the History of a Young Lady* (London: J. Rivington, 1768–69) and *Pamela; or Virtue Rewarded* (London: Harrison & Co., 1785), Frances Brooke, *The History of Emily Montague* (London: J. Dodsley, 1769), Susanna Rowson, *Charlotte Temple: A Tale of Truth* (Philadelphia: Matthew Carey, 1797), Anna Bleecker, *The History of Maria Kittle* (Hartford, Conn.: E. Babcock, 1797).

64. Keatinge, *Authentic Account,* 4.

65. Friedrich Schiller, *The Ghost-seer; or Apparitionist* (New York: T. and J. Swords, 1796), and *The Ghost of John Young the Homicide, who was executed the 17th of August last for the Murder of Robert Barwick* (New York, 1797). Elizabeth Drinker, the Philadelphia diarist, noted on January 5, 1804, that she had read *The Ghost Seer; or Apparitionist.* Elaine Forman Crane, ed., *The Diary of Elizabeth Drinker,* 3 vols. (Boston: Northeastern University Press, 1991), 3:1789.

66. "On the Different Species of Phobia," *Weekly Magazine of Original Essays, Fugitive Pieces, and Interesting Intelligence* (Philadelphia), 1798, 4.

67. Inigo Barlow, Anne Ker, et al., *The Three Ghosts of the Forest, a Tale of Horror. An Original Romance* (London: D. N. Shury, 1803); John Tregortha, *News from the Invisible World; or Interesting Anecdotes of the Dead: containing a particular survey of the most remarkable . . . accounts of apparitions, ghosts, spectres, dreams . . . visions* (Burslem, 1808); M. G. Lewis, *Tales of Terror! Or More Ghosts, Forming a Complete Phantasmagoria* (London: T. Maiden, 1802).

68. Regina Maria Roche, *The Children of the Abbey* (London, 1796). As John Greenleaf Whittier wrote, "I have noticed in our thrifty, money-loving community, that there is a very common notion that the disposal of an estate contrary to the known wishes of the testator is the most potent spell of all others for raising a Yankee ghost." See Whittier, *The Supernaturalism of New England* (Baltimore, 1993 [1847]), 13.

69. On the gothic novel see Maggie Kilgour, *The Rise of the Gothic Novel* (New York: Routledge, 1995), 12; Neil Cornwell, "European Gothic," in *A Companion to the Gothic,* ed. David Punter (Malden, Mass: Blackwell Publishers, 2000), 28–29; Markman Ellis, *The History of Gothic Fiction* (Edinburgh: Edinburgh University Press, 2000). For gothic novels with the themes described above see, for example, Horace Walpole, *The Castle of Otranto* (London, 1764, and New York, 1801), and Ann Radcliffe, *The Mysteries of Udolpho* (London: G. G. and J. Robinson, 1794, and Boston: Samuel Etheridge, 1795). This last is one of many gothic works enjoyed by Elizabeth Drinker. See Crane, *Diary of Elizabeth Drinker,* 1:694.

70. Radcliffe, *Mysteries of Udolpho,* 507. And as Christopher Maclachlan explains in his introduction to Matthew Lewis's *The Monk,* Lewis "re-asserts the role of the supernatural in Gothic fiction as a device to inspire fear of forces beyond human understanding. What these forces are is left unspoken—do they really exist, or are they projections of the psyche?" Matthew Lewis, *The Monk: A Romance* ([London, 1796] New York: Penguin, 1998), xxiii.

71. *Northern Whig,* July 25, 1809.

72. *American Magazine of Wonders, and Marvellous Chronicle,* 2 vols. (New York, 1809).

73. Burton, *Narratives of Criminal Trials in Scotland,* 2:107.

74. Will of Thomas Harris, August 25, 1791, MdHR 18, 471–3 [C1496–24, 2/3/4/31], MSA.

75. "An Act respecting Apprentices" (1786), in *Laws of Maryland, 1785–1791* (Annapolis: Frederick Green), in Archives of Maryland (online), 204:181. An orphan was a child whose father was deceased.

76. My thanks to Michael Zuckerman for his interpretation of Mary Harris's role.

77. Patriarch or not, ghosts seem to have had a warm relationship with the Briggs family. In 1673, the ghost of Rebecca Briggs Cornell appealed to her brother, John Briggs, in an infamous Rhode Island matricide case about which I wrote some years ago. (*Killed Strangely: The Death of Rebecca Cornell,* Ithaca, N.Y.: Cornell University Press, 2002). Whether William Briggs of Maryland was descended from John Briggs of Portsmouth, Rhode Island, cannot be determined, although in another literary fantasy I see the story of Rebecca's ghost handed down in the Briggs family from generation to generation, with William Briggs taking a cue from it as a way to resolve the problem of his friend's property. Without giving away any personal reflections on the supernatural, I would only add that the first name on my class roster in spring '07 was William Briggs, a young man who turned out to be a descendant of the Rhode Island Briggs family.

78. Judith Richardson, *Possessions: The History and Uses of Haunting in the Hudson Valley* (Cambridge, Mass: Harvard University Press, 2003), 123, 26.

Epilogue

1. Alexis de Tocqueville, *Democracy in America,* trans. Henry Reeve (Boston: J. Allyn, 1876), 176. The full quotation is as follows: "It is a strange thing, the authority which is accorded to the intervention of a court of justice by the general opinion of mankind! It clings to the mere formalities of justice, and gives a bodily influence to the shadow of the law."

2. Edwin Wolf, *The Book Culture of a Colonial American City: Philadelphia Books, Bookmen, and Booksellers* (New York: Clarendon Press, 1988), chap. 4, "Lawyers and Law Books," esp. 132 and 151; Edmund Burke, *Speech of Edmund Burke, Esq. on Moving His Resolution for Conciliation with the Colonies, March 22, 1775* (London, 1775), 30. For an analysis of reader preference see David D. Hall and Elizabeth Carroll Reilly, "Practices of Reading: Part II, Customers and the Market for Books," in *The Colonial Book in the Atlantic World,* ed. Hugh Amory and David D. Hall (New York: Cambridge University Press, 2000), 390.

3. Andrew J. King, "Constructing Gender: Sexual Slander in Nineteenth-Century America," *Law and History Review* 13, no. 1 (1995): 73.

4. *Vermont Gazette (Bennington),* May 4, 1801, p. 4. The writer of the article is referring to the American Revolution.

5. Sharon Block, *Rape and Sexual Power in Early America* (Chapel Hill: University of North Carolina Press, 2006), 147–50, 196.

6. On this topic see Bruce H. Mann, *Republic of Debtors: Bankruptcy in the Age of American Independence* (Cambridge, Mass.: Harvard University Press, 2002).

7. For a detailed examination of the importance of entail in Virginia see Holly Brewer, "Entailing Aristocracy in Colonial Virginia: 'Ancient Feudal Restraints' and Revolutionary Reform," *William and Mary Quarterly* 54, no. 2 (April 1997): 307–46.

8. de Tocqueville, *Democracy in America,* 316.

9. This issue is discussed in the introduction to Christopher L. Tomlins and Bruce H. Mann, eds., *The Many Legalities of Early America* (Chapel Hill: University of North Carolina Press, 2001), 1–23, esp. 6–7, 19–20.

INDEX